THE NEW
BIBLE HANDBOOK

First Published March 1947
Reprinted February 1948

MADE AND PRINTED IN GREAT BRITAIN BY
THE STANHOPE PRESS LIMITED (A STAPLES
PRESS COMPANY) : ROCHESTER KENT

THE NEW
BIBLE HANDBOOK

EDITED BY

THE REV. G. T. MANLEY, M.A.
Sometime Fellow of Christ's College, Cambridge

ASSISTED BY

THE REV. G. C. ROBINSON, B.A., B.D., AND
THE REV. A. M. STIBBS, M.A.

LONDON
THE INTER-VARSITY FELLOWSHIP
1948

CONTENTS

A detailed analysis of the chapters will be found at the beginning of each part.

PART FOUR: THE NEW TESTAMENT

PREFACE

FOR some years past, students of the Bible have felt the need of a new and up-to-date Handbook which would combine a belief in its plenary inspiration with sound scholarship. Important additions have been made to our knowledge of the language, history and religion of Palestine and the surrounding nations; and linguistic and archæological discoveries have seriously modified the views of a former generation, causing a reaction in favour of a more constructive criticism.

The present volume is intended for all who are ready to give serious attention to a right approach to, and a right understanding of the Bible. For this reason, the more familiar Authorized Version has been followed and Greek and Hebrew words have been transliterated. In order to keep the price within the limits necessary for a wide circulation certain things have been omitted. Adequate maps can be found in most Bibles, and the I.V.F. Bibliography, *A Guide to Christain Reading*, can be consulted for further reading.

The task originally assigned to those who are mainly responsible for the production of the book could not have been carried out without the willing help of a number of contributors. Their names are given on pages viii and ix. Their work calls for a warm tribute of thanks from both the editors and the publishers; for the time which they have so generously and freely expended and the care which they have taken in the preparation of their contributions all concerned are in great debt, and the more so as all the work has been undertaken voluntarily.

The editors have been at pains to secure accuracy. But they are, of course, open to constructive suggestions. In view of the possibility of future editions, scholarly criticism and help in correcting any mistakes which may have escaped their notice, will be welcome.

No body of men can approach a task of this sort without realizing their own unworthiness. If prophets and apostles felt their unfitness to deliver the Word of the Lord, how much more should we handle that Word with humility and prayer. May He who inspired it use this humble effort as an instrument to fulfil its purpose of conviction, correction and instruction in righteousness.

G. T. MANLEY.
G. C. ROBINSON.
A. M. STIBBS.

vii

LIST OF CONTRIBUTORS

General Editor

THE REV. G. T. MANLEY, M.A., sometime Fellow of Christ's College, Cambridge.

Assistant Editors

THE REV. G. C. ROBINSON, B.A., B.D., Young People's Secretary, Baptist Missionary Society.

THE REV. A. M. STIBBS, M.A., Vice-Principal of Oak Hill Theological College.

Other Contributors

B. F. C. ATKINSON, M.A., PH.D., Under-Librarian in the University Library, Cambridge.

THE VERY REV. S. BARTON BABBAGE, M.A., PH.D., Dean of Sydney, N.S.W.

THE REV. G. R. BEASLEY-MURRAY, B.D., M.TH., Minister of Ilford Baptist Church.

THE REV. H. A. G. BELBEN, M.A., B.D., Chaplain and Lecturer in Divinity at Southlands College.

F. F. BRUCE, M.A., DIP.HEB., Head of the Department of Biblical History and Literature in the University of Sheffield.

THE REV. PROF. J. H. S. BURLEIGH, B.LITT., D.D., Regius Professor of Ecclesiastical History, University of Edinburgh.

THE REV. J. C. CONNELL, M.A., Minister of Rayner's Lane Baptist Church, Harrow.

THE REV. F. COLQUHOUN, M.A., Editorial Secretary, National Church League.

THE REV. PROF. F. DAVIDSON, M.A., B.D., D.D., Professor of Biblical Criticism, United Original Secession Church of Scotland.

THE LATE REV. T. W. FAWTHROP, D.D., D.LIT., F.R.G.S.

THE REV. PROF. R. F. HETTLINGER, M.A., Wycliffe College, Toronto.

THE REV. R. G. G. HOOPER, B.A., B.D., Tutor at London College of Divinity.

THE REV. E. F. KEVAN, B.D., M.TH., Principal, London Bible College.

THE REV. D. B. KNOX, B.A., B.D., Tutor at Moore Theological College, Sydney, N.S.W.

THE REV. G. J. C. MARCHANT, M.A., Curate of St. Andrew-the-Less, Cambridge.

THE REV. A. W. H. MOULE, M.A., Rector of Woolhampton, Berkshire.

THE REV. W. C. G. PROCTOR, B.A., B.D., Rector of Harold's Cross, Dublin, and Lecturer in the Divinity School, Trinity College, Dublin.

THE REV. W. A. REES-JONES, M.A., B.Sc., Rector of St. George's, Stamford, Lincs.

THE REV. PROF. A. ROSS, M.A., B.D., Professor of New Testament Exegesis, Free Church College, Edinburgh.

THE REV. W. J. SAWLE, B.D., Secretary, Church Association.

THE REV. L. E. H. STEPHENS-HODGE, M.A., Rector of Hatch Beauchamp with Beercrocombe, Somerset.

THE REV. H. WALLWORK, M.A., Lecturer in Christian Ethics and New Testament Greek, B.C.M. and T. College, Bristol.

THE REV. J. STAFFORD WRIGHT, M.A., Senior Tutor, Oak Hill College, Southgate.

LIST OF ABBREVIATIONS

Books of the Old Testament: Gn., Ex., Lv., Nu., Dt., Jos., Jdg., Ru., 1, 2 Sa., 1, 2 Ki., 1, 2 Ch., Ezr., Ne., Est., Jb., Ps. (Pss.), Pr., Ec., Ct., Is., Je., La., Ezk., Dn., Ho., Joel, Am., Ob., Jon., Mi., Na., Hab., Zp., Hg., Zc., Mal.

Books of the New Testament: Mt., Mk., Lk., Jn., Acts, Rom., 1, 2 Cor., Gal., Eph., Phil., Col., 1, 2 Thes., 1, 2 Tim., Tit., Phm., Heb., Jas., 1, 2 Pet., 1, 2, 3 Jn., Jude, Rev.

Books of the Apocrypha: Spelled in full except Ecclus. for Ecclesiasticus, and Macc. for Maccabees.

Aram.	Aramaic.
A.V.	Authorized Version (1611).
c.	about (with dates).
cf.	compare.
f., ff.	following verse(s) or page(s).
Gk.	Greek.
Heb.	Hebrew.
Int. Crit. Comm.	The International Critical Commentary.
LXX	Septuagint Version.
mg.	Margin.
Moff.	Moffatt's translation.
MS., MSS.	Manuscript(s).
op. cit.	cited above.
P.B.V.	Prayer Book Version.
R.V.	Revised Version (1885).

In general, the Authorized Version of 1611 has been used for quotations from the Bible. Where the translation has been taken from some other version, this is normally noted. In one or two places, however, notably in that part of the book dealing with the New Testament, contributors, in order to make some point clearer, have made their own translation of the passages quoted.

x

INTRODUCTION

THE purpose of this Handbook is to help those who read the Bible to enter into a fuller understanding of its meaning, and thus to learn the will of God and to experience a closer sense of communion with Christ Himself. For the words which epitomize the message of the Gospel of John are applicable to the entire volume of sacred Scripture. 'These are written, that ye might believe that Jesus is the Christ, the Son of God; and that believing ye might have life through His name.' There is a danger, of course, that books *about* the Bible may usurp the Bible's place: the reader must continually be on his guard, therefore, against the temptation to spend on other books time which could more profitably have been spent on *the* Book itself.

Beyond the pages of the Bible, it is the Lord whom the Christian seeks; and there is still an Emmaus road experience for the soul to whom the risen Christ, 'beginning at Moses and all the prophets' expounds 'in all the Scriptures the things concerning Himself'. This experience, however, will come only to those who recognize their need for such spiritual enlightenment. The full meaning of Scripture, the truth it was written to reveal, can become clear to us only as the Spirit of God gives us insight and enables us to understand. We need, therefore, to approach all Bible study in prayerful dependence upon God. It is also necessary to remember that the Spirit of God reveals the divine truth not to satisfy curiosity or mere intellectual interest, but to promote active obedience. Theoretical assent alone will not do. What is required is a practical faith and a responsive readiness personally to apply and to obey the truth discerned.

This privilege of being able to understand by the anointing of the Spirit is God's gift to every believer. Yet experience shows that no one individual alone can see all truth. It is only in fellowship with others that he can hope to grasp the wealth and wonder of the divine purposes (Eph. iii. 18). This is why direct, positive help can be obtained from a Handbook of this kind, in which guidance is offered on a number of matters which are bound to be encountered in serious Bible reading. The Spirit of God uses Christians to help one another. God has made us interdependent, able to help one another and needing to be helped by one another.

Again, we must recognize that study of the Scriptures must be thorough and systematic if it is to be effective. The Bible does not yield its choicest fruits to the casual reader. We therefore recommend that this Handbook should be used in close conjunction with some scheme of systematic study, such as that published by the Inter-Varsity Fellowship under the title *Search the Scriptures*.[1] This particular course presupposes the use of a Bible Handbook, and in a revised edition, the first volume of which has recently been published, direct references are given to the present volume.

No greater blessing could visit our land than a revival of serious Bible reading. The Christian believer especially requires the sustenance of 'the bread which cometh down from heaven', and it has rightly been asserted that the reason for lost spirituality can often be traced back to neglect of God's Word. Said John Chrysostom: 'This is the cause of all our evils, not knowing the Scriptures.' Wherefore, 'resort to the same and read it'.

[1] This course guides the student through the whole Bible in three years. Passages are set for each day's study, two or three questions are asked, and brief notes are included to explain difficult or obscure passages.

PART ONE

THE BIBLE AS A WHOLE

CONTENTS OF PART ONE

CHAPTER I

INSPIRATION AND AUTHORITY

B Y universal consent the Bible is the most wonderful book in the world. It is not like any other book. It makes the greatest claims, exerts the greatest influence, is the most widely read, is the best loved, and has been the most hated of all books. It has been banned and burned, and yet it lives and spreads.

It contains most wonderful histories, but is yet no history book; it is a treasury of truth concerning right and wrong, but it is not a text-book of ethics; it goes deeper than any other into the problems of life, but in no sense is it a hand-book of philosophy.

It is an Eastern book, and yet is universal in its appeal; it is so simple that a child can paddle safely in its shallows, but so profound that it provides deep waters for the strongest to swim in. Penned by many writers through the course of centuries, it possesses a remarkable unity; although given in many parts and divers fashions, it is marvellously complete; the product of antiquity, it is applicable to every side of modern life.

What is this book, and what is its secret? It is like God's work in nature with its lofty mountain ranges and its smiling Alpine valleys rich with flowers, so different from the cities built by man; it bears upon its face the impress of the Creator's hand.

Upon the title page of the Authorized Version is the inscription 'The Holy Bible, containing the Old and New Testaments', and in the accompanying dedication it is called 'God's sacred Word', 'the Holy Scriptures', and 'God's holy Truth'.

It contains thirty-nine books of the Old Testament (or Covenant) and twenty-seven of the New.[1] These form the Bible, the 'books' *par excellence* (Gk. *biblia*, books). These books have been acknowledged by all sections of the Christian church in all ages to be the divinely inspired foundation of the Christian faith. In order to discover their nature and value we must begin by examining the claims which they make for themselves.

[1] See Chapter III.

3

THE CLAIMS OF THE BIBLE

(a) The teaching of Christ

The Old and New Testaments are inseparably bound together: in the Old Testament the New is concealed, in the New Testament the Old is revealed (Augustine). Christ Himself bore such testimony to the Old Testament that to deny its inspiration is to offer a direct challenge to the authority of His teaching.

He associated the words of the former Scriptures with His own, expanding, fulfilling and confirming them as words which should never pass away (Mt. v. 17, 18, xxiv. 35; Jn. v. 46, 47). He appealed to them as to a divine, and therefore final authority (Mt. xix. 4, 5; Mk. vii. 9-13; Jn. v. 37). '*It is written* is His final justification of courses of action, the ground on which He bases principles.'[1] To difficult questions He finds an authoritative answer from the Old Testament; He quotes its history with unquestioning confidence, and brings into prominence some of its less conspicuous but vital passages (*e.g.* Lv. xix. 18: see Mt. xix. 19, etc.).

He used the Scriptures to repel Satan, to correct the Pharisees, to instruct His disciples, to confirm His mission, and to pour out His soul on the Cross. Our Lord gave His *imprimatur* to the three recognized divisions of the Old Testament, the Law, the Prophets, and the Writings (Lk. xxiv. 44). He Himself kept the Law and encouraged others to observe its teaching and to keep its precepts (Mt. xxiii. 2, 3; Mk. i. 44; Lk. x. 26). He testified to the divine mission of the prophets (Lk. xi. 49; cf. 2 Ch. xxiv. 18-22) and, by word and deed, insisted that the prophetic Scriptures *must* be fulfilled (Mk. xiv. 27, 49; Lk. xxi. 32; Jn. xiii. 18, xvii. 12). He ascribed the writing of a Psalm to the inspiration of the Holy Spirit (Mk. xii. 36). His sayings abound with Old Testament imagery, and His quotations from it were frequent as He neared the cross and after His resurrection (Lk. xxiv. 45). It is difficult to see how any stronger endorsement could have been given to its divine origin and authority than that which His words and deeds supply.

His teaching on this subject cannot be ascribed to 'accommodation' to the ignorance of His hearers (could this explain His rebukes of Satan?) or to the limitations of His humanity (could this have applied after His resurrection?). The authority of Scripture is so interwoven with His life and doctrine that it can

[1] Swete, *The Holy Spirit in the New Testament*, p. 330.

neither be eliminated nor explained away by any doctrine of *kenosis*.[1] For whilst He asserted the limitation of His knowledge as Son of Man (Mk. xiii. 32), He claimed supreme authority for His teaching (Mk. xiii. 31, cf. Mk. i. 22; Jn. xii. 48-50). 'His statements are never tentative; His predictions are made with unqualified confidence; there is no sign of the slightest confession of error in anything He taught.'[2]

(b) The teaching of the book itself

That which Christ taught concerning the Old Testament corresponds closely with the claims made by the writers themselves. Moses claims to record the words of the Lord (Gn. i. 3; Ex. xxiv. 4; Dt. xxix. 1, xxxi. 26), and later writers confirm this claim (Jos. viii. 31; 2 Ki. xiv. 6; Pss. xix. 7-11, cxix. 1). The prophets claim to have their calling from God, and to speak His message: they do not speak their own thoughts, but proclaim, 'Thus saith the Lord' (1 Sa. iii. 15-21; Is. i. 2, vi. 9; Je. i. 4-9, vi. 9, xxxvi. 2; Mi. vi. 1).

What is true of the Old Testament is equally so of the words of Christ Himself. They are spoken with authority (Mt. vii. 29); they are spirit and life; they were not His own but received from the Father (Jn. vi. 63, xvii. 8).

It is in the nature of the case that the testimony to the divine origin of the books of the New Testament should be less explicit than to those which had been long in use; yet few would grant the claim of inspiration to the Old Testament and refuse it to the New. Christ taught clearly that the older Scriptures pointed to Him and awaited fulfilment (Mt. viii. 17).

The Law and the Prophets were to have a sequel (Lk. xvi. 16). He dispensed words of eternal life which should never pass away, and the message He committed to His disciples was for all nations and until the end of the age (Mt. xxiv. 35, xxviii. 20; Mk. xiv. 9; Lk. xxiv. 47). For the work of witness committed to them He promised them His Spirit to assist their memories and to guide them into all truth (Jn. xiv. 26, xv. 26, xvi. 13; Acts i. 8), a promise which was duly fulfilled (Acts xv. 28; 1 Cor. ii. 12, 13; Eph. iii. 5; 1 Jn. v. 6). From time to time the voice of the Lord was heard from heaven directing them (Acts x. 13, xxii. 21), and finally He sent His revelation of things to come to John by His angel (Rev. i. 1).

The New Testament writers claim that they are guided by the

[1] See p. 42.
[2] J. W. Wenham, *Evangelical Quarterly*, April, 1945.

B

Spirit (1 Cor. ii. 13; 1 Pet. i. 12; Rev. i. 10), and expect obedience to their teaching (1 Cor. xiv. 37; 2 Thes. iii. 14). They know that their message is the word of God (1 Thes. ii. 13), received by revelation from Him (Gal. i. 12, ii. 2; Rev. i. 1), and Peter ranks Paul's Epistles among the inspired Scriptures (2 Pet. iii. 16). Finally the apostles and evangelists follow their Master in their treatment of the Old Testament. Its contents are the 'oracles of God' (Rom. iii. 2; cf. Acts vii. 38), and, after quoting Gen. ii. and Ps. xcv., the writer to the Hebrews refers to them as the 'word of God' (iv. 4, 7, 12). The words of Scripture are quoted as a final court of appeal (Mk. xv. 28; Lk. ii. 23, iii. 4; Jn. xix. 24; Acts i. 16, iv. 25, xiii. 34; Rom. xv. 8-12; Heb. i. 1; Jas. ii. 23; 2 Pet. i. 21). Thus from Genesis to Revelation the Bible makes the tremendous claim that in its words God has spoken to man.

REVELATION

(a) Its meaning and possibility

The word 'revelation' (*apocalypsis*, unveiling) means the drawing away of a veil from that which had been previously hidden in mystery (Rom. xvi. 25; Rev. i. 1). In this sense Christ was revealed when first He took upon Himself human flesh, and will be so revealed again when He comes in glory (Lk. ii. 32 R.V.; 1 Pet. i. 13). In the same sense the Spirit is said to reveal to the individual soul some hidden truth (1 Cor. xiv. 26). Philosophers have denied the possibility of revelation. How can the Infinite, they have said, communicate with the finite, the Creator with the creature? Can absolute truth be expressed in the relative terms of human language? To which we may reply that, although man cannot by searching find out God (Jb. xi. 7), yet God, the all-loving and all-wise, may find a way to communicate with men. The traveller describes the unknown in terms of the known, and the father teaches the child line upon line. So God in the incarnate, and through the written, Word has condescended to convey His thoughts to mankind.

It is evident that, if there be a revelation, the initiative must lie with God. For even the inner thoughts of a man, no one but the man himself can communicate (1 Cor. ii. 11); and as Irenaeus said, 'The Lord taught us that no one can know God, unless God Himself be the teacher; that is, without God, God cannot be known.'

God has in fact so come to our help: we open the pages of the

Bible and we find ourselves there confronted 'with a strange new world, the world of God'.[1]

(b) How the revelation came

The writers of the Old Testament believed that God spoke to them. In ancient times, we are told, God spoke 'in the prophets by divers portions and in divers manners' (Heb. i. 1 R.V.). The word of the Lord came to Abraham in a vision (Gn. xv. 1), to Moses out of the midst of the burning bush (Ex. iii. 4), to Aaron and Miriam out of the cloudy pillar (Nu. xii. 6), to the child Samuel by a voice in the night (1 Sa. iii. 4), to David through Nathan as God's chosen messenger (2 Sa. xii. 1).

By voices and visions and dreams God called and sent His messengers, 'rising early and sending them' (Je. xxv. 4, cf. Lk. xi. 49). He committed to them His message to deliver to the people, and they fearlessly proclaimed 'Thus saith the Lord' (Ex. iv. 22; Nu. xxiv. 13; Jos. vii. 13; Is. vi. 7, 8; Je. i. 8; Am. ii. 11; Mal. i. 2).

In the end of those days God spoke in His Son: the only-begotten in the bosom of the Father declared Him whom no eye had seen (Jn. i. 18). Even He spake not of Himself, but as He was taught of the Father (Jn. viii. 28); and, though expressed in simple Aramaic, His words were spirit and life (Jn. vi. 63).

The disciples bear testimony that they heard the word of the Father out of the heavens (Mk. i. 11, ix. 7; Jn. xii. 28; 2 Pet. i. 17); Paul received the word of the glorified Christ in open vision by day, or in the silence of the night (Acts ix. 4, xxiii. 11); by the voice of a fellow disciple or by means of an angelic messenger (Acts xxi. 11, xxvii. 24). We have already noted that the 'revelation of Jesus Christ' was sent and signified to John by an angel (Rev. i. 1).

What we have in the Gospels is not a mere biography of Jesus, nor a bare record of facts, but it is the 'testimony of Jesus' (Rev. i. 2, 9), the complement of the 'Word of God'. It is the ordained witness (Acts i. 8) of those who, having known Jesus 'after the flesh', now know Him as the ascended and eternal Son of God. One disciple declares the things which he himself has seen and heard (1 Jn. i. 3; Jn. xxi. 24), another writes an orderly account of those things which had been delivered by eye witnesses of the Word (Lk. i. 2, 3).

The New Testament writers testify to the gospel of the grace of God (Acts xx. 24), how the Father sent the Son to be the Saviour

[1] Barth, *The Word of God and the Word of Man*, p. 33.

of the world (1 Jn. iv. 14); their testimony is the spirit of prophecy (Rev. xix. 10), and whosoever receives their testimony sets to his seal that God is true (Jn. iii. 33).

It is in this fashion that God has found a way to convey His message to mankind, which we now have, expressed in human language and written for our learning, in the pages of the Bible (Rom. xv. 4). We proceed to consider the work of the Spirit in and through the Scriptures, or, in other words, their inspiration.

INSPIRATION

(a) The work of the Holy Spirit

When Paul wrote to Timothy that 'all scripture is given by inspiration of God' (2 Tim. iii. 16),[1] it is beyond doubt that he referred to the 'holy writings' (verse 15) of the Old Testament, the sacred literature which was able to make the reader wise unto salvation. By calling them inspired (*theopneustos*, God-breathed) he taught that 'the breath of God was in each "Scripture" as man's breath is in his words, making them to be the vehicle of his thought'.[2]

That the Old Testament was the work of the Holy Spirit was the convinced belief of the Christian church from the beginning, and that the Holy Ghost 'spake by the prophets' was a primitive element in the Eastern Creed. 'The Scriptures were given by the Holy Spirit' wrote Clement of Rome at the end of the first century. The prophets themselves were conscious that they were controlled by a power stronger than their own (Is. viii. 11, lxi. 1; Jer. i. 9; Ezk. iii. 4); they were indeed borne along by the Spirit of God (2 Pet. i. 21).

Much thought and labour have been expended upon the endeavour further to define inspiration, namely the mode whereby the Spirit operated upon the minds of the writers. Athenagoras likened His action to that of a flute-player making his flute vocal and tuneful.[3] The process of inspiration was assuredly not mechanical, for man is not a machine, nor does his Maker treat him as such. He called men to be His messengers, and committed to them His message, but it is delivered through the medium of their personalities, and its transmission is coloured by their characters and circumstances.

---

[1] The alternative renderings in R.V. and R.V. mg. do not affect the meaning of the words, or their reference to the *whole* of the Old Testament.

[2] Moule, *The Second Epistle to Timothy*, (R.T.S.) p. 123.

[3] Swete, *The Holy Spirit in the Ancient Church*, p. 45.

Certain features characterize the divine message as it came to Abraham which remind us of his flocks and pastures as he journeyed along the highway which led from Haran through the land of promise; the scene changes when the narrative of Joseph carries us to the land of Egypt, and again as we march with Moses through the wilderness and hear the thunders of Sinai. How different are the sweet songs of David, the incisive addresses of Amos, the plaintive pleadings of Jeremiah, Luke's carefully ordered narratives, or the compelling logic and loving exhortations of Paul. How thankful we should be for the human element in the Bible, and how worthy it is of study. We gain much from the four-fold portrait of Christ in the Gospels, each adding life to the picture; and faith is confirmed in that we have the testimony not only of Paul, but of James and Peter, John and Jude. But although in Scripture the human side is everywhere prominent, the divine is always dominant.

(b) The divine and human elements inseparable

The divine and human elements cannot be separated: we cannot say that this is human and that divine. The Bible is sometimes described as the record of a revelation; it is that, but it is more, for the record itself is an inspired part of the revelation. It is likewise sometimes said that the Bible contains the Word of God, which is true; but it is also true that it *is* the Word of God. There are not two parts as of a picture within a frame, one the work of the artist and the other of the picture dealer. God has not added His own words to those of the prophets, but has spoken *through* the prophets. The Holy Spirit did not give them a message, and then abandon them to add what they thought fit. It is well for us that it is so; for it would be the utmost folly to think that ignorant and sinful man could judge and say, 'this part is human and that divine; this is record and that revelation'. This would be to fall into Satan's snare and to set up ourselves as gods (Gn. iii. 5). It is our part to receive with meekness the engrafted word (Jas. i. 21), as He has been pleased to give it to us through those whom He has chosen to be His instruments and endowed with His Spirit for their work.

(c) Verbal inspiration

The expression 'verbal inspiration' is not to be found in the Bible, but the thought, as Lightfoot says, 'is involved in the conception of any inspiration at all, because words are at once the instruments of carrying on, and the means of expressing ideas'; more-

over, a particular word may be important and even crucial (see
Mt. xii. 37; Jn. x. 35; Gal. iii. 16). The 'judicious' Hooker said
that the Scriptures were with such perfection planned that they
contained neither a word too little or too much, and that the
authors 'neither spoke nor wrote one word of their own, but
uttered syllable by syllable as the Spirit put it into their mouths'.[1]

Yet the Christian does not think of his sacred books as the
Moslem thinks of the Quran, who believes that it loses its virtue
if translated into another tongue; nor does he regard it as a
Hindu does the Veda, as a charm which possesses no power but
in Sanskrit. On the contrary, the Bible revels in translation, and
the Christian rejoices to carry it to other races in their mother
tongue. For the real value of words lies not in their literal form,
but in their spirit and meaning, and in the living message they
are intended to convey. The Bible is verbally inspired in this sense
that, as Gregory said, it conveys to us 'the heart of God in the
words of God', in those 'sayings of God' (logia) which were the
greatest treasure of the Jews (Rom. iii. 2), and in those words of
our Redeemer which are 'spirit and life' (Jn. vi. 63).

But though the words are inspired, they are to be received,
under the new covenant, not in the letter but in the spirit, not as
carved mechanically in precise, unalterable characters upon hard
stone, but as a living message to the heart of man.

Considered thus, verbal differences or apparent discrepancies
here and there between various accounts of the same incident need
not surprise or perplex us; for as the double view of a stereoscope
gives perspective to the picture, so the presentation of varying
aspects of the same character or event enables its reality to be
better understood.

Even when the evangelists record differently the sayings of
Christ we do not give up our belief in their inspiration; for the
variations, due in part to translation from the Aramaic and in
part to the different impressions made on those who heard them,
actually supplement each other and illuminate the whole, as is
notably the case, for example, in the threefold account of the
Transfiguration, where each narrative helps to confirm our faith
in the facts, and has something to add by way of enrichment to
the picture.

(d) The witness of the Spirit

The process of inspiration, which is the work of the Holy Spirit,
did not end when the Bible was first committed to writing; it is

[1] Sermon V, p. 4.

only completed as the Spirit applies the Word to each believing soul.

This fact, which the reformers called the 'inward witness of the Spirit' (*testimonium Spiritus internum*) supplies the answer to the question frequently asked, How may we know that the Bible is truly the Word of God? No human witness can settle this question, the Word must be self-authenticating, and the only adequate testimony is that of the divine Spirit. Then, when God speaks, man can but listen: 'Yea, let God be true and every man a liar' (Rom. iii. 2-4). 'He that hath an ear let him hear what the Spirit saith' (Rev. iii. 6).

Christian experience endorses this teaching. Augustine records how, before his conversion, the Scriptures seemed to him inferior to much of the literature of Rome, but afterwards they became his delight and joy, difficulties disappeared, and he saw in them the truth, the inspired Word of God.

Where there is no faith the Bible may be studied as literature, or history, or even as theology, yet without spiritual profit. Just as the wireless waves create no impression upon the receiver which is not tuned in, so, in such a case, the voice of God will not be heard speaking through the written Word (Heb. iv. 2). But when a man is born again, the Bible becomes to him a new book. Then, by the Spirit's influence, it is seen as it were *from the inside*, and as the glory of stained windows is revealed by the sun shining through them, so that which before seemed dull and commonplace is filled with new meaning and beauty.

The necessity of faith does not mean that the intellect is laid aside; on the contrary it is quickened and is never so effective as when listening to the Redeemer's voice. Now the Holy Spirit who inspired the Scriptures acts as their divine interpreter; it is He who 'inspireth the true meaning unto them that with humility and diligence seek for it' (Chrysostom).

(e) The Living Word

Whilst we affirm that the Bible *is* in itself the inspired Word of God, yet, in another sense, its message *becomes* the Word of the living God to the individual when it is received by faith, and begets new life within the soul (1 Pet. i. 23, 25; 1 Cor. ii. 12, 15; 1 Thes. ii. 13).

In this sense it is not something we possess, it is rather something which possesses us. It is living and powerful, and a critic of thought and will (Heb. iv. 12). Professor Romanes gave his testimony that in his agnostic days, when he began to examine the

Bible, he suddenly became aware that it was examining him. It instructs, convicts and corrects (2 Tim. iii. 16), and the wisdom which it imparts is divine.

The written Word is God's instrument which lives and abides, and by which His voice still speaks directly to the soul. The Word therefore comes to us with *authority*, and into the nature and scope of this authority we must now inquire.

AUTHORITY

(a) *Its nature*

The source of the authority that belongs to the Bible is God Himself. Its essential truth is a consequence of its divine origin. Christ Himself stated, 'Thy word is truth' (Jn. xvii. 17).

Augustine attributed God's provision of a written revelation to the inability of mankind to find Him through human reason. 'Since then we were too weak by the light of reason to find out truth, and for this very cause needed the authority of holy writ, I had now begun to believe that Thou never wouldst have given such excellency of authority to that Scripture throughout all lands, hadst thou not willed that through it Thou shouldst be believed, and through it sought.'

Bishop Chillingworth, a thoughtful writer of the seventeenth century, put the matter thus: 'Reason will convince any man, unless he be of a perverse mind, that Scripture is the Word of God, and then no reason can be greater than this; God says so, therefore it is true.'

The authority of Scripture, however, is not held in Protestant opinion to supersede or exclude the use of reason. But the human mind should not set itself above the Word, or pick and choose what it will, and what it will not, follow; but realizing that all human reason is limited and imperfect, will find its highest exercise in the endeavour to understand its teaching, to appropriate its promises and to obey its commands, accounting it, as Isaac Newton said, 'the most sublime philosophy'.

Belief in the divine origin of the Bible decided the attitude towards it adopted by the Reformers. They placed it above traditions of the church, which can have no force of obligation unless they can be proved by holy writ; and above the authority of General Councils, since they are not entirely governed, as they should be, by the Spirit and Word of God.

Holy Scripture is the ultimate authority; one Scripture must be interpreted by another, nor may one be so interpreted as to contradict another.

This authority resides in the Bible as a whole. The interconnection between the Old and New Testaments is too strong and penetrating for it ever to be possible to accept the one as the Word of God and reject the other. When Christ rebuked Satan with the words, 'It is written, man shall not live by bread alone, but by every word that proceedeth out of the mouth of God' (Mt. iv. 4), He was quoting Moses' words from the book of Deuteronomy, so uniting the old and new dispensations.

(b) How the Old and New Testaments are related

In reading the Old Testament, it must be remembered that it differs from the New Testament because of its incomplete, temporary and preparatory character; it is related to it as a highway leading to its destination. The Law and the Prophets were until John; since then the Kingdom of God is preached and men press into it (Lk. xvi. 16). The Prophets prepare the way of the Lord, the Gospels tell of His birth and lead up to His cross and resurrection, the other books look back to these, and forward to His return.

1. The Old Testament must be read in the light of the New. The true meaning of the Mosaic Law is found in Mt. v.-vii., where its moral content is expounded and expanded, and summed up in the golden rule (vii. 12). We should not think of the Law after the manner of the Pharisees, as a collection of trivial rules, but as a call to love God and our neighbour (Mt. xxii. 40), a lamp and light by which to walk, a storehouse of wisdom and gracious promises, the delight and rejoicing of the heart (Ps. cxix.). The civil statutes, like the proverbial philosophy of Israel, were an inspired selection from the common property of the ancient world, adapted to the needs of the people of God from age to age. The tabernacle, with its sacrifices and ceremonial was, as the Epistle to the Hebrews teaches, a pre-figuring of Christ and His High-priestly work.

The prophets were sent by God to teach the people and to be the forerunners of Christ (Mk. i. 2, 3); from Abraham onwards they looked forward to His 'day', and predicted His sufferings and entrance into glory (Lk. xxiv. 25, 26; Jn. viii. 56; Acts iii. 21-24). The historical books cannot be treated better than by following the example of Christ and His apostles, accepting their narratives without demur, and seeing in them the revelation of God's mighty deeds and righteous judgments (Lk. xvii. 26-29; Acts vii.), and the miracles they contain as parallel to those of the Gospels, wrought in mercy by the same almighty hand.

2. The Old Testament is equally necessary in order to grasp the full significance of the New, which by hundreds of citations and references appeals to its authority so that, if that be denied, much of the apostolic teaching is invalidated. The New Testament is the sequel to the Old and, as such, the heir of its distinctive ideas. The holiness and righteousness of God, His judgment and His mercy, His redeeming purpose and the remission of sins through the shedding of blood, His Spirit and His anointed King were all first revealed to Moses and the prophets, whose teaching lies behind and explains the meaning of these terms in the Christian dispensation.[1]

Moreover, Jesus Christ according to the flesh was the Son of David, the Son of Abraham, the promised seed, the heir to David's throne, and the glory of God's people Israel (Is. ix. 7; Je. xxiii. 5; Mt. i. 1; Lk. i. 32; Acts xiii. 22; Gal. iii. 16). He is the second Adam, and there is not a name in the long line of His genealogy, nor any event in the Old Testament story of redemption which does not illuminate in greater or lesser degree His wonderful Person and work.

(c) Its range

In applying the authority of the Bible it is important to keep within the range of its purpose. It was never intended to be a compendium of knowledge, nor to save us from study or research. Therefore we should not go to the Bible to learn astronomy even though an astronomer of reputation[2] has asserted that it contains not a single astronomical error. In the same way we may believe that the Levitical rules for health possessed divine sanction and show a remarkable insight into the principles of medicine, without thinking that they were intended for use in Europe to-day. The Reformers, in their day, found it necessary to point out that the civil ordinances laid down for Israel, whilst ordained of God, were not meant to be binding upon all people for all time. So we in our day may believe that the disciples were guided by the Spirit to have all things in common, without thinking that this was meant to teach 'communism'.

On the other hand, it is the supreme and decisive standard in all matters of faith and practice. In every matter that concerns his spiritual welfare the Christian should consult the Scriptures and, having ascertained their teaching, should accept it as 'certain and infallible truth revealed by God, who by reason of

---

[1] See Snaith, *Distinctive Ideas of the Old Testament.*
[2] E. W. Maunder, *The Astronomy of the Bible.*

His infinite knowledge cannot be deceived, and by reason of His transcendent holiness cannot deceive'.[1] The word 'infallible' raises a difficulty in many minds and is deserving of careful consideration.

(d) An infallible guide

To call the Bible infallible does not mean that it renders the reader infallible, but that, when rightly understood, it will never lead him astray. Two implications seem to be involved in our Lord's saying to the Sadducees: 'Do ye not therefore err, because ye know not the Scriptures, neither the power of God?' (Mk. xii. 24). In the first place He attributed their error to ignorance or misunderstanding of the Scriptures and of God's almighty power, and He also implied that a true knowledge of the Scriptures would surely lead them aright.

Lack of faith and wisdom may hinder our apprehension of the Bible's true meaning. The language of the East is more flexible and pictorial than our own, and we may not always rightly determine what is intended as historical fact and what as parable. Even the most devout students have not always agreed as to the exact relation between historical background and dramatic setting in poetical books like Job and Canticles. Again, it would be rash to assert that the inspired writers who copied genealogies or scraps of learning from ancient records would necessarily be led to correct them in the manner dear to Western minds of the twentieth century.

But such cautions as to the interpretation of Scripture are no challenge to its infallible truth. Many students indeed have concluded that the Bible *cannot* be infallible because it is the work of fallible human beings, and because of the defects and discrepancies which they find in the present text. But the latter consideration does not apply to what was originally written, and the former is not a logical consequence; for it must be self-evident that God *could* preserve the writers from error.

The question of infallibility cannot be decided by *a priori* reasoning. It must ultimately depend upon what is revealed, and its reception requires both faith in the power of God and spiritual understanding. In the last analysis, God alone can be witness to Himself.[2]

[1] Pearson, *On the Creed*, p. 16.
[2] A very reverent and scholarly treatment of the subject will be found in *The Infallible Word*, compiled by the staff of the Westminster Theological Seminary, Philadelphia, and published in Great Britain by the Tyndale Press.

Augustine has some wise words for our guidance. After long deliberation he reached this conclusion: 'I do not doubt that their authors therein made no mistake and set forth nothing which might mislead. If in one of these books I stumble upon something which seems opposed to the truth, I have no hesitation in saying that either my copy is faulty, or that the translator has not fully grasped what was said, or that I myself have not understood.'[1]

When we have done our best, unresolved difficulties will remain, as they do in the world of science and every realm of human thought; yet we shall find spiritual food in that which we do understand, and that which we do not will stimulate our further study.

(e) The incarnate and the written Word

The Christian who is guided by the teaching of the New Testament will be in no danger of 'Bibliolatry', nor of setting its authority above that of Christ, who is the divine Son of God and alone to be worshipped. But neither will he join with those who deny that the Bible is 'God's Word written', and who assert in contrast that 'God's message was spoken in its finished and final form through a Person rather than through a book'.

It is easy to fall into confusion of thought on this subject. That the supreme and ultimate revelation of God was in His Son, Jesus Christ, is a fundamental tenet of Christianity, and no authority can exceed that of His words. But His words (and His deeds), which were the objects of direct experience for the apostles, are made known to us only through their testimony, preserved in the pages of the Gospels. For us these writings, and not the primary experiences of the first disciples, are 'the finished and final form' of the message. The Christian revelation did not reach completion till after Pentecost and the writing of the New Testament, and our belief in its inspiration 'finds its justification in the promises of divine assistance made by our Lord to the apostles and their company, and the special gift of the Spirit possessed by the apostolic age'.[2] Unless the truth of the New Testament can be guaranteed we are left adrift on a sea of speculation. One critic may deny the virgin birth, and another the bodily resurrection of our Lord, whilst a third may rob us of some of His most precious sayings, until nothing is left to us but the attenuated Christ of the imagination of any critic whom we choose to follow.

It should be evident that the revelation happens in the Scrip-

---

[1] *Epistles* LXXXII.
[2] Swete, *The Holy Spirit in the New Testament*, p. 389.

tures we have, and not in something we try to get at behind them. It is through the book that we know the Person, and because of the Person that we have received the book. The incarnate and the written Word mutually support each other.

THE BIBLE DOWN THE AGES

It remains to say a word about the influence which the Bible has exercised in the world since its completion in the first century of our era.

Whilst the books of the New Testament were being written, the message they contain was received as the Word of God (1 Thes. ii. 13), because it was attested by the Old Testament Scriptures (Acts ii. 16, xvii. 2, 3, 11) and by the 'signs' that followed (Mk. xvi. 20; Acts v. 12, xix. 18-20). The signs ceased, but the witness of fulfilled prophecy and of the Spirit remained.

During the second century the Old Testament was received as divinely inspired by Gentile philosophers and other converts on the authority of Christ and His disciples; whilst the New Testament writings gradually won their way to acceptance upon an equal footing; Irenaeus speaks of them as 'spoken by God's Word and His Spirit',[1] and Origen[2] describes the Evangelists, through the aid of the Spirit, as 'incapable of error or lapse of memory'. The burning of Scriptures by Diocletian and other persecutors could not hinder the growing hold they had upon the Christian church. In spite of spiritual declension in East and West, the Bible was copied and translated far and wide.

With the revival of learning in the fifteenth century, it became the foundation of study in the schools and universities. At the dawn of the Reformation Henry VIII in 1538 ordered the provision of a Bible in English for every parish church. J. R. Green, in his *Short History of the English People*, describes what followed in these words: 'It was read in church and read at home, and everywhere its words, as they fell on ears which custom had not deadened, kindled a startling enthusiasm. . . . No greater change ever passed over a nation. England became the people of a book, and that book was the Bible.' Writing of the authorized version published in 1611, G. M. Trevelyan says that the effect of its study 'upon the national character, imagination and intelligence for nearly three centuries to come was greater than that of any literary movement in our annals, or any religious movement

[1] *Adv. Haer.* 2. 28.
[2] Commenting on Mt. xvi. 12.

since the coming of St. Augustine'.[1] It would be easy to multiply this testimony by quotations from modern writers and speakers.

The past century has seen an immense expansion in missionary work, and with it translations of the Bible have circulated in all lands. In India it is more widely read than any other book, and is frequently upon the lips of educated Moslems who have never read the Quran and of Hindus who are ignorant of the Vedas. In Uganda it is the foundation book of those who can read, and has raised the Baganda to the leading place among the Bantu races. In China it is treasured by many in high position. Here are the words of the Chinese generalissimo, Chiang Kai Shek, when taken prisoner by bandits in 1937: 'I have now been a Christian for nearly ten years, and during that time I have been a constant reader of the Bible. Never before has this sacred book been so interesting to me as during my two weeks' captivity in Sian. . . . From my captors I asked but for one thing, a copy of the Bible.'

Truly we may say, 'All thy commandments are truth. Concerning thy testimonies, I have known of old that thou hast founded them for ever' (Ps. cxix. 151, 152).

[1] *The History of England*, p. 367.

CHAPTER II

THE TEXT

A MONG the consequences of the intensive study of the text of the Old and New Testaments undertaken by scholars of the last three generations, one of the most important is the conviction based on irrefutable evidence that we hold in our hands to-day a Bible which differs in no substantial particular from the originals of the various books as they came from the hands of their authors. Differences of reading are of course inevitable in the case of writings copied by hand for many centuries, but in no case is any doctrine affected by these variations. In the case of the Old Testament the careful copying of the Jewish scribes has preserved the text with remarkable accuracy; while in that of the New Testament we have Professor F. J. A. Hort's[1] word that, putting aside insignificant variations of grammar or spelling, not more than one thousandth part of the whole is affected by differences of reading.

THE OLD TESTAMENT

While it is possible that the book of Genesis contains elements going back to primitive times, written originally on tablets in Babylonian cuneiform, the language of the Old Testament is classical Hebrew, the spoken form of which was in use by the Jews from about the fourteenth century B.C. or earlier until the Babylonian captivity at the beginning of the sixth. The only exceptions are one verse in Jeremiah and portions of the books of Daniel and Ezra,[2] which are written in Aramaic, a Semitic language akin to Hebrew, named from Aram or Syria, the country bordering upon Palestine on the north-east, where the Jews came into closest contact with this language during the kingdom period. A dialect of this language may have been the speech of the patriarchs. At the time of the exile and onwards it superseded Hebrew as the language of Palestine and became the *lingua franca* of the Middle East. Later it was gradually superseded by Greek. Aramaic was the language habitually spoken by our Lord and His disciples.

[1] *New Testament in Original Greek*, ed. B. F. Westcott and F. J. A. Hort, Vol. II, Introduction (1881), p. 2.
[2] See pp. 180, 233.

MSS. of the Hebrew Old Testament

No extant MS. can be dated earlier than the ninth century A.D. There is a ninth-century MS. of the Pentateuch in the British Museum, one of the Prophets in Leningrad dated 916, and a large number more in Russia. At Cambridge there is a Hebrew MS. dated 856, but scholars consider the dating to be erroneous.

All extant Hebrew MSS. of the Old Testament contain what is known as the Massoretic text. The Massoretes were Jewish Rabbis and scholars who edited the Hebrew Old Testament during the seventh century A.D. and onwards. They reduced the text to uniformity and assured its permanence by meticulous rules for the direction of copyists. When a book had been copied, the number of letters in the exemplar and copy had to be counted and if a discrepancy occurred the copy was rejected. The Massoretes added the present vowel-points to the text, thus greatly adding to the intelligibility of a consonantal text but sometimes perpetuating incorrect meanings. The extreme care taken of the text by the Massoretes accounts for the late date of our extant MSS., there being no need to preserve older copies when their exact identity with the later ones had been guaranteed.

The edition of the Massoretes was based upon the *Talmud*, which was an explanation and commentary upon the Old Testament dating from about A.D. 270 to 500. Thus the Massoretic text, which is the official Jewish text, has handed down the Hebrew text current in the second century A.D., which was substantially the text known and used in the time of our Lord. Behind the *Talmud* lie the *Targums*, which are Aramaic paraphrases of the Hebrew text and belong to the third and fourth centuries A.D. The text used for the purposes of these paraphrases was that current in Palestine in the first century B.C. It differs slightly from the Massoretic text on which our versions are based.

Versions of the Old Testament

One of the most important of Old Testament recensions, which can conveniently be grouped with the versions, is the Samaritan Pentateuch, probably originating in the eighth century B.C. in the circumstances described in 2 Ki. xvii. Copies of it exist dating from the tenth and thirteenth centuries A.D. or even earlier, some at least having been copied from the MS. now existing at Nablus, Palestine, which is thought by some to go back to the early centuries of the Christian era. The text differs from the Massoretic in about six thousand places, the majority of the differences being unimportant grammatical ones. Of the remaining differences

some have been deliberately effected (e.g. *Gerizim* for *Ebal* in
Dt. xxvii. 4); some consist of explanations or repetitions; while
others show genuine differences of reading. The Samaritan
readings are sometimes confirmed by the Septuagint (see below),
and about thirty-five of them are regarded as superior to those of
the Massoretic text.

The Greek version ('version' is the technical term for a translation) of the Old Testament known as the *Septuagint* is of outstanding importance. Its translation was begun in Alexandria in
the third century B.C. and it became the recognized Bible of the
Greek-speaking Jews. Its importance as a check upon the
Massoretic text can be readily understood. It was adopted and
used by the Christian church as the recognized version of the
Old Testament. This caused its rejection by the Jews, and a new
translation into Greek from the current Hebrew text, characterized
by extreme literalness, was made by the Rabbi Onkelos about
A.D. 150. In the course of the second century a further translation
was made by Theodotion, said to have been a Hebrew Christian,
also from the current Hebrew text, but using great freedom.
About the year 200 a fourth translation into Greek was made by
Symmachus. All four translations were arranged together in
columns with the Hebrew text and Greek transliteration by Origen
during the course of the third century, his work being known as
the Hexapla. The text of the original Septuagint was edited by
Origen himself. The Alexandrian version represents, of course,
a Hebrew text several centuries older than the Massoretic and it
differs considerably from it, least in the Pentateuch, most appreci-
ably in Samuel and Kings. The order of the sections in the book
of Jeremiah is different, and about one-sixth of the book of Job
is omitted. The opinion of most scholars is that where the
Septuagint differs from the Hebrew it is sometimes right because
it is supported here and there by the Samaritan, but that generally
speaking the Massoretic text is the more reliable of the two.

Almost the whole of the Greek Old Testament is contained both
in the Codex Vaticanus, in the Vatican Library at Rome, and the
Codex Alexandrinus, in the British Museum, and considerable
parts in the Codex Sinaiticus, discovered by Tischendorf in 1844
and now also in the British Museum. These great codices date
from the fourth or fifth centuries. The Codex Ephraemi, at Paris,
also comprises a fragment of a very ancient copy. In addition to
these great codices there are about eighteen uncial MSS. dating
from the fifth to the ninth centuries and over three hundred
cursives. It should perhaps be explained that 'codex' is the

technical term for a book of the form which we now use as opposed to a roll, which was the form in the ancient world.

Other versions of the Old Testament were made during the early centuries of the Christian era. The Syriac, known as the *Peshitta*, was made during the second or third century. It was taken from the Hebrew text but revised in the light of the Septuagint and cannot therefore be relied upon in the matter of variant readings. The two Coptic versions, *Bohairic* and *Sahidic*, appeared in the third century and were probably taken from the Septuagint. There were also Ethiopic, Gothic, Armenian, Arabic, Georgian and Slavonic versions, but none are of high value for purposes of textual criticism. The version known as the Old Latin was made probably in North Africa during the second century A.D. It was taken from the Septuagint and survives incompletely, its value for textual purposes being less in the case of the Old Testament than in that of the New. Finally comes the Latin version known as the Vulgate, the Bible of the Middle Ages and the official version of the Roman Catholic Church to-day. It is mainly the work of Jerome and consists partly of direct translation from the Hebrew, partly of revision of the Old Latin with reference to the Greek, and, in most of the Apocrypha, of the Old Latin version unrevised.

THE NEW TESTAMENT

Over four thousand MSS. of the New Testament or of parts of it are extant. The process of transmission divides itself into three periods, that of the *papyri* (from the first to the fourth century), that of the *uncials* (from the fourth to the ninth), and that of the *cursives* (from the ninth to the fifteenth). It should be clearly understood that the evidence for the text of the New Testament is far more abundant than it is for any other work that has come down to us from the ancient world.

Papyrus period

The common material for writing purposes at the beginning of the Christian era was the stem of the papyrus reed suitably treated. The plant grew profusely on the banks of the Nile. Many remains of documents written upon papyrus have been discovered during the last fifty years in Egypt, among them fragments of MSS. of the New Testament. One of the most remarkable of these discoveries has been that of three papyrus codices dating from the third century and containing a large part of the New Testament. They were found about 1930 and purchased by Mr. A. Chester Beatty. The whole of the New Testament can seldom, if ever, have been

contained in a single codex or upon a single roll during this period.
The Christian Church, though increasing in strength and influence, remained an underground movement within the Roman
Empire until the fourth century. Possession of a Bible or of part of
it was dangerous during times of persecution. Individual Christians generally belonged to the poorer classes. This means that
copies of the Scriptures must have been often hastily made by
persons unable to distinguish marginal glosses from the genuine
text. The possibilities of confusion arising from such circumstances
can be easily imagined. It is remarkable that so few of these
possible confusions actually occurred.

Uncial period

The whole aspect of the problem of the transmission of the text
changed when Christianity was given official patronage in the
fourth century. The emperors made it their business to discover
and preserve the best text, and the great vellum codices came into
existence. The script in this period is generally that known as
'uncial' in which most of the characters are written in the form
which would now be recognized as capital letters. This type of
hand is clear and may be beautiful. At a later period uncial
script, for a variety of reasons, fell out of fashion and was succeeded
by various types of cursive script.

Cursive period

A cursive script is a running hand used for ordinary purposes,
e.g. for writing letters. Some of these hands are difficult to
decipher. The value of the cursive MSS. to the textual critic lies
in their number, which provides many checks upon the text. The
cursive MSS. do not supply any type of text unknown in the
previous periods, but an important variant reading is preserved
from time to time in one or other of them.

Types of text

In thinking of the different types of text into which scholars have
divided the material we should always bear in mind the comparative unimportance of the majority of variations. In 1881
Westcott and Hort divided the text into four types of families.
The first group is that known as the *Syrian* because it was believed
to have originated at Antioch, though more recently the name
Byzantine has been preferred. It is substantially the text of the
Codex Alexandrinus (early fifth century). It was the text of the
first printed edition of the Greek New Testament, that of Erasmus
produced at Basle in 1516. It is that of the third edition of the
Parisian printer, Stephanus, which appeared in 1550, based upon

Erasmus, and of the Elzevir edition of 1624, which scarcely differs from it. It is known as the 'received text', and has been that of all subsequent editions of the Greek New Testament until the publication of the modern critical editions. It was derived by Erasmus from a few late MSS., the most important of the great codices not having been yet discovered.

Another type of text is known as the *neutral* or *Alexandrian*. It is substantially the text of the great Codex Vaticanus and the Codex Sinaiticus. Westcott and Hort placed emphatic reliance upon it, and it has been thought to be the nearest to the original of all texts which survive.

Mention should be made of the type of text which is known as *western* because it is the text of the Old Latin version and appears in Latin MSS. or those which have both Greek text and a Latin version. It is not now thought to have originated in the west. The chief representative of this text is the Codex Bezae, at Cambridge, which contains the Gospels and Acts.

The tendency of scholars since the days of Westcott and Hort has been further to subdivide to the extent of recognizing five[1] types instead of four, but to regard the types as less independent than formerly. Certain families of MSS. are thought to be of greater importance than others, and there are scholars who consider it reasonably certain that the original text may be found wherever a given group of two or more of these families agree.

Versions of the New Testament

The earliest of these is the *Diatessaron* of Tatian, a harmony of the four Gospels made in the second century, for the use of the Syriac churches, but whether originally in Greek or Syriac is not known. It is extant to-day in an Arabic translation, and a fragment of it in Greek has been recently discovered. It is based on the western type of text and was probably compiled in Rome.

The old Syriac version of the Gospels probably dates from about the year 200. Its basic text was perhaps of the neutral group, though it shows some western readings which it may have derived from the *Diatessaron*. Some suppose it to represent an independent textual type. The official version of the Syriac churches from the fifth century onwards was that known as the *Peshitta*. Its text is more akin to the group known as Syrian than to any other.

There are at least five ancient Egyptian versions representing

---

[1] These are (1) the *Alexandrian*, (2) the *western*, (3) the *Caesarean* (represented by the Koridethi Gospels and the Chester Beatty papyri), (4) the *Antiochian* (represented by the old Syriac version), and (5) the *Byzantine*.

different dialects of the Coptic language. The two principal ones are the *Bohairic*, in the dialect of lower Egypt, and the *Sahidic*, showing a few western affinities. The remaining three versions seem to be based on the Sahidic.

Other ancient versions are the *Armenian*, dating from the fifth century, the text of which is mixed, the *Georgian*, with a text known as Caesarean, the *Gothic*, dating from the fourth century, based on a text of Syrian type, and the *Ethiopic*, dating from the sixth or seventh.

In the west we have the Old Latin versions, the earliest of which was made for the use of the North African churches. There were variations of this in use in Italy and elsewhere. The Old Latin versions were in existence in the fourth century and must be distinguished from the great version of Jerome, still current as the official version of the Roman Church, and known as the Vulgate. They are not of very great importance for our knowledge of the transmission of the text. Jerome's Vulgate, which dates from the time of the fourth and fifth centuries, seems to have been compiled from Greek MSS. of a neutral type, though it contains western readings owing to the influence of the Old Latin.

English versions

A few versions of the Psalms and Gospels were made in Anglo-Saxon times. The Norman conquest put an end to translations of Scripture into the vernacular for three hundred years owing to the influence of Continental ecclesiastics and the use of French by the upper and professional classes. In the fourteenth century translation was resumed and versions were made in Middle English of the Psalms, the Apocalypse, the Pauline Epistles, the Acts and the Catholic Epistles previous to the Wycliffite versions. There were two of these, neither being directly the work of Wycliffe personally. The later of the two superseded the earlier and must have been widely used in the country until the Reformation.

In the sixteenth century came the translations of Tyndale and Coverdale, and several other versions based upon them, of which the most popular was the Geneva version, published in 1560. These culminated in the great Authorized Version of 1611, a masterpiece of literary style and skill which embedded itself in the life and literature of the English people. The Revised Version of 1881-84, though based upon superior MSS., has not succeeded in replacing the Authorized Version in popular favour. Modern translations used to a considerable extent are those of Dr. Weymouth and Dr. Moffatt.

CHAPTER III

THE CANON

I. THE OLD TESTAMENT

THE root meaning of the word 'canon' (Gk. *kanon*) is a 'rule' or 'standard' by which a thing is measured. From this it came to be applied to 'that which is measured' by an authoritative standard. The word may be applied to the books of Scripture in both senses since they are (1) a God-given rule and guide, and (2) those which conform to the standard of inspiration. However the use of 'canonical' as applied to Scripture arose, it is clear that its books are authoritative, not because any body of men has made them so, but because they already bore the stamp of their divine origin, which was recognized as distinguishing them from all other books.

With this view of the meaning of the word 'canon', that it signifies 'the authoritative Word', we may trace its development from the earliest expressions of belief in such authority.

LIMITS OF THE CANON

The Protestant Church accepts as canonical identically the same books as the Jewish Church. The Roman Church, since the Council of Trent (1563), includes also the books of the Apocrypha. The order in the English Bible is that of the LXX, but in the Hebrew Bible the books are divided into three groups: (*a*) The Law (*Torah*), Genesis to Deuteronomy; (*b*) The Prophets (*Nebiim*), sub-divided into (1) the Former Prophets (Joshua, Judges, Samuel, Kings), (2) the Latter Prophets (Isaiah, Jeremiah, Ezekiel, and the Book of the Twelve, Hosea to Malachi); (*c*) The Writings (*Kethubim*), called in the LXX the *Hagiographa*, the remaining books of our canon including Daniel (see Lk. xxiv. 44).

These three divisions are evidence of three stages by which first the Law, then the Prophets, and finally the Writings were included in the canon. But it is not evidence that this was the chronological sequence in the order of their composition. The word '*Torah*' meaning 'teaching', was early applied to denote the first five books of the Bible (Ho. viii. 12), which were always recognized by the Jews as the work of Moses the Lawgiver.[1]

The function of a prophet was that of one whose life was devoted

---

[1] See Chapter IX.

to revealing the messages of God and His purpose for His people. Foretelling the future constituted only a small portion of his message. The revelation was given largely through the word which was preached and later set down in writing; but it came also through the written record of the way in which God dealt with mankind. Hence the books which we would call *historical* were rightly included by the Jews among the *prophetical* books, both because their authors were prophets (e.g. Nathan, 1 Ch. xxix. 29; and Isaiah, 2 Ch. xxxii. 32), and because their contents are truly a prophetic message.

The books of Chronicles, Ezra and Nehemiah were excluded from the Prophets by virtue of their authorship, none of them being by prophets in the technical sense. Of the Psalms, many are anonymous, and others are ascribed to David, the king. He is called a prophet in the New Testament, as also is Daniel, but in that general sense in which this title is there applied to all *inspired* writers, whatever may have been their technical function. Proverbs, Ecclesiastes, and the Song of Songs are ascribed to Solomon, again a king. Job and Esther are anonymous. Ruth and Lamentations, which now appear among the 'Writings', were probably at first attached to other books, Ruth to Judges, and Lamentations to Jeremiah, and so would have been included in the Prophets when the grouping was first made. Later they were transferred to the Writings so as to be with the other three of the group of five called the 'volumes' (*Megilloth*, cf. Ps. xl. 7), viz. Esther, the Song of Solomon and Ecclesiastes.

HOW THE CANON WAS FORMED

The books were classified according to the status of their authors in the divine dispensation. The ground upon which their authority was accepted by the people was that they were manifestly the utterances of men inspired by God to reveal His word.

Accepting the claim of the Pentateuch to be the work of Moses, we can see that the laws, as soon as they were issued, were intended to be respected as the decrees of God Himself, and were therefore committed to writing and preserved that they might be both a reminder of the nature of these decrees and a witness to the fact that the people had accepted them as such. (See Ex. xxiv. 3, 4; cf. Mk. vii. 9, 10; Heb. ix. 18-20.) Later generations continued to regard the law of Moses as the commandments of God (Jos. i. 7, 8; xi. 15; Jdg. iii. 4; 1 Ki. ii. 3; 2 Ki. xiv. 6; 2 Ch. xxiii. 18). The history gives only scattered references to the actual performance of the Mosaic law; for, as Moses predicted (Dt. xxxi. 27), the people for long periods grossly neglected it and fell into the evil ways of their neighbours. Yet its authority was recognized by their spiritual leaders (e.g. Samuel, David, Solomon, and Hezekiah) and it was the *recognition* of its authority, not the issue of a new authority, which provoked Josiah's great distress upon finding how long it had been neglected (2 Ki. xxii. 11).

After the time of Moses other laws were issued by men of God. These were similarly committed to writing and preserved because, from the first, they were regarded as being binding upon the people (Jos. xxiv. 26, 27; 1 Sa. x. 25).

When we examine the prophetical books we find that the prophets themselves manifestly believed that they spoke with authority. 'Thus saith the Lord', is the common preface to their oracles. The people were taught to accept this claim and to distinguish between those who made it falsely and those who were truly authorized by the Lord (Dt. xiii. 1-5, xviii. 18-22; Zc. xiii. 3). If the spoken word was accepted as soon as it was uttered, how much more those oracles which the prophet himself was led to record because of their permanent value (Is. viii. 16).

The book of Jeremiah gives a clear picture of how his prophecies came to be written down (Je. xxxvi.). Thus, through each successive generation, a body of writings was being continually built up, which was accepted by the faithful in Israel as the authoritative word of the Lord and as the revelation of the divine will. Not only in the prophet's own day was his word so accepted, but later generations referred to the authority of the words of the prophets who preceded them (2 Ki. xvii. 13; Je. vii. 25; Dn. ix. 2; Zc. i. 4). The *historical* books which the prophets also wrote would be reverenced as much as the written records of their *preaching* and on the same grounds, namely, on the authority of the author as being a man divinely commissioned to be a revealer of the purposes of God.

The Old Testament itself provides little evidence of the grounds upon which the authority of the Writings was accepted, but we know that by New Testament times it was already customary to describe at least some of these Writings as the utterances of the Holy Spirit (Acts i. 16). At what stage in their history this ascription was given to these particular books remains in obscurity, but we may be confident that the reason for their reception into the canon was that they were commonly regarded as the authoritative oracles of God. Where their authors were not known, the characteristics of the books were sufficient to stamp them as divinely inspired.

STAGES OF COMPLETION

(a) The Law

The Old Testament canon was a body of Scripture, continually growing, yet complete at each stage, beginning with the edicts and records of the first lawgiver (Ex. xxiv. 3, 4; Dt. xxxi. 9-11; Jos. viii. 34, 35) and increased by the works of each successive prophet. Some think the promulgation of 'the book of the law' (taken to be Deuteronomy) by Josiah to be the first stage in the growth of the canon, and that a second stage was reached when Ezra 'read in the book of the law of God' to the people (Ne. viii. 18). We should rather regard the solemn reading of the law by Josiah, and later by Ezra, as occasions when that which had already been accepted for centuries as a document of sacred authority was brought again to the minds and impressed upon the wills of a people who, through pressure of events and neglect on the part of preceding generations, were in danger of losing sight of their responsibility towards God.[1] That Ezra made no mention of the writings of the prophets was due to the occasion; for it was to the precise commandments of the Law that he wished to bind the people in a pledge of obedience.

The existence of the Samaritan version of the Pentateuch, which owes its origin to the times of Hezekiah or earlier[2] affords evidence that the *Torah* was acknowledged by both Israel and Judah before the fall of Samaria, and probably before the division of the kingdom. Other books had been written by then, including Joshua and Judges, later grouped among the Prophets, together with the Davidic Psalms. These constituted the nucleus of the second and third divisions of the canon.

(b) The Prophets

We may dismiss the legend, found in 2 Esdras xiv. 19-48, that all the books of Scripture having perished by fire, Ezra was inspired to re-write them in forty days. Nor is there any sound evidence for the late tradition that the canon was edited and fixed by 'the men of the Great Synagogue', a body of 120 members presided over by Ezra.

The statement in 2 Mac. ii. 13 that 'Nehemiah . . . founding a library, gathered together the books about the kings and

---

[1] See Dt. xvii. 18; 1 Sam. x. 25; 2 Ch. xxxi. 3, and also on p. 118.
[2] See p. 120.

prophets, and the books of David, and letters of kings about sacred gifts' (R.V.), may indicate that Nehemiah played some part in the collection of the sacred books, other than the *Torah*, into a united body of Scripture. This would contain at least the greater part of the section known as 'the Prophets', and would include also some at least of the psalms of David. But such a collection may well have been in process of formation in the time of Daniel, for he refers to 'the books' (ix. 2) and these might have included more than the writings of Jeremiah which he specifically quotes.

The canon of the Prophets must have been closed when it became apparent that the voice of prophecy had been withdrawn, and perhaps we can see in Zc. xiii. 2-5 and Mal. iv. 5, the latest of the prophetical books, a foreshadowing of the termination of the era of true prophecy, which may have prepared the people to expect no further oracles of this kind. Certainly in the time of the Maccabees they were aware that the spirit of prophecy had long since departed (1 Macc. ix. 27), although faith looked to the future when a 'faithful prophet' should arise (xiv. 41).

Evidently they were well able to distinguish between the divine word and the human pronouncements of which there was no lack at that time. The canon was closed not by the arbitrary decision of council or scribe, but by the absence of any further prophetic voice.

(c) The Writings

There is little evidence for the date at which the *Kethubim* were accounted canonical. It may be that, as their authors were not prophets in the full sense of the word, these books were not received into the canon until it became evident that they also were written by 'holy men of God . . . moved by the Holy Ghost'. But 'The Wisdom of Jesus ben Sirach' (Ecclesiasticus) written in about 200 B.C. includes, in chapters xliv.-xlix., references to all the books of the Law and of the Prophets, and to part of the Writings. The 'Twelve Prophets' were by this time grouped into one section. The writer's grandson, in the prologue to his translation of the book into Greek (132 B.C.) mentions three times 'the Law and the Prophets and the other books of our fathers' as having been carefully studied by his grandfather. It is clear, therefore, that by 200 B.C., or at least by 132 B.C., the division of the canon into its three sections must have been fixed, and that it contained most, if not all, of what we now know as the canonical books.

THE CANON AT THE COMMENCEMENT OF THE CHRISTIAN ERA

By the commencement of the Christian era the word 'Scripture' had come to mean a fixed body of divinely inspired writings, the authority of which was fully recognized. This was the sense in which the word was understood by the Lord and His contemporaries when He said, for example, 'the scripture cannot be broken' (Jn. x. 34, 35). By many other similar references to and quotations from the Old Testament He endued it with His authority as the one complete revelation of the divine will. It is true that He gave no exact statement of the names or number of the books, but it was to the whole field of Scripture that He referred Cleopas and his friend (Lk. xxiv.) if they were to have an understanding of the events concerning the Messiah. In verse 27 of that chapter He speaks of 'Moses and all the prophets', and, in verse 44, of the Law of Moses, the Prophets, and the Psalms (see above).

The New Testament writers refer to all the canonical books of the Old Testament except Obadiah, Nahum, Ezra, Nehemiah, Esther, Song of Songs, and Ecclesiastes. However, Nahum and Obadiah formed part of one volume, *The Book of the Twelve Prophets*, which is amply quoted; Esther, Song of Solomon, and Ecclesiastes belonged to a complete group of five, the *Megilloth*, one of which was recited at each of five festivals of the Jewish Church. Ezra and Nehemiah originally formed one book with Chronicles.

Josephus, writing about A.D. 100 (*Contra Apionem*, i. 8), declares, 'For we have not an innumerable multitude of books among us, disagreeing from, and contradicting one another, but only twenty-two books which contain the records of all the past times; which are justly believed to be divine; and of them five belong to Moses, which contain his laws and the traditions of the origin of mankind until his death. . . . The prophets wrote down what was done in their time in thirteen books. The remaining four books contain hymns to God, and precepts for the conduct of human life.' The twenty-two books correspond exactly with the number in our present Canon if we consider that the twelve minor prophets counted as one book, that Ezra and Nehemiah were one, that Ruth was joined to Judges, and Lamentations to Jeremiah. Josephus' grouping is similar to that of the LXX, which counts Daniel among the prophets and Ezra to Job among the propheticohistorical books. Josephus goes on to say that later writings did not possess equal authority because 'there hath not been an exact succession of prophets since that time'. He emphasizes also the respect with which the Scriptures were held. 'For during so many ages . . . no one has been so bold as either to add anything to them, to take anything from them or to make any change in them; but it is become natural to all Jews . . . to esteem these books to contain divine doctrines, and to persist in them, and if occasion be, willingly to die for them.' These statements of Josephus, reflecting as they do the popular belief of his time, accord with the claim made above, that the canonicity of the books depended upon the divine authority of their authors, and that the general acceptance of their canonicity preceded any decision of the schools, although such a decision was probably made at the Council of Jamnia, c. A.D. 90, at which the limits of the canon already accepted by general consent received endorsement by that official body.

The proof that the leaders of Israel were divinely guided in their selection of books to be received into the Canon is to be seen in the result. In contrast with the ancient literature of other Eastern races the Bible is markedly free from polytheistic absurdities or vain boasting on the part of its heroes. It contains historical records and genealogies, laws and prophecies, psalms and proverbs, yet it is one whole, so constituted by its dominant theme, God's revelation of Himself, preparing the way for the coming of His Son to redeem mankind.

II. THE NEW TESTAMENT

THE QUESTIONS INVOLVED

THE meaning given earlier in this chapter to the word 'canon', applies equally to the New Testament, and implies the recognition of certain books as a part of the inspired and authoritative Scriptures, bearing the divine imprimatur as the Word of God. In both cases this recognition came, not through formal decisions, or suddenly, but as the result of a long and gradual process, worked out among the people of God guided by the Holy Spirit as they read and meditated upon the writings of prophets and apostles and heard God speaking through them. The formation of the canon was the end and not the beginning of this process.

For the Christian of to-day two questions are involved, namely, (1) Why should I believe that these books, and these alone are inspired? and (2) How did they come to be so regarded by the early church? In the case of the New Testament the answer to these questions is not quite the same as that given in respect of the Old. For, when our Lord lived on the earth, He and His disciples already possessed a Bible which, in common with the Jewish people, they revered as holy Scripture and quoted as having divine authority. As we have already seen, this alone would be a sufficient reason why we should reverence the ancient Scriptures as did our Master. But for the twenty-seven books of the New Testament we have no such guarantee. On the other hand, we have more abundant evidence regarding the writings and subsequent history of the New Testament books, and we can see more clearly how their ultimate collection into a canon of Scripture fulfilled the Lord's promise that the Holy Spirit should guide His followers into all truth.

The two questions of the *how* and *why* of the canon are closely related, and when the historical process has been described, the reasons why we should be satisfied with its result will appear.

THE HISTORICAL PROCESS

It will be convenient to divide the history into five periods, marking stages in the process by which the New Testament came to its present position, although this gives an appearance of artificiality to a growth which was essentially natural. The spread of the knowledge of the sacred literature, and the deepening understanding of its meaning and inspired character, were not confined to any one period, but went on continuously and uninterruptedly throughout three centuries. We may nevertheless get a clearer view of it by marking the following stages.

1. In the first century the various books were written, copied, and first disseminated in the churches.

2. In the first half of the second century they became more generally known, were read in churches and quoted with authority.

3. In the second half of the second century they were given a place beside the Old Testament as 'Scripture', translated, and made the subject of commentaries.

4. In the third century they were collected into one whole, were spoken of as the New Testament, and by a sifting process were separated from other Christian literature.

5. In the fourth century the writings of the Fathers state that the conclusions reached were universally accepted by all Christian people: in other words, the canon became fixed.

The first century. The Scriptures written

Information about the several books of the New Testament will be
found in the Introductions. It is uncertain when the 'words of the
Lord' (Acts xx. 35; 1 Cor. vii. 10) were first committed to writing.
Some think it was during His lifetime, or it may have been soon
afterwards. But it is certain that, when Luke commenced the
writing of his Gospel about the year 58, many had already taken
this work in hand (Lk. i. 1). Paul's Epistle to the Galatians may
have been written as early as A.D. 49, and those to the Thessalonians not later than 53. The Epistle of James must have existed
before his death in 62; Paul's other Epistles and those of Peter
before 68. The greater part of the New Testament was in writing
before the fall of Jerusalem (A.D. 70) wrought such great changes in
the Christian church. That some of Paul's letters were then
already in circulation is witnessed by 2 Pet. iii. 15, 16. The
Revelation of St. John is variously ascribed to the reign of Nero
or of Domitian, and his Gospel and Epistles, probably the last
books of the New Testament to be written, to the closing years of
the century.

The earliest Christian writings outside the New Testament all
show acquaintance with the Gospels and Epistles, either quoting
them or using their words with more or less exactitude. Clement
of Rome (*c.* A.D. 96) quotes 1 Corinthians by name, and shows a
knowledge of other parts of the New Testament; the Epistle of
Barnabas quotes the words, 'Many are called but few are chosen',
with the introduction 'as it is written'. Clement, Barnabas and
Ignatius all draw a clear line of demarcation between their own
and the apostolic writings, to which they attribute inspiration and
authority (1 Clem. i. 47; Ign. *Ad Rom.* iv).

These writers confirm the New Testament by revealing a state
of things in the Christian churches at the end of the first century
which corresponds exactly with that which it would lead us to
suppose. In addition they afford evidence that thus early the
Gospels and Epistles were being circulated and honoured in East
and West.

First half of the second century. The Scriptures read in churches

As we enter the second century Papias (*c.* 140), himself a hearer
of John the Apostle, bears witness to the way in which the living
voice of 'the elders' was being replaced by the authority of the
written word. About the same time, the writings of the heretic
Marcion show that he used the Gospel of Luke and ten of the

Epistles of Paul, and knew of the Apocalypse. Justin Martyr (148) refers to the 'memoirs of the apostles and their followers' (*Dial.* 103), which were read in churches, a custom which was then 'well established' in Rome, and so widespread in the next generation that 'we cannot refuse to carry back its origin some distance before the appearance of Marcion'.[1]

In the writings of this period distinct references can be found to all the books of the New Testament except six or seven of the shorter Epistles. The witness to their authority comes from heretics as well as from the orthodox. Basilides (125) quotes the New Testament as 'Scriptures' and uses the words 'It is written' to introduce a quotation.

Second half of the second century. Translations and commentaries

The second half of the second century was a time of rapid expansion and great development in the Christian Church. Christianity spread throughout the Roman Empire and beyond its confines; Pantaenus is said to have travelled to India and to have found there a Gospel of Matthew in Hebrew which had been brought by the Apostle Bartholomew. The ingathering of men of different races into the church, and the increasing competence of Christian scholars, led to the translation of the Scriptures into new languages. The Old Latin version for the people of North Africa, the Syriac for those of the East, and the early Coptic translations in Egypt can all be traced back to the second century.

Commentaries also began to appear. Papias wrote his *Commentary on Dominical Oracles* about 140[2], Heracleon also wrote a commentary on the Gospels, and Melito, Bishop of Sardis (165), one on the Apocalypse. Shortly afterwards Tatian, a disciple of Justin Martyr, wrote the Diatessaron, a harmony of the four Gospels, which were now recognized as possessing unique authority.

The Muratorian fragment (*c.* 170) contains a list of the books of the New Testament in which the Acts is ascribed to Luke, and the 'fourth Gospel' and the Apocalypse to the apostle John: five of our present books are missing from this list, but, as the MS. is incomplete, no safe deduction can be drawn from this. Irenaeus (180) freely quotes the Gospels and Epistles as 'Scripture'. About the end of the century Clement of Alexandria (150-220) wrote his *Outlines*, a commentary in seven volumes on the books of the New

---

[1] Gwatkin, *Early Church History*, I, p. 256.
[2] Gwatkin, *op. cit.*, I, p. 282.

Testament, including Jude and the other catholic Epistles, together with the addition of the Epistle of Barnabas and the Apocalypse of Peter.

The third century. The books of the New Testament collected and separated

The next century saw great advances in Christian learning and intellectual ability. Origen was a prodigious worker, and is said to have employed seven stenographers who worked for him by turn, besides seven copyists and sundry girls to make fair copies.[1]

Besides his famous *Hexapla*, or sixfold copy of the text of the Old Testament in Hebrew and Greek, he revised the text of the New Testament, defended its inspiration, and wrote commentaries and homilies upon most of its books, and, which is significant, upon no others. At Alexandria, Jerusalem, Caesarea, Antioch, Rome and elsewhere libraries began to be formed of which manuscripts of the Scriptures and commentaries upon them made up an important part. It was Tertullian (*c.* 200) who first called the Christian Scriptures the 'New Testament', thus placing them on the same level of inspiration with those of the former dispensation.

The collection of the Gospels and other writings into one volume, their translation into other languages, their recognition as the authority of the Christian faith, and the doctrine of inspiration all combined to make it important to distinguish clearly between the inspired Scriptures and other Christian books which had long been read for edification. The latter consisted primarily of the Apostolic Fathers, the writings of those who had been in touch with the Apostles, the Epistles of Clement, Barnabas, Hermas, Ignatius and Polycarp, and the *Didache*. Some of these were reckoned as inspired by some persons and at various times, but none generally or continuously. A third class of writings had also begun to appear in the shape of apocryphal Gospels and other spurious writings, such as the Gospels of the Infancy and the Apocalypse of Peter. These things, together with the growth of heresies and false doctrine, emphasized the need for an authoritative standard of doctrine, and led to the sifting and separating process by which the books of the New Testament were distinguished from all others, which is the equivalent of the formation of the canon.

The tests applied were, on the one hand, the consensus of church opinion and practice, and, on the other, internal evidence of apostolic authorship and authority. The last doubts which

[1] Gwatkin, *op. cit.*, II, p. 194.

needed to be dispelled concerned books like 2 Peter and the Revelation of St. John, the genuineness of which was questioned by some because of the differences of style between them and the other writings of these apostles.

The fourth century. The canon settled

At the beginning of the fourth century the majority, and before its close all, of the churches had accepted the canon of the New Testament as we have it to-day. Eusebius[1] gives us a balanced statement of how the matter stood in his day (316).

1. Universally 'agreed' to be canonical were the four Gospels, Acts, the Epistles of Paul (including Hebrews, though of doubtful authorship), 1 Peter, 1 John, Revelation.

2. 'Disputed' by some, though admitted by the majority and by Eusebius himself, James, 2 Peter (doubtfully) 2 and 3 John and Jude.

3. 'Spurious', The Acts of Paul, the Didache and the Shepherd of Hermas. He adds a fourth list of writings which are 'heretical and absurd'.

A generation later Athanasius accepted the whole New Testament as we have it, and in A.D. 397 the Third Council of Carthage ordered that 'besides the canonical Scriptures nothing be read in the church under the title of the divine Scriptures'. From thence onward all controversy died out. As we look back on the long process by which the books were written, disseminated, collected, and finally recognized as the Word of God, we can only be filled with wonder and praise for the overruling Providence which brought this about.

CONCLUSION

Although the books included in the canon were thus agreed upon, Christian scholars throughout the ages have never ceased to ask themselves afresh, as we do to-day, why they should reach the same conclusion.

Augustine found the answer in the character of the books themselves, in the consensus of Christian opinion, and in the testimony of those churches which had preserved a continuous apostolic tradition. In the days of the Reformation, when every aspect of the Christian faith had to pass through the crucible of criticism, the books of the Bible formed no exception. Luther went so far as to place Hebrews, James, Jude and the Apocalypse at the end of his German translation of the New Testament, seeing that these four

[1] *Eccl. Hist.*, III, 25.

were less universally accepted by the early church, whilst asserting that the remainder contained all things necessary to salvation. Calvin found a basis for his belief in the 'inward testimony of the Spirit', both in the individual and in the church, to all the Scriptures. We have a great heritage, and the same reasons which convinced the wisest of our predecessors may well convince and satisfy us. We know that many, who were eye witnesses of the events recorded, died rather than deny the things which they had seen and heard, and we have before us their testimony contained in writing of contemporary origin. We can trace the way in which the claim of these Scriptures to inspiration was examined and approved by Christian scholars of many lands and in critical ages; we have the internal evidence of fulfilled prophecy, and their grand unity. Finally we have the witness of the Spirit in our hearts.

The New Testament has survived all criticism and stood every test. One supreme test remains and lies ready to hand, that of practical application; for the word of God was given in order that the Christian might live by it (Mt. iv. 4). It is when he obeys its precepts, follows its guidance, puts his trust in its promises, and finds his Saviour in every part, that the truth breaks in upon his soul that it contains not a word too little or too much (Rev. xxii. 18, 19).

APPENDIX TO CHAPTER III

The Apocrypha

ORIGIN

THE Apocrypha ('hidden' or 'secret') is the name given to fourteen books found in the Vulgate, but not in the Hebrew canon. They are 1 and 2 Esdras, Tobit, Judith, additions to Esther, the Wisdom of Solomon, Ecclesiasticus, Baruch, The Song of the Three Children, the story of Susanna, Bel and the Dragon, the Prayer of Manasses, and 1 and 2 Maccabees. There is abundant evidence that they were never received into the Jewish canon, nor reckoned as part of the inspired Scriptures either by Jew or Christian in the early centuries of our era (Josephus, Melito, Origen). They have no place in the Massoretic text, nor were any Targums attached to them. They are nowhere cited in the New Testament.

Their origin is obscure; some date from the second century B.C., others belong to the first or second century A.D. They do not appear to have been included at first in the LXX, but they found their way gradually into later copies, being inserted in places that seemed appropriate, and so came to be included by Jerome in the Vulgate.

They vary greatly in character and value, from accurate history and lofty thoughts to worthless legends and dreary writing. Even a cursory glance reveals the gulf that divides them from the inspired Scriptures. For this reason, and because they found no place in the Jewish canon, or in New Testament quotation, the Reformers distinguished them sharply from the Old Testament; but they allowed certain portions to be read in churches for example of life and instruction of manners, like homilies, hymns, and other writings.

CONTENTS

1 Esdras is our book of Ezra with accretions; 2 Esdras consists of apocalyptic visions partly Jewish, partly Christian. Tobit and Judith are romantic, but fictitious, narratives of a Jewish hero and heroine. The seven extra chapters of Esther merely expand the story from professedly original documents. Wisdom is an imitation of Proverbs; it contains some noble passages, e.g. iii. 2-9, iv. 9-11, on the life of the righteous after death, and vii., viii., in praise of wisdom. Ecclesiasticus, or the Wisdom of Jesus, the son of Sirach, was written about 200 B.C. in Hebrew and translated by his grandson into Greek in 132 B.C. The passage xliv.-l. 21, in praise of famous men, is finely written. Baruch is a feeble imitation of Old Testament prophecy.

The Song of the Three Children (the 'Benedicite') was inserted after Dan. iii. 23, the story of Susanna prefixed to the same book, and that of Bel and the Dragon, in which the wisdom of Daniel is praised, after chap. xii. The Prayer of Manasses is a compilation of Old Testament passages. The first book of Maccabees, probably written about 100 B.C., is valuable as a history of the Maccabaean revolt.[1] The second book deals with a portion of the same period, but is inferior as a record, mixed with legend, and of little worth.

[1] See p. 28off.

CHAPTER IV

MODERN CRITICISM

THE USE OF TERMS

THE higher criticism of the Bible has been the cause of much controversy, and it is desirable to understand how this has come about. Criticism, in its grammatical sense, means no more than the exercise of judgment. When applied to literature, 'textual criticism' refers to the study of ancient manuscripts in order to recover the best original text; whereas 'higher criticism' is the term used for the discussion of date, authorship, etc., by means of internal and external evidence.

Used in this neutral sense, Biblical criticism, both textual and higher, is something not only permissible, but commendable, if pursued in a reverent and scholarly fashion. In the proper sense of the word, critical studies have been pursued by the early Fathers, by the Reformers and by Christian scholars up to the present day, all of whom have been fully persuaded of the divine authority of the Scriptures. But in the period which followed the 'destructive theology of the latter half of the eighteenth century' (Delitzsch), there arose a school of criticism in conformity with it. Early studies by Eichhorn (1783), De Wette (1805), and Ewald (1823) resulted in a 'documentary hypothesis' of the Pentateuch which assigned its origin to the combination of a series of documents, the first of which was not committed to writing until four or five centuries after the death of Moses. In the latter half of the nineteenth century, after many changes and adaptions, this hypothesis began to take on a stable form at the hands of two brilliant Hebrew scholars, Graf and Wellhausen.

Not believing in the possibility of miracle they elaborated a theory which pictures the religion of Israel as a gradual evolution from primitive animism, through a stage when Jehovah was taken as a tribal god, like the gods of the heathen, until, under the influence of the later prophets, a lofty level of monotheism was reached. The whole Old Testament was radically affected by this theory; the 'sources' of the various books were dated in accordance with it, using as a criterion the stage of the development which they were thought to reflect. The late dating of the documents opened the way for attributing their supernatural elements to the growth of myth or legend, and the history was completely reconstructed from this point of view.

A detailed view of the hypothesis as it affects the Pentateuch will be found in chapter IX; here it will suffice to note three of its fundamental characteristics.

1. *The Priestly legislation* (P) is said to be *post-exilic*. The Levitical law is assumed to be not Mosaic, but a priestly development during, and after, the exile.

2. *The Deuteronomic Code* (D), and allied documents, are assigned to the *prophetic period*, and the restriction of worship to a central sanctuary to the reform of Josiah.

3. *The history prior to the monarchy* is regarded as built up of *traditions* upon which little reliance can be placed.

REACTION TO WELLHAUSEN'S THEORY IN GREAT BRITAIN

These conclusions were at first rejected by British theologians because of their rationalistic and revolutionary character. But they had been built up with great ability and infinite pains; they seemed to explain certain facts and to remove some difficulties; their background harmonized with the evolutionary philosophy which reached the height of its popularity towards the close of the nineteenth century; and they soon found supporters.

In 1891 Professor Driver published his *Literature of the Old Testament* closely following the lines laid down by Wellhausen. Soon a group of scholars proclaimed the new teaching as the latest outcome of 'modern scholarship', and from that time it has gradually found entrance into the text-books for theological colleges and permeated the general religious life of this country. The general view of the Old Testament as set out by Professor Driver, and later by Oesterley and Robinson in three companion volumes, is often spoken of as 'modern criticism' (though now nearly a century old), and in what follows it will sometimes be referred to by this designation.

If it be thought surprising that theories so radical and propounded by professed rationalists should be so readily accepted, the following reasons, in addition to those mentioned above, may be offered in explanation.

1. The whole-hearted adoption of the documentary analysis by Robertson Smith and Driver, two of the best Hebrew scholars of the day, gave it an excellent start. As they based their opinion on linguistic and literary grounds, this tended to make others think

that it was a matter for experts, whose advice should be followed, and obscured the connection with the rationalistic outlook of its authors.

Both these British scholars held official positions in the church. In England Driver's statement that his conclusions 'did not affect the authority or the inspiration of the Scriptures'[1] reassured many.

In Scotland there was strong opposition: Robertson Smith was tried for heresy and deprived of his professorship. This savoured of persecution, was ascribed to prejudice, and in the end reacted in his favour. The desire to be in the forefront of scholarship attracted many younger scholars to the new ideas. They followed easily in the tracks which Wellhausen had traced out and Driver had popularized, and soon it was possible to proclaim the system as the 'assured results' of the higher criticism.

2. At first the most strenuous opposition came from those who clung most rigidly to traditional ideas and interpretations. This was easily ascribed to prejudice. Their appeal to the authority of Christ was met by a doctrine of the *kenosis*, or human limitation of our Lord's knowledge, which waived aside His teaching as limited by the current ideas of His environment, and therefore irrelevant.

At a somewhat later date, when scholars of repute such as Professors Sayce and Orr, in this country, and Hommel, Dahse, Troelstra and others on the Continent, met the critics on their own ground, and exposed the weakness of their arguments in detail, they were treated as an insignificant minority who could safely be ignored.

3. The whole system had been worked out with characteristic German thoroughness, and with conspicuous imagination and ability. Under opposition its weak points were discovered and adjustments made, until it assumed the form of a coherent and well-compacted structure. Within this framework there was much material that was both true and valuable, especially that which threw light upon the setting and original meaning of the Scriptures. In giving a welcome to this, many orthodox people failed to distinguish the true from the false, and so accepted the whole without discerning whither it was leading them.

4. During the closing years of the nineteenth century the attack on the New Testament by the Tübingen school from a similar standpoint had been met by the researches and arguments of great New Testament scholars such as Salmon, Westcott, and Lightfoot. At that time the citadel of the New Testament seemed

[1] Driver, *Literature of the Old Testament*, 1st Ed., p. x.

safe, and the defence of the Old Testament history and miracles appeared of secondary importance.

Further experience has shown this appearance to be fallacious, for the same spirit of scepticism underlies much recent criticism of the New Testament and has produced a 'modernist' school which claims to uphold the Christian creed whilst denying its miraculous elements, including the virgin birth, and bodily resurrection of our Lord.

A MODERN VIEW

Some recent writers attempt to combine an evangelical faith in the New Testament with Wellhausen's view of the Old. Their belief in the miracles of Christ clears them of the charge of rationalism, but they cannot so easily be acquitted of inconsistency. They, in fact, adopt a double standard. Whilst maintaining that the significance of events like the crucifixion and resurrection of Christ depends upon their having actually happened, they minimize the need of historical support for the miraculous events of the redemption story of the older dispensation.

Certainly Canon Phythian Adams[1] attempts to find a factual basis for the miracles of the Exodus, making rather large demands upon volcanic and electric phenomena for this purpose, but he concludes also that 'no voice, sublime and terrible' was heard from Sinai, and admits that 'a mass of legends' is found in the Pentateuch, from which the extraction of historical truth is very largely a matter of conjecture. But if no voice were heard from Sinai, what credibility can be attached to the narratives of the baptism and the transfiguration? And if miracles are no more than a 'miraculous coincidence' of events, how are we to explain the feeding of the five thousand, or the raising of Lazarus?

It is not possible to detach the religious significance of facts from the question of their history. Christ and His apostles quote from the Old Testament historical instances of God's actions as revealing His character, with the implication that the record can be relied upon. This is something vastly different from treating it as a mass of legends, and the difference should not be glossed over or ignored.

Dr. Wheeler Robinson quite reasonably protests against 'timidly conservative' formulations of the history which 'ask us to believe more than the Hebrews themselves ever believed'. What

[1] *The Call of Israel, passim.*

we wish to state here is that what they believed, both writers and readers, is far removed from the modern view just described.

PRESUPPOSITIONS

The questions raised by modern criticism involve issues so deeply affecting the Christian faith that it is impossible to approach them without presuppositions derived either from human reason, or from Christian experience. Those who have been strongly influenced by the doctrine of evolution would expect to see in all religion a slow upward development from primitive beginnings: whilst those who are more impressed by the miracle of divine grace triumphing over human weakness will find no difficulty in believing that God could reveal Himself as easily to Moses as to the later prophets. One who has been fascinated with Wellhausen's ingenious guesses and sceptical spirit could attribute the tabernacle to the fancy of some late writer; on the other hand, one imbued with the spirit of the Epistle to the Hebrews would believe in its reality and see in its ordinances a divine 'pattern'.

Those who think the Old Testament worthless as history cannot view questions concerning it in the same light as others who regard it as 'unequalled as a source of knowledge about the history of civilization in one important region of the ancient world'.[1]

It is the same with the documentary hypothesis, and the methods which support it. A life spent in the study of the niceties of Hebrew vocabulary and style predisposes the mind to build a theory upon the use of special words and expressions, whereas those whose thoughts are cast in a more logical mould will be sceptical of a method which cannot stand the test of application to modern literature.

In their search for truth, both advocates and opponents of Wellhausen's theories come to their consideration with certain convictions already formed, which influence their conclusions.

THE RATIONALISM UNDERLYING THE WELLHAUSEN THEORY

The various parts of the critical theory are bound together by a logical connection which should not be overlooked. Those who began by rejecting the miraculous looked upon the accounts of miracle as either legend or myth, and were logically bound to work out a theory of the documents and the religious development

[1] Danby, *The Study of Theology*, p. 192.

according with their evolutionary ideas. This involved the abandonment of the story of revelation as told in the Bible, and the reconstruction of what was conceived to be the true history which lies behind its fables and traditions. The documentary analysis rendered this possible by affixing to each document, or fragment, a date corresponding with the critic's view of the history and religious progress. Thereby a book which purports to be a true narrative derived from contemporary sources was turned into a late compilation derived from varying traditions, myths and legends.

All this is logical enough once the original premise is granted that no such thing as miracle exists. It is strange, however, that so many who are themselves opposed to rationalism should fail to perceive that the converse of this process is just as much a logical necessity. Those who accept, and think they are bound on literary grounds to accept, the documentary analysis with the corresponding dates, sooner or later awake to find themselves with a Bible purged from miracle and prediction, untrustworthy as history, and utterly different from what it claims to be.

The more closely this matter is examined, the more evident it will become that we have here two *systems of thought*, each more or less coherent in itself, and each bound up with the general standpoint adopted. This is why those who try to compromise between the two find themselves involved in inconsistency and instability. It also explains why scholars like W. H. Green, Orr, and Allis, starting from the same facts and with an equal knowledge of Hebrew, reach exactly opposite conclusions to those of Wellhausen or Driver.[1]

Of course, if the methods of the latter are really demonstrative they must be followed in the interests of truth: but we now proceed to show that this is far from being the case.

FALLACIES VITIATING THE METHODS OF MODERN CRITICISM

(a) Lack of external evidence

At the outset liberal criticism requires us to accept as real a number of documents, authors and compilers without the slightest scrap of external evidence. If ever they did exist outside the imagination of the critics, they have not left behind them any

[1] The same is true in New Testament criticism of the views of Westcott, Moule and W. Temple on the one hand, and those of Streeter or Dibelius on the other.

trace either in literature or in Hebrew tradition, tenacious as that tradition is of the memory of its great names. When we consider the power and originality of these writings and their deep effect on the national life, this alone is sufficient to discredit the theory. Nor has any Old Testament critic 'offered to explain how the diverse documents of the Pentateuch, which they discover or create, acquired their sanctity and authority'.[1] Is it really probable that the name of the author of Deuteronomy was completely forgotten, whereas those of the minor prophets of the eighth century B.C. were so carefully preserved?

The zeal and enthusiasm of certain scholars has tended constantly to increase the number of these hypothetical individuals, and this to an indefinite extent. Wherever a difficulty exists, or the theory requires, the analysis is continued by means of 'more and more complex surgical operations upon J. or E. or upon any of their now rapidly increasing progeny'.[2]

This multiplication of imaginary authors must be distinguished from the use of earlier sources of information by the authors of the historical books, which is not in dispute. What is hard to believe is that the choicest flowers of Hebrew literature should have been produced as a patchwork of fragments from unknown or forgotten writers, rather than owe their origin to the great historical figures with whose names they have been connected by an unbroken chain of tradition.

(b) Unsound foundations

Wellhausen built his critical theory largely upon two foundations, both of which have proved to be unsound.[3] The first was that writing was unknown before the days of the monarchy. The narratives of the Old Testament, in consequence, were thought of as being handed down for long ages by oral tradition. The second was that the religion of Israel began as a totemistic animism, ascended through a stage of polytheism closely parallel to that of their Canaanite neighbours, and became monotheistic only in the prophetic era.[4]

The first of these assumptions has been demonstrated to be false, and is now generally abandoned. In Abraham's city of Ur and in his day writing was commonly practised. The existence of early

[1] Robertson, Temple and Torah, p. 6.
[2] Phythian Adams, Call of Israel, p. 58.
[3] For a full examination of the theory and a justification of this statement see Allis, The Five Books of Moses, pp. 127-202.
[4] See Chapter IX.

inscriptions containing law-codes prove that the laws of a people are among the first things to be reduced to writing, and Sir L. Woolley has pictured Abraham supplying his family with a selection of written laws for their guidance. The Babylonians of that time certainly observed the seventh day, and many of the precepts of the Mosaic law find a parallel in Hammurabi's code. Therefore, the command given to Moses in Ex. xxxiv. 27 to *write* the law is intrinsically natural and probable.

Genealogies were carefully kept on inscribed tablets long before Abraham's day, and, so far from being a sign of post-exilic writing, probably constitute the oldest elements of the Bible.

Nor were the days of the settlement in Palestine, though in many respects rough and rude, devoid of culture, as Wellhausen supposed, for many records and much correspondence of that period have been found, both in Babylonian cuneiform and in the ancient Hebrew script.

Dr. E. Robertson, Professor of Semitic Languages in Manchester University, in a series of scholarly monographs, has argued that the whole Pentateuch existed in writing in, or before, the days of Samuel.[1]

The second of these assumptions, that the religion of the Old Testament was the product of a natural ascent from animism, has no more basis in fact. The idea that man was gradually mounting upward from the ape to the angel was more popular in Darwin's day than now, since the recrudescence of barbarism in two great wars has destroyed so many utopian dreams.

Much evidence exists to indicate how widespread has been religious degeneration. The extravagant polytheism of India was certainly such, for the Sanskrit literature shows an approach to monotheism the further back it goes in time. The common origin of the name for the God-Father in Latin, Greek and Sanskrit (*Ju-piter*, *Zeus pater*, *Dyaus pitar*) points to the worship of the supreme God as Father in the dim past before the separation of the Aryan races.

Professor Snaith, in emphasizing the uniqueness of Old Testament religion, calls on Hebrew scholars to 'awake out of our semi-hypnosis, induced by the desire for comprehensiveness and broad mindedness, and by the attractiveness of . . . studies in early comparative religion and native custom'.[2] Moreover, evidence has been accumulating during recent years that even among the

---

[1] *Temple and Torah* (1941), *The Priestly Code* (1942), *The Riddle of the Torah* (1943), *The Pentateuchal Problem* (1945).
[2] *Distinctive Ideas of the Old Testament*, p. 13.

primitive animistic people of the present day there was originally a general and widespread belief in a 'high God', the supreme Being, the Father and Creator of the world.[1]

Among the Semitic races from early time El appears generally as the 'name for the High God, the great Deity who is supreme over all and distinct from all lower gods and lesser spirits'.[2]

Dr. Langdon, Professor of Assyriology at Oxford, has declared his conviction that 'both in Sumerian and Semitic religions monotheism preceded polytheism and belief in good and evil spirits'. He adds, 'I therefore reject the modernistic theory absolutely. Early Canaanitish and Hebrew religions are far beyond primitive totemism (if it ever existed among them) in the period when any definite information can be obtained about them'.[3]

We need not hesitate therefore to accept the scriptural statement that, amid the prevailing corruption of mankind, a purer monotheistic faith was maintained by individuals such as Enoch and Noah, Abraham and Jacob. Something of the struggle between this faith and the surrounding polytheism is reflected in the life of the latter (Gn. xxxi. 19, xxxv. 2; cf. Jos. xxiv. 2).

(c) The dating of documents is dependent upon the theory of religious development

The only safe means of fixing dates is through facts recorded in the documents themselves or derived from the monuments. The critical theorists, with little regard for history or tradition, fix the date of each chapter or verse according to its 'religious outlook'. If this be 'universal', origin in the Persian period is denoted; if the law is mentioned, the date cannot be earlier than the exile; and only those parts which are coloured by 'crude ideas of Jehovah' are allowed to belong to the monarchy.

This involves considerable re-adjustment of the evidence. Jeremiah's insistence on the sabbath, for instance (Je. xvii. 21-27) is dealt with as a later interpolation.[4] The ideas of Is. xxiv.-xxvii. are considered too advanced for Isaiah's time, so they too are an interpolation belonging to the exile, or 300 B.C., or even later (critics differ),[5] although Delitzsch says that all possible grounds

---

[1] See Zwemer, *The Origin of Religion*; W. Schmidt, *Origin and Growth of Religion*.

[2] Snaith, *op. cit.*, p. 47.

[3] *Semitic Mythology*, pp. xviii and 93

[4] Oesterley and Robinson, *Introduction to the Books of the Old Testament*, p. 299.

[5] Oesterley and Robinson, *op. cit.*, p. 253.

combine to indicate Isaiah's authorship if it be once granted that
'no human critics can determine *a priori* the measure of divine
revelation'. In like manner one reason given for the late date of
P is the absence of reference to the Levitical law in the prophetical
writings. To strengthen this argument various passages which
indicate a knowledge of the law, and have every appearance of
genuineness, are stated to be later interpolations.[1]

Another difficulty which the critical theory has to surmount is
the presence of elements, such as the genealogies, which have
every appearance of being very ancient. It is conceded, for
instance, that 'there are very early elements in P',[2] but the late
date is maintained nevertheless. No explanation is offered why
these genealogies were overlooked, or neglected, by J and E, who
are supposed to be so much earlier.

At one time it was the fashion to see in the account of the flood
in Genesis a re-shaping of Babylonian legends undertaken by an
exilic author. Further study has shown their independence, and
now it is conceded that 'the creation and flood narratives in P are
derived from a source which . . . must go back to an early period in
Canaanite culture, though they were profoundly modified in the
course of centuries, and now bear little resemblance to what must
have been their original form'.[3] No shadow of proof for the latter
part of this confident statement is given, but it is needed to
reconcile the late date of P with the early character of its contents.
There is, moreover, a very subjective element in dating the documents by means of the writer's 'outlook'. This is witnessed by the
various dates assigned by different critics to the book of Deuteronomy,[4] to say nothing of speculations about the Psalms.

This subjective character manifests itself also in the reconstruction of the history, where all is a sea of conjecture. Quite a literature exists, for example,[5] upon theories of the 'real' origin of the
ark and its contents, and other matters where no external standard
exists to check the imagination.

(d) The method of analysis is by nature arbitrary and indeterminate

It is certain that some of the Old Testament writers made use of
existing documents, for such are mentioned by name (e.g.

---

[1] Orr, *Problem of the Old Testament*, p. 305. See also Chapter VIII.
[2] Oesterley and Robinson, *op. cit.*, p. 40.
[3] Oesterley and Robinson, *op. cit.*, p. 56.
[4] The time of Samuel (Robertson); the early monarchy (A. C. Welch); the
reign of Josiah (Wellhausen); the exile (Kennett).
[5] See Phythian Adams, *The Call of Israel*, p. 81.

2 Sa. i. 18), and it is legitimate to point to evidences of such use. But this is quite different from the postulation of documents, otherwise quite unknown, or of schools of Deuteronomic or priestly writers. In the latter case the analysis cannot be effected until the style of each separate document is *assumed*; and this is by nature arbitrary.

Even when an author's style is well known from his acknow-ledged writings, the determination as to whether a document is his or not is difficult enough, as is witnessed by the great variety of opinion obtaining among critics as to Pauline or Johannine writings. But where a book which has the reputation and appearance of having but one author has to be divided among four, the whole process must *depend upon the initial assumptions* regarding their respective styles and vocabularies, and every change in these assumptions must vary the analysis accordingly. The analysis is therefore entirely subject to the critic's choice of assumptions.

Thus we have it laid down that the style of P is 'sophisticated' and 'legal', and on this ground the passages in Genesis com-mencing with the words 'These are the generations of . . .' are assigned to P. When, as we have seen above, the early nature of these passages has to be acknowledged, it is assumed that their form has been 'profoundly modified' in the course of centuries (though in fact they retain their primitive appearance). It would be much more natural to assume that these genealogies were a characteristic of J or E, but then an entirely different analysis would result. The use of the divine names, once relied upon as a clue to the analysis, has proved an *ignis fatuus* which has led the critics into a whole quagmire of difficulties from which they find it hard to extricate themselves.[1] They have come to admit its weakness, and after the early chapters of Exodus it is wisely abandoned.[2] Were the same guide followed in Isaiah, the use of the name the 'Holy One of Israel' would prove the unity of that book. The counting of words also can be shown to produce widely different results according to the way in which it is employed.[3] Some minute analysis has been accomplished by assigning alternative names of persons or places to different authors (for example, Horeb to E, and Sinai to P and J), but it is evident that by simply reversing the choice the P and J passages become E, and vice versa.

---

[1] See Troelstra, *The Name of God in the Pentateuch.*
[2] Oesterley and Robinson, *op. cit.*, p. 32.
[3] See Allis, *op. cit.*, p. 77.

Upon this question of 'style' Professor G. A. Smith says, ' "facts" of style will be regarded with suspicion by anyone who knows how they are employed on both sides'.[1] As an example of this, the *difference* of style between Is. i.-xxxix. and xl.-lxvi. is frequently given as a proof of dual authorship, but others say that the writer of the later chapters *imitated* Isaiah's style, or that at a later time they were added to the earlier part because they were thought to be Isaiah's.

The assumption underlying much of the analysis, that no writer can use more than one style, is fundamentally false. Newton wrote on mathematics and prophecy, and treated these subjects very differently; Scott wrote in poetry and prose. The critics allow that Hammurabi left behind him both narratives of his exploits and codes of laws; why may not Moses have done the same?[2]

The agreement among scholars of the critical school upon the style and outlook of P and the reconstruction of the Priestly document is urged as a reason for its acceptance.[3] But how has this consensus of opinion been attained? Prior to Wellhausen there was much disagreement until, by the change over of a large number of passages, and the splitting up of verses, a fairly coherent scheme was obtained. The unanimity of those who have since adopted it no more proves its truth than the unanimity of those who reject it proves the contrary.

DUPLICATE NARRATIVES

Among the reasons for postulating a combination of parts from several documents Professor Driver puts first that 'the same event is doubly recorded',[4] and, at first sight, the list of these alleged duplicates appears formidable.

No doubt Moses and the prophetical historians had more than one source of information, and traces of duplication can perhaps be seen, although any assertion about their limits must be conjectural. Examination of the so-called duplicates, however, shows that the very great majority of them are either (1) expansions, where the second part supplements the former, or (2) concerned with *different* events having something in common, or (3) entirely fictitious, being created by an artificial division of a single story. A complete examination of those in the Pentateuch will be found

---

[1] *Isaiah*, Vol. I, p. 402.
[2] See also Chapter IX.
[3] Oesterley and Robinson, *op. cit.*, p. 29.
[4] *Op. cit.*, p. 6.

in Allis, *The Five Books of Moses*, chs. IV. and V., but a few examples here will show the fallacy of the arguments built upon their supposed existence.

1. As an obvious instance of 'expansion', the grand cosmic scenes of creation in Gn. i.-ii. 4, apparently vouchsafed in vision to Moses himself, are followed naturally by the story of the beginnings of the human race in ii. 4-25. Were the latter taken from an ancient tablet this would account for the change of style.

As a second instance, in Gn. xxvii., xxviii. 1, 2, where Rebecca sends Jacob away to avoid his brother's anger and then gives him instructions to seek a wife from his own people, there is really neither repetition nor duplication, but mere sequence.

2. A 'doublet' is stated to exist in Ex. xx. 4-6 and xxxiv. 7, 17, and a 'contradiction' asserted between the 'graven' image of the former and the 'molten' image of the latter. The occasions are clearly different, and the reason for the change of wording is rendered obvious by a reference to xxxii. 8.

3. The search for doublets has resulted in the division of many narratives into parts, after the fashion of a jig-saw puzzle, the 'doublet' being created by the process itself.

An example of this is found in Gn. xxxvii., which is chosen in some text-books as a conspicuous case of a doublet. The analysis splits the chapter into twenty-six fragments, of which three consist of only a part of a verse. In one place the meaning is changed by the way in which verse 28 is divided. A contradiction is discovered because the merchants are called both Midianites and Ishmaelites, although a reference to Jdg. viii. 24-26 shows that the chiefs of Midian were itinerant merchant men, and were also known as Ishmaelites. A similar overlapping of racial names is found in the inscriptions (but not then used to make doublets). The actions of Reuben and Judah which follow on one another naturally enough in the story are assigned to different documents and presented as another contradiction. The whole is well described by Professor Orr as an 'exercise of misplaced ingenuity'.[1]

THE REDACTOR AND HIS IMPOSSIBLE TASK

A consideration of the task imposed upon the various compilers or redactors, who interwove these portions with each other, reveals another weakness in the whole system. No little ingenuity and ability must be attributed to them for the construction of books of such power out of so great a variety of sources.

[1] *Problem of the Old Testament*, 1st Ed., p. 237. See also p. 131.

The analysis is justified on a variety of grounds, differences of style and diction, duplicate accounts, interruptions in the narrative, divergences and contradictions. Yet in proportion as these afford argument *for* the analysis, they provide arguments of equal strength *against* the synthesis.

If the compiler had two complete narratives before him, we can understand his using them in turn; but what was his reason for this strange selection of fragments first from one and then from the other? For instance, it is easy to see the reason why, when, as in Gen. v. 29, the name Jehovah occurs in the middle of an E narrative, it should be put down to an insertion from J. But what motive could have induced the compiler to pick out this tiny portion and substitute it for the corresponding verse in E? Can this be considered probable? Then if he had, for instance, two differing accounts of the flood, why did he select from each such portions as to leave the whole with 'glaring contradictions'?[1] Was he too obtuse to see them, or too careless to care about them? Still more inexplicable is it why he should select from three documents, J, E and P, twenty-six fragments, and weave them together to create a *duplicate*, certainly of great interest, but, according to the critical theory, so inconsistent with itself.

To take a further example, Ex. vi. 2- vii. 14 is assigned to P and said to be a duplicate of Ex. iii. It contains genealogies (a sign of P) and interrupts the narrative which flows evenly from vi. 1 to vii. 15. Why did the redactor then insert it here, when it could have been so placed that it did *not* interrupt the narrative so abruptly? If he knew that the injunctions in Ex. iii. and vi. were really divergent accounts of the *same* event, why should he have made them appear different? If he thought they were different, was he not probably right?

Great stress is laid upon Ex. vi. 3 as supplying the reason why 'P scrupulously avoids the use of the name Yahweh in the account of the creation and the story of the patriarchs'. According to the hypothesis the redactor, who had before him the whole of the P document and not the few scraps he has preserved for us, should have known this. Was it not then very inconsiderate of him to throw in so much of the J, E material as completely to obscure this important fact?

That the earlier books did undergo limited additions and revisions is probable, but that they were on this scale and of this character is utterly impossible.

'All history', writes Kegel, 'can hardly produce a more comic

[1] Oesterley and Robinson, *op. cit.*, p. 27.

c

figure than this ever-helpful redactor of Old Testament texts who is by turns incredibly stupid and remarkably cunning.'[1]

FURTHER WEAKNESSES OF MODERN CRITICISM

It remains to point out briefly some further weaknesses in the critical theories:

1. It has been pointed out above that the principles on which the analysis of the text is conducted are *incapable of general application*.[2] This is a serious challenge to their validity.

2. The argument from silence, notoriously precarious, is relied upon in important matters (e.g. attention is drawn to the scarcity of references to the Mosaic law in the historical books). The same is true concerning doubtful interpretations of individual texts such as Ex. vi. 3 or Je. vii. 22.

3. Reliance is placed upon the occurrence of certain 'Aramaisms' and other words to prove the later date of the passage or book containing them. Further research is continually bringing to light examples of the early use of such words and expressions.[3]

4. Kegel and others have accused Wellhausen and others of taking liberties with the text in order to support their contentions.[4]

5. The facts of archaeology have shaken many critical conclusions and supported few of them: they show no acquaintance with J, E, D or P, and with supreme indifference have supported all parts of the historical books alike.

6. The theories, which are essentially divisive, fail utterly to account for the unity of plan and purpose running through the individual books, and the whole Bible. Such results do not come from haphazard collecting of traditions, and the interweaving of fragments culled from them.

7. More serious is the way in which destructive criticism denies the claims to contain God's special revelation which the books make for themselves. This revelation forms the basis of much New Testament teaching. By eliminating the predictive elements it leaves as a standing and unexplained wonder how it has come about that so many of the predictions have been fulfilled, both those relating to Christ Himself, to which He and the evangelists call attention, and others concerning the nations, already fulfilled

---

[1] *Away from Wellhausen*, p. 62.

[2] See also Allis, *op. cit.*, pp. 55, 69, 87.

[3] See Allis, *op. cit.*, pp. 77, 214; and R. D. Wilson, *Is the Higher Criticism Scholarly?*

[4] See Kegel, *Away from Wellhausen*, Ch. II, and references there to Wiener; Troelstra, *op. cit.*, p. 31.

or about the Jewish race, its dispersion and sufferings, some of which have come to pass before our very eyes.

RECENT CHANGE OF OPINION

It is not easy to break away from a system of thought which has once taken hold of the popular mind. A great literature has come into existence in support of what is designated 'modern criticism', and a complex system of thought built up round about it. To pull down an edifice erected with so much labour and scholarship, and to set up another on surer foundations cannot be done in a day. But support for the attempt has come from some unexpected quarters.

Whilst there is still too great a readiness to accept the criticism as 'scientific' and to see 'traditionalism' in all opposition to it, there is an increasing protest against the scepticism inherent in so much recent writing. Canon Phythian Adams has raised his protest against 'radical reconstructions' of the history, has insisted upon the essential truth of the stories of the patriarchs, and protested against the idea that it should be thought impossible to look upon Abraham as a monotheist, quoting Bohl in his support.[1]

Even more definitely, Professor Snaith thinks that literary analysis, where pressed too far, 'does more harm than good. Even the good order J, E, D and P may corrupt the scholarly world'. He also protests against the modern study of the history of religion, by 'the new scientific method, with its rigid evolutionary hypothesis', and casts scorn upon the supposed necessity that Hebrew religion should progress along the 'common path beginning with pre-animism or with ghost-worship, and thence through all the orthodox stages of the Tylor-Spencer-Frazer school of primitive religion'. In the preface to his *Distinctive Ideas of the Old Testament* he pleads that Christian teachers should make up their minds that 'the Bible really is the Word of God, and the Old Testament an integral part of it'.[2]

Such statements are the more significant coming from authors who nevertheless hold to many of the critical views. Professor Danby questions 'how much of this literary analysis will continue to be accepted as sound. . . . Much of it is subjective'[3]: and Professor E. Robertson goes further still when he speaks of the

---

[1] *The Fulness of Israel*, pp. 69, 81.
[2] Pp. 9, 13, 29.
[3] *The Study of Theology*, p. 201.

'sinister shadow' cast on the Old Testament by the Graf-Well-hausen hypothesis, and adds, perhaps too optimistically, 'It is a shadow which the great majority of the present Old Testament scholars would wish to see removed.'[1]

A system reared upon foundations which are logically unsound and spiritually false cannot be saved from ultimate collapse, in spite of all the labour spent on it.[2]

[1] *The Priestly Code*, p. 23.

[2] Although this chapter has been devoted mainly to the liberal criticism of the Old Testament, the same principles apply to much recent criticism of the Gospels and other New Testament books, reference to which will be found in the various introductions included in Part IV. The clash is between the same two systems of thought—that which believes in miracle and in the divine inspiration of Scripture, and that which doubts or rejects both.

CHAPTER V

MIRACLES

THE MIRACLES OF THE OLD TESTAMENT

THE proper approach to miracle is in the Old Testament. Here all nature, including life itself, is represented as depending entirely on God's will for its continuance. But God is shown to be carrying out great purposes, and nature must therefore serve to realize His purposes; the idea of nature being governed by fixed 'laws' is, therefore, superfluous. 'Every event in Nature is looked at merely as a single act of God's free will, rain and sunshine as well as earthquake and prodigy. Consequently the essence of a miracle is not that it is "unnatural", but that it is a specially clear and striking proof of God's power, and of the freedom He exercises in furthering His objects.'[1]

This brings us at once to the first and all-controlling principle of miracle; it is a personal act of God. Miracles belong to the supposition of theism.

We find, next, that the miracles of the Bible always have a moral and spiritual setting. Those who tear them away from the fabric into which they are woven, and judge them in that isolated way, have simply never faced the real issue presented by them. Miracles are striking incidents, connected with moral ends, which occur at the word of God or in answer to the prayers of His servants. They inspire awe as well as wonder, for they bring us into the presence of the living God.

It is by these principles that we are to appreciate at their true value the miracles of the deliverance at the Red Sea, the destruction of Korah, Dathan and Abiram, the healing of the plague-stricken people through beholding the brazen serpent, the speaking of Balaam's ass, and those miracles of Elisha, which some are inclined to call trivial, such as the making of the axehead to float, and the elimination of the poison from the pottage. All these miracles were signs to Israel that Jehovah was not a far-off God, but one who was intimately concerned in all their affairs. The Israelites were surrounded by peoples whose 'gods' were visible

[1] S chultz, *Old Testament Theology*, Vol. II, pp. 192, 193.

and tangible: their own God was invisible. Without these miracles Jehovah would have been an abstraction.

The most searching investigation of the documents of the Old Testament tends to restore them to a date much nearer to the times which they record. The evidential value of the Old Testament is, therefore, far greater than it has been popular to suppose. It is true that the evidence for each separate miracle recorded in the Old Testament is not of the same kind or degree as that which can be produced for those in the New. This, however, does not detract either from their credibility or from their value. They harmonize with their moral context, and are consonant with the whole idea of the ever present and active Jehovah of whom the Old Testament is the recorded revelation. We reach a proper appreciation of even the less significant miracles when we understand them, first of all, in their relation to the general Old Testament representation of the all-sustaining activity of God, and when, in the second place, we regard them in the light that is thrown back upon them by the perfect revelation of God in the person and work of our Lord Jesus Christ.

THE MIRACLES OF THE NEW TESTAMENT

This leads us on to a consideration of the New Testament miracles. The evidence for the Gospel miracles is unimpeachable. The records of them are sober, balanced, without extravagance, and free from that kind of enthusiasm which mars the value of evidence. Luke has been vindicated as a most painstaking and accurate historian, and no solid grounds have been established for denying the reliability of the other evangelists.[1]

The suggestion that the miracle-stories are a later adornment of the truth will stand neither historical nor literary criticism. The documents were issued early enough for any errors within them to be detected and exposed by those who had been alive at the time of the events described, and no ground, other than the philosophical objection that they are impossible, exists for eliminating the miracles from the narratives.

There have been many attempts in modern times to recast the Gospel narratives and to recover what the authors have imagined to be the real Jesus of history, free from legendary embellishments, the purely human rabbi whom the crowds followed for his teaching.

[1] See Chapter XIX.

What has been the result of these attempts? It has been found that the teaching and the miracles are so interwoven the one with the other that, unless the history is mutilated in the most arbitrary manner, it is necessary to accept or reject both the teaching and the miracles. One illustration of this must suffice, though many more might be given. The Sermon on the Mount is the part of our Lord's teaching which is the most widely applauded, and it is the one thing which the supporters of a non-miraculous Jesus are usually willing to accept. At the close of this recorded sermon Jesus challenged His hearers by saying, 'Many will say to me in that day, Lord, Lord, have we not prophesied in thy name? and in thy name have cast out devils? and in thy name done many wonderful works? And then will I profess unto them, I never knew you' (Mt. vii. 22-23). These words could have been uttered only if miracles were generally acknowledged to have been worked in His name.

The presence of miracles in the story of God's self-revelation is what we should expect. Revelation and miracle belong to the same realm. This is most clear in the case of the Gospel miracles. We might say that in an account of such a Person with such divine claims it is not the presence but the absence of miracles which would need to be explained.

THE RESURRECTION

The miracle of all miracles is the resurrection of Christ. Let this once be admitted, and support is at once given to all the others. It is not surprising, therefore, that the opponents of miracle should have concentrated their attack upon the Christian faith at this point. The evidence for the resurrection of Christ stands like a rock amid all these wild storms of debate. Swoons, visions, frauds, mistakes, tradition, hallucination, creative faith, pious invention, these and other equally untenable hypotheses have been put forward only to fall back broken on the strong historical evidence which the New Testament and Christian history provide. It is certain from the writings of Paul and of Luke, his companion, that, at the time when Stephen was stoned and Paul was persecuting the church, the whole body of Christians, whether in Jerusalem, Damascus, or Antioch, believed in Christ's resurrection from the dead as a fundamental article of their faith.

Of the list of witnesses which Paul gives in 1 Cor. xv. he had met Peter and James certainly, and probably many others in the early days of his new-found faith. The accounts by the four evangelists

of the finding of the empty tomb, first by the women and then by
Peter and John, are so markedly independent, naïve and circum-
stantial that to attribute them to pious invention is to violate every
law of evidence. That tomb never became a place of pilgrimage,
the 'first day of the week' was observed as a day of prayer and
worship, men laid down their lives for testifying to 'the things
which they had seen and heard', and the course of the subsequent
history took precisely the form which the reality of the resurrection requires—a form which it is impossible to explain on any
other basis. It may be noted further that the evidence for the
resurrection is derived from the same sources, and stands on the
same level as that for the passion: there can be no reason for
denying the one which does not apply to the other.

The resurrection of Christ is thus the touch-stone of all miracle.
It introduced the principle of miracle into Christianity in its
most pronounced form. All that is needed after the acceptance
of this supreme miracle is to examine the other Christian miracles
in the light of their evidence.

Miracles are still the glory of the Christian faith. They represent the very heart of the divine relationship to the world. They
indicate that God has an interest in the world, and are a denial
that God, in deistic fashion, has made the world and left it to go
on as best it can. He upholds 'all things by the word of His power'
(Heb. i. 3).

MIRACLE AND NATURAL LAW

Miracles are not a breach of the laws of nature, but, on the contrary, must be regarded as the bringing back of order into a
disordered world. Spinoza argued that miracles were contrary to
the very conception of God as all-wise, and maintained that they
implied an imperfect creation, which thing, *ex hypothesi*, could not
be admitted. The reply to Spinoza is plain. This world has lost
its original 'goodness'; the order of things has been rudely broken
by sin. Sin, with its attendant evils, is called *a-nomia*, 'lawlessness',
or that which is contrary to law (1 Jn. iii. 4). Miracle, on the
other hand, comes in from a higher and purer world to restore the
broken harmonies of earth, whereby the divine order is re-
established, if only for a brief, prophetic moment.

The discussion of miracle has been confused by considerable
ambiguity of terms. The real stumbling-block is the ambiguity of
the word 'law'. The word is too often used as if a law were capable
of doing or preventing something. A law of nature is simply an

abbreviated statement of the results of many observations and experiments. It is a statement and only a statement: it has no power of effecting the thing which it states. Presented in popular language, it is a law that the sun rises every morning; but that 'law', as such, has no power to cause the sun to rise. Therefore, when we are tempted to use the phrases, 'suspension of law', 'violation of law', 'interposition of higher law', we are making sounds without meaning. The determinative element in nature resides neither in natural 'law' nor in matter, but in mind. If this be admitted, then the freedom of mind is a real factor in the way things are to be conceived. To the believer in a personal God who creates and sustains all things the mind behind the universe is the mind of God and He is the God of order. The observed uniformities merely represent God's *usual* method of working in nature; but it must not be forgotten that God is free in His own world. Paul's question on this subject is very apposite, when he asks Agrippa, 'Why should it be thought a thing incredible with you, that *God* should raise the dead?' (Acts xxvi. 8). God may produce an extraordinary act by His own direct volition, if He deems it desirable for the end in view. The laws of nature are uniform only because He so wills, and their uniformity continues only so long as He wills.

SCIENCE AND MIRACLE NOT OPPOSED

Nevertheless the uniformity in nature is so real and so vast in extent as to produce in many minds a strong prejudice against the miraculous. An unbalanced view of physical science, and the extension of its laws to moral and spiritual spheres where they do not and cannot apply, has led to a feeling that free-will must be an illusion, and that all things are mechanically and inexorably determined. But those who hold to the supremacy of moral and spiritual realities may be encouraged by more recent developments in science. The theory of a closed universe, which rules out all possibility of interference by any force other than those which can be accounted for on mechanistic principles, is now being destroyed from within science itself. What is matter? What is force? What is the real nature of cause? Materialistic answers to these questions are now rejected by the sciences. It is coming to be seen that 'matter' approximates to 'spirit', and that the boundary line is difficult to determine. It is well known that some of the greatest scientists have been believers in the Christian miracles. It is enough to mention Newton, Faraday, Simpson,

Kelvin, and Lister; and to these could be added the names of men still living. Kelvin stated that, in his view, science not only admitted, but positively demanded, the existence of a Creator, and, more recently, Sir James Jeans has called it a scientific certainty that 'there must have been what we may describe as a "creation" at a time not infinitely remote'.[1] Sir Arthur Eddington also, from the point of view of atomic theory, has protested against a determinist view of the universe and declared that 'the idea of a universal mind or logos would be a fairly plausible inference from the present state of scientific theory'.[2] It cannot therefore be held that modern science sustains any valid objection to the occurrence of the miraculous.

The steady accumulation of facts in the domain of psychotherapy has shown the influence of mind over matter both in the production and in the healing of disease. Psycho-therapeutics by no means explains miracles, but it is an aspect of enquiry which throws light on the essentially spiritual constitution of the universe and its theological subordination to the mind of God. It has been shown that mind may exert over the organic processes of the body an influence which might seem to the uninitiated little short of miraculous. Under certain conditions, especially in the hypnotic state, the production of blisters and marks on the skin (stigmata) have been determined by verbal suggestion, and the complete suppression of pain, and the elimination of inflammation can be produced by the same means.[3]

PHILOSOPHICAL OBJECTIONS

Such facts and questions as these drive us to the conclusion that the problem of miracle is not really a scientific one, but a philosophical one. The problem is concerned not with how nature moves, but with the question of that original impulse which set nature moving and now keeps it moving. The former question is the province of science: the latter problem belongs to philosophy.

The real issue at stake in discussing any miracle is the Christian doctrine of the world, namely, that the material exists for the spiritual. This is what is commonly known as a teleological conception of the universe, the belief that everything in it is sub-

---

[1] *The Mysterious Universe*, p. 144.
[2] *The Nature of the Physical World*, p. 338. See also T. C. Hammond, *Reasoning Faith*.
[3] McDougall, *Body and Mind*, p. 351.

ordinated to 'purpose'. Purpose is inherent in the universe, and purpose is of the essence of miracle: purpose thus unites miracle to the very order of the universe.

DEFINITION OF MIRACLE

We are now in some kind of position to attempt a definition of that which we call miracle. Dr. James Orr defines it as 'any deviation from, or transcendence of, the order of nature due to the interposition of a supernatural cause'.[1] This definition, however, does not seem to go far enough: it stops short just at the point where we need it to go on. It places miracle in the category of the mysterious, and nothing more.

Dr. J. H. Bernard[2] carries us further when he says: 'A miracle may be described as an event manifesting purpose, occurring in the physical world, which cannot be accounted for by any of its known forces, and which, therefore, we ascribe to a spiritual cause. It is an interference with the ordinary action of the forces of nature on the part of the author of nature—an event brought about, not by any observed combination of physical forces, but by a direct divine volition.' The chief points concerned in this definition are focussed in the three New Testament words for miracles: (a) *dunameis*, meaning 'powers'; (b) *terata*, meaning 'wonders'; and (c) *semeia*, meaning 'signs'. (See Acts ii. 22.) We have in miracle, therefore, a mighty *work*, evoking *wonder*, but at the same time conveying a *meaning*. It is the act of divine will in miracle that makes it of any significance for faith, and which also gives to miracle its harmonious place in the divine scheme of things. Miracles are the effects of causes that belong to the 'impending' world (Hebrews vi. 5), a world divided from us by such a thin veil that it breaks through upon us from time to time at the bidding of Him whose home it is.

OBJECTIONS OF HUME AND HUXLEY

We have little space in which to consider Hume's argument that 'no testimony is sufficient to establish a miracle, *unless* the testimony be of such a kind that its falsehood would be *more miraculous than the fact which it endeavours to establish*. Or, briefly, it is contrary to experience that a miracle should be true, but not contrary to experience that testimony should be false'.[3] The outstanding

[1] *The Faith of a Modern Christian*, p. 65.
[2] Hastings' *Dictionary of the Bible*, Vol. III, p. 384.
[3] *Essays*, Vol. II, p. 93.

weakness of this argument is that it proves too much. It would prove that the Jesus of history never existed, for He is as unique as any of His works. But this is not the only flaw in Hume's argument, which involves many logical fallacies which were exposed and answered in Paley's *Evidences of Christianity*.

T. H. Huxley took up the question of evidence in a different manner. He admitted, rather subtly, the possibility of miracles, but demanded a type of evidence which would amount to 'scientific demonstration'. In the case of the feeding of the five thousand, for example, it was Huxley's view that in order to establish the miracle, the loaves and fishes would have to be weighed before and after the event, besides collecting evidence that everyone's hunger was satisfied.[1] This is to ask for a type of evidence which, in the nature of the case, is impossible. We may agree that, since the course of nature is orderly, we should require *more* evidence for a miracle than for ordinary matters of everyday experience; but that is a very different thing from requiring 'scientific demonstration'. All we need for the overcoming of any antecedent improbability which might arise from our general experience is the evidence of divine purpose.

SPURIOUS MIRACLES

Before we leave this subject there remain still to be considered those other occurrences which are alleged to be miracles. There are those of mediaeval times, the miracles of the 'saints'; there are the 'wonders' of spiritualism, and those of oriental heathen religions. Are we justified in taking it for granted that ecclesiastical, or Roman Catholic, or spiritualistic miracles did not happen, but those of Elisha, for example, did?

It is to be noted that the early Fathers of the church made a frank confession that miracles were not occurring within their experience, that is, of a kind and significance like those of the Gospels.

T. H. Huxley[2] recounts at length some of the extraordinary miracles alleged to have occurred in connection with one Eginhard, of the eighth century, who tells the story of the 'Translation of the blessed martyrs Marcellinus and Petrus'. After describing these marvels, which include those of exuding blood and various 'cures', Huxley asks why we do not believe in Eginhard's miracles when, at the same time, we accept those of the Gospels. He claims that the documentary evidence for Eginhard is superior to that of

[1] *Essays: Science and Christian Tradition*, p. 203.
[2] *Op. cit.*, pp. 160 ff.

the Gospels, and that we are inconsistent in the rejection of the former and the acceptance of the latter. Our answer is plain and straightforward. Admitting, for the sake of argument, that Eginhard's marvels have good documentary evidence, we reply that this is surely the only aspect of the matter in which 'superiority' can be claimed. Huxley gives his own case away. He himself shows that the whole context of the alleged miracles is one of fraud, imposture, and superstition. The moral baseness of the episodes and the low level of purpose with which the miracles are invoked put such 'marvels' in a totally different category from those in the Scriptures.

Huxley compares the age of the New Testament with the period of the mediaeval miracles, and declares that there was the same general expectation of the marvellous in Judaism as there was in the eighth century A.D. This, however, is contrary to all the evidence. The Pharisees refused to believe that a man born blind could receive his sight, and the news of the resurrection was greeted with incredulity not only by the Jewish authorities, but at first by the disciples themselves.

The reasons why we reject the alleged miracles of later ages is that in themselves they bear no resemblance to divine miracles as they appear in the Scripture, and that the evidence for them is in most cases wholly inadequate.

Those in the apocryphal Gospels are puerile and absurd, those of mediaeval saints are pointless. The motives and characteristics of the mediaeval miracles are grossly inferior to those of the Scripture record: the same is true of the practices of spiritualism to-day. The Gospel miracles support a great faith; but what are we to say of those which are alleged to have been wrought in support of such doctrines as the 'immaculate conception' of the Virgin Mary, or the fatuous products of the modern spiritualist séance?

When we come to consider the question of evidence, the superiority of the Gospel miracles is most clearly demonstrated. Most of the miracles attributed to the saints were so attributed long after their death; indeed, the notion prevailed that the saint was expected to have performed miracles. If, therefore, no miracles were recorded in his history, they seem to have been 'supplied' by later admirers. But, apart from this latter procedure, the mediaeval miracles are mostly lacking in contemporary evidence. Such evidence as has been adduced is patently tendentious and worthless, and in many cases has been proved false and counterfeit.

'We reject the mass of later miracles', says Mozley, 'because they want evidence; *not because our argument obliges us to reject all later miracles whether they have evidence or not.*'[1]

There is yet another point, however, that must not be over-looked. The Bible here and there refers to 'lying wonders' (Dt. xiii. 1-3; 2 Thess. ii. 9), and teaches that events transcending the power of man may be brought about by spiritual agencies for an evil purpose. The subject is full of mystery, but the principle is clear that, as the true miracle attests a doctrine, so the truth of the doctrine and the evidence of divine purpose are needed to prove the divine origin of the miracle. So when Christ was accused of casting out devils by Beelzebub (Mt. xii. 24), He appealed to their beneficent design and result to prove the contrary.

MIRACLES AND DOCTRINE

We must now turn to the positive value of the miraculous. Miracles are evidential in value. When taken in their doctrinal context they give support to that doctrine.

A cautionary word must be said here, however: 'a miracle does not prove the truth of a doctrine, or the divine mission of him that brings it to pass. That which alone it claims for him at the first is a right to be listened to; it puts him in the alternative of being from heaven or from hell. The doctrine must first commend itself to the conscience as being *good*, and only then can the miracle seal it as *divine*.'[2] 'To the law and to the testimony: if they speak not according to this word, it is because there is no light in them' (Is. viii. 20). No amount of miracle can prove the divine origin of that which cannot pass this test. Both doctrine and miracle have their own marks of verity within them, and it is only when this is so that either of them may be used to substantiate the other.

Miracles are given to confirm the authority of the messenger, and only indirectly to authenticate the message. In this way miracles have been of the utmost value in the long course of God's revelation of Himself; for by them He has been pleased to endorse and confirm the authority of the bearers of His revelation. Pharaoh did well when he demanded a miracle of Moses (Ex. vii. 9-10), and Ahaz was guilty of a grievous sin when he despised the proffered sign from God (Is. vii. 10-13). The bringer of new and supernatural truth must be able to show his credentials. Nico-

[1] J. B. Mozley, *On Miracles*, pp. 181, 182.
[2] Trench, *Notes on the Miracles of our Lord*, p. 27.

demus was right when he said to Jesus, 'We know that thou art a teacher come from God: for no man can do these miracles that thou doest, except God be with him' (Jn. iii. 2). The works of Jesus, in conjunction with the divine quality of His ministry, had demonstrated that He was 'from God', and, on the basis of this, Nicodemus was prepared to be taught anything more that such a divinely commissioned teacher was able to tell him.

MIRACLES A VEHICLE OF REVELATION

Miracles, however, are much more than credentials; they are organically connected with the revelation to which they belong. They are not given by God to act merely as a town crier's bell to attract attention to the announcements that follow. Miracles are a means of revelation; they are vitally related to revelation and are themselves part of revelation. The miracles of Christ were the deed of which the gospel was the word. Our Lord revealed that He was the Saviour by doing the works of a Saviour, by healing men and women of their diseases of both body and soul. Miracles were not performed in order to stun men into faith: they were primarily addressed to faith, although, where despised, they constituted a ground of condemnation. That is why it is recorded of our Lord's home country that He did not many mighty works there because of their unbelief (Mt. xiii. 58). Miracles were wrought as part of a revelation. Thus when our Lord had said, 'I am the light of the world', He straightway proceeded to heal the blind man (Jn. ix. 5-7); and when He had said to Martha, 'I am the resurrection, and the life', He forthwith called Lazarus out of the grave (Jn. xi. 25, 43). His comment on the feeding of the five thousand was the profound claim, 'I am the bread of life' (Jn. vi. 35). It has been well argued by Dr. R. E. D. Clark[1] that miracle furnishes a link between the God of revelation and the God of creation. In our Lord's revelation of God it was appropriate that so many of His miracles—the evidence of the Creator's working—should have been the means by which works of mercy and love were performed. As a result of our Lord's miracles it becomes reasonable to trust His explicit statements about God's care for His creation. Supremely, then, the miracles are themselves a revelation of God in Christ. The wonderful life and the wonderful works of Christ are inseparable: they are one thing. Our Lord said, 'If I do not the works of my Father, believe me not. But if

[1] *Evangelical Quarterly*, July, 1936, p. 240.

1 do, though ye believe not me, believe the works: that ye may know, and believe, that the Father is in me, and I in him' (Jn. x 37-38).

The true miracle in its function as a 'sign' is thus a vehicle of revelation, and not merely an evidential addition. It is being 'increasingly realized', says Dr. Wace,[1] 'that miracles, so far from being an excrescence on Christian faith, are indissolubly bound up with it, and that there is a complete unity in the manifestation of the divine nature, which is recorded in the Scriptures'.

Before we close this section on the evidential value of miracles there is one important reservation to be made. Great and real as is the value of miracles, both as the attestation and vehicle of revelation, they can never be a substitute for faith. Christian assurance is not grounded on some absolute demonstration objectively given: it is not something which is mathematically proven. Our Lord rebuked what He perceived to be a wrong attitude of mind when He said, 'Except ye see signs and wonders, ye will not believe' (Jn. iv. 48).

The attempt, made by would-be defenders of the Christian faith, to substitute some objective and formal proof, when the heart of man cannot be finally satisfied with anything less than a moral and spiritual one, is to do the soul an injury, and to sow the seeds of future unbelief. The assurance of the believer rests upon God, not through the external testimony of miracles, but through the internal testimony of the Holy Spirit. 'The Spirit himself beareth witness with our spirit' (Rom. viii. 16, R.V.), and this is the final authority through which conviction reaches the heart.

[1] *International Standard Bible Encyclopaedia*, p. 2066.

CHAPTER VI

PRINCIPLES OF INTERPRETATION

THE purpose of this chapter is to give some elementary guidance and practical suggestions to those who are prepared to be workers in the school of scriptural understanding. This goal of true understanding is not one easily reached. Its pursuit requires prayerful diligence, painstaking labour and sustained quest.

UNDERSTANDING THE TEXT

1. *Make full use of commentaries, modern translations, paraphrases, etc.* It is a mistake to rest satisfied with nothing but the Authorized Version. A fresh translation or paraphrase, read at length at a sitting, often gives one some fresh insight into the meaning of a book or passage. The detailed explanation of meaning which is provided in commentaries can also greatly enrich understanding.

2. *Aim to discover the true meaning of the original text.* This should be one's immediate goal. Its pursuit is the more important because fancy easily runs riot. There is a real danger lest we see in Scripture not what is really there, but only a reflection of our own ideas, or a fancied endorsement of our own prejudices.

The sense of Scripture is determined by the words. Therefore every single word matters; and the more so if we believe that divine inspiration extends to the words and has secured the selection of peculiarly appropriate ones. Special notice should be taken of the fact that some words acquire a special or new meaning in Scripture from scriptural usage alone, and in consequence of the progress and enlargement of the content of revelation.

Where it is impossible to become expert in the original languages of Greek and Hebrew, it is possible, as a good second best, to go halfway, and to get nearer to a more accurate understanding by the use of the many aids specially prepared to help such limited study; e.g. an analytical concordance with transliterations of the original words in roman script.

3. *Discover the significance to the original readers.* This is a very important rule. One needs to set oneself to enter into the writer's mind and environment, his reaction to prevailing conditions, and his conscious purpose in writing. This involves acquaintance with

the background and the historical setting. It is as a help to such understanding that this handbook is written.

4. *Discover the character of the composition*, e.g. whether history or allegory, prose or poetry, narrative or discourse, soliloquy or dialogue, etc. Do not necessarily rely upon chapter or other divisions which are no part of the original, and may sometimes be inappropriate. Seek to recognize the obvious and possibly declared connection of any statement or passage with what precedes or follows.

5. *Discover the form of expression*, e.g. whether literal or figurative, actual or metaphorical. Figurative terms should not be taken literally. Note whether statements are indicative or interrogative or imperative, definite or conditioned, actual or hypothetical. Aim to appreciate the allusions, figures and expressions which are related to the customs, circumstances, etc., of the original readers. Here the help of commentaries and of scholarly investigation is obviously necessary.

6. *Recognize the character of divine revelation* as given in and through history. God has spoken not just in words, but in and through the lives of men, and most of all in and through the life, death and resurrection of His Son incarnate. Therefore, what matters equally with the words of the prophets, and in the end more than the words, are the deeds or events which they interpret. Christianity is a historic revelation. Therefore, the original literal and historical meaning of Scripture is of fundamental importance.

INTERPRETING THE TEXT

The Christian's use of the Bible does not end when he has succeeded in understanding the text. In fact it is only then that the more direct Christian use of it can begin.

1. *Interpret straightforwardly*, i.e. according to what the text actually says. Words must be taken in their proper sense. There is no normal justification for letting the words of Scripture mean something to us which they do not mean in their Bible setting. We should beware of an excessive or needless literalism and of a fanciful or an evasive spiritualization. Clear distinction should be made between words which are the dogmatic utterances of God and of God's messengers, and words of others, e.g. of Satan, which are recorded for our edification, but not necessarily for our acceptance.

2. *Interpret the part in relation to the whole.* The meaning of a word or phrase is often modified by the connection in which it is used. So the setting of a word must be allowed to determine its particu-

lar sense and significance. Attention should also be given to the character and purpose of the whole book or section in which the words come.

Similarly there should be continual recognition of the unity of the scriptural revelation as a whole. One ought, therefore, to beware of the tendency just to regard each book independently. Rather one should constantly aim to get beyond the contributions of particular passages or single books to a properly developed understanding of the general consent and consistent teaching of Scripture as a whole.

3. *Recognize the general purpose of all Scripture*, viz., to reveal the ways of God with men and for men, particularly His salvation for sinful men. Only those who recognize this can use Scripture rightly. For its words are not intended to provide light on all subjects, nor to answer all men's questions. They are addressed to a particular need and end.

4. *Regard Christ as the main subject of all Scripture.* Holy Scripture bears witness in all its parts to Christ, and to His comings as the Man to men, whether to save or to judge. He is the great subject and final agent of both revelation and redemption. In this historic work He is supremely God's word of salvation. The written Word is but the complement or the reflection of the living Word. Without Him it would not exist. In Him alone are its true unity and fulfilment to be found. Therefore, all study of the Scriptures should be centred in Him. He is the one all-sufficient key to their right interpretation.

5. *Interpret Scripture by Scripture.* Use the Old Testament for the understanding of the New Testament, and interpret the Old Testament in relation and subordination to the New Testament. It is clear that the New Testament writers believed that the Old Testament Scriptures were divinely intended to help them to understand the gospel of Jesus Christ. Also, in general, Scripture should be compared with Scripture in order to let Scripture itself check and confirm one's interpretation of Scripture. Consistent obedience to this rule will mean that one passage of Scripture will not be so interpreted as to conflict with another. Heresies commonly start from an exaggerated interpretation of one side of truth.

6. *Recognize that the truth is infinite and many-sided.* There may be more than one aspect or point of view, e.g. Christ is both 'the Lion' and 'the Lamb' (Rev. v. 5, 6). Opposite aspects of infinite truth inevitably appear to finite minds to be contradictory and irreconcilable. The humble and reverent student of divine revelation will recognize with Charles Simeon that 'the truth is

not in the middle, and not in one extreme, but in both extremes'.

7. *Recognize individual limitations*, and respect the judgment of other believers, particularly the consensus of the saints. Remember not only that human understanding is at the best still finite, but also that individual ability to grasp the fulness of truth is still more limited. It is wise to treat with respect interpretations held by others, particularly when such interpretations have for long been accepted by most, if not all, of God's people. Do not be dogmatic in matters over which the equally devout disagree.

8. *Seek the enlightenment and the testimony of the Holy Spirit.* This is of primary and universal importance. It is only by the illumination of the Spirit that we can discern revealed truth, and only by His sanction or witness that we can know its certainty as 'of God'. He is the only adequate Teacher for the right exposition of His own inspired text-book.

SPECIAL RULES FOR THE INTERPRETATION OF PARABLES, AND OF ALL SCRIPTURE WHICH IS FIGURATIVE OR ALLEGORICAL

1. *Concentrate attention on the central point or main teaching.* Keep all the details subordinate to the main impression of the picture as a whole. Remember that, in all figurative representations, there is much that is mere costume or setting. So do not (except in special cases) attempt to find a spiritual significance in every detail. Such detailed correspondence should not be pursued without very clear scriptural justification. Occasionally our Lord did do it (see Mt. xiii. 3-9, 18-23, 24-30, 36-43). But contrast His application of the parable of the Good Samaritan (see Lk. x. 37). And note that there are some parables in which it is quite impossible to find correspondence in every detail.

2. *Base all doctrine on direct statements of Scripture.* A figure is in character additional and illustrative only. So it should never be made the main basis of an article of faith. Rather one should seek explicit Scriptural authority for the interpretation or application of types, figures, and parables. The mere perception of analogy will not suffice. One must make sure independently that the idea derived from the figure is itself scriptural truth.

PRACTICAL RULES FOR USING THE BIBLE FOR CHRISTIAN LIVING

1. *Use the Bible as a rule of faith and conduct.* Seek for scriptural ground and justification in principle for all that you believe and

do as a Christian. For instance, aim to know what the Bible teaches about God's way of salvation for sinful men; and be sure that you grasp clearly those revealed truths which are of primary importance for man's eternal well-being. Similarly, strive to be prepared to give a scriptural answer as a reason for the faith that is in you (1 Pet. iii. 15). Seek from the Bible to discover not only what Christians believe, but why; so that you may be able to answer men's questions without hesitation, and to justify your own Christian confidence.

2. *Regard the Bible as a handbook of personal religion*, a daily means of grace, and regularly use it as such. God still speaks to the seeking soul in and through His written Word. So do not read the Bible merely as a detached spectator. Aim most of all to discover spiritual truth which is capable of immediate personal application to your own condition, needs, and circumstances. Be on the look-out continually for things to do which the teaching of Scripture demands. In other words, be a doer of the Word, and not a reader only.

3. *Recognize the place of individual conscience and judgment.* Scripture only speaks to every man according to the measure of his entrance into light; and that is the point at which he must respond to its further challenge if he is to progress in its understanding.

4. *Recognize the need for continual return to, and fresh reformation according to, the Word of God.* There is constant need for a continual coming back to God to examine oneself afresh in the light of His Word, to be convicted of the beginnings of sinful decline, to be made aware of fresh ways in which advance in holiness and love is now possible.

5. *Recognize the unceasing possibility of further progress in understanding and obedience.* It never becomes any of us to relax our quest as though we had arrived at full knowledge or perfect performance. There is always room and always need to discover more; and then to walk in the fresh light gained.

PART TWO
THE OLD TESTAMENT

CONTENTS OF PART TWO

CHAPTER VII

THE HISTORICAL BACKGROUND

MODERN ARCHAEOLOGICAL DISCOVERY

UNTIL the last century all our knowledge of the ancient world either came from the Bible or was derived from the writings of historians such as Josephus or Herodotus, or from the literary traditions of Greece, India and other nations. But, in recent years, archaeological research has thrown a flood of light upon the early history of mankind. Great monuments had long borne their silent witness when early in the nineteenth century the decipherment of the Egyptian hieroglyphics opened up a new era. Layard's excavations in Mesopotamia came soon after, and then the discovery of the key to the Babylonian cuneiform writing, until at last the way was open to the recovery and translation of the manifold records of the past.

The Egyptian hieroglyphics, originally pictures, stand each for a word or syllable, and are mostly found engraved upon stone or other hard material. The Babylonian cuneiform writing is also made up of symbols each representing a single syllable. These consist of groups of wedge-shaped ('cuneiform') lines, variously arranged, and chiefly occur on tablets of clay. The ancient scribe would choose a clod of clay from the Euphrates or the Nile, reduce it to the size required, smooth it to a flat surface, and whilst it was still moist stab it with an iron stylus having a wedge-shaped end, so impressing the characters upon the clay. This was then hardened in the sun or baked in an oven, when it acquired a durability which has preserved it through thousands of years. Thousands of these tablets dug up out of the sand, together with the inscriptions on monuments, rocks, or the walls of buildings now tell us the story of the past, sometimes in legend or poetry, and sometimes in contemporary records of accurately dated history. Among the tablets have been found commercial receipts and contracts, official instructions, personal and official correspondence, catalogues, law-books, and all other things for which writing is used by civilized peoples. Apart from written material, much information has been gathered by observation and inference from the temples, houses and tombs that have been excavated, and from the objects found in them. Household vessels, weapons and instruments, ornaments of gold, silver and precious stones, pictures of hunting, warfare, or agriculture, the model of a boat or of a bakery, a harp, or a hairpin, all have added to our knowledge of the life and customs of the distant past.

'Digging up the past', as Sir Leonard Woolley calls it, has become a scientific process.[1] Some 'Tell', or mound of ancient ruins, is selected, shafts are sunk, probings made and surface rubbish removed. Then the treasures that lie below are gradually revealed. These mounds, marking the sites of ancient cities, are often of a considerable height owing to the Eastern habit, when a city had fallen into decay, of building afresh upon its ruins. Thus each Tell consists of layer upon layer of remains, the more recent above and the more ancient below. In excavating at Jericho, for example, ruins were found near the surface belonging to the Byzantine period, below them those of the city built by Hiel the Bethelite (1 Ki. xvi. 34); then came a wide-spread layer of charred remains of inhabited houses, mixed with objects of the fifteenth century B.C., the city with brick walls built upon stone foundations which was burned by Joshua (Jos. vi. 24); lower down still, and therefore earlier, were found traces of a fortified city dating back before 2,000 B.C.; then a layer with primitive pottery and polished flint instruments of the neolithic period; and, finally, rude flint instruments of the palaeolithic age scattered over a floor of beaten earth, with its witness to human occupation in prehistoric times.[2]

The date of these remains can be decided in part by the relative position in which they are found, by an inscription, a coin or a dated scarab; in part also by the character of the objects themselves. As in this country the existence of Roman bricks, or the style of architecture, acts as a guide to the date of a building, so, in the East, the building material used, or the kind of vessels and instruments discovered, can be used to fix the period to which the discoveries belong. Fifty years ago in Palestine, Professor Flinders Petrie made a special study of thousands of pieces of pottery which had been dug up, carefully noting the place and accompaniments of each, and classifying them in groups. In this way it was established that, in any given period and region, a definite type of pottery was used, and these types now afford 'the best criterion that an archaeologist can have'.[3] Although it is seldom possible to fix an exact date, yet the sequence-dating can be carried out with very considerable

[1] *Digging Up the Past*, Pelican Series.
[2] For further examples see Garstang, *Joshua and Judges*, pp. 359 ff.
[3] Woolley, *op. cit.*, p. 28.

accuracy. Thus we can speak of things belonging to the early, middle, or late bronze age in Palestine, denoting by these terms periods commencing at 2,500, 2,000, and 1,600 B.C. respectively.[1]

Before the introduction of metals man used instruments of flint. At first in the palaeolithic, or old stone, age, these were roughly chipped and crude, but later, in the neolithic period, weapons and other objects of finely polished and worked flints reveal a more advanced civilization.

Such traces of human life are found all over Europe as well as in Asia, but they do not mark the same period in all places. In Mesopotamia the neolithic age came to a close in the fourth millennium B.C., in Palestine some centuries later, and in Britain it lasted nearly until the Christian era. Attempts at the dating of palaeolithic remains are highly speculative and the estimates differ widely.[2]

THE TRANSMISSION OF THE RECORD

These discoveries have greatly modified earlier views as to the date and the credibility of the sacred records. Wellhausen regarded the patriarchal narratives as legendary and Abraham as a creature of the imagination, but to-day Sir Leonard Woolley tells us that the fact of Abraham's existence is 'vouched for by written documents almost, if not quite, contemporary with him'.[3] Inscriptions have been recovered, both in Egypt and Mesopotamia, dating back to before 3,000 B.C.,[4] and codes of laws belonging to the patriarchal age have been dug up. 'Possibly', Sir Leonard Woolley says, 'Abraham may have put down in writing for the benefit of his household so much of the familiar laws of Sumer . . . as he thought applicable to their nomad life'.[5] Tablets have also been found, both in Babylonia and Egypt, containing genealogies and family histories, like those occurring in the book of Genesis. Moreover, these are sometimes furnished with headings, such as we meet with in the phrase, 'these are the generations of ——' or 'the book of the generations of Adam' (Gn. ii. 4, v. 1). *Sepher*, the word for 'book' means a record or register and the name 'Kirjath-Sepher', or city of records, in Jos. xv. 15 indicates that such records were carefully stored. This has given rise to the belief that the genealogies were copied by

---

[1] Garstang, *op. cit.*, p. 52, note.
[2] See A. Rendle Short, *Modern Discovery and the Bible*, p. 80.
[3] *Abraham*, p. 41.
[4] *Ur of the Chaldees*, p. 95.
[5] *Abraham*, p. 32.

Moses from tablets of patriarchal origin, which had been preserved by Abraham and his descendants.[1] It may be noted that spec al care has been taken to preserve the promises of a 'seed' to Eve, to Abraham, Isaac, and Jacob; and the genealogies belong to those to whom these promises were made. The marked change in the narrative which takes place at Gn. xii., the fulness of detail and family character of what follows, and the plainness of speech with which the weakness, doubts and mistakes of Abraham and Jacob are laid bare, would alone suggest that the narrative came originally from their hands. Other features raise this to a probability. A striking resemblance has been shown to exist between the actions of Abraham and Jacob and the laws and customs now known to have prevailed in their days among the neighbouring peoples. For example an ancient Hurrian tablet says that possession of a father-in-law's household gods gave a son-in-law title to be regarded as his legitimate heir, which explains the motive of Rachel's theft of the 'images' (Gen. xxxi. 34).[2] A similar correspondence with Egyptian customs and modes of thought[3] can be seen in the life of Joseph and in the book of Exodus.

The same is true regarding the earliest Bible references to 'books' and 'writing'. Many ancient genealogies have been brought to light (cf. Gn. v. 1) and codes of law (cf. Ex. xxiv. 4; Dt. xxxi. 26), whilst from the earliest times records were kept of wars (cf. Nu. xxi. 14; 2 Ch. xii. 15). There is no reason, therefore, for doubting that the 'books' referred to contained similar contemporary records. References to the materials used are likewise confirmed by archaeology; pottery has been found inscribed with an ink which could have been washed off (cf. Nu. v. 23), iron pens were in use (Je. xvii. 1), and both Egypt and Babylon employed professional scribes (Jdg. v. 14).[4] Two kinds of writing have already been mentioned, the hieroglyphic and the cuneiform, but a third kind is now known to have been in use among the Semites from the time of Moses, or before, namely, an alphabet similar in type to, but different in form from, the square Hebrew letters of a later age, which may be called the proto-Hebrew script. The first specimens were found at Serabit, in the Sinai desert, in connection with the turquoise mines which had

[1] Naville, *Archaeology of the Old Testament*, Chs. I, II; P. J. Wiseman, *New Discoveries in Babylonia about Genesis*.

[2] Kenyon, *The Bible and Archaeology*, pp. 268, 269.

[3] See Chapter IV, and Yahuda, *Language of the Pentateuch*, and *Accuracy of the Bible*.

[4] See Duncan, *Accuracy of the Old Testament*, Ch. I.

been worked by Semitic workmen in the employ of the Egyptian kings. Other writings in this script have been found at Byblos, Gezer, Bethshemesh, and Lachish; the dates assigned to them varying between 2,000 and 1,500 B.C.[1]

At Ras Shamra, near the Syrian coast, a whole library has been unearthed of tablets using an alphabet of twenty-nine cuneiform characters, in a language akin to Hebrew. It is implied in Deuteronomy (vi. 9, xxiv. 1) that writing was in use among the Hebrews; and the foregoing evidence, though leaving much that is obscure, places no hindrance in the way of believing this to have been the case.

FROM THE CREATION TO THE FLOOD[2]

The book of Genesis traces the story of God's dealing with the human race from 'the beginning' (an expression possibly borrowed from the Egyptian for 'primeval time'): the first four sections, or tablets, commencing i. 1, ii. 4, v. 1, and vi. 9, include the whole antediluvian period. Many ancient traditions of the creation and the flood exist. Zoroaster tells in the Zend-Avesta of the creation, in order, of the sky, water, plants and animals, and mankind; and of a Paradise where God set a brother and sister to be the ancestors of mankind. These were created perfect, but were corrupted by the evil spirit and fell; then later comes a chronicle of the flood and the ark.[3]

The Babylonian stories of the creation and flood are found in the Gilgamesh Epic, the oldest form of which is inscribed on a tablet of six columns belonging to the third millennium B.C. In it the primitive innocence of man in Paradise is described, the creation is connected with the flood, and the flood with the sin of man; a great ship is prepared in which one human family is saved, and there are other points of similarity. But the differences are even more striking. The Babylonian stories bristle with polytheistic extravagances and lack the simplicity, the moral character, and the lofty monotheism of the Bible story. Sir Wallis Budge, a high authority, gives it as his decided opinion that 'the account of the flood given in the book of Genesis is not borrowed from the Babylonian version as has been so often stated'.[4]

A fragment found at Boghaz Keui of an independent story of

---

[1] Kenyon, *op. cit.*, p. 266.
[2] See also Chapter IX, under *Genesis*.
[3] Zwemer, *Origin of Religion*, p. 111.
[4] *Babylonian Life and History*, p. 86.

the flood belonging to the Hurrians (see below) gives the name of the hero as Nahmoliel, which might be a longer form of Noah. The common origin of all these accounts must go back to a very early time, probably to the event itself.

It has long been known that the historian Berossus (280 B.C.) recorded the Babylonian belief in the flood, and gave a list of ten kings who reigned before the flood for a period of twelve *sars*, or 432,000 years, the last of whom, Xisuthros, made an ark in which he and his family were saved, after which he offered sacrifices on a mountain and was received up into heaven. Inscriptions have now been discovered referring to these ten rulers, but giving different names and length of days. No connection can be traced between these and the ten ancestors of Noah with the exception of Enmeduranki (=Evedorachos of Berossus)=Enoch.

The excavations at Ur and Kish have added to our knowledge. The sinking of a deep shaft at Ur in 1929 which penetrated down to the virgin soil through deposits of various kinds, revealed a layer of eight feet of alluvial clay, entirely free from fragments of any kind, below which pottery of a primitive type again appeared mixed with neolithic flint instruments. This, with similar phenomena at Kish, led Woolley to the conclusion that the deposit could be due only to a flood of quite exceptional dimensions, which had completely wiped out an earlier race and culture, and was, indeed, the flood of the Bible story and of Sumerian history and legend.[1] Whether the flood covered only the inhabited world as known to Noah, or had a much wider range may, in the present state of our knowledge, be left an open question.

Beneath the flood layer, and at corresponding levels, Woolley ound in association with flint instruments, tokens of civilization, painted pottery, some objects of clay impressed with the owner's seal, and a single brick. These finds confirmed the Sumerian tradition that, before the flood, their ancestors had come in from a hilly country to the East, had subdued the previous inhabitants, and brought with them the arts of agriculture, working of metal, and writing. The Eden of Genesis iii. is probably the same word as the Babylonian *Edinnu*, which denotes a plateau or steppe, and is found in the name Sippara of Edinnu (cf. Gn. ii. 8).

What can be learned concerning the antediluvian period from the dim light thrown upon it by these discoveries? They confirm the statements that, even then, cities were built (Gn. iv. 17),[2]

---

[1] *Ur of the Chaldees*, p. 29.

[2] 'The remarkable statement of Gn. iv. 17, has been amply confirmed by the excavations'. Snaith, *Distinctive Ideas of the Old Testament*, p. 28.

and that metal instruments were in use (v. 22). It has recently been brought to light that the land which lies east of the upper reaches of the Tigris was known by the Kassites as Cush[1] which implies that the river Gihon (Gen. ii. 13, R.V.) was the Araxes, and that Eden was in the region assigned to it by Sumerian tradition, at the head waters of the great rivers of Mesopotamia.

In the present state of our knowledge it is not safe to speculate as to the deductions to be drawn from the widespread traces of human remains or as to the duration of the neolithic or palaeolithic ages[2]; nor is it wise to insist upon any particular interpretation, literal or otherwise, of the numerical data of the early genealogies in Genesis.

According to the numbers in the Septuagint version of Gen. xi. the date of the Noachian flood would be some time prior to 3,200 B.C., Woolley tentatively suggests 3,500 B.C. or earlier. It is significant that the period immediately following saw a sudden and simultaneous outburst of civilization in the early Minoan age in Crete, under Menes in Egypt and in Mesopotamia about 3,400 B.C.

FROM THE FLOOD TO THE CALL OF ABRAHAM

As real history emerges we find two races established in the Mesopotamian plain, the Accadians, who were Semites, to the North, and the Sumerians, a non-Semitic race, to the South, and amongst their most ancient cities Accad (Agade), Erech, Ur and Babel (or Babylon) (Gn. x. 10). From graves at Ur, dated soon after the flood, have been recovered beautifully worked ornaments of gold and precious stones, some apparently brought from distant India. There is evidence also of skill in music (see Gn. iv. 21), a knowledge of astronomy, and the widespread use of writing.

Then came an age of ambitious building, with great palaces and temples. The pyramids of Egypt were reared in the first half of the third millennium B.C., and the great palaces at Knossos about the same time.

In Gn. x. we have a very early account of the various races of mankind, and their geographical position. The fact that there is no mention of the 'Arabs' by name testifies to its antiquity. It must be remembered that, in the Biblical genealogies, names are frequently omitted (as in Mt. i.), that the word 'son' may stand

---

[1] The name survives in Hindu-Kush. See *Expository Times*, December, 1940.
[2] See Macalister, *A Century of Excavation in Palestine*, p. 224-247.

for a grandson or other descendant, and that their repetition frequently has some special object in view. It is not possible to connect all the fragments of history recoverable from the earliest Babylonian records with the equally fragmentary material in the two chapters of Genesis (x., xi.) which contain all that the Bible tells us of more than a thousand years; but there is no actual conflict, and the very bareness of the Bible account is in harmony with its early origin and historical character. The striking correspondence between the story of the building of the Tower of Babel with what archaeology has revealed of the structure and history of the Babylonian Ziggurats cannot be accidental, and we need not doubt that we have here a piece of primitive history. Ziggurats were pyramid temples, made of sunbaked bricks and using bitumen (the original Babylonian word for this has been preserved in the Hebrew text) for mortar, rising in terraces to a great height. There are many records of the repair of these buildings in some of which the words occur, 'its top shall reach to heaven'. The ruined base of a Ziggurat at Babel has been discovered. Moses draws attention to the use of materials which are different from those of Egyptian architecture (Gn. xi. 3). Among the great figures of those early years, some centuries after the flood, was a great king Sargon of Agade, who began to reign in that city about the year 2,650 B.C. He conquered the whole of Mesopotamia, and tradition asserts that he even crossed the Mediterranean Sea and conquered Cyprus. Woolley says, 'he was identified, and perhaps rightly, with the Nimrod of the Old Testament who founded Caleh and was a mighty hunter before the Lord'.[1] Coming nearer to the days of Abraham the inscriptions supply dated lists of the kings of Babylon and other cities. The sixth king of the first dynasty in Babylon was Hammurabi, whom Woolley and other authorities identify with the Amraphel of Gn. xiv. (Hammurapi-el). Apart from this identification, the monuments and excavations give us a fairly clear picture of Ur of the Chaldees, and the wider world of that day.

THE WORLD IN ABRAHAM'S DAY

(a) The City of Ur

Excavation in Ur has laid bare whole streets of the time of Abraham, with two-storied houses, some of them showing a considerable degree of comfort and refinement. There are temples also, and tablets have been found containing hymns that once were

[1] *Ur of the Chaldees*, p. 77.

sung in them. Literary achievement is proved by the existence of libraries and dictionaries, mathematical tables, and even copy-books for learners. On one tablet the name of Abram was found, and it appears to refer to a small farmer of a somewhat earlier time.

One famous monument, of which a cast can be seen in the British Museum, contains Hammurabi's law code, which includes many precepts parallel to the Mosaic law, with some important differences.[1] Other records reveal an elaborate system of government administration, and great commercial activity. The archives in one temple included receipts from the priests for gifts and offerings to the god, cheese, a herd of sheep, a bale of wool, a quantity of copper from abroad, gold for the idol, and oil for the doors. There was also a register of workers, and a monthly balance sheet of accounts.[2] Abraham, therefore, in his youth, found himself a citizen of no mean city; the world was already old in his day.

(b) The route to Egypt

When he left Ur for Haran, and later received the call to go forth from thence, he followed a route that had been traversed by many others, for there was much commerce between one nation and another. Wares brought from Persia and India on one side, and from distant Crete on the other, have been found in Babylonia. Cedar was imported from Lebanon, and asphalt for building from the Dead Sea. At Mari, on the way between Ur and Haran, tablets, religious, commercial and relative to metal-working, have been discovered, also the ruins of a palace which might possibly have afforded shelter to Abraham on his journey.[3]

A well-known wall painting on a tomb of about 2,100 B.C. at Beni Hassan, in Egypt, depicts a party of thirty-seven Semites, under a leader named Abishua, bringing products of their country to an Egyptian official in return for the corn of Egypt. They are armed with spears, clubs and bows, and an ass carries a lyre of Asiatic pattern, and a pannier of goods. Other inscriptions refer to 'gum from the land of Canaan', and to balm and myrrh for embalming, and 'Syrian slaves' brought from Damascus, by the ancient route which passed through Dothan (cf. Gn. xxxvii. 17, xliii. 11). Scarabs of an earlier date, about 2,300 B.C., and an inscribed cylinder found under Mount Ophel show that, even

---

[1] See p. 136.
[2] Woolley, Ur of the Chaldees, p. 171.
[3] Allis, The Five Books of Moses, p. 208.

D

then, Egypt and Babylon were connected by a route which passed through Jerusalem; and an Egyptian story of the same period tells of a prince who fled into Palestine and dwelt there in the hill country enjoying its wine and honey and finding for himself a bride from amongst its people.

(c) Habiru, Amorites and Hittites

We are told in Gn. xiv. 13 that Abram was a *Hebrew* (*ibri*), and in x. 21 that Shem was the father of all the 'sons of Eber'. The meaning of this name is said to be 'wanderer', but, whatever its derivation, it is evidently used here in a wider sense than in later times when it was restricted to the children of Israel: and it suggests that Abram, in his travels, might have met with other men of his own race. Inscriptions of Rim-Sin, the predecessor of Hammurabi, tell of the employment of Habiru (the same word) as mercenary soldiers, and the name occurs in Babylonian texts from Mari of the same period, in Hittite records from Boghaz-Keui, and in Hurrian texts from Nuzi.[1]

It is also said that Abram dwelt 'in the plain of Mamre the *Amorite*' and was confederate with him and his brothers. This word, which may mean 'mountaineer', also seems to have been used sometimes in a more general (see Gn. xv. 16, xlviii. 22) and at others in a narrower sense.[2] Sargon of Agade claimed to bear rule over the Amurru who dwelt in the 'western land' and the claim was renewed by Hammurabi. They seem to have been a Semitic race who, before Abraham's day, surged into Palestine and imposed their language upon the earlier inhabitants who belonged to a Hamitic stock. The inscriptions describe them as mountain dwellers, and excavation has shown that their cities, which in Joshua's time existed in the hill country on both sides of the Jordan (Nu. xxi. 21; Dt. iii. 5; Jos. xiii.), contained well-planned houses with granaries, water conduits, underground passages and drainage systems.

The *Hittites* or 'Hatti' (Egyptian *Kheta*) whose very existence was once doubted by critics, are now known to have been a powerful race, giving rise to a powerful kingdom. They invaded and plundered Babylon about 1,800 B.C., and, at a later period, warred on equal terms with the monarchs of Egypt. Their capital at Boghaz-Keui was first excavated in 1906,[3] and a large quantity

---

[1] Kenyon, *op. cit.*, p. 277.
[2] See Garstang, *op. cit.*, p. 123.
[3] See Kenyon, *op. cit.*, pp. 81-96; Marston, *The Bible is True*, Chs. XIII, XVI.

of cuneiform tablets in the Hittite and other languages has been found. These have given the key to the Hittite tongue. They spoke an Indo-European language which shows affinities with old Latin, and migrated from the East. Babylonian tradition refers to an irruption of Hatti, *c.* 2,000 B.C. Their kingdom extended at one time from Cappadocia to the Euphrates in the East and to Kadesh on the Orontes in the south. The 'sons of Heth' whom Abraham encountered (Gn. xxiii. 3) were doubtless immigrants from the north.

Such were the peoples in and around Canaan. 'It is safe to say that the general effect of the discoveries has been to confirm the substantial accuracy of the picture of life in Canaan in the second millennium B.C. as described in the patriarchal narratives of Genesis'.[1]

FROM ABRAHAM TO MOSES

(a) *The call of Abraham*

This call forms a clear dividing line in the book of Genesis. The preceding chapters are in the nature of a summary, centuries being passed over in a few sentences; the succeeding ones expand into personal narratives which have all the appearance of autobiographies.

The archaic character of Gn. xiv. is recognized on all hands. Amraphel, who is there mentioned, is, as stated above, possibly to be identified with Hammurabi. Names equivalent or similar to Chedorlaomer and Arioch have been found in lists of the Kings of Elam and Larsa (Ellasar), but the identifications are uncertain. 'Tidal . . . might be Tudkhaliah, king of the Hittites'.[2] Petrie gave it as his opinion that no writer after the time of Joshua could have described the places named in Gn. xiv. in the terms there used, and Dr. N. Glueck, who made extensive explorations in Transjordan, has stated that the archaeological facts agree completely with the account of the cities of the plain contained in that chapter.[3]

(b) *The Hyksos*

At some time during the patriarchal age Egypt was invaded by the Hyksos (*Haq-shasu,* 'desert princes') or shepherd kings, who were the rulers of the thirteenth to the seventeenth dynasties.

---

[1] Hooke, *Record and Revelation,* p. 372.
[2] Kenyon, *The Bible and Archaeology,* p. 121.
[3] *The Other Side of the Jordan,* p. 114.

Whilst there is general agreement as to the end of the Hyksos rule about 1,580 B.C., there is considerable diversity of opinion about its commencement (Petrie, 2,370 B.C.; S. A. Cook, *c.* 2,000 B.C.; others later). Excavation in Palestine, at Lachish and Jericho, at Debir, Hebron and Gerar, shows that the cave-dwellers who inhabited these city sites in early times were succeeded about 2,000 B.C. by a race who lived in well-built houses, possessed stone cities (e.g. at Jericho), used finely ornamented pottery, and fenced their cities with an elaborate and characteristic type of fortification. This consisted of a mound some twenty feet high, with a smooth, sloping, outer surface, surrounded by a fosse, the only entrance to the fortified city being by means of a long, sloping causeway leading up to and over the mound. Such, no doubt, were the cities 'walled and very great' (Nu. xiii. 28; Dt. ix. 1) reported upon by the spies.

The pressure of Semitic influences upon Southern Palestine and Egypt is reflected in the story of the patriarchs. Abram goes down to Egypt for corn (Gn. xii. 10), he finds at Gerar a Semitic king, though having a captain with an Egyptian name (xx. 2, xxi. 22), and Ishmael finds a wife in Egypt (xxi. 21). The site of Gerar has been excavated and it has been observed that the 'palace' is situated on an eminence immediately overlooking the only suitable camping ground, still used by the Bedouin for their tents (xxvi. 8).

(c) The sojourn of Israel in Egypt

With the entry of Joseph into Egypt the narrative in Genesis at once takes on a strongly Egyptian colouring.[1] The monuments illustrate the many colours, the vesture of fine linen, signet ring and golden chain bestowed upon the royal favourite, horses and waggons and chariots. They contain stories of dreams and interpretations, of Canaanite slaves raised to high office, of disastrous famines when stores of corn were collected and distributed to the people through a series of years, and of grants of pasturage to immigrant Asiatic shepherds. Although the name of Joseph has not been discovered the Bible story conforms in many details to the conditions of the time and place.

(d) The oppression

The expulsion of the Hyksos was followed by a dynasty of native rulers (the eighteenth) who left great monuments behind them and extended the empire of Egypt over Nubia to the south and

[1] See Chapter IX, under *Genesis.*

to the north over Palestine.   Among them was 'the new King which knew not Joseph' (Ex. i. 8).

A wall engraving of this period pictures the building at Karnak of the temple of Amon with slave-gangs, apparently Semites, hard at work.   Over them stands the slave-driver, the inscription running, 'the taskmaster saith to his labourers, "the rod is in my hand, be not idle" '.   An ancient papyrus also contains the complaint of an Egyptian contractor, 'I am not provided with anything, there are no men for making bricks, and there is no straw in the district'.   The word for 'officers' in Ex. v. (*shoterim*) corresponds with the Egyptian word for writer, which is the usual title given to the supervisors who kept the tally of hours worked by the slaves, for which they had to account to the taskmasters under whom they worked.

(e) The Exodus

Hat-shep-sut, daughter of Thothmes I, a princess of great personality, was probably the 'daughter of Pharaoh' who brought up Moses.   The Pharaoh of the oppression appears to have been her brother, Thothmes III, a powerful monarch, many of whose buildings and inscriptions remain, one of which can be seen in 'Cleopatra's Needle', now on the bank of the Thames.   A pylon at Karnak gives a list of his conquests in Palestine, in which more than a score of cities are mentioned which occur in the Bible story. He extended his conquests to Carchemish on the Euphrates, and by breaking the power of the Hittites and Amorites he prepared the way all unconsciously for the conquest of Canaan by Joshua.   Garstang[1] interprets the 'hornet' of Jos. xxiv. 12 as the Egyptian power, a hornet being part of the hieroglyph representing the sovereignty of Pharaoh.   Thothmes III was succeeded (1447 B.C.) by Amenhotep II, the Pharaoh of the Exodus.

THE WILDERNESS WANDERINGS

The wanderings of the Israelites in the wilderness cannot be identified with certainty.   The inscriptions at Serabit, and other facts, indicate that a line of communication existed from Egypt, through the Sinai peninsula, to the land of Midian east of the gulf of Akaba.   It was not the entirely inhospitable region that some have supposed; even in the Sinai desert there are traces of former fertility, and in the mountains of Midian there must have been abundance of pasture (see Ex. ii. 16).   It may be noted that the

[1] *Op. cit.*, p. 258.

name Kadesh, which means 'holy', or 'separated', may have been given to more than one place where the tabernacle halted.

In the narratives in Exodus and Numbers the influence of Egypt can be clearly traced. The account of the plagues is redolent of the Nile, the reference to the 'foundation' of Egypt (Ex. ix. 16, 24) finds an exact parallel in an inscription of Thothmes III, and brazen mirrors such as the women brought for the making of the laver (Ex. xxxviii. 8) have recently been recovered dating from the same time.[1] Its contemporary character is also to be inferred from the archaic character of the legal code or 'judgments' of chs. xxi.-xxiii. which are evidently applicable to a simple people engaged in agriculture. Several of them find a parallel in Hammurabi's code which was then centuries old. (So Ex. xxi. 16, 23, 28, 29, xxii. 2, 10, 12, 13.)[2] Some may represent widespread customs of that time; others, such as those protecting the rights of the first-born and prescribing the right treatment of slaves, seem to be unique. Their exact relationship to earlier or contemporary systems is not easy to determine; what is certain is their primitive character.

THE CONQUEST OF PALESTINE (1,400-1,010 B.C.)[3]

Concerning the books of Joshua and Judges, Prof. Garstang has said that after years of study he is convinced 'that not only were these records in general founded upon fact, but they must have been derived from earlier writings, almost contemporary with the events described, so detailed and reliable is their information'.[4]

(a) The Fall of Jericho

Little can Joshua have thought when he gave the command to burn the city of Jericho that he was providing scholars of three thousand years afterwards with a means of determining with accuracy the date of his action. Yet so it was. Excavations at Jericho reveal clear evidence of its destruction by fire; charred bricks and timber, with household vessels, and bins full of corn proved that this disaster had fallen upon the city when inhabited. Below the fire-layer was found a city of the Hyksos period (see above), which had been destroyed and rebuilt about 1,600 B.C., together with characteristic pottery of a somewhat later date. In

---

[1] For other instances see Naville, *Archaeology of the Old Testament*, Chs. III, IV; and Yahuda, *Accuracy of the Bible*, pp. 65-130.

[2] Kenyon, *The Bible and Archaeology*, pp. 122-124.

[3] See Chapter X, under *Joshua and Judges*.

[4] *Op. cit.*, p. viii. Prof. Garstang, however, excepts certain 'priestly insertions' of later date.

a cemetery adjoining the city, pottery of a similar kind was found, and a few scarabs, up to and including the reign of Amenhotep III (1,411-1,375 B.C.), but none later. This, together with the absence of Mykenaean deposits in the occupation layers and other details, suggested a date for the burning of *c.* 1,400 B.C. which harmonizes with the statement in 1 Ki. vi. 1. This date may therefore 'be accepted with confidence as satisfying three conditions, the archaeological requirements, the Biblical data, and parallels between the records of Israel and Egypt, too consistent and too complete to be founded upon mere coincidence'.[1]

The defences of the city consisted of two walls built of brick, the outer one six feet thick, the inner about twelve feet, and five yards apart, the intervening space being bridged with timber, upon which houses had been built. Only one gate was discovered. On the west side the outer wall had fallen down the slope outside, and much of the inner wall also, with the remains of buildings between the walls. Houses alongside the wall had been burned to the ground, and their roofs had fallen in upon the household pottery within.

The pottery above the fire-layer belonged to a much later period, about the ninth century B.C., showing that centuries had elapsed before the city was rebuilt (1 Ki. xvi. 34). The dates above are based upon the examination of nearly 100,000 pieces of pottery and scores of scarabs. They receive further confirmation from the fact that signs of destruction by fire at the same time have been found at Bethel, Hazor, and other cities mentioned in the book of Joshua.[2]

(b) *Contemporary Events*

The shadow of Egypt lay over the land of Palestine all the days of Joshua's conquest and through the long period of unrest which followed. The reign of Amenhotep III (1,411-1,375 B.C.) was perhaps the period of Egypt's greatest material splendour. Thothmes III (see above) had already extended his conquests far beyond Palestine to the Hittite Kingdom and the banks of the Euphrates. If the records of Amenhotep upon the magnificent temples of Luxor may be trusted, the whole of this region looked

---

[1] Garstang, *Joshua and Judges*, pp. 66, 130, 388. 'This may be said now to be the prevalent view of the date of the Exodus' (Kenyon, *op. cit.*, p. 74). Albright and others adhere to a date in the thirteenth century B.C., and claim that the results of recent researches in Edom and Moab support this view. See also S. A. Cook, *Introduction to the Bible*, p. 213.

[2] Garstang, *op. cit.*, p. 54 ff., pp. 130-133.

up to him as its overlord. The earliest of the Tel-el-Amarna
tablets (see below) belong to his reign and reveal the kings of these
northern regions suing for his favour.

He was succeeded by Akhenaten (or Amenhotep IV), one of the
most striking figures in Egyptian history. Acting under some
unknown influence, possibly connected with the Hebrew religion,
he endeavoured to establish a kind of monotheism in place of the
prevailing idolatry, and his addresses to the deity approach in
some places the language of the Psalms. He was a seer rather than
a conqueror, and Hittite and other kings who had rendered
obsequious obedience to his predecessor now threw off the mask,
and asserted their independence, and began to reconquer neighbouring territories. A vivid picture of Palestine in those days,
which are also the later days of Joshua's life, is presented in the
tablets discovered at Tel el Amarna, in Egypt. They are written
in Babylonian cuneiform, a fact which demonstrates the influence
exerted on Palestine by the two great powers between which it
lay.

In them the priest-kings of Palestine implore Akhenaten as their
suzerain to come to their aid against hordes of Semitic invaders
whom they describe as Habiru. One of the letters is from Abdi-
Khiba, king of Urusalim (Jerusalem) and reads, 'The Habiru are
occupying the King's cities. There remains not one prince to my
lord the King, everyone is ruined.' Similar appeals for help were
sent from Gezer, Askelon and Megiddo. Who were these invaders?
Since Prof. Garstang's discoveries at Jericho, scholars of different
schools of thought have accepted his conclusions that these are the
Hebrews under Joshua. The name of Joshua actually occurs on
one tablet, but the reference is uncertain. [1]

The conclusion, however, is almost inevitable that here we have
a view of the invasion of Palestine by the children of Israel as seen
by the Canaanite, the Amorite and the Jebusite.

(c) The Ras Shamra tablets: the Hurrians

Light from a different angle has been shed on the conditions
prevailing on the northern border of Canaan at the time of the
Hebrew occupation by discoveries at Ras Shamra (near the
Syrian coast), Nuzi (east of the Tigris) and elsewhere. These have
revealed the existence of a race known to the Egyptians as Hurri,
and appearing in the Bible as Horites (Gn. xiv. 6, xxxvi. 20, 29;
Dt. ii. 12). Some scholars think also that Hivites represents a

[1] See p. 157.

scribal error for Horites. At the time of the Exodus, they seem to have been distributed over Mesopotamia, Syria and Palestine, whither they had migrated from the Armenian highlands.

Many of the tablets found at Ras Shamra (or Ugarit) were written during the reign of a king named Nigmed, probably in the fifteenth century B.C., the period of Hurrian influence, and are of a religious character. The supreme God is referred to as El, and the land of Canaan is called 'the whole land of El'—but the religion was polytheistic, and El had a wife Asherat, whose name often appears in the plural form Asherim (see Ex. xxxiv. 13, R.V.). There are many parallels with Scripture language, including references to a 'chief of the priests', to 'the bread of God' (Lv. xxi. 21), tithes, and to burnt, trespass, and peace offerings.[1] Customs are described which the law of Moses forbids, as for example the seething of a kid in its mother's milk (Ex. xxiii. 19). The Hebrew record, nevertheless, presents a striking contrast by the complete absence of any female god, or of stories of many gods intriguing or fighting with each other, or of the mythical extravagances which are found in the tablets.

THE JUDGES[2]

The inscriptions at Karnak and Luxor, the ancient Thebes and the capital of Upper Egypt, show how, during the whole period of the Judges, Egyptian influence extended over Palestine and beyond. Those by Thothmes III before the Exodus, picture his triumphal progress past Gaza, Taanach and Megiddo in his campaign against the Hittites, whom he forced to pay tribute. A century later the exploits of Seti I and Rameses II are illustrated by pictures in which the characteristic appearance and methods of warfare of the Hittites can be clearly seen.

Prof. Garstang has pointed out[3] that the periods when the author of Judges says that 'the land had rest' correspond closely with the reign of powerful Pharaohs; the eighty years rest in iii. 30 to the reign of Rameses II, and the forty years rest in viii. 28 to that of Rameses III. The intermediate periods of anarchy, oppression and deliverance synchronize with times of disturbance or weakness in Egypt, when its control did not extend beyond its own limits. Although the inspired writer makes no mention of

[1] J. W. Jack, *The Ras Shamra Tablets*; Marston, *The Bible Comes Alive*.
[2] See Chapter X, under *Judges*.
[3] *Joshua and Judges*, p. 64.

Egypt, an omission which appears to be deliberate, yet, under God's over-ruling providence, this correspondence was not accidental.

Among the things which excavation has revealed belonging to this period have been many Canaanite shrines, high places, 'Asherim', and other objects of worship, confirming the accuracy of the scriptural description of the prevalent idolatry and barbarism.[1] In 1909, Professor Macalister excavated Gezer, the site being certainly identified by his finding on a rock the inscription, 'the boundary of Gezer'. Among the ruins there were found, with other signs of Moloch worship, earthen jars with the bones of infants who had been burned in sacrifices to the god (Lv. xviii. 21). The children of Israel, through lack of faith, failed to subdue the people of the land, but settled down among them, intermarried with them and fell into their evil ways; and such traces of the life of that period as remain confirm this picture.

The Philistines

It was at this time that the Philistines invaded the land from Crete (Caphtor, see Gn. x. 14; Am. ix. 7; Je. xlvii. 4), which accords with Greek tradition. Their original home was probably in Asia Minor. In the temple of Medinet Hebu are pictures of a great naval battle between Rameses III and Philistine invaders, who seem to have attacked Egypt by sea and land. In the south they settled in Ashkelon, Ashdod, Gath, Ekron, and Gaza, and in the north were found as far as Bethshan (1 Sa. xxxi. 10).

Their cities, the remains of which are found just above an excavation level which shows traces of Egyptian occupation, reveal a state of prosperity and a comparatively high civilization. They appear to have been exceptionally well provided with powerful armour.[2] Until recently it was often assumed that the use of iron was not introduced into Palestine before the time of the monarchy. But at Gerar, Gezer, and elsewhere ironwork has been found, including hoes and plough points; and smelting furnaces, smaller furnaces for making and tempering swords, and moulds for chariot wheels and other purposes have also been discovered, all dating from the times of the Judges (see Dt. iii. 11; Jdg. i. 19).

DAVID AND SOLOMON

After the death of Rameses III the Egyptian empire declined, priests and kings struggling for dominance. Babylon and Assyria

[1] For examples, see Duncan, *Accuracy of the Old Testament*, Ch. XII.
[2] Macalister, *A Century of Excavation in Palestine*, pp. 162 ff; cf. 1 Sa. xiii, 19-22, xvii. 3.

were fully occupied with their own internal affairs and their mutual rivalries, and the times were ripe for the rise of the Israelites under David and Solomon to a height of political power and prosperity which was the greatest in all their history. Making Jerusalem his capital, David brought the whole nation under one central, efficient and benevolent government, whilst his armies extended his dominions beyond Damascus on the north and to the gulf of Akaba in the south.

Excavation in and around Jerusalem has verified and illustrated what the books of Samuel and Kings tell of the building work of David and Solomon. Mount Ophel, to the south-east of the temple area, has been shown to be the site of the 'city of David', and the gutter (*tsinnor*), or shaft by which Joab obtained access to the city has been opened out. The upper parts of the Jebusite stone bastion, Millo, and David's tower (2 Sa. v. 9), have been uncovered, and many parts of David's building and repairs identified[1] (1 Ki. xi. 27).

The temples of Solomon, Zerubbabel and Herod have long since disappeared (Mt. xxiv. 2), but the undoubted site of the threshing-floor of Araunah the Jebusite, on which stood the altar of burnt offering, can still be seen under the Dome of the Rock, miscalled the Mosque of Omar. A thrill passes through the Christian visitor as he beholds this place, with the cave beneath, and the channel through which the blood of the sacrifices drained away; or as he paces over the temple area, built up around the ridge of the hill on the huge foundation stones laid by Solomon, some of which can still be seen. Signs of Phoenician workmanship were discovered by Sir Charles Warren corresponding with those on the oldest ruins of Tyre, the prophecies concerning which have also long since been fulfilled.

Those were days when Israel proudly lifted up its head among the nations, whether warring with Syria (2 Sa. x. 15), maintaining commerce on equal terms with Tyre (1 Ki. vii.), or contracting a royal marriage with an Egyptian princess (1 Ki. iii. 1).

THE DIVIDED KINGDOM AND THE FALL OF SAMARIA

(a) The division of the kingdom

When Jeroboam fled into Egypt, shortly before the death of Solomon, a strong ruler, Shishak, had come to the throne, who reasserted his nation's power. In Rehoboam's fifth year, he came up against Jerusalem, showing that the Pharaohs had not

---

[1] Macalister, *op. cit.*, pp. 99-104, 171-177; Duncan, *op. cit.*, Chs. X, XI.

abandoned their claim to suzerainty over Palestine (see 1 Ki. ix. 16 and xi. 14-22). On the wall of one of the courts of the great temple at Karnak he has pictured this campaign and given a list of 156 places subdued, including Megiddo, Jerusalem, and one called 'the field of Abram'. The luxury of Solomon and the folly of Rehoboam now bore their fruit; the kingdom was divided, and the glory departed.

(b) The Syrian power and influence

From this time the power of Egypt steadily declined, until it was only a shadow of its former self. In the annals of Israel it is scarcely mentioned, and in place of it we find increasing references to Syria and Assyria. Of these, Syria, though less powerful, yet being the nearer neighbour, came into closer contact for the next two centuries with both the northern and southern kingdoms, sometimes as friend and sometimes as foe. Syria or Aram (lit. 'highlands') is an ill-defined region including the upper valley of the Euphrates, lying to the north-east of Palestine, and was inhabited from early times by a Semitic race speaking *Aramaic*, a language which is closely akin to Hebrew. They worshipped a god called *Hadad*, a name which occurs in Ben-hadad and other compounds. After the exile, Aramaic became the common speech of the Jews, but owing to the close contact between the peoples 'Aramaisms' found their way into spoken Hebrew in early times, and their existence is now known to be unreliable as a proof of date.

The city of Damascus, which later became the capital of the Syrian kingdom, goes back to remote antiquity (Gn. xv. 2). It paid tribute to Thothmes III, is mentioned in the Tel el Amarna tablets, and came under the rule of king David (2 Sa. viii. 6). It soon regained its independence, and became the centre of a state which rapidly grew to power.

Thus it was that Asa's appeal to the king of Syria for help against Baasha, king of Israel (1 Ki. xv. 16-20), met with a ready response from a ruler desirous to extend his influence. Israel now came under the power of Syria, and for a century onwards was subject to attack from her more powerful neighbour (see 1 Ki. xx.). But Israel's loss was not Judah's gain, for she also became dependent on Syria.

(c) Ahab, king in Samaria

The foreign connections of the kings of Israel and Judah seldom brought them anything but evil. Ahab took to wife Jezebel, the daughter of the king of Sidon, and, though this seems to have proved a political and commercial advantage, it was spiritually disastrous. His father, Omri, formerly 'captain of the host', had usurped the kingdom, and built a new capital on the hill of Samaria, which Ahab restored and rebuilt, setting up an ivory palace, and imitating the luxury of his heathen neighbours (1 Ki. xvi. 24, xxii. 39). Excavation has exposed the 'Gate of Samaria' with its mighty bastions, and the site of Ahab's palace has yielded carved panels of ivory, a vase fragment bearing the cartouche of an Egyptian king contemporary with Ahab, and cosmetic vessels in abundance (2 Ki. ix. 30). The pool of Samaria (1 Ki. xxii. 38) has been identified, and a list of Ahab's stewards discovered, amongst which the name of Obadiah is to be seen (1 Ki. xviii. 3).

The famous monument known as the Moabite stone, erected by Mesha, king of Moab (2 Ki. i. 1, iii. 4) and now in the Louvre, gives a picture of Israel in those days as seen by an enemy. In the inscription the words occur 'Omri, king of Israel, opposed Moab many days. Omri's son followed him, and also said, "I will oppress Moab". In my days Chemosh[1] said, "I will see my desire on him and his house" and Israel surely perished for ever'. A list of towns recovered from Omri is added, which includes Nebo and Medeba (Is. xv. 2), Horonaim and Kiriathaim (Is. xv. 5; Je. xlviii. 1).

(d) The rise of Assyria

From the time of Ahab onwards Assyria takes a larger place in the Bible story. About two centuries after Hammurabi's death a new dynasty, the Kassites, ruled in Babylon, and at this time the chiefs of Assyria threw off their suzerainty and founded an independent kingdom. From then the two kingdoms of Assyria and Babylon existed side by side, sometimes one and sometimes the other gaining the predominance.

Another famous monument, the 'black obelisk', records the victories of Shalmaneser III, who ruled over Assyria in the ninth century. Its inscriptions claim a victory at Qarqar (853 B.C.) against an alliance which included 'Ahab of the land of Israel' and Ben-hadad of Syria, and later (842 B.C.) over Hazael of Syria (1 Ki. xix. 15; 2 Ki. viii. 9-15). It also records the tribute paid to him by 'Jehu, son of Omri'.

The breaking of the power of Syria may partly account for the material prosperity of Israel under Jeroboam II. At Megiddo a

---

[1] See Nu xxi. 29; 2 Ki. iii. 4, 5, 27; Am ii. i.

jasper seal has been found with a Hebrew inscription, 'belonging
to Shema, servant of Jeroboam', probably an officer of this king.
After the death of Jeroboam, Samaria was the scene of revolution
and counter-revolution, and hastened to its doom.

Once again a king of Judah called in a foreign prince to the
undoing not only of Israel, but of Judah also. Refusing the
advice of Isaiah (Is. vii.) to put his trust in Jehovah, Ahaz sought
the help of Tiglath-Pileser III, the king of Assyria (2 Ki. xvi. 6-9).
This monarch had already subdued Babylon and reigned there
under the name of Pul. From thence he had already invaded
Palestine, and king Uzziah is four times mentioned in his records
(2 Ki. xv. 19, 29). These records tell us how in response to
Ahaz's request he now marched against Damascus and took it, and
then went on to attack Israel. He 'overthrew Paqaha (Pekah) their
king and placed Ausi'a (Hosea) over them'. This was in the year
734 B.C., and twelve years later, in 722-1, came the final catastrophe, following on Hosea's conspiracy with So (Sabaka), king of
Egypt. 'The Assyrian method of quelling rebellion was short and
effective; the towns and villages of the rebels were burned, the
rebels themselves were slain, or burnt alive, or impaled, and their
women and cattle and sheep were carried off into captivity. The
Assyrians were a brutally cruel people. . . .'[1]

The fall of Samaria is thus chronicled in the annals of Sargon:
'In the beginning of my reign, the city of Samaria I besieged; I
captured; 27,820 of its inhabitants I carried away' (2 Ki. xviii. 10;
Is. xx. 1). The mention of Sargon by Isaiah was once thought to
be a mistake, but it is now known that whilst the king, Shalmaneser V, was besieging Samaria, Sargon seized the throne,
reduced Samaria and warred also against Lachish and Ashdod.
During his time Merodach-Baladan (2 Ki. xx. 12) seized the throne
of Babylon and reigned there until driven out by Sargon in
709 B.C.

THE LAST DAYS OF THE KINGDOM (721-586 B.C.)

The Assyrian power was now at its height, and for a century
constituted a terror 'from the north' (Is. xiv. 31; Je. i. 14, iv. 6)
for Palestine and its neighbours. Sennacherib, who reigned from
705-681, has recorded his campaign against southern Palestine,
and, in his writings, the names of the court officials of Assyria find
an explanation. The Rabshakeh (2 Ki. xviii. 17) was the prime
minister or vizier, the Tartan (Is. xx. 1) the commander-in-chief,
the Rab-saris the chief noble (2 Ki. xviii. 17), and the Rab-mag

---

[1] Budge, *Babylonian Life and History*, p. 46.

the chief of the Magi (Je. xxxix. 3). The siege of Lachish is pictured (2 Ki. xviii. 14) with the description, 'Sennacherib sits on the throne, whilst the spoil of Lakis passes before him'. The deliverance of Jeusalem is indirectly confirmed by the absence of any claim to its conquest, whilst the statement is made, 'Hezekiah, like a caged bird, I shut up in Jerusalem'.[1] The disaster which fell upon his army is mentioned both by Herodotus and Berossus; the former attributes it to a host of mice, sent by the gods.

It was probably in connection with the siege of Sennacherib that Hezekiah made the conduits which safeguarded the water supply of Jerusalem from enemy attack (2 Ki. xx. 20; see also Is. vii. 3, xxii. 8-11). These pools and conduits have been fully investigated, and in the heart of the Siloam tunnel Sir Charles Warren discovered the contemporary inscription made by Hezekiah's workmen.[2]

Sennacherib, having been murdered by two of his sons, was succeeded by Esarhaddon (2 Ki. xix. 36, 37). A prism recording the circumstances of his accession, and accusing his brothers of 'drawing the sword godlessly' was found at Kuyunjik.[3] This monarch, of whom a great bas-relief portrait may be seen in the British Museum, and who re-peopled northern Palestine from the cities of Mesopotamia (2 Ki. xvii. 24; Ezr. iv. 2), records 'Manasseh', 'of the city of Judah' among his vassals. He displayed a zeal for religion in restoring the temple services and re-establishing the priestly orders in Babylon, which throws an interesting sidelight on his action in sending the priest to Samaria (2 Ki. xvii. 27). It may have been through this priest that the Samaritans received their first copy of the Pentateuch, and learned the primitive customs which they have preserved up to the present day.

The power of Egypt had long been on the decline. Ahaz had found it a 'bruised reed' (2 Ki. xviii. 21); Hezekiah was taught not to lean upon it. Esarhaddon carried his campaigns into Egypt itself, overcoming Tirhaka, its Ethiopian king, and taking Memphis (2 Ki. xix. 9). Yet under Pharaoh-Necho it raised its head again, and he marched against Assyria. Josiah, a tributary to Assyria, opposed him and was slain at Megiddo (612 B.C.) But Assyria also was weakened by attacks from Scythian tribes, whom Herodotus describes as particularly active at this time (see Je. i. 14) and offered no serious opposition. On his return, Necho deposed Jehoahaz and set Jehoiakim on the throne.

---

[1] Kenyon, *op. cit.*, p. 50 f.
[2] Duncan, *op. cit.*, pp. 166-124.
[3] Campbell Thompson, *Prisms of Esarhaddon and Ashurbanipal.*

THE EXILE (586-537 B.C.)

(a) Babylon, God's instrument of judgment

A new era was opening for the eastern world, and events marched forward with great rapidity. The rising power of Babylon showed itself during the reign of Nabopolassar (625-604), who married his son Nebuchadnezzar[1] to the daughter of Astyages, King of the Medes. He recovered the independence of Babylon, and took Nineveh in 612 B.C. Soon after, Nabopolassar sent his son on an expedition against Egypt. A great battle took place at Carchemish (605 B.C.) when the Egyptian forces were decisively routed and Babylon became mistress of the eastern world. From this date Jeremiah, guided by the Spirit of God, endeavoured in vain to persuade the princes of Judah to find their peace in subjection to Babylon. His advice was disregarded, and although Jehoiakim and Jehoiachin in succession were forced into submission, the weak-minded Zedekiah again rebelled, looking with a fatal persistency to Egypt for help. This led to the siege of Jerusalem by Nebuchadnezzar, and its capture and destruction in 586 B.C. The last Pharaoh to be named in the Old Testament is Hophra, whose name occurs in Jeremiah's prophecy that Egypt, like Israel, shall fall under the hand of Babylon (Je. xliii. 8-13, xliv. 30, xlvi. 14; see also Ezk. xxx.). During the present century the researches of Sir Flinders Petrie at Tahpanhes have shown how these predictions were fulfilled to the letter.[2]

(b) The exile and return

For fifty years the Bible scene moves to Babylon, where already some of the leaders of the people had spent many years in exile under Nebuchadnezzar (2 Ki. xxiv. 15). This king was a great builder, as his inscriptions abundantly testify. 'He rebuilt his capital so thoroughly that modern excavators could scarcely find any trace of buildings older than his time—"Is not this great Babylon, that I have built for the house of the kingdom by the might of my power, and for the honour of my majesty?" '[3] The Tower of Babel, which he restored, and which had been rebuilt many times since its first foundation, the famous hanging gardens described by Diodorus and Strabo, and the wells from which they were watered by means of a hydraulic screw, the bridge 500 feet

---

[1] Nebuchadrezzar (Je. xxi. 2) appears to be the more correct form of his name.

[2] *Egypt and Israel*, p. 85-93.

[3] Woolley, *Ur of the Chaldees*, p. 185.

long which he built over the Euphrates and the approach which he paved, the temples of Bel and Nebo (Is. xlvi. 1, 2) which he restored and adorned, the ruins of these and of much else have been identified. The double walls (Je. li. 58), each twenty-four feet wide, with an intervening space of ninety feet, extend for ten miles round the city. Nebuchadnezzar was proud of his work and has left abundant inscriptions, which fully confirm the impression of Babylon's greatness gained from the book of Daniel.

Nebuchadnezzar also restored the temples at Ur, and here it was that Sir L. Woolley discovered what he describes as a novelty in the worship of those days. A large open space had been created, at one side of which was a statue base, the whole being evidently intended for the setting up of a statue for 'a form of congregational worship which all his subjects are obliged to attend'. He regards the correspondence between the facts of the ruins and the story in Dn. iii. as 'so striking' as to prove their connection.[1]

Until recent years the critical school rejected the book of Daniel with contempt as unhistorical. Amongst other reasons given for this was the fact that Belshazzar's name could nowhere be found in the inscriptions. But cylinders have been discovered which prove beyond doubt that Belshazzar was the eldest son of Nabonidus. Four of these contain his father's prayers for him. It is also made plain that he was, before his father's death, acting as regent, or second ruler in the kingdom, which accounts for Dn. v. 29, where Daniel is called *third* ruler. Three contract tablets of Belshazzar have also been found, enclosed in clay envelopes, sealed and signed, and deposited in earthen jars (see Je. xxxii. 14). What Sir L. Woolley describes as the 'nunnery' of Belshazzar's priestess sister has been found at Ur, with many interesting inscriptions and remains.[2] Together these discoveries have removed many of the historical objections previously urged against the book of Daniel, and a reaction in its favour has followed.[3]

Babylon fell with tragic suddenness (539 B.C.). It would appear that Nabonidus was first defeated in the field, and that later the troops of Cyrus, under his general Gobryas, having diverted the course of the river, and perhaps being aided by treachery, gained access to the fort and palace which were situated on the western bank, that Belshazzar was put to death, and Darius appointed in

---

[1] *Op. cit.*, pp. 195 ff.
[2] *Op. cit.*, p. 199.
[3] Daniel, *Int. Crit. Comm.*, pp. 58, 109.

his place. The latter is usually regarded as identical with Gobryas.[1]

Cyrus adopted a policy of religious appeasement, and restored various shrines. Referring to one of these, Woolley writes, 'The inscription on the bricks has a familiar ring; "the great gods have delivered all the lands into my hand", it begins, and we think of the proclamation of Cyrus in the book of Ezra.'[2] The edict of Cyrus for the restoration of the temple soon followed.

So the kingdoms rise and wane, and their history proves that 'the most high ruleth in the kingdom of men, and giveth it to whomsoever He will' (Dn. iv. 32).

THE PERSIAN PERIOD (539-331 B.C.)

In his vision of the great image Daniel foresaw four world empires, and the second of these, that of the 'Medes and Persians', lasted from the time of Cyrus until it was overthrown by Alexander of Greece (539-331).

Cyrus died in 529 B.C. and was succeeded by Cambyses, who conquered Egypt, Smerdis (522), and Darius Hystaspes (521-486). During their reigns the temple was rebuilt by Sheshbazzar and Zerubbabel (Ezr. i-vi.; Hg. i., ii.), amidst opposition and after many delays.

Darius was succeeded by Xerxes (the Ahasuerus of Esther) in 486, and in 464 by Artaxerxes Longimanus who commissioned Nehemiah to rebuild the wall of Jerusalem, a task he completed in 445. The foundations of this wall have been traced through more than half their course, and can still be seen in many places. When Bishop Gobat built his school in Jerusalem in the last century, the foundation of the outer wall was afforded by the ledge of rock cut out by Nehemiah's workmen, the traces of whose implements upon the scarped face of the rock could be clearly seen.

A sidelight upon this period is thrown by papyri discovered at Elephantine near Aswan, emanating from a Jewish colony which traced its settlement there to the time before the Persian conquests, that is, to the period of the exile or earlier (see Je. xliv. 1; Zp. iii. 10). They are written in Aramaic (see Is. xix. 18-22), and range in date from 471-407 B.C. In the last-named year a letter was sent to the Persian governor of Judaea saying that the temple of the Lord (Yahu), with its roof of cedar wood, had been destroyed, and begging that it might be rebuilt. This letter

---

[1] Budge, *op. cit.*, pp. 54, 65.
[2] *Op. cit.*, p. 205; see Ezr. i. 2.

refers to Sanballat as governor of Samaria and to Johanan as high priest in Jerusalem (Ezr. x. 6; Ne. iv. 1, 2); and it expresses their distress that the priests have been unable to bring to the temple 'meal offerings, incense and burnt offerings', as in days of old. Their worship nevertheless was mixed with debasing idolatry, for as it was with those of Jeremiah's days (xliv. 14-28), whose descendants they may have been, they knew and kept the ceremonial law, but did not serve the Lord with their whole heart.

CONCLUSION

Into the framework of external history as revealed by the monuments and records of the past, that of Israel fits exactly. We can see reflected in the Bible story the conditions of life and travel in the second millennium B.C., the might of Egypt in the eighteenth and nineteenth dynasties, the influence on Israel of the Hittites, Syrians and other surrounding tribes and nations, and the rise and fall of Assyria and Babylon.

What is true of the history is equally true of the language in which it is written, for, as a great linguist has declared, it everywhere displays the footprints of the nations, who introduced their ideas at the very times at which the various books were written.

The results of archeological research 'confirm what faith would suggest, that the Bible can do nothing but gain from an increase of knowledge'.[1]

APPENDIX TO CHAPTER VII

Outline Chronology of the Old Testament

THE outline chronology which follows is intended to give a bird's-eye view of the sequence of the main events in the history of Israel, as affected by that of the surrounding nations.

Authorities differ widely as regards some of the earlier dates, and, even after David's accession to the kingdom, there are considerable discrepancies. Those here given are mainly based on S. A. Cook's volume, *The Old Testament, A Reinterpretation*. The numbers given in the books of Kings have been to some extent corrupted in the course of transmission, and it is not always certain when the periods given are successive and where they overlap. The same is equally, or more, true of the fragmentary records derived from the monuments.

Kenyon, *op. cit.*, p. 279.

Nevertheless, the dates given here and in the text may be relied upon as sufficiently accurate for an understanding of the order in which the events occurred.

DATE B.C.	ISRAEL	THE NATIONS
c. 3500[1]		The Flood
c. 3400		First dynasty in Egypt, first Minoan dynasty in Crete
c. 3100[1]		First dynasty in Ur
c. 2650[1]		Sargon of Agade
c. 2000	Abraham enters Canaan	Hammurabi
		XIIth dynasty in Egypt
c. 1785	Jacob goes down to Egypt	
c. 1580		Expulsion of the Hyksos
1501		Thothmes III
1447		Amenhotep II
c. 1440	The Exodus	
1411		Amenhotep III
c. 1400	Fall of Jericho	
1300-1234		Rameses II
1202-1170		Rameses III
c. 1050	Samuel	
c. 1010	David (accession)	
974	Solomon	
c. 970	Dedication of the Temple	
937	Division of the Kingdom	

[1] Sir L. Woolley.

DATE B.C.	JUDAH	ISRAEL	THE NATIONS
937	Rehoboam	Jeroboam I	
875		Ahab	
872	Jehoshaphat		
853			Battle of Qarqar
783		Jeroboam II	
780	Uzziah		
745			Tiglath Pileser III (Pul), King of Assyria
727			Shalmaneser V of Assyria
726	Hezekiah		
722-1		Fall of Samaria	

DATE B.C.	JUDAH	THE NATIONS
705		Sennacherib of Assyria
700	Sennacherib's siege of Jerusalem	
681		Esarhaddon of Assyria
669		Ashurbanipal
637	Josiah	
612		Fall of Nineveh
608	Jehoiakim	
605		Battle of Carchemish
604		Nebuchadnezzar II, King of Babylon
597	Zedekiah	
586	Fall of Jerusalem	

DATE B.C.	THE JEWS	THE NATIONS
550		Cyrus, King of Media and Persia
539		Cyrus takes Babylon
537	Return under Zerub-babel	
521		Darius Hystaspes, King of Persia
520	Zechariah and Haggai prophesy	
464		Artaxerxes Longimanus
458	Ezra	
445	First Mission of Nehemiah	
433	Second Mission of Nehemiah	
331		Alexander defeats Persia, and visits Jerusalem
323		Death of Alexander. Seleucid dynasty in Syria, Ptolemies in Egypt
c. 250	LXX commenced under Ptolemy Philadelphus	
167	Antiochus Epiphanes desecrates the temple	
165	Judas Maccabaeus cleanses the temple	
53	Pompey takes Jerusalem	
37	Herod the Great made King of the Jews	

CHAPTER VIII

THE OLD TESTAMENT STORY

OLD Testament history cannot rightly be studied in isolation: it can be understood only in the light of the New Testament which completes and fulfils it. In the words of a contemporary scholar, 'the two Testaments . . . are one in the sense in which the parts of a musical cadence are one. Without the final chord it is incomplete, a process which does not reach its goal; on the other hand, the final chord, however beautiful it may be as a chord, is robbed of its full significance without the chord that should precede it. The two Testaments are one in that they form a single whole'. Both Testaments are a record of God's self-revelation to man, which culminated in the fulness of time in the personal revelation in Jesus Christ.

The God of the Scripture is always the living God, and consequently He reveals Himself in His acts. It is the intention of this chapter to outline the purpose and character of the revelation of God, 'who at sundry times and in divers manners spake in time past unto the fathers by the prophets'. It will be clear that God is at once both the Creator-Lord and the Redeemer-Saviour, who acts in holy judgment and saving mercy to redeem men from sin, and to win them into loving fellowship with Himself. It will be apparent, further, that the purpose of God's self-revelation is ever to create a holy people, a people for His own peculiar possession. This is progressively accomplished through the calling and election of a family, a nation, a kingdom, and a remnant out of the kingdom, until the remnant itself is finally reconstituted and recreated in Jesus Christ. So the New Testament sums up all that has gone before in the Old Testament revelation: 'Ye are a chosen generation, a royal priesthood, an holy nation, a peculiar people . . .' (1 Pet. ii. 9).

PATRIARCHAL HISTORY

The Old Testament opens with a majestic description of the creation of the universe as the sphere of God's self-revelation. Man is created in the divine image as the climax of the work of creation. The book of Genesis is, as the name implies, the book of origins, and in rapid pen-pictures an account is given of man's temptation and fall, the entrance of sin and death, the growth of lawlessness and corruption, until judgment inevitably falls in the flood. The preservation of Noah demonstrates that the way of blessing is none other than the path of obedience, and that faith is a trustful response to the revelation which has been given: 'By faith Noah, being warned of God of things not seen as yet . . . prepared an ark to the saving of his house . . . and became heir of the righteousness which is by faith' (Heb. xi. 7; cf. Acts x. 34, 35).

An event of paramount importance is the call of Abram in Ur of the Chaldees, a city which has been painstakingly excavated through the labours of Sir Leonard Woolley. About the year 2000 B.C. Abram, at the call of God, journeys forth to Haran and then to Canaan, living as a pastoral nomad (cf. Acts vii. 2). This call was of decisive spiritual significance: it was a witness to the initiative which God exercises in electing for Himself a people from pagan darkness. In the record of Abraham's subsequent journeyings, the sacred narrative impinges on contemporary secular history (Gn. xiv.).[1] But the Bible is not concerned with history as such, but rather with the purpose of God to create for Himself a people of His own possession, and this purpose is furthered in the successive elections of Isaac and Jacob and Joseph. These 'calls' were not dependent on birth or merit: they originated solely in the grace and mercy of the sovereign Lord, who saved and redeemed them.

THE EXODUS

The book of Exodus opens with the providential preparation and training of Moses to be God's servant to deliver Israel from Egyptian bondage. The Israelites, who were originally welcomed to the fertile valley of the Nile during a famine in Canaan, found themselves reduced to serfdom when a change in dynasty resulted in a change of policy towards them (cf. Acts vii. 18). Moses was the chosen instrument to effect deliverance, and, after the accomplishment of a series of fearful and dramatic plagues, the Israelites escaped. Their immediate destination was the mount of Sinai, and there, with awe-inspiring solemnity, a covenant was entered into between God and His people. The ground of the covenant was the redemption from Egypt, which, as always, was not the result of any moral or material superiority that the Israelites possessed over other nations, but was solely the result of God's free and unconditioned love towards them (Dt. vii. 7ff.). Un-

[1] See Chapter VII, p. 84.

deserved grace demands gratitude in the recipient, and the people were called to obedience in return. 'Ye shall be holy, for I, the Lord your God, am holy.' The Decalogue summarized the divine standards of holiness which were required of the people of God. Henceforward the profession of religious worship was indissolubly associated with the practice of morality, while the blessings of God were conditional upon obedience and service. At the same time sacrifice was ordained as the visible means whereby the guilty might find pardon. It was a powerful reminder that the wages of sin is death, and that without the shedding of blood is no remission.

The government of God's people was so organized that Moses was prophet and lawgiver, and consequently the divine mouthpiece, while Aaron occupied the priest's office. By disobedience Moses forfeited the privilege of entering the Promised Land, and on his death, Joshua was raised to lead the people. The divine presence was manifested in the crossing of the river Jordan, and in the circumstances of Jericho's capture about the year 1400 B.C.[1] Despite explicit directives, sin and compromise resulted in an imperfect subjugation of the land, which, in turn, led to lawlessness and apostasy. The twelve tribes were allocated to various portions of the land, but their foothold was insecure and their sense of corporate loyalty weak. God punished their persistent sin by servitude, until in penitence they cried unto Him for deliverance and 'judges' were sent to save them.

THE MONARCHY

Samuel, the last of the judges, had combined the functions of military leader, prophet, and priest, but when the people demanded the establishment of a monarchy, the theocratic system of government came to an end. Henceforward the religious and the civil leadership were separated, in theory, if not in practice. The theocratic system of government had emphasized the unique relationship which existed between God and His people—the fact that God Himself was their Ruler and King: although the relationship still existed, its distinctiveness was obscured by the establishment of a human intermediary, and Israel approximated in political form more closely to the surrounding nations. In obedience to the command of God, Samuel anointed Saul to be king, and devoted himself to his priestly and prophetic duties. This dual leadership was shattered when Saul trespassed upon the priestly functions, and further, when he disobeyed the direct

[1] See Chapter VII, p. 91.

commandments of God. David, a youthful Bethlehemite shepherd, was called of God and anointed by Samuel to assume the military leadership of Israel. Saul, conscious of his alienation from God, sought solace in spiritualism, and was slain ignominiously in battle. David was faced with the challenge of disunity: at first acknowledged only by Judah, his military prowess and conciliatory policy won him the loyalty of the northern tribes. He consolidated this political victory by capturing Jerusalem from the Jebusites in the seventh year of his reign, thus providing his kingdom with a natural capital. But Jerusalem was more than a political centre: it also became the religious centre with the establishment of the central sanctuary. Thus Zion, the place which God had elected above all others to hallow with His presence, became the focus for worship and sacrifice. To subsequent generations, this period, when the enemies of Israel were subdued, when the ark was brought up to Jerusalem, and when the Psalter was begun, was seen to foreshadow the messianic age. But it was around the person of the king that the messianic promises were concentrated, and David was seen to pre-figure the ideal King, the bright and morning star, who would be the root and offspring of David (Acts xiii. 23; Rev. xxii. 16).

Solomon succeeded his father and was entrusted with the high privilege of building the temple. His regime was outwardly magnificent and successful, with the construction of both the temple and the palace (although, significantly enough, the material splendour of the palace exceeded that of the temple), the fortification of Jerusalem, and the development of foreign trade. But the outward façade rested on corrupt foundations. Solomon's licentiousness and immorality led to the introduction of many foreign wives accompanied by their heathen idols, while his grandiose building schemes, necessitating forced labour, produced profound social discontent. The cumulative effect of these things was soon to become apparent.

THE DIVIDED KINGDOM

On the death of Solomon in 937 B.C., the northern tribes gave expression to their discontent and dissatisfaction. Rehoboam, Solomon's son, foolishly advised, refused to make concessions, with the result that the northern tribes revolted under Jeroboam. Thus the united kingdom had barely survived three generations. The kingdoms of Judah and Israel were now subject to fluctuating fortunes at the hands of a succession of unworthy rulers, who un-

wisely essayed to play a part in the rivalries of the great powers in
the Middle and Near East. The geographical position of Palestine
was an added danger, so that the land became ravaged with the
tumults of war. Prophets unavailingly sought to recall the
kingdoms to their true destiny as the people of God, but oppor-
tunism and expediency triumphed over principle and right, until
the cup of iniquity was full.

(a) *The northern kingdom*

In the northern kingdom of Israel a series of military *coups d'état*
hastened the road to ruin. During Ahab's reign Elijah exercised
his prophetic ministry, and on a memorable occasion on Carmel,
God vindicated His servant in a decisive contest with the prophets
of Baal. But the lesson was unheeded, and Elijah was commanded
to anoint Jehu in the place of the apostate Ahab. This action was
a clear and forceful reminder that the prophet lived under the
direct authority of God, while the civil power was only derived.
Elijah's mantle descended on Elisha, who was faced with the same
problems of religious syncretism and idolatry. In the year 783 B.C.
Jeroboam II ascended the throne, inaugurating a reign of
military greatness and commercial prosperity comparable to the
glory of Solomon's reign. But outward success was accompanied
by evil within, and the degradation and destitution of the poor,
together with the ostentatious luxury of the rich, cried aloud for
redress. Amos, an uncompromising prophet of righteousness, was
sent from the southern kingdom to rebuke the social injustices of
Israelite society. He was conscious that he had been called by the
inscrutable will of God to perform this task: 'I was no prophet,
neither was I a prophet's son; but I was an herdman . . . and the
Lord took me as I followed the flock, and the Lord said unto me,
Go, prophesy unto my people Israel.' Despite the continued
prophetic witness that repentance alone could avert catastrophe,
there was an unspiritual confidence in formal religion, and a
failure to realize that the privilege of being God's people implies
the responsibility of being a holy people. Moral and spiritual
deterioration continued, until the Assyrians invaded the kingdom,
capturing Samaria in 721 B.C., and in accordance with the
custom of the time, deporting the people to captivity.

(b) *The southern kingdom*

The sequence of events in the southern kingdom of Judah was not
strikingly dissimilar, although the judgment was longer delayed.
The prosperity of the northern kingdom under Jeroboam II

found a parallel in the long protracted reign of Uzziah. In the year that the latter died, Isaiah saw his vision of the holy God, and was overwhelmed by a sense of his own personal sin and the corporate sin of Judah. Cleansed by divine grace, he heard the call to service. His message developed out of his own initial experience: the whole land was corrupted with sin, and renewal was possible only through repentance and divine forgiveness. In the realm of politics he advocated a policy of strict neutrality. Judah could be preserved only if she trusted implicitly in God and foreswore all political entanglements. The seductive appeal of an Egyptian alliance must be resisted. During the reign of Hezekiah, when the Assyrian army under Sennacherib threatened Jerusalem itself, his policy of quiet reliance on God was dramatically vindicated. A sudden scourge swept the Assyrian army and Sennacherib was forced to retire. Nevertheless Judah remained impenitent, and finally Isaiah saw that the nation could be purified only through a judgment of fire and blood in which a remnant would be refined. After suffering, healing would follow through the mediation of One who should bear vicariously the sins of the people (Is. liii.). The experience of captivity would also reveal the futility of idolatry, and the essential nothingness of idols, so that never again would Judah succumb to this snare.

But in the meantime idolatry and corruption persisted during the ensuing reigns, apart from a brief promise of reform under Josiah. In his reign (637-608 B.C.) 'the book of the law' was discovered during repairs in the temple, and, as the extensive religious reformation which followed indicated, it included a rediscovery of the instructions in Deuteronomy concerning the centralization of worship (2 Ki. xxii.). But Josiah's tragic dea:n at Megiddo, fighting against the Egyptians, was the signal for a relapse to the old ways. It was at this time that Jeremiah commenced his prophetic ministry. He insisted that idolatry was a twofold declension: a departure from God, and a pursuit of false gods. This was God's complaint: 'My people have committed two evils; they have forsaken Me the fountain of living waters, and hewed them out cisterns, broken cisterns, that can hold no water' (Je. ii. 13). He, too, saw the inevitability of judgment, and prophesied that a captivity of seventy years would ensue in Babylon (Je. xxv. 11). This would be for their ultimate salvation (cf. Heb. xii. 11). In the furnace of suffering a remnant should be refined, and, regenerated with a new heart, they would serve God in their own land (Je. xxiv. 6-7). Judah's final decline was rapid, being precipitated by a hopeless revolt against the over-lordship of Babylon. Nebuchadnezzar marched to wreak a fearful judgment: Jerusalem was captured and destroyed in 586 B.C.; Zedekiah was blinded and led captive to Babylon; and very many were deported.

THE CAPTIVITY

In captivity God did not desert His people. Ezekiel interpreted the will of God to the exiles who sat down and wept by the waters of Babylon (Ps. cxxxvii.). He declared that, when God's anger and indignation were past, a remnant should return, and this remnant should be regenerated and made anew by the impartation of a new spirit. So a new covenant, inward and personal, would accomplish that which the old legalistic covenant had been unable to achieve. In the meantime, the exiles were to live a peaceful and settled existence until the captivity ended. The book of Daniel, with its immortal stories of unflinching fidelity to God and His service, has reference to this period of Israel's history. One significant development took place at this time under the good hand of God. Temple worship no longer being possible, the people turned to the worship of God in prayer and the reading of the Torah, a development which ultimately, in the form of synagogue worship, found a permanent place in Jewish life.

THE RETURN

Cyrus, the Persian, was the unknowing instrument to fulfil the purpose of God in the redemption of His people. It was the policy of Cyrus to grant facilities for repatriation to deported peoples, and, in accordance with his practice, a decree was made in 537 B.C., a short time after the capture of Babylon, by which the Jews were granted permission to return to their own land. A scene of desolation greeted their return. But a powerful stimulus was given to the dispirited and impoverished exiles by the prophets Haggai and Zechariah, who encouraged the people to rebuild the second temple, the foundation of which was laid in 520 B.C. Later, under the lead of Ezra (c. 458 B.C.) and Nehemiah (445-433 B.C.), a happy combination of church and state, the law was re-established and the walls of the city rebuilt.

So in post-exilic days prophet, priest and statesman combined in the systematic endeavour to insist on moral purity and ritual cleanliness. Mixed marriages were forcibly dissolved, usury and swearing were condemned, and sabbath observance was enforced. The prophets looked forward to that day when a fountain should be 'opened to the house of David and to the inhabitants of Jerusalem for sin and for uncleanness' (Zech. xiii. 1), and when the very bells of the horses should be inscribed with 'holiness unto the Lord' (Zech. xiv. 20).

The canon of the Old Testament closes with the searching challenge of Malachi addressed to priests and people alike, and the gracious promise: 'Unto you that fear My Name shall the Sun of Righteousness arise with healing in His wings.'

CHAPTER IX

THE PENTATEUCH

AUTHORSHIP

THERE are two views of the origin of the Pentateuch. The first takes the five books at their face value, and ascribes the bulk of them to Moses. The second holds that they are a blend of documents that gradually came together during a period that extends from pre-Mosaic times down to about 400 B.C. The former view held the field without challenge until the end of the eighteenth century; from that date the alternative theory has gradually come to the fore. Although the holders of the second have never agreed about the dating and division of the documents, they are agreed in ascribing no more than a fraction of the books to Moses himself.

This theory established a hold on the universities and colleges at the beginning of this century, a fact which has prejudiced the consideration of evidence to the contrary which has since been steadily accumulating.

WHAT THE BOOKS CLAIM

The testimony of any book to its own authorship cannot lightly be set aside, and it is the more valuable when there is a large amount of incidental suggestion as well as direct assertion. Now three of these five books contain references to Moses as a writer and recorder. In Ex. xvii. 8-14 Moses sets down a record of the battle against Amalek; in Ex. xxiv. 4, 7 he writes the terms of the covenant (i.e. xxi.-xxiii., with possibly chapter xx.) and reads them from a book to all the people; in Nu. xxxiii. 2 he keeps a record of the travels of the people. Dt. xxxi. 9-12, 24-26 (cf. xxviii. 58-61) is even more definite. Here Moses is definitely declared to have written down the law as it is given in Deuteronomy, and to have laid the book by the side of the ark.

The fact that these are the only direct references to Moses as author need not surprise us. Twice he is declared to have recorded contemporary history, and twice to have written down the divinely given law. Therefore he could quite well have written down the rest of the history and the other laws. This applies with special force to the latter, since most of them were given by God to Moses himself in the first instance. If he received them, and if, by reason of his education in Egypt, he was well qualified to write them, we are entitled to conclude that he did in fact write them.

Thus the last four books of the Pentateuch contain an implicit claim to be from the pen of Moses; and no one has yet maintained that Genesis does not form a unity with the other four books. Commentators of every school agree that the same authorship may be traced in Genesis as in the other four. Hence, if Moses is accepted as the author of the legal sections, he may safely be accepted as the author of Genesis.

The terms 'author' and 'authorship' must, however, be used with qualifications. By 'authorship' is meant merely that Moses wrote the books, and the term does not convey the idea that he received them as directly dictated by God, or in any other particular manner. It leaves open the question of how God revealed His will through Moses. Sometimes it appears to have been by a direct voice; at other times it may have been through an inward impression that set the divine seal upon the adoption of laws that had long been recognized amongst the Semitic peoples.

As regards Genesis, Moses wrote chiefly as a compiler. Like other historians, he made use of earlier records which were contemporary with the events that they describe. In many cases he probably acted as translator and interpreter, making the old stories plain for the people of his day.

The general Mosaic authorship is also consistent with a few later additions, such as Nu. xii. 3, xxi. 14, and the account of Moses' death, and such as those designed to help the reader or to make the books up to date, e.g. Gn. xii. 6, xiii. 7, and parts of xxxvi. 9-43. Old place names may have been modernized, just as a modern historian, when writing about Roman times, might call the Roman town of Aquae Sulis by the modern name 'Bath'. Ex. i. 11 supplies a probable example of this, for according to the best available evidence no Pharaoh named Rameses ruled before Moses' day, whereas it is known that Rameses II (1300-1225 B.C.) frequently claimed credit for the work of his predecessors, and renamed cities after himself. Thus it is probable that Moses here wrote the original name, but, when this name had become obsolete, the modern name was substituted for it.

Some also have supposed that certain small additions were made to the laws themselves from time to time, to meet any problem which had not arisen during the time of Moses. The whole law could still be called 'Mosaic' in the sense that the few additions were incorporated into the general Mosaic framework.

These considerations offer an adequate explanation of the small number of passages which, for one reason or another, Moses could not have penned himself. Taking the Pentateuch, then, at its own valuation, it is clear that apart from a few later additions it suggests no other author or compiler for itself than Moses. The assertion of the book itself should therefore be accepted unless adequate proof to the contrary can be adduced, and what is to be said on this side must now be considered.

THE WELLHAUSEN HYPOTHESIS

There is no need here to outline the origin, history and growth of what is now generally known as the Wellhausen Hypothesis. Attention is called elsewhere in this volume to its materialistic bias and the anti-supernatural theories that frequently underlie it. [1] This bias does not settle the question of the truth or error of its conclusions, which is to be considered here.

The following outline represents the general conclusions of such representative scholars as J. Wellhausen, S. R. Driver, W. O. E. Oesterley and T. H. Robinson. It is possible to give only general conclusions, since there is often considerable disagreement over matters of detail.

A time is imagined when the Israelites had no written records, but in the towns, and round the camp fires, stories were told of ancient times and of the great things that God had done. The sacred places and sanctuaries up and down the land were centres round which stories collected, and these sanctuaries would vie with each other in tracing their origins to a theophany made to one of the heroes of old, or to some action of one of these heroes. The priests of the sanctuaries were often called upon to make legal and moral decisions, and such decisions were remembered, and formed a small body of *Torah* or 'law'.

Two writers between 900 and 750 B.C. put some of these stories and laws into writing. The earlier of the two is known as J, since he believed that the sacred name Jehovah (or Yahweh)[2] was known to mankind from the earliest days. He was chiefly interested in the southern kingdom, and in its people and sanctuaries. His view of God is simple and childlike. Jehovah moulds men out of clay, walks in the garden, and comes down to see the builders of

---

[1] See Chapter IV, *Modern Criticism*.

[2] The form Yahweh represents the original pronunciation and is used in many modern works. In the A.V. it is generally translated 'LORD'.

E

Babel. This writer is interested in the derivation of names, such as those of Adam, and Jacob's sons. His stories enforce the lesson that God punishes sin and rewards righteousness.

The second writer, E, is more interested in the northern kingdom, though he is also familiar with Egyptian matters. He does not believe that the name Jehovah was known before the revelation to Moses at the burning bush (Ex. iii. 14, 15). Hence he confines himself to the title Elohim before this date. His view of God is less anthropomorphic, and he prefers to make God reveal His will through dreams (Gn. xx. 3) or voices from heaven (Gn. xxi. 17).

Both J and E contain a body of laws supposed to have been given to Moses on the mountain. E's version is commonly known as 'The Book of the Covenant' and occurs in Ex. xx. 22-xxiii. 19. J's version is similar, though shorter, and is found in Ex. xxxiv. 10-28.

J and E may be regarded as the work of two individuals, or each of the documents as the result of a whole school of writers. At an early date J and E were combined into a single book. Sometimes the compiler kept the sections of the two documents separate, but they 'are sometimes so closely interwoven as to defy accurate and certain disentanglement'.[1]

The next document is known as D, since it constitutes the greater part of Deuteronomy. D has affinities with E, and hence with the north. It may be identified with the book of the law that was found in the temple in the reign of Josiah in 621 B.C. (2 Ki. xxii. xxiii.). The reason for this identification is that Josiah's reforms are along the lines laid down in D, especially with regard to the one sanctuary where Jehovah might be worshipped. It is conjectured that the book was compiled by a group of spiritually-minded men in the northern kingdom who had some connection with the eighth century prophets, especially with Hosea. The writers have a strongly humanitarian outlook, with much sympathy for the poor and oppressed. The same school of writers worked over the history and the earlier laws (but not Genesis) and made certain additions and comments.[2]

A further document is found in Lv. xvii.-xxvi., and deals mainly with ceremonial purity. Hence it is referred to as H, standing for holiness. There are close resemblances between H and Ezekiel, and it used to be held that Ezekiel preceded H. But some writers now believe that Ezekiel is dependent upon H, and even that H

[1] Oesterley and Robinson, *Introduction to the Books of the Old Testament*, p. 47.
[2] Oesterley and Robinson, *op. cit.*, pp. 47, 48.

precedes D, though, whereas D is to be connected with the north, H belongs to the south.[1]

Finally a document, P, or the Priestly Code, was produced. P is marked by the 'rather stilted, yet dignified, style, the orderly arrangement, the fondness for exact details in numbers and in dates, the careful genealogies, and the interest in all things concerned with ritual.'[2] Like E, P does not believe that the name Jehovah was known in the times of Genesis, and he has his own version of the giving of the name in Exodus vi. 3. Typical examples of P are the orderly creation story of Gn. i. 1-ii. 4, the details of the tabernacle and the ritual of the sacrifices.

Whatever earlier material P contains, its final form is the product of the Priestly party during the exile. Being cut off from the temple, and surrounded by paganism, they laboured to build up a Jewish exclusiveness and to emphasize and remodel everything in Jewish history and worship that would make a distinction between Judaism and paganism. P is commonly supposed to be the law book that was read to the nation by Ezra in Ne. viii. According to the modern dating of Ezra this would be about 398 B.C.[3]

Last of all, some compiler or group of compilers welded all the documents into the complete whole that forms our present Pentateuch. Editorial additions and revisions were sometimes necessary, and some portions were more patchy than others. 'But early in the second century B.C. the law was regarded as a single whole, with, apparently, no suspicion of its composite origin. We shall not greatly err, then, if we assign its final completion to a date not later than 300 B.C.'[4]

EXTERNAL EVIDENCE

The admission quoted in the preceding paragraph is important. It is a fact that 'early in the second century B.C. the law was regarded as a single whole, with, apparently, no suspicion of its composite origin'; and seeing that the Pentateuch would be the first part of the Old Testament to be translated into Greek, the same must have been true in the third century when that trans-

---

[1] Oesterley and Robinson, *op. cit.*, pp. 49, 50, 52, 53.

[2] Oesterley and Robinson, *op. cit.*, p. 51.

[3] This dating is based on the view, first put forward by Van Hoonacker, that the Artaxerxes of Ezra is Artaxerxes II. The dating of Ezra above in chapters VII and VIII (*c.* 458 B.C.) follows the traditional view that he was Artaxerxes I.

[4] Oesterley and Robinson, *op. cit.*, p. 63.

lation was commenced. But this is hard to reconcile with its completion only a few years before.

Religious beliefs and practices have always tended to become fixed, especially among the Jews, and any innovation has provoked violent opposition. Is it credible that a whole corpus of law was imposed on the nation in the name of Moses without any record of the novel demands being even questioned?

This problem becomes particularly acute in the light of the existence of the Samaritan Pentateuch.[1] Apart from differences of reading, this is essentially the same as the Pentateuch of the Massoretic Text and the Septuagint. Hence it is obvious that either this had its origin after the date when the Pentateuch, according to the modern critical theory, was completed, or else that the whole of that theory needs radical revision.

The copy of the Pentateuch which is treasured in Nablus by the little Samaritan community is written in letters of gold and in the ancient script used before the square Hebrew letters came to be employed about the commencement of the Christian era. It bears a note that it was written in the thirteenth year of the occupation of Palestine by 'Abisha the son of Phinehas the son of Eleazer the son of Aaron'; and this no doubt enshrines a very ancient tradition. Several copies exist in the John Rylands Library, Manchester, one of which Professor Robertson places 'several centuries' earlier than another dated A.D. 1211.

Discounting the tradition, scholars have suggested various dates when the Pentateuch first came into the possession of the Samaritan community. It is said that (1) it represents a copy (or copies) retained in the northern kingdom from the days of Rehoboam, or (2) it was brought by the priest mentioned in 2 Ki. xvii. 28, who was sent to instruct the mixed population of Israelites and immigrants 'how they should fear the Lord'.

It is unnecessary to point out that if any of these suppositions be true, the whole critical theory of the dating falls to the ground.

Josephus has a story (*Antiq.* xi. 7, 8) that, in the time of Alexander the Great (c. 330 B.C.), a certain Manasseh who was brother of the high priest, married a daughter of Sanballat and was expelled from Jerusalem, whereupon Sanballat built him a temple on Mount Gerizim. Some have thought, therefore, that the Pentateuch was carried to the Samaritans by this Manasseh. But it appears from Ne. xiii. 28 that Josephus has mistaken the date, which should be placed about 430 B.C. But this also is disastrous for those who date the introduction of P into Palestine

[1] See pp. 20, 99; and Finn, *Unity of the Pentateuch*, p. 402.

some thirty years later, and the completion of the Pentateuch later still. Nor is this supposition likely in itself, since it involves the reception by the Samaritans of a law book from their bitter enemies, and one which imposed on them those very restrictions which were a main cause of the enmity!

The alternative to accepting the date given by Josephus involves the very uncritical proceeding of inventing another Sanballat who re-enacted the story recorded in Ne. xiii. Nor would it entirely remove the difficulty, for the enmity between the Jews and the Samaritans was then no less, and the completed Pentateuch was still, according to the theory, only a recent composition.

Those who accept Wellhausen's theory have yet another difficulty to overcome, for they maintain that it can be shown by their system of analysis that the book of Joshua can be divided among the same authors, J, E, D, and P, and must therefore have originally constituted with them one whole. Why then did not the Samaritans accept it as such? The answer is given that the Jews separated Joshua from the other books, because of the wide gulf which seemed to divide it from them, but that the division was wholly artificial. No shadow of external evidence, however, can be adduced in support of this. The very word Pentateuch, used by early Christian writers (e.g. Origen, Tertullian) is associated with an ancient Jewish saying that these books are 'the five-fifths of the law'.

A careful examination of some hundreds of Old Testament passages relating to the laws and sacrifices shows that reference is made to very much that is contained in the first five books, but there is not the slightest hint that Joshua was ever counted one with them.

If we accept the account the books give of themselves these difficulties vanish and the facts admit of a natural explanation. The suggestion put forward by Prof. E. Robertson[1] that Samuel and the schools of the prophets were responsible for the completion of the Pentateuch is free from most of the objections just considered, and important as evidence against any later date; but whatever part may have been played by Samuel or anyone else in finally arranging the Pentateuch, it remains true that no other name has been associated with it than that of Moses. In this respect it may be contrasted with the Psalms. Although traditionally associated with David, the titles have handed down many other names as connected with them. But, in the whole range of Hebrew literature, no Jewish writer is found defending or disputing any tradition regarding the Pentateuch.

[1] *Temple and Torah*, *The Riddle of the Torah* and *The Pentateuchal Problem*.

LINGUISTIC EVIDENCE

In a handbook of this size it is not possible to write about this in
detail. Those who are interested are referred to Prof. R. Dick
Wilson's books, *A Scientific Investigation of the Old Testament* and
Is the Higher Criticism Scholarly? Prof. Dick Wilson was a philologist
with a wide grasp of the languages of the ancient East. Very
strong linguistic support for the conservative view is provided
by the fact that, although Persian words are found in Chronicles,
Ezra, Nehemiah, Esther, and Daniel, none are found in the
Priestly Code, although the Code is supposed to have come from
the school associated with Ezra. From another standpoint, Prof.
A. S. Yahuda has shown that there are many marks of Egyptian
influence on the language and thought of the Pentateuch, as is to
be expected if Moses were the author.

No one would deny that there are differences of style and
expression in the Pentateuch, but these can quite well be accounted
for by the fact that in Genesis Moses made use of earlier documents from different authors, and also that differences of theme
inevitably involve difference of style and vocabulary. It is not
sound criticism to pick out all the more formal passages, such as
genealogies, solemn covenants, and ritual directions, and to
postulate a different author for these passages on the ground of
the more precise and formal vocabulary that is found there.

INTERNAL EVIDENCE

The argument for multiple authorship furnished by the alleged
discrepancies and disagreements is double-edged. Modern
scholars have supplied us with a sufficient number of compilers
and redactors who have 'worked over' the material in order to
produce a harmonious whole. Did none of them detect the contradictions so frequently stated to be 'obvious'? On the other hand,
it is a fair rule of criticism that the more obvious a discrepancy
may appear on the surface, the more likely it is to be no discrepancy at all, but capable of a simple explanation were all the
facts before us which were known to the author or compiler.

Much of the disagreement alleged is fictitious. As an example,
a careful study of the laws will prove that they form a consistent
whole, if the record be taken as true, as the following outline
indicates.

1. *The ten commandments* (Ex. xx.), afford a moral code delivered by Jehovah to the assembly in an audible voice (Dt. v. 22).

2. In Ex. xx. 22-xxiii. 33, xxiv. 3-9, God declares through Moses certain religious, moral and social precepts to form the *basis of a covenant,* which the people accept.

3. In Ex. xxiv. 12-xxxi., Moses receives the *ten commandments in written form,* together with detailed instructions for the tabernacle.

4. The *covenant is restated* in Ex. xxxiv. 10-27, the people having broken it by their worship of the golden calf. Since only the Godward side had been broken, this is the side that is restated, with fresh warnings against idolatry.

5. In Leviticus *instructions for the life and worship* of a people called to be holy are received by Moses in the tabernacle, and recorded in a form perhaps intended as a handbook for the priests.

6. The legal sections of Numbers record sundry laws and *directions for the body politic.*

7. Deuteronomy contains a *summary of the laws* given when the majority of those living had not been present at Sinai, *a popular exposition in preparation for their entry into the promised land.*

To the Christian it is not unimportant that Jesus Christ accepted the Jewish tradition. That He was well acquainted with the Pentateuch cannot be denied, for He ascribes the legal portions to Moses (Mt. viii. 4, xix. 8; Mk. vii. 10; Lk. xx. 37; Jn. vii. 19). He rebuked the Jews for holding 'the traditions of men', but never classed their attribution of the law to Moses among them. If the difficulties, discrepancies and crudities were so great as some would have us believe, surely Christ's searching eye could not have overlooked them.

It is not suggested that there are no difficulties,[1] nor is it suggested that internal evidence alone can *prove* Mosaic authorship. But making due allowance for oriental modes of thought and for the unknown factors of so distant a time in the world's history, it is contended that a fair reading of the record reveals nothing irreconcileable with the view that the Pentateuch, substantially as it has been handed down to us, was written by Moses, or compiled from contemporary documents, written mainly by him.

[1] Many of these are dealt with in *The Five Books of Moses* by Prof. O. Allis.

GENESIS

AUTHORSHIP, DATE AND CIRCUMSTANCES

THE question of authorship has already been discussed in the introduction to this section, but a few further points may be added. In speaking of Moses as the author of Genesis it must be borne in mind that the narratives go back to much earlier times, and many of them can best be regarded as family records handed down from father to son, such as undoubtedly existed among the civilized nations of the ancient world.[1]

The patriarchal narratives may not improbably have been brought into Egypt by Jacob and his sons, which would account for the fulness of detail in the lives of Abraham and Jacob. It is certain that the early chapters bear traces of Babylonian influence, and the fact that they probably underwent translation has to be remembered in respect of literary problems. The Egyptian influence can be discerned throughout,[2] and it can best be accounted for by supposing that Moses compiled Genesis during his stay in Egypt.

ANALYSIS

i.-v.	The creation and early days of the human race.
vi.-ix.	The flood.
x., xi.	The origins of the nations.
xii.-xxiii.	Life of Abraham.
xxiv.-xxvi.	Life of Isaac.
xxvii.-xxxvi.	Life of Jacob.
xxxvii.-l.	Last days of Jacob and life of Joseph.

CONTENTS

The book of Genesis shares with the whole Bible the characteristic that the narratives are selected, not for their interest or political importance, but for the relation they bear to God's great redemptive purpose, and for the light they throw upon His dealings with mankind.

Beginning with the creation of the universe we are told of the creation of man in the image of God, in order that the world might be peopled with beings who would walk in His ways. Then follows the entrance of sin into the world, and, as wickedness

---

[1] See P. J. Wiseman, *New Discoveries in Babylonia about Genesis.*
[2] A. S. Yahuda, *Language of the Pentateuch*, and *Accuracy of the Bible.*

increased, the judgment of the flood. Yet in the midst of the evil the record is preserved of Enoch who walked with God, and of righteous Noah, who with his family was preserved in the ark.

From the first hint of a coming Saviour and Conqueror in iii. 15, we see God preparing a people to be the vehicle of His ultimate revelation of Himself to the world in love. The covenant with Abraham concerns not only his descendants, but blessing to all mankind through Abraham's seed (xii. 2, 3; cf. Gal. iii. 16). The line of blessing is continued through Isaac and Jacob, and we may trace in the carefully preserved genealogies the value attached to the promised inheritance of blessing.

Jacob's sons are kept together to form a nation of tribes who shall be known as God's people; and Judah is chosen to hold the sceptre till 'He come whose it is' (xlix. 10, R.V. mg.). The whole book must be read in the light of the New Testament in order to learn its lessons of faith (Heb. xi.), of God's purpose to build Himself a spiritual temple (Acts vii.), to see how Christ's priesthood was foreshadowed (Heb. vii.), and to connect man's beginning in the garden of Eden with his ultimate goal in the paradise of God (Rev. xxii.).

The Creation

The external world history as it is revealed in the monuments of the past will be found in Chapter VII. Here notes are given on special parts of the Bible story with a view to their better understanding.

The story of the Creation is given in two consecutive accounts (i. 1-ii. 3 and ii. 4-25); the opening words of ii. 4 should be read, as in all the parallel passages, as belonging to *what follows*.[1] The first account is cosmic in its significance; its setting is markedly Egyptian (note the mention of *tannin* or 'crocodiles', not 'whales', in verse 21) and may represent a vision vouchsafed to Moses. The second gives the commencement of the human story as seen from Adam's view-point, and certainly represents a very primitive tradition. The former corresponds in a remarkable way with the discoveries of science, as for instance in the priority of light, the velocity of which is a fundamental element in Einstein's theory of relativity. The stages in which water and land, vegetation, water life, flying creatures, animals and man appear correspond closely with the geological record. Whilst this chapter was certainly not written to teach science or to save the labours of

[1] See Allis, *The Five Books of Moses*, p. 50.

research, it is not reasonable to suppose that the writer hit upon these things by mere chance or derived them from Babylonian myths by a process of purification, which would be more miraculous than any view of the inspiration of the record.

The word *day* need not be understood literally, nor was it always so understood in Hebrew literature (see, for example, Is. ii. 12, and cf. Jn. v. 17 and Heb. iv. 3 ff. in respect of the seventh day. See also 2 Pet. iii. 8). The days may represent the stages in the revelation, or periods of time; in any case they represent an orderly progress.

The 'creation' of matter, of life and of man are clearly implied (i. 1, 21, 27) though it is hazardous to stress the difference of the two Hebrew words 'created' and 'made'. The emphasis of this wonderful chapter, which fittingly opens the divine record, is upon *God* as the creator of all things, and of man in His own image.[1] If the account in chapter ii. represents the primeval tradition, it must have been preserved orally, or possibly in writing, through Noah. It is supplementary to the former, and not contradictory. The animals are here introduced to show that there was no companion suitable for man among them, and both plants and animals are considered in relation to their usefulness. It is commonly held to-day that civilized man and the art of cultivation date from about the period assigned by the Bible to Adam. It is therefore perfectly possible that Gn. ii. had special reference originally to plants used for cultivation. The geographical detail is dealt with on pp. 82, 83.

The Genealogies

In Chapter v. we have the first of a series of formal genealogies, and are led to inquire whence they came. No one acquainted with Hebrew thought will imagine that they were *invented*, and scholars generally accept their origin as very ancient. They cannot be made the basis for calculating dates, nor are they ever used in the later books for this purpose. Their purpose is to inculcate spiritual lessons, amongst which is the faithfulness of God to the *heirs* of promise. Luke traces the natural ancestry of Christ to Adam, the first man; Matthew follows the royal line through to Abraham. In the latter genealogy it may be observed that some names are omitted to round off the list into three groups of fourteen, and it is possible that in chapter v. we have only a selection of the more important names.

[1] A full discussion will be found in Rendle Short, *Modern Discovery and the Bible,* or Sir Ambrose Fleming, *Evolution or Creation.*

The Antiquity of Man

The discovery of skeletons (or parts of them) of Neanderthal and other races of man, or man-like beings, raises questions to which, in our present state of knowledge, no final answer can be given. The immense periods of antiquity assigned to these by some anthropologists rest on very insecure foundations and the more sober-minded speak with great caution of all pre-historic remains. Some writers have thought that the creation of Adam should be pushed far back and that these 'hominids' may be degenerate races; others regard them as sub-human, and that from the creation of Adam, into whom the spirit of God was breathed, the human race proper, capable of communion with God, took its beginning.[1]

The Fall

Chapters ii. and iii. have much in common with the two closing chapters of Revelation, and in both it is hard to say where the literal ends and the symbolic begins. Yet the story of the Fall can never be read by any Christian who realizes his own sinfulness without the deep conviction of its essential truth, and it is in-wrought into the doctrine of the New Testament (Rom. v. 12; 1 Cor. xv. 21; Rev. ii. 7). Adam was created as a God-centred being, who should derive his life on every side from God, and find his chief end in communion with God. He was at the same time created free to choose to know good and evil and to be the arbiter of his own life to that extent, and hence with the possibility of becoming self-centred. Through pride he fell, and became, as Brunner terms it, 'Man in Revolt'; the result being disorganization and death. This does not require us to believe that no animals died before the Fall, but means that the death of man was the penalty of sin.

In iii. 15 there is the primeval promise of redemption, which was fulfilled on Calvary, when, though it was the hour of the power of darkness, the prince of this world was cast out (Lk. xxii. 53; Jn. xii. 31; Rev. xii. 9, 11). In iii. 21 the record emphasizes the fact that God made 'coats of skins', with the suggestion that the sacrifice of life was needed to make a 'covering' for their sin and shame.

The Flood[2]

The critics divide the account of the flood between P and J and, by dissecting the narrative, create 'doublets' and 'contradictions',

[1] See p. 79, also Sir Ambrose Fleming, *The Origin of Mankind*.
[2] See also p. 81.

particularly as to its duration and the number of clean animals entering the ark, the difficulties being capable of easy explanation when the story is read as one whole.[1] It may be noted that the Babylonian story of the flood, from which some critics say this is derived, contains elements parallel to both P and J! The command in vii. 2, 3 is an amplification of that in vi. 19 (the clean animals perhaps being needed for food), and the modes of reckoning are sometimes by the number of days, at others by dates.

The tradition of a flood is widespread among the nations of the world, and the geological evidence has been held by Sir Henry Howorth and other eminent scientists to indicate that the flood was universal.[2] On the other hand, the evidence for a flood of quite exceptional magnitude in the valley of the Euphrates, at a later period, may point to a judgment falling only upon that central area of the world's early inhabitants. It is to be noted that the two words translated 'earth' in the A.V. (*adamah* and *erets*) are elsewhere translated 'ground' (e.g. Gn. ii. 6, 7) and 'land' (Gn. ii. 11) and by no means imply universality; nor need the stocks of animals be interpreted to mean more than those which would suffice for a new beginning.

The spread of mankind[3]

Chapter x. tells of the origin of certain nations, such as would be known in Abraham's day.[4] It undoubtedly contains some very ancient ethnology and genealogy. Chapters x. and xi. are not, on the one hand, to be treated as folk-lore, nor, on the other, as modern scientific treatises. They form the link between Noah and Abraham through the line of Shem, and there is absolutely no reason to doubt their historical basis. The confusion of tongues may be referred to in x. 25; the manner in which it was effected is not stated. Some have thought that resistance to a divine command to spread abroad (ix. 7, 19) is indicated in xi. 4.

It is significant that from this point Babylon occupies a prominent place over against the people of God (cf. Je. li. 7, 8; Rev. xviii. 2). The statement in xi. 1 need not be taken as contradicting the reference to many 'tongues' in x. 31, since the word *erets* (earth) may refer only to one locality.[5]

---

[1] Allis, *op. cit.*, pp. 95-99.

[2] See paper by Lieut. Col. Davies, D.Sc., F.G.S., *Transactions of the Victoria Institute*, 1930.   [3] See also p. 83.

[4] See two papers by G. R. Gair, *Transactions of the Victoria Institute*, 1934 and 1936.

[5] See Pinches, *Old Testament in the Light of the Monuments*, p. 133.

Abraham

After xi. 9 Genesis leaves the story of the nations to concern itself with the line from which the children of Israel sprang, and so comes to the story of Abraham.[1] The migration of Terah and Abraham to Haran in the north (xi. 31) may have been one of many such movements of the Aramaean peoples with whom the Habiru or Hebrews were connected. This is confirmed by Gn. xxv. 20 and Dt. xxvi. 5 (R.V. mg.).

In chapter xiv. we have an ancient record in which the story suddenly introduces great historical figures. Of Melchizedek nothing is known but what is here recorded. It was not uncommon in those days for the office of priest and king to be combined; and it would appear that, like Abraham, he had preserved the knowledge of the one true God. He thus became a type of the Messiah (Ps. cx.; Heb. v.-vii.).

The name of God here used, *El Elyon*, appears in Scripture, especially where, as Dr. Kuyper says, 'men stand outside the covenant of grace'; i.e. where the sphere of God's revelation touches the Gentile world (see Nu. xxiv. 16; Dn. iii. 26).

It may here be remarked that in i.-xvii. four designations of God are to be found,[2] each with its own distinct connotation and appropriateness. God (*El*, or *Elohim*) is used as a common noun, to denote deity as such, and so is constantly applied to the gods of the heathen. The Lord (or *Jehovah*) is the proper name, so to speak, of the true God (Gn. iv. 26; Ex. iii. 15; Dt. xxxii. 3; Jn. xvii. 6), especially appropriate when reference is made to His Person, His characteristics and His covenant relationship with His people, and to the full revelation of His redemptive power in the deliverance from Egypt (Ex. vi. 3). He appears to Abraham (xvii. 1) as *El Shaddai*, the Almighty or All-sufficient, when the long delayed promise of a son is repeated and about to be fulfilled, and again under this title to Jacob (xxxv. 11, xlviii. 3) to assure him that what He promised He was able to perform.[3]

In studying the unfolding revelation of God, the several promises to Abraham should be noted.

1. In xii. 1-3 (see Acts iii. 25; Gal. iii. 8) the promise is first national, that he will become a great nation, and then universal, that he shall be the source of blessing to the whole world.

2. In xv. 1-6 there is the promise of an heir and the gift of the land, which is sealed by a sacrifice. His response is quoted as an

---

[1] See p. 84.
[2] See Troelstra, *The Name of God*.
[3] See Ch. VII, p. 50.

instance of justifying faith in Rom. iv.; Gal. iii. 6; Jas. ii. 23. There is a prophecy of the deliverance from Egypt (verses 13-16; Acts vii. 7, 8).

3. In chapter xvii. the particular 'seed' is promised (cf. Gal. iii. 16), and the sign of circumcision is ordained.

4. In chapter xxii., after his faith has been tested in the offering of Isaac, the promises are renewed, his faith having been 'justified by works' (Jas. ii. 21, 22).

In xvii. 5, where we have the change of name from Abram to Abraham, we have an example of the Hebrew love of a play upon names ('Father of a multitude', Ab-hamon), another of which is found in Isaac (Gn. xvii. 19, R.V. mg.). These plays upon names are not to be read as scientific etymology, but rather as if one should say, 'You are called Richard, because you will become rich'.

Circumcision was given as a sign, although already an existing custom, just as previously the 'bow in the cloud' was given as a memorial of God's promise.

The testing of Abraham's faith in the command to offer Isaac has been represented as an imitation of the child sacrifices of the surrounding heathen, to which it has little resemblance. It was not a test of Abraham's love, but of his faith, as interpreted in Jas. ii. 21 and Heb. xi. 17-19. His faith was victorious, and the incident provided a wonderful type of Christ's substitutionary sacrifice (Jn. iii. 16).

Jacob

The life of Isaac is lightly passed over, and is followed by that of Jacob, which reads like an autobiography; and such it doubtless was in its original form. His craftiness, his ill-treatment of his brother, his favouritism of Joseph are nowhere praised, but plainly exposed; and equally plain is the punishment he experienced, his years of exile, his trickery repaid, and his sorrows and trials through his sons. No biographer of a later age could ever have penned this record, nor romancer invented it. Yet in spite of his many faults, his faith in the promise of God (xxv. 23), in which his mother had instructed him, was outstanding, and, like a lamp, lighted up his path to the very end (Heb. xi. 21). He was rightly named Israel (xxxii. 28), and his life story is an encouragement to every repentant sinner.

Joseph and his brethren

Various stories are told about the sons of Jacob, but the chief purpose of Genesis now is to show how the nation went down into

Egypt, and how God planned to deliver them there. Thus the chief interest is concentrated on Joseph. Chapter xxxvii. is regarded as affording strong support to the modern theory of the composition of the Pentateuch. It is thought that the concluding portion especially shows signs of being composed of contradictory documents. The verses are divided between J and E as follows:

J: verses 2-4, 12-18, 21, 25b-27, 28b, 31-35.

E: verses 5-11, 19, 20, 22-25a, 28a (to 'pit'), 28c-30, 36.

Reading the J account by itself, Joseph's life is saved by Judah, and he is sold by his brethren to the Ishmaelites without being placed in the pit. In the E account his life is saved by Reuben, and his brethren put him in the pit, from which later he is kidnapped by a passing company of Midianites.

But the story can be read consistently as it stands. Reuben suggests putting Joseph into the pit so that later he can rescue him secretly. Judah later suggests removing him from certain death in the pit, and selling him for money. The Bible leaves us to assume that Reuben had temporarily left the others, so that he did not know of the transaction. The difficulty of the Ishmaelites and Midianites turns on the question of whether the term could be used interchangeably of any groups of people. Both were descended from Abraham (xxv. 2), which probably means that each of the sons of Abraham would have a number of followers to form the nucleus of a clan. The clan of Ishmael started first, and the lesser clans might well have been grouped round Ishmael for some time. The evidence of Jdg. viii. 24 cannot be ignored. There we read of Midianites who were also Ishmaelites. Why the writer here uses the names alternately we cannot tell, but similar variations for no apparent reason can be paralleled in English literature.[1]

As against the critical division of the documents here, we may note that, although E is not supposed to know of any sale of Joseph by his brothers, yet in xlv. 4, 5, which is in an E section, Joseph says that his brothers sold him.

Joseph in Egypt

Professor Yahuda and others have shown that there is strong Egyptian influence in the narratives of Joseph in Egypt. It is possible that part of the story was originally written in Egyptian. Since the incidents take place in non-Jewish surroundings, the general name for God, *Elohim*, is used, the only exceptions being

[1] See Allis, *op. cit.*, pp. 69 f.

chapter xxxix., which obviously belongs to the private memoirs of Joseph, and xlix. 18, where Jacob uses the covenant name.

One or two, out of many, examples of Egyptian influence may be noted.

1. The king of Egypt is simply called 'Pharaoh', with no name added. This was the Egyptian custom between the eighteenth and nineteenth centuries B.C. By the time of Solomon the custom was to add the phrase 'king of Egypt' or the name of the Pharaoh, e.g. 1 Ki. ix. 16; 2 Ki. xxiii. 29.

2. In xli. 14 it is mentioned that Joseph shaved himself before coming into Pharaoh's presence. This was the correct etiquette in Egypt, in contrast to the Semitic idea of the beard as a mark of dignity.

3. In xlii. 30, 33, and frequently in xliii., Joseph is called 'the man'. This was the title of the vizier; he was the first man in the country, since Pharaoh himself ranked as divine. Joseph fulfilled all the duties of a vizier, as is seen from a tomb inscription of about a century later, in which such duties are described. Early Egyptian pictures show the vizier with the golden chain mentioned in xli. 42.[1]

Towards the end of this book the messianic promise shines out clearly once more in the blessing of Judah (xlix. 10). Here Judah is pictured as a king holding his sceptre like a standard between his feet. He holds the monarchy in trust 'until Shiloh come'. This latter phrase has been interpreted in a messianic sense by Jews and Christians from early times, though most of these ancient commentators do not seem to have read the word 'Shiloh', which is nowhere else used as a title of significance, but to have followed variant readings. The R.V. mg. suggests likely readings, and we may translate either 'Until that which is his shall come', or more probably, 'Till he come whose it is'. The close parallel in Ezk. xxi. 27 ('until he come whose right it is') suggests the latter rendering is probably correct.[2]

THEMES FOR STUDY

1. Among all the great themes of the Bible, of which can you trace the 'beginning' in Genesis?

[1] For these and other points, see A. S. Yahuda, *The Accuracy of the Bible*, S. L. Caiger, *Bible and Spade*, J. Garrow Duncan, *New Light on Hebrew Origins*.

[2] Another interpretation equates 'Shiloh' with Babylonian *shêlu*, 'prince'. See *Exp. Times* xxxvi. (1925), p. 477.

2. God chose to be called the 'God of Abraham, of Isaac and of Jacob' (Ex. iii. 6, 15; Mt. xxii. 32). What reasons for this choice are suggested by the history?

3. What foreshadowings are there in the life of Jacob of the special calling and election of the people of Israel (cf. Is. xliv. 1, 2; Je. xxx. 10; Ho. xi. 1)?

4. Study the sacrifices recorded in Genesis in relation to the Sacrifice on Calvary.

5. What features in the career and character of Joseph justify us in regarding him as a type of Christ?

6. Study the names of God recorded in chapters i., ii., xiv., xvii., xxxi., xlviii., xlix. In the light of the occasions where they are used, what do they suggest as to the character of God?

EXODUS

AUTHORSHIP, DATE AND CIRCUMSTANCES

IN this book Moses is said to have written the account of the battle with Amalek (xvii. 14) and 'all the words of the Lord' that were spoken on the Mount (xxiv. 4). It may be presumed also that Moses wrote down the specifications of the tabernacle for Bezaleel and Aholiab to follow (xxv. 9, xxxvi. 1). Thus the book itself indicates a claim to Mosaic authorship.

The arguments of those who make the tabernacle sections the work of P during the Exile are here especially difficult to follow. The plan of the tabernacle and its furniture is not the same as that of the temple, and it is difficult to understand the mentality of a writer (or writers) who longed for the restoration of Solomon's temple, and yet invented an elaborate tabernacle, different from the temple, and ascribed it to the direct revelation of God.[1]

The book opens in Egypt more than eighty years before the Exodus (vii. 7), and ends a year after the Exodus (xl. 2; cf. Nu. i. 1), with the setting up of the tabernacle. The date of the Exodus can be determined not only from the Bible itself but from archaeological discoveries, especially from the excavations at Jericho.[2] It took place in the middle of the fifteenth century, probably at the beginning of the reign of Amenhotep II.

---

[1] See also under *Deuteronomy*, p. 147.
[2] See Chapter VII, *The Historical Background*.

ANALYSIS

CONTENTS

Whereas the book of Genesis begins with the creation of man in conditions of innocence and beauty, and tells of his fall and continuance in sin, this second book of the Bible tells the story of Israel's bondage and redemption, and provides many pictures of the salvation wrought by our great High Priest, worthy of more glory than Moses as being the Son of God (Heb. iii. 1-6). The Passover (1 Cor. v. 7), the Manna (Jn. vi. 32), the Smitten Rock (1 Cor. x. 4), and the Offerings (Heb. x. 11, 12) all speak of Christ and His atoning work.

Exodus falls roughly into two sections, chapters i.-xix., which are chiefly narrative, and chapters xx.-xl., which are mostly made up of laws and regulations. The narratives are notable for the miracles they contain. In regard to these some allowances must be made for oriental modes of thought and expression, and views differ as to the extent to which God may have used natural forces to work these signs. It has been suggested, for instance, that the turning of the Nile water into 'blood' was due to volcanic action near the sources of the river releasing some red substance into the water, so rendering it poisonous; and attention has been called to the poisoning of all the streams on one side of the island of St. Pierre at the time of the eruption of 1902.[1] The five following plagues, on this explanation, might have followed as a consequence of this poisoning.

In regard to the death of the first-born (chapter xi., xii.) the Bible suggests some specially deadly epidemic. If the Exodus occurred in the reign of Amenhotep II, there is evidence that his first-born son died. His successor was Thothmes IV, who was not his first-born; for an inscription on a granite slab says that the future Thothmes IV, when a boy, dreamed that the Sphinx told him that he would one day be king of Egypt. Obviously there would be no significance in this dream if he were the natural heir.[2] In chapter xv. it should be noted that we are dealing with poetry.

The Law

As we enter upon the system of laws laid down in this and the subsequent book, we have every justification, both from the narrative itself and from the teaching of Christ and His apostles, for regarding it as the direct revelation of God (Ps. xix. 7; Mk. vii. 9; Rom. vii. 12, 14; Heb. viii. 5, 9). In considering its purpose the conditions of the time should be borne in mind. The children of Israel were being called from a state of servile bondage to be a nation under theocratic rule. They had to be taught by direct statement, by statutes and ordinances, and by mighty works, that Jehovah was not like the gods of Egypt; they had to be taught that God was in their midst, and that He was holy; they needed to have the moral law before them in a simple and intelligible form.

Moreover, it was necessary that the law should be a 'figure' and 'shadow' of the good things to come (Heb. ix. 8, 9, x. 1), and be a divine pattern of the heavenly things which were fulfilled in Christ. Paul called it a 'schoolmaster' to lead men to Him (Gal. iii. 24).

The particular precepts of the law may be classified as spiritual, moral and social, involving the love of God and of one's neighbour.

The spiritual precepts, including much of the ceremonial law, throw light upon God's character, and teach man obedience and the beauty of holiness. The altar of incense was a constant lesson in prayer, the shewbread portrayed the need of constant communion, the candlestick the need of heavenly light, the pillar of cloud and fire the need of God's guidance.

The moral law is summed up in the ten commandments, as apposite to-day as then, and is expanded in Ex. xx. 22-xxiii. 33,

---

[1] Phythian Adams, *The Call of Israel*, pp. 161, 162.
[2] Marston, *The Bible Comes Alive*, p. 68.

(known as the 'book of the covenant'), into many details, some of universal and some of special application. The Rabbis classified the various precepts of the law under the headings of the ten commandments.

The social laws chiefly look on to the beginnings of Israel's national existence in the promised land. Since the people were expecting to enter the land almost immediately, it is natural to find laws dealing with houses, lands, and property.

The ceremonial law was fulfilled in Christ, so that the need for its priesthood and sacrifices has passed away, and the details of civil rule do not apply to the complex civilizations of our time. The underlying principles remain, however, and their study and practice would bring about a far better world than that in which we live.

By ascribing the whole law to the direct guidance and revelation of God, the mistake must not be made of thinking that it contains no elements which go back before Moses' time. The prohibition of murder goes back to the beginning, as does the whole moral law. Many of the social statutes find a parallel in the records of the surrounding countries, and some go back to Abraham's day, or even before. But they are confirmed, or restated, at Sinai.

A comparison is often drawn between the laws of Moses and the laws of Hammurabi[1] who reigned in Babylonia about 2,000 B.C. Towards the end of his reign he had a code of laws inscribed on a pillar some seven feet high by two feet in diameter. This stone was taken by the Elamites in the twelfth century B.C. and set up as a trophy at Susa, where it was discovered at the beginning of the present century. Some of these laws were more ancient still. For it is recorded that about 2,700 B.C. a king named Urukagina had promulgated a code which has not been preserved.

Hammurabi's code contains 282 laws, which occupy thirty pages in an English translation. They deal in order with theft, burglary, robbery, land, buildings, landlord and tenant, traders and their agents, public houses, debts, divorce, inheritance, adoption, damages for assault, medical fees, building and the builder's responsibility if the house is defective, hiring fees for workmen, animals, and goods, and, finally, slaves.

The parallels and the differences between the laws of Hammurabi and those of Moses are interesting. In general it may be said that the latter lay greater stress on the protection of persons, the former on the importance of property, and that whereas the

[1] See Chapter VII, p. 84.

Babylonian code makes important distinctions between the treatment of a 'gentleman' and a 'plebian', the scriptural code would have rich and poor treated alike, being merciful to the needy and the oppressed.

The following selections will give some idea of the nature of Hammurabi's code:

Law 117. When a free man has been sold for debt, he shall be released after three years (cf. Ex. xxi. 2-6).

Law 195. The penalty for striking one's father is the loss of both hands (cf. Ex. xxi. 15).

Law 206. If a man injures another accidentally in a quarrel, he must pay the doctor's bill (cf. Ex. xxi. 18, 19).

Law 268. If an accident occurs to the sheep in a sheepfold, 'the hired shepherd shall clear himself before God', and the owner of the fold shall meet the damage (cf. Ex. xxii. 10, 11).

Those sections of Exodus that govern man's approach to God are on a different footing from the social regulations. Here it was necessary that the people should realize the righteous holiness of God, at a time when the tendency of the eastern religions was towards a degraded and sensual worship. Moreover, the regulated approach to God through the ritual of the tabernacle stood for something more than could be realized at the time. The Epistle to the Hebrews gives an introduction to the true interpretation of the tabernacle types. Early fathers and Christian scholars since have added further interpretations; and whilst it may be granted that some of the latter owe more to the fancy of the expositor than to the original text, there remains enough which is too striking in its applicability to be the result of mere chance. The man of faith is compelled to see in the ordinances of the first covenant a figure and pattern of heavenly things designed as such by the Holy Spirit (Heb. ix. 1, 8, 9, 23).

THEMES FOR STUDY

1. How far are the spiritual and moral principles that underlie each law realized in our national and personal life?

2. Study Heb. viii.-x., with its interpretation of the tabernacle in the light of Jesus Christ.

LEVITICUS

AUTHORSHIP, DATE AND CIRCUMSTANCES

THOSE who assign the greater part of Leviticus to the 'priestly code', and make it subsequent to the book of Ezekiel, give as reasons: (1) the parallels with that book[1] which they regard as indicating the origin of certain parts, and (2) the detailed and formal nature of the Levitical system.

Elaborate ritual, however, is not necessarily a mark of lateness of date, for the religious ceremonies of the great civilizations of Mosaic and pre-Mosaic times were carefully regulated. The recently discovered *Ras Shamra* tablets, which date from the time of the Exodus and reflect earlier usage, refer to trespass offerings, and have other points of resemblance to Leviticus.[2]

There is, therefore, no adequate reason to doubt the early date and Mosaic authorship of this book. The section xvii.-xxvi., known as the law of holiness (or holiness code), is acknowledged, even by those who deny the Mosaic authorship, to contain archaic features, some dating it earlier than Deuteronomy.[3]   In these chapters are found instructions for the priests about the daily life of the people, the majority of whom must have been illiterate, and dependent for such instruction upon those who could read.

God spoke in Exodus from the thunders of Sinai, but now that Israel has entered into covenant relationship with Him, He makes the further revelation in the quiet of 'The Tent of Meeting' (Lv. i. 1). A comparison of Ex. xl. 2 with Nu. i. 1 gives the exact month during which these instructions were received. Fifty-six times in these twenty-seven chapters is the claim repeated that Jehovah imparted these laws to Moses. The denial of their Mosaic origin, therefore, is a direct challenge to the truth of these statements.

The prophets and sacrifice

There are a few references in the prophets which have led some to suppose that they knew nothing of a law of sacrifice imposed upon Israel at Sinai. Rightly interpreted in the light of similar passages (e.g. 1 Sa. xv. 22; Ps. xl. 6; Is. i. 11) they teach a very different lesson. The prophets are concerned with an attitude of mind which held that God desired sacrifice as an end in itself, and that

[1] See Chapter XII, under *Ezekiel*.
[2] See Marston, *The Bible Comes Alive*, p. 74 and also Chapter VII, p. 92.
[3] Oesterley and Robinson, *op. cit.*, p. 52 f.

consequently a multitude of sacrifices was a substitute for righteousness of life. The forceful language of the prophets must be interpreted comparatively. This is clear from Ho. vi. 6, 'I desired mercy, and not sacrifice; and the knowledge of God *more than* burnt offerings'. The same interpretation holds good for Mi. vi. 6-8. The question in Am. v. 25 admits of an affirmative, and not a negative, answer, as is pointed out by Oesterley in his book, *Sacrifices in Ancient Israel*. But even if a negative answer is to be supplied, it is possible that, during the forty years in the wilderness, private sacrifices were almost non-existent owing to shortage of cattle.[1] Je. vii. 21-23 present a difficulty at first sight. Commentators, however, have pointed out that the words translated 'concerning' in verse 22 are in some places translated 'for the sake of', or 'because of' (e.g. Gn. xii. 17; Dt. iv. 21).[2] This gives much better sense here. God says that He did not speak to the fathers for the sake of sacrifices, but for the sake of obedience.

ANALYSIS

i. 1-vi. 7.	The laws of the offerings. Burnt offering (i.); meal offering (ii.); peace offering (iii.); sin offering (iv. 1-v. 13); trespass offering (v. 14-vi. 7).
vi. 8-vii. 38.	Instructions for the priests in connection with the same offerings.
viii., ix.	The consecration of the priests.
x.	The death of Nadab and Abihu.
xi.-xv.	Laws about uncleanness and purification: clean and unclean beasts (xi.); childbirth (xii.); leprosy (xiii., xiv.); issues (xv.).
xvi.	The day of atonement.
xvii.-xx.	Various social and religious practices for the people.
xxi., xxii.	Instructions for the priests.
xxiii.-xxv.	The calendar of sacred seasons.
xxvi.	The blessings of obedience and the evil of disobedience.
xxvii.	Laws concerning vows.

---

[1] Or again the force may be comparative, 'Did you offer Me sacrifices alone, and not also obedience of heart?' (See W. R. Harper in *Int. Crit. Comm.*)

[2] So L. E. Binns in *The Westminster Commentary*.

CONTENTS

As Genesis describes man's ruin, and Exodus his redemption, so
Leviticus lays down the way of life for a redeemed people. It
concerns the daily walk of the man who would be holy, and
reminds him that a purely humanitarian conduct is not sufficient.
God is concerned that man should admit His claims over the
whole of life, and should be holy in spirit, soul, and body. It is
profitable for the Christian to study the laws in Leviticus in the
light of the deep spiritual principles involved, which take on a new
meaning when applied to the person and work of Jesus Christ.

There are three outstanding features:

(a) The offerings; (b) atonement by blood; (c) The priesthood.

(a) The offerings

The Epistle to the Hebrews teaches that the offerings were typical
of Jesus Christ's offering of Himself (Heb. ix. 23, x. 12) and these
can be studied in various commentaries.[1] The burnt offering
exhibits Christ in His perfection, offering Himself wholly on the
cross; the meal offering (so R.V. more correctly than A.V. 'meat
offering') is His perfectly blended character as the bread of life;
the peace offering signifies the enjoyment of the peace that He has
made; the sin offering shows Christ as the One who was made
to be sin for us (Rom. viii. 3, R.V.); the guilt offering indicates
Christ as atoning even for sins which admitted of some restitution.

(b) Atonement by blood

This is strongly insisted on in Leviticus. A key passage is xvii. 11
(note particularly the R.V.). The blood on the altar makes atonement for sins, because it is life being given for life that has been
forfeited through sin. The blood is valid for atonement only when
it is poured out on the altar in death; it has otherwise no efficacy.
Similarly, in the New Testament the blood of Jesus Christ refers
always to His blood poured out on the cross.

Various ritual actions are prescribed for the blood. It is
poured out on and around the altar (i. 5, iv. 7, etc.), signifying
utter devotion to God in death; and it is sprinkled on or before the
veil in the tabernacle (iv. 6), signifying that Christ's human body

[1] Kellogg (1901) or Andrew Bonar (c. 1870) on *Leviticus*; Andrew Jukes on
The Offerings.

(Heb. x. 20) must be marked with the blood of sacrifice. This thought comes out again in the directions for the day of atonement, when the high priest goes within the veil, carrying the blood which denotes a finished sacrifice. A further mysterious use of the blood is also seen when even the most sacred parts of the tabernacle are sprinkled with blood to cleanse them, because or their presence in the midst of a sinful people (xvi. 14-19). The application in Heb. ix. 23, 24 gives a hint that the whole universe, including 'heavenly things', needs the effects of the atonement.

In the cleansing of the leper, the man has to be sprinkled with blood (xiv. 6, 7), one illustration of the statement in Heb. ix. 22, R.V.: 'According to the law, I may almost say, all things are cleansed with blood, and apart from shedding of blood there is no remission.'

(c) The Aaronic priesthood

The Epistle to the Hebrews expounds the typical nature of the Aaronic priesthood by carefully working out the details of the high priest's action on the day of atonement (Lv. xvi.; Heb. ix., x.). Christ by His one perfect offering, the one sacrifice for sins for ever, once offered, has rendered all further sacerdotal ministry unnecessary and invalid.

The type of Aaron supplements that of Melchizedek (Heb. v. 6), that of the priest supplements that of the offerings and that of the tabernacle. The united witness of all is required to show forth the full glory of Christ.

In addition to those parts of the book which have a special fulfilment in Jesus Christ, the laws of cleanness and uncleanness have an interest of their own. Medical writers have shown that good reasons underlie the laws of cleanness and uncleanness.[1] They are far from being irrational taboos. God wished His people to be the very best in spirit, mind and body, and to this end it was necessary to have regulations for each department of their life. One of the main needs was the prevention of disease, infection, and epidemics. Some of the laws in Leviticus should be studied from this point of view. Thus xi. 32-37 deals with the treatment of vessels or utensils which come into contact with the dead body of any unclean creature. The things must be thoroughly washed or even destroyed, and no food or drink that has been in contact with them must be used. This regulation applies to the unclean creatures only after they are dead (verse 32), and was intended to

---

[1] See especially Rendle Short, *Modern Discovery and the Bible*, Chapter VI.

prevent contamination from contact with decomposing bodies. That this is so appears from verses 39, 40, where personal contact with the dead body even of a clean animal must be followed by a temporary isolation and thorough washing.

The sacrifices might easily have formed a breeding place for flies, with the consequent spread of germs. Quite apart from the spiritual significance of the rules for the sacrifices, it is possible to see a hygienic necessity in them. Nothing was to be left lying exposed. The sacrifice was burnt on the altar, or, if only a part was burnt, the remainder was eaten as soon as possible (vii. 15-18). Other parts were taken out of the camp and destroyed by fire (iv. 11, 12). One might hazard a guess that other refuse from the camp was burnt here also. The blood was poured at the base of the altar, and would drain into the sand or earth, and no doubt would repeatedly have fresh earth sprinkled over it. In these ways the very real danger of fly-borne disease was kept down to a minimum.

One dangerous disease was leprosy. There was no known cure for it, but it could be kept from spreading by isolation, and in Lv. xiii. this is the way that the disease was treated from the moment that it was suspected in any individual. Centuries later it was the way in which leprosy was stamped out in Britain.

The laws of clean and unclean beasts are interesting. In the main, modern experience agrees with the restrictions of Lv. xi. It has often been pointed out, for example, that, whereas we can eat pork safely to-day, it is a meat that quickly deteriorates and becomes dangerous if it is not killed and kept under proper conditions. The law of Moses was wise to ban it.

One of the so-called 'mistakes' of Moses occurs in xi. 5, 6, where he stated that the coney (or rock badger) and the hare chew the cud, whereas actually they are not ruminants at all. But the regulations here are devised for easy observation: and, since these animals appear to chew the cud, that was sufficient. The days of microscopes and dissecting instruments had not yet come.

THEMES FOR STUDY

1. Consider leprosy and other forms of uncleanness mentioned in this book as types of sin.

2. Study the aspects of the work of Jesus Christ which the various sacrifices and offerings reveal.

NUMBERS

AUTHORSHIP, DATE AND CIRCUMSTANCES

THIS book, like the two preceding, combines incident and statute. Unless it be pronounced impossible that the statutes could have been given as the narrative suggests, or that no author could record both, this affords a further argument for the unity and contemporary character of the Pentateuch. The story follows on naturally to record the commencement and closing scenes of the wilderness wanderings, no dates being stated between the second and the fortieth year.

The mention of individuals, and of names afterwards forgotten, the snatches of primitive song in chapter xxi., the laws which according to their entire contents have reference to a situation which in times later than Moses had ceased to exist, the frequent references to Egypt and its food, and the very difficulty caused by the quantity of the materials for the tabernacle and the numbers of the people, all testify to its being a writing of the Mosaic age.

The Hebrew title of the book means 'in the wilderness'. This word should not mislead the reader into thinking of nothing but a sandy desert. In the Sinai peninsula to-day there are oases and streams of water. Geological and historical evidence points to an even greater amount of vegetation in the past.

Rithmah means the 'place of juniper trees', and *Hazeroth* means 'villages' or fenced encampments (xxxiii. 18). The shepherds of Midian found pasture and water for their flocks (Ex. ii. 15, 16) and these would be more abundant as the lands of Midian and Edom were approached (xxxiii. 37).

The ordering of the camp (ii.) does not prove that the Israelites kept in one compact body all the time, but various groups with their flocks would seek out pastures and return. (See below, under *Journeyings.*)

ANALYSIS

i., ii.	Number of the tribes and order in the camp.
iii., iv.	Service of the Levites.
v.-viii.	Laws of separation; Nazirites; offerings and consecration of the Levites.
ix., x.	The first passover and onward march.
xi., xii.	Complaining and rebellion; seventy elders appointed. Further murmuring.

CONTENTS

Although this book sets forth plainly enough the hardships, the murmurings, the lapses into sin, and the stiff-necked and rebellious character of the people, the real theme is the long-suffering and the mercy of Jehovah, and how He led them safely through the howling wilderness and into the promised land (Ps. lxxviii.).

The person and character of Moses stand out in the narrative, but he is only a servant in the house (Heb. iii. 5). God is the supreme ruler and law-giver; the theocracy is being established. Following on the punishment for the people's rebellion (xiv.), He comforts them with a renewed promise of the land to which He will bring them (xv. 2), and gives them a law for those days.

The numbering of the men of war (i.) constitutes them a nation; the ordering of the camp makes them a body politic, and the consecration of the Levites binds them into a religious community. The second numbering, ending with its memorial of those who had died in the wilderness (xxvi. 65) is a solemn reminder of the loss caused by lack of faith, and how, nevertheless, God does not forsake, but graciously restores His people.

The journeyings

Chapter xxxiii. gives an outline list of the places that the Israelites passed through during the forty years, but the route cannot be plotted with certainty, since not more than twelve of the forty-two names can be identified. After passing through the south of the Sinai peninsula, and then north to Kadesh Barnea, they turned to the south again, and for thirty-eight years wandered to the south and east of the Gulf of Akaba. How far they went into the Hejaz area of Arabia is not known. *Kadesh* (holy) may have been a name applied to more than one place connected with the tabernacle, at one of which there appears to have been a notable spring called *En-mishpat*, the 'fountain of judgment' (Gn. xiv. 7).

The number of the Israelites

The number of the men over twenty years of age who came out of Egypt is given as 603,550 (i. 46; cf. Ex. xii. 37, 38), which would correspond with a total population of about two millions. These figures have been described as incredible and purely artificial. They certainly present a problem; for instance, it is difficult to reconcile these figures with the small number of Levites (22,000, iii. 21-39) and of the first-born males (22,273, iii. 43). But whatever is the solution of the problems they raise, they present an appearance as far as possible removed from artificial. It would be nearer the truth to say that they are almost certainly derived from some ancient record, the mere fact of the difficulties they raise being enough to clear them of the charge of invention or artificiality.

Prof. Flinders Petrie[1] maintained that the word 'thousand', denoted by the Hebrew *Eleph*, should be read here and in Ex. xii. as 'families' or 'groups' as in Jdg. vi. 15 (cf. Jos. xxii. 14, R.V. mg.; 1 Sa. xxiii. 23; Mi. v. 2). But while this removes some difficulties it introduces others. More probable is Wiener's suggestion that in the process of copying the numbers have been corrupted by well-meaning scribes.

In all cases of such figures it is well to remember that the reconciliation can be made only when *all* the factors concerned are known. In this instance it may be noted that the supernatural elements are closely interwoven with the history. The exceptionally large number of the people (Ex. i. 9), and the miraculous nature of God's provision for them (Dt. viii. 3, 4) are emphasized. Those who are prepared to believe in the possibility of miracle

---

[1] *Egypt and Israel*, p. 42.

need have no hesitation in accepting the narrative as it stands whatever may be the correct interpretation of its details.

Balaam.

At the end of the wilderness wanderings the most striking story is that of Balaam. He was one who had a personal knowledge of Jehovah. He speaks of himself as coming from Aram (xxiii. 7), and the history says that the king of Moab sent for him to Pethor, 'which is by the river (i.e. Euphrates) to the land of the children of his people' (xxii. 5, R.V.). The indication is that Balaam came from the Padan-Aram district, perhaps from Haran, where Abram and his family spent some time (Gn. xi. 31) and where Laban lived (Gn. xxviii. 5). Possibly he was descended from Laban. His words are represented as prophecies delivered under the form of a trance or as recording what he had seen in a trance (xxiv. 3, 4). Definite references to the future occur in the last prophecy (xxiv. 15-24). Some of them are puzzling, but the 'star out of Jacob' appears to be a messianic allusion.

Scholars of the Wellhausen school have commonly dated these oracles in the ninth century, but Prof. W. F. Albright has recently demonstrated that the allusions in them do not demand a date later than the time of Balaam.[1]

The story of how Balaam's ass spoke has been described as a piece of folk-lore. It may, however, be taken literally, or to mean that the prophet was led to receive an impression of words coming from the ass. The former is the more natural interpretation of 2 Pet. ii. 16, but the fact that the ass is there described as 'dumb' might suggest that the words existed in Balaam's perception alone.

THEMES FOR STUDY

1. 'These things happened unto them by way of example' (1 Cor. x. 11, R.V.). What encouragements and warnings can be derived from the stories in this book?

2. What types and prophecies of Jesus Christ does it contain?

DEUTERONOMY

AUTHORSHIP, DATE AND CIRCUMSTANCES

THIS book purports to give the substance of addresses given by Moses to the people of Israel shortly before their entrance into

[1] Paper printed in *Journal of Biblical Literature*, September, 1944.

Canaan, together with an appendix giving an account of his death. There is no valid reason for denying this claim.

1. The claim is made expressly and emphatically, with details of time and place (i. 1-6, iv. 44-46, xxix. 1). If these statements be not true, it is difficult to acquit their author of forgery.

2. The words are instinct with the warm solicitude of a great leader for the people whose experiences he had shared. It is characterized by an integrity and unity of thought, and by an air of reality entirely suited to the circumstances, and to no other time or place.

3. The geographical details of chapters i.-x. bear every sign of an ancient record, as do the frequent references to Egypt.

4. The modifications of the Levitical law in view of the future residence in the land, and the prospects of victory and peace never fully realized, are not likely to have been invented.

5. There is no touch of the myth or legendary accretion which would arise in an oral tradition handed down through centuries, nor of the fancy or extravagance of an inventor.

The unity of the book is often challenged in respect of chapters xxxii. and xxxiii., the song and blessing of Moses. These are ascribed to another author and date, but without adequate reason. The song has a parallel in Ex. xv. and takes up the thoughts of the greatness of God and Israel's tendency to rebellion, which run through the earlier part of the book. Its poetical form would render it easy to memorize in a way that would be impossible for the whole book.

The blessing is appropriate to the occasion, and natural on the lips of one who was in a real sense the father of his people. The name Jeshurun ('little righteous one') is held to be a diminutive of endearment for Israel, and, as such, pathetically natural to Moses in his old age. The obscurity of the allusions is a sign of its archaic origin. The closing chapter, xxxiv., is obviously by a later hand.

As against the Mosaic authorship and approximately Mosaic date, Wellhausen, and those who follow him, ascribe Deuteronomy to the reign of Josiah, or somewhat earlier, and its authorship to a company of devout priests, possibly in exile in the northern kingdom, who compiled it on the basis of older material. The book was then either lost or deliberately concealed in the temple, where it was found by Hilkiah the priest when Josiah ordered the cleansing of the house of God, and became the basis of the reformation that followed (2 Ki. xxii., xxiii.).

The reasons given for this late date are its prophetic tone and standpoint, certain alleged inconsistencies with the Levitical legislation, and, in particular, that the 'law of the central sanctuary' contained in it was previously unknown and was promulgated for the first time in Josiah's reign.

Since the whole critical structure is founded upon the dating of J, E, D, and P to correspond with the early monarchy, the prophetic period, and the Exile or after, it is of interest that of recent years scholars who accept the documentary analysis have challenged the above date. Professor A. C. Welch places a large part of the book much earlier, Hölscher and Kennett relegate it to the Exile, and Professor Edward Robertson[1] thinks it was completed in its present form by Samuel. The variety of these conclusions is an indication of their speculative character. The question of the central sanctuary is dealt with below.

In xxxi. 9-12, 24 Moses is said to have written down 'this law' so that it could be read aloud every seven years. This might have referred only to the legal portions, but is more naturally applied to the whole book (see i. 5 and Jos. i. 8). Priests of a later age would scarcely have left this reference so indefinite.

ANALYSIS

i.-iv. 43. Introductory speech, recalling past experiences.

iv. 44-xi. The ten commandments, and exhortations to obedience, with special reference to the first two commandments.

xii.-xxvi. A summary of the laws as they affect the people, including the place and manner of sacrifice, clean and unclean meats, the yearly feasts, the duties of the king, and other ordinances, social, judicial and religious.

xxvii.-xxx. The blessings and the curses, and solemn affirmations.

xxxi.-xxxiv. The writing of the law, Moses' song, blessing and death.

CONTENTS

Many unnecessary difficulties in the reading of this book may be avoided by bearing in mind the circumstances of the people addressed, and the objects which Moses had in view.

[1] See p. 121.

It was now forty years after the giving of the law at Sinai, and all those then over twenty years of age had died (Nu. xiv. 29-33, xxvi. 64, 65). Moses, therefore, gives to the new generation a summary of the past history and an exposition of the laws fitted to the capacity of the whole congregation, and enforced with spiritual warmth and tender pleading.

Leviticus had already been written as a handbook for priests and Levites, and the discourses recorded in Deuteronomy centre on love towards God and one's neighbour (Dt. vi. 4, 5, xv. 7; cf. Mk. xii. 29 ff.). The ten commandments are repeated in chapter v., and what follows might be regarded as largely a commentary upon them.

The contents of the previous books are taken for granted, as, for example, in Dt. xxiv. 8, 9 referring to Lv. xiii. 6, xiv. 2 and to Nu. xii. 10. This one instance would suffice to show that Leviticus was not *later* than Deuteronomy; and the difference of purpose accounts for the fewness of more definite references in the latter book to the former.

In view of the fact that the people were on the eve of exchanging their wandering life for settlement in the land, certain modifications in the laws may be noticed. Thus Dt. xii. allows more liberty in the killing of food than Lv. xvii.; Dt. xvi. adds the note of rejoicing to the directions of Lv. xxiii.; Dt. xv. adds the merciful idea of the release from debt to that of rest contained in Lv. xxv.

An evangelical note of the love of God for His people, and His care for the poor and needy pervades this 'second' putting forth of the law. The particular laws should not be regarded as intended to bind a yoke upon the people. They had come through a time of trial (viii. 3) and now, because of His love for them (vii. 8), God gives them His statutes and judgments to enable them to walk in His ways (viii. 6), and to do them good (viii. 16). The precepts are humane and pre-eminently sane.

Priests and Levites

The priests were all Levites, but not all Levites were priests; as bishops, priests and deacons are all 'clergy' though of different orders. So, in Deuteronomy, the expression 'the priests the Levites' (five times), 'the priests the sons of Levi' (twice), and 'priests' (seven times), all refer to the same persons. In xx. 2 'the priest' may refer to the high priest. The Levites also are mentioned fourteen times, where the reference is sometimes to the tribe as a whole. It is not necessary to read any contradiction into the more general statements in Deuteronomy and the more detailed directions in Leviticus.[1]

The central sanctuary

The teaching of Deuteronomy concerning the centralization of worship assumes special importance because of the contention of many scholars that the ordinance was unknown before Josiah's day, and that, in earlier times, sacrificing at 'high places' was freely permitted, contrary to what is stated in the Pentateuch. But a careful examination of the statements of the Old Testament regarding the place of sacrifice will show, on the contrary, that, *if taken in their context,* they form a natural and consistent whole. Any difficulties that remain are trifling when compared with those involved in the above supposition.

1. In the days of the patriarchs altars were built at various times, either at places where a servant of God had made an extended stay (Gn. xii. 8), or where God had specially manifested His presence (Gn. xxxv. 7).

After the deliverance from Egypt Moses built an altar at Rephidim to commemorate the victory over Amalek (Ex. xvii. 15). Shortly after this Moses was given an ordinance concerning such altars (Ex. xx. 22-26). This passage (attributed to J or E) has been interpreted as contrary to the later laws of D and P. But when taken in connection with the narrative in which it stands, it is seen to contain a general injunction to avoid idolatry and an immediate direction for the time before the tabernacle was erected, such as was carried out by Moses soon afterwards (Ex. xxiv. 4, 5). Together with these is a promise of God's blessing, 'in every place where I record my Name' (Ex. xx. 24).

The phrase 'in every place' might be read 'in all the places' and refer to the promised land; so it might indicate future theophanies (see Jdg. vi. 24; 2 Sa. xxiv. 25), or it might mean every place where the tabernacle should rest, with a forward look to Shiloh and Jerusalem (Je. vii. 12). But it is as far as possible removed from the 'high places' which subsequently became a snare to the people.[2]

2. After the erection of the tabernacle, explicit directions are given in Lv. xvii. for animals offered in sacrifice (verses 1-7) and those permitted for food (verses 10-16). The law of the peace offerings (Lv. iii., vii. 11-21) allowed the offerers to eat the meat

[1] See Finn, *Unity of the Pentateuch,* Chapter XIX; Allis, *The Five Books o/ Moses,* pp. 183-192; Chapter XII, under *Ezekiel.*
[2] Allis, op. cit., pp. 176-182.

after certain parts had been duly offered on the altar. Otherwise they killed the animals and ate them in the ordinary way.

The reference to 'devils' (R.V. 'he-goats' or 'satyrs') in Lv. xvii. 7 relates to superstitious and idolatrous customs which were evidently prevalent, but the exact nature of which is obscure.[1] The weaning of the people from idolatry was one of the chief objects of the Levitical laws.

3. Deuteronomy forms the next step, when the previous regulations are reviewed, and plans made for the time when the people should be settled in Canaan and have rest from their enemies (Dt. xii. 10); then sacrifices shall be offered at 'the place which the Lord your God shall choose to cause His name to dwell there' (verse 11, R.V.).

A certain indefiniteness is attached to the chosen 'place'; its primary reference appears to be to the tabernacle, which soon after the conquest was established at Shiloh (Jos. xviii. 1). The erection of a great altar beyond the Jordan by the two and a half tribes (Jos. xxii.) met with a determined protest from the rest under the leadership of Phinehas, until it was explained that it was not intended for a rival sanctuary, but as a memorial. The contemporaneous character of this account is sufficiently evident.

4. In the unsettled days of the Judges there was great ignorance of the law, and frequent apostasy; 'every man did that which was right in his own eyes' (Jdg. xxi. 25). It was the duty of the priests to teach the people (Dt. xxxi. 9-13): and the parents were to teach their children, and write portions of the law in prominent places (vi. 6-9). But even in loyal households this can have applied only to the more important precepts (as in Jewry to-day). Complete copies of the law were doubtless rare; one would be preserved near the ark in Shiloh, and from this and a few others the people would be instructed (see Dt. xxxi. 9-13 and 1 Sa. i. 3). Among the less godly the worship at 'the high places' was not only unorthodox, but frequently, perhaps mainly, idolatrous.

5. Shiloh lost its significance through the capture of the ark by the Philistines (1 Sa. iv.), and from then until the building of the temple there was constant warfare. The peaceful conditions visualized in Dt. xii. did not obtain, and Samuel offered sacrifice at Mizpah (1 Sa. vii. 9) and elsewhere, and Solomon at Gibeon (1 Ki. iii. 4). In this connection the sacrifices at high places are excused on this very ground (verses 2, 3).

6. The complete unification of the people under Solomon, the

[1] See Kellogg, *Leviticus*, pp. 368-372.

establishment of peace and the building of the temple brought about the conditions necessary for the centralization of worship with Jerusalem as the centre. Offerings at the high places were still made, but henceforth were constantly reprobated.

7. Upon the division of the kingdom the conditions changed again. Jeroboam set up sanctuaries at Bethel and Dan, to prevent the pious from going down to Jerusalem. In the northern kingdom altars to Jehovah were erected in many places, and Elijah bewailed their destruction as a mark of apostasy (1 Ki. xviii. 30, xix. 10). In Judah also worship at the high places continued sometimes directed to Jehovah, but more often to the gods of the land. Such practices were encouraged by Ahaz (2 Ki. xvi. 4) but under Hezekiah they were put down with a strong hand (2 Ki. xviii. 4).

8. It is not surprising that the idolatry practised for fifty-seven years under Manasseh and continued under his son Amon, had caused the law to be all but forgotten. That the action taken following the discovery in the temple of the book of the law (2 Ki. xxii. 8) was not an innovation, but a reformation in the true sense, is evidenced both by the preceding account, and by the expression used. 'The book of the law' (not a law-book or a roll of laws) cannot mean anything else, either grammatically or historically, than the Mosaic book of the law (the Pentateuch). The expression shows that the allusion is to something already known, and not to anything which had come to light for the first time.

The testimony of Jeremiah (vii. 12-14) with its explicit reference to Dt. xii. 11 and to Shiloh is an additional proof that Josiah was not promulgating something new, but causing the people to return to a law laid down by Moses, kept for a while, and then departed from, by their fathers. The very vagueness of the law in Deuteronomy is an indication of its genuineness. There is no satisfactory reason why the alleged compilers in Josiah's reign should have stopped short of naming Jerusalem.

Relation to the New Testament

Deuteronomy contains one direct messianic prophecy. God promised Moses that He would raise up a prophet like unto him (xviii. 15-19), and the reference to this in the later addition of xxxiv. 10-12 indicates that a personal fulfilment was looked for. The words are applied to Christ by Peter in Acts iii. 22, and by Stephen in Acts vii. 37.

<hr>

[1] Keil, *Kings*, pp. 477, 478.

As prophet, Christ declared the Father in a manner that was constant and immediate (Jn. i. 18; Nu. xii. 6-8; Dt. xxxiv. 10), and as a mediator, He instituted a better and enduring covenant (Heb. ix. 15-28).

Deuteronomy is quoted or referred to in the New Testament some eighty times. This is more than any other book. (Note especially Rom. x. 6-8; Heb. xii. 29, xiii. 5.) From it came all our Lord's defence against the tempter (Dt. vi. 13, 16, viii. 3; Mt. iv. 4, 7, 10); and the first part of His summary of the law and the prophets (vi. 4, 5; Mt. xxii. 37, 38).

THEMES FOR STUDY

1. Note the New Testament references to Deuteronomy with the aid of a reference Bible, and sum up the teaching they contain.

2. Gather together, and summarize, the passages which teach God's love and care for His people, for the poor and for the oppressed.

CHAPTER X

HEBREW HISTORY

UNDER the title of historical books we may include Joshua, Judges, Ruth, 1, 2 Samuel, 1, 2 Kings, 1, 2 Chronicles, Ezra-Nehemiah, and Esther. Of these the five latter are included in the Hebrew text under the *Writings*; the others are grouped as the *Former Prophets*, a description the significance of which must not be overlooked.[1] Joshua, Judges and Ruth and the books of Samuel lead up to the establishment of the monarchy; Kings and Chronicles carry the story in parallel accounts up to the captivity; Ezra and Nehemiah tell the story of the return; Esther falls in the Persian period.

Excepting Ezra and Nehemiah, the books, strictly speaking, are anonymous. Joshua and Samuel no doubt owe much of their material to these leaders (cf. 1 Ch. xxix. 29), but were evidently compiled after their death. Many prophetic writings and chronicles are quoted as sources of information; and, in general, these books bear every evidence of a care for accuracy similar to that which Luke manifested when writing his Gospel (Lk. i. 1-4).

They are also like Luke's Gospel in that they are no mere history. Whether they record the experience of individuals or of the nation, *God's* dealings with them constitute the subject. God's covenant with Abraham, Isaac, and Jacob influences the form and content of the genealogies which are included, and is the reason for the inclusion of many incidents which unfold the story of its fulfilment. In the history of Israel the material is specially selected in order to emphasize their redemption from the bondage of Egypt, their calling and election as God's chosen people, and their function as the recipients of His oracles (Rom. iii. 2).

The reigns of kings are assessed according to whether they did right *in the sight of the Lord* and walked in the steps of David their father, or did evil like Jeroboam, the son of Nebat. Room is found not only for the deeds and characters of great national heroes—Joshua, Samuel, David, Solomon, and others—but also for the words of the otherwise unknown Micaiah, the son of Imlah, and the stories of the humble women who ministered to Elijah and Elisha.

So these books relate the wonderful *acts of God* (Ps. cxi. 4), how

[1] See pp. 156, 209.

He put down the mighty from their seat and exalted the humble
and meek. They reveal His holiness, His long-suffering, His
compassion, His readiness to pardon the penitent, His seeking
of the lost and His joy at their return. They relate the experiences of prophets and how they fulfilled their commissions.
They correspond in their record of *deeds* to the truths proclaimed
in the prophetical books in *words*. They give not only the predictions, but their fulfilment. They grant us an insight into the
working out of God's great redemptive purpose in history, and
show how the way was prepared for the coming of His Son.

In them, as in the prophetical books, we see a progress of
thought from Israel as a chosen nation, to that true Israel within
Israel, the faithful remnant; and then even within that remnant
a pointing forward to the chosen servant, the Branch, the son of
David, God's well-beloved Son. The history as well as the
prophecy points forward constantly, like a series of signposts, to
the One who should come. The genealogies and the events
form a historical chain which links God's primal purpose in
Adam with His ultimate purpose for mankind in Christ.

The treatment of the Old Testament history by Christ should
be carefully studied. He never cast doubt either upon its main
outlines or its minutest details. He mentions the incident of
David and the shewbread (Mk. ii. 26), the glory of Solomon
(Mt. vi. 29), the visit of the Queen of Sheba (Mt. xii. 42), Elijah's
mission to the widow of Zarephath (Lk. iv. 26) and the healing of
Naaman (Lk. iv. 27). Even radical critics admit that He believed
in its historical truthfulness, and we may unhesitatingly do the
same.

It is, nevertheless, not as history, but as *revelation* that these
books are chiefly treated in the New Testament, and should be
studied by the Christian. They are cited as revealing God's
character in His deeds, His gracious promises from generation to
generation, and His redemptive purpose in Christ, the Son of
David; and finally they tell how the sending of His prophets and
the rejection of their message (Mt. xxi. 33-46) led on to the
sending of His Son.

JOSHUA

AUTHORSHIP, DATE AND CIRCUMSTANCES

Standing as it does at the head of the first part of the second
section of the Hebrew Bible, the *Former Prophets*, the book of
Joshua forms a link between the 'law' (i.e. the *Torah*, or Instruc-

tion) and its articulation in practice as recorded in the later history. The continuity of style and purpose with the preceding books has led many recent critics to class it with them as the last book of the Hexateuch (see i. 8, xxiv. 26), but references to 'the Book of the Law' in viii. 31 and xxiii. 6 plainly point to a separate and independent scriptural authority.

There is nothing in the historical books, beginning with Joshua, to suggest that they are not on the same level of inspiration as the others, just as the Gospels and Acts are no less inspired than the Epistles. Their description as the *Former Prophets* is due not merely to the nature of their teaching and contents, but to the fact that they were recorded by prophets and seers (cf. 1 Ch. xxix. 29), some contemporary with the events thus related, and others using contemporary sources. They bear witness to the mighty acts of the living God, and display acquaintance with His purposes for, and dealings with, His people, both individually and nationally. In other parts of the Bible they are alluded to and quoted as veracious history and an essential part of those Scriptures that make us wise unto salvation.

Joshua's right to its place in the Old Testament canon has never been disputed. There are various references to its contents in later books (1 Ch. ii. 7, xii. 15; Ps. xliv., lxviii., lxxviii., cxiv.; Is. xxviii. 21; Hab. iii. 11-13). Procopius, a reliable authority of the sixth century, relates that there was an inscription at Tingis in Mauretania which ran, 'We are they (i.e. refugees) who fled from the face of Joshua, the robber, the son of Nun.'

The name Joshua denotes rather the hero than the writer of the book, although Jewish tradition held him to be the author. It had no 'author' in the sense of one setting out to write a story, but was an account of events of such outstanding importance and significance that the agency of Joshua in causing them to be written cannot be ruled out, seeing that writing was certainly possible at that time (viii. 32, xxiv. 26). The expression 'to this day' occurs some fourteen times. In three places (xxii. 3 and xxiii. 8, 9) it would fall within Joshua's life-span. The details given are often so minute as plainly to be from the hand of a contemporary (e.g. xv. 6, xviii. 17). By comparing xv. 63 with 2 Sa. v. 7-9 and xvi. 10 with 1 Ki. ix. 16, and by noting the absence of any reference to the division of the kingdom, the completion of the book before the days of Rehoboam may be inferred.

Few parts of the Bible hang so closely together as the first twelve chapters. Such discrepancies as appear on the surface

between certain statements in this part and the remainder of the
book vanish when the text is carefully examined and when regard
is had to such statements as xi. 18; 'Joshua made war a long time
with all those kings'. In such a 'war of movement' the picture
was continually changing; new factors and fresh problems constantly appeared with the lapse of time, and with the change
from battles with the united army of Israel to the tribal settlement.
There is, for example, no contradiction between xii. 10 and xv. 63
if it be borne in mind that 'Jerusalem' in the former refers to the
city and in the latter to the administrative district (see also xv. 8).
There is again a time-interval between xi. 23 and xix. 51.

Accepting the date of the Exodus as 1440 B.C.,[1] Keil's suggestion that it was compiled by 'one of the elders that outlived
Joshua' is attractive and, besides, would give a date consistent
with the recurrence of the words 'unto this day'. This is much
more probable than the oral transmission through the centuries of
all the detail contained in the body of the book. The notices in
the Tel el Amarna tablets of the invasion of Palestine by the
children of Israel, there called Habiru, cannot compare for
historical value with the account in the book of Joshua. Sir
Charles Marston writes:[2] 'It has become clear that the Tel el
Amarna letters contain enemy versions of Joshua's invasion,
written by Canaanite, Amorite, and Jebusite chiefs. The trouble
is to fit them into the course of events. They extend over forty
years, and numbers of people, of whom we know nothing, are
mentioned in them. The name of Joshua actually occurs on one
of the tablets in the following setting: "As the king my Lord
liveth, Job is not in Pella. For two months he has been hiding.
Ask then Benjamin, ask then Tadua, ask then *Joshua*." At the
same time the letters do show the unsettled state of the native
population and their defection from their nominal rulers consequent upon the sweeping victories of Joshua.'

Familiarity with the map is essential to a proper understanding
of the situation at the period. From north to south stretched the
central highlands, the main mountainous area including Shechem,
Shiloh, Bethel, Jerusalem and Hebron; and between this and the
Mediterranean the foothills (*Shephelah*) and the maritime plain.
Along the latter ran the Egyptian high-road north to Megiddo and
thence to Hazor and the east. 'The *Shephelah* . . . formed a
screen as well as a barrier, as though the passing of Pharoah's
armies remained unseen, the coming and going of his messengers

---

[1] See 1 Ki. vi. 1; Garstang, *Joshua and Judges*, p. 147. See also Chapter VII.
[2] *The Bible Comes Alive*, p. 93.

unnoticed.'[1] During the forty years wandering the grip of Egypt
had relaxed somewhat, but there were still small garrisons at
points skirting the above road and inland. In securing a foothold
in these key positions events attended by such amazing phenomena
occurred that Joshua saw in them, quite rightly, the hand of God.

ANALYSIS

i.-v.	Preparations for the conquest. Jordan crossed.
vi.-viii.	Jericho and Ai taken. Achan's sin.
ix.-xii.	Further acts of conquest. Compromise with Gibeon.
xiii.-xix.	Distribution of the tribes.
xx.-xxii.	Cities of refuge, Levitical cities, return of the two-and-a-half tribes.
xxiii., xxiv.	Joshua's exhortations and death.

CONTENTS

The book of Joshua follows up the history after Deuteronomy
somewhat as the book of Acts follows on the Gospels. The record
shows how obedience and loyalty met with success just as the book
of Judges shows that apostasy brought failure in its wake. To be
understood and appreciated aright it must be approached in the
spirit of, and with something of the faith of, the warrior-chief who
is its subject. This is aptly illustrated in the episode of the spies
(Nu. xiii., xiv. 6-10; Dt. i. 38), all of whom, including Joshua
himself, were confronted with the same evidence of impregna-
bility and difficulty, but did not all share the same faith in the
destiny of Israel. The faith of Joshua and Caleb that the land was
good, and that there was no cause for fear if only the Lord were
with them, expanded by Moses into a creed for the people in
Dt. iv. 34 ff., vi. 4 ff., xi. 18 ff., was the rationale of the whole
forward movement of the nation. Thus the record demands from
the Christian reader a faith and insight like that which inspired
Israel's leaders, and brought them into the promised land.

The book is not free from difficulties for the modern reader.
Joshua's command to the sun to stand still (x. 12, mg. 'be silent')
over Gibeon has been a stumbling block to many, yet the record

---

[1] Garstang, *op. cit.*, p. 91.

has every sign of being contemporaneous, and something more than poetic imagery must be conceded. As with the 'darkness over the land' at the Crucifixion, the miracle cannot be dissociated from the importance of the occasion. E. W. Maunder has given his view of the astronomical character of this event,[1] but however explained there is no need to doubt its occurrence.

Another difficulty is felt concerning the command for the wholesale destruction of the Canaanite population as at Ai (viii. 2, cf. vi. 21). Yet no thoughtful believer in God can survey the field of history without seeing that God *does* judge nations as well as individuals, not only Assyria and Babylon, as foretold by the prophets, but even the peoples of our modern world. The Lord Jesus Christ, whose tenderness cannot be impugned, teaches this quite plainly (Lk. xvii. 26-30), and the sins of the Canaanites were no less heinous than those of the cities of the plain. The same Son of Man revealed to His servant John, the apostle of love, that He goes forth 'in righteousness to judge and make war' (Rev. xix. 11-16). When studied in the light of the New Testament, 'passages which were once a difficulty may be found to teach us humbling lessons of our own shortness of vision, of our inadequate ideas of God's holiness and hatred of sin, and of God's infinite mercy in Christ in sparing us from those evils which we most righteously have deserved.'[2]

In general we may say that the book records the *acts* in which Joshua was conscious of divine aid; the *facts* concerning the progress made towards the final goal; and finally the *effects* of permanent significance. Joshua's headquarters were first established at Gilgal (iv. 19), and afterwards advanced from there to Shiloh (xviii. 9) and Shechem (xxiv. 1). The sacred ark, the symbol of the presence of God, is moved forward to each of the stations in turn, to be found, after the period of the Judges, at Shiloh (1 Sa. 1).

The book teaches the importance of obedience to the divine law with its moral requirements for those who would be instruments of the divine will; and further, of the necessity of complete self-dedication (xiv. 9) to that end. In the early part especially, it is full of most valuable spiritual teaching. The story of Rahab and the spies, the crossing of Jordan, and other stirring events all have meaning beyond historical facts, telling us of the conditions under which God's greatest spiritual blessings are gained or forfeited.

---

[1] *Trans. Victoria Inst.*, Vol. LIII (1921). See also Garstang, *op. cit.*, p. 179.
[2] See H. E. Guillebaud, *Some Moral Difficulties of the Bible*, p. 135, where the whole subject of the Old Testament warfare is fully discussed.

THEMES FOR STUDY

1. List the promises God gave to Joshua and note the conditions on which they depended. Study the promised land as the type of the Spirit-filled life.

2. What do you consider is the spiritual meaning of the 'crossing of Jordan'? Note that it is the necessary condition before God can do wonders in us. What is its relation to the two main purposes of the miracle as stated in iii. 10 and iv. 23, 24 (R.V.)?

3. Examine the spiritual dangers of compromise as illustrated in the story of the Gibeonites. Note Joshua's faithfulness and compare Ps. xv.

4. Examine Joshua as a type of Christ (Heb. iv. 8). Consider his name, his leading the people of God to the land of promise, his succeeding Moses (as gospel succeeds the law, Acts xiii. 39).

5. What New Testament parallels are suggested by the stones of witness, the promised possession, circumcision, the cities of refuge?

JUDGES

AUTHORSHIP, DATE AND CIRCUMSTANCES

RABBINIC tradition[1] asserts that 'Samuel wrote his book and Judges and Ruth'. Despite the fact that the early Christian Fathers accepted this, no weight can be attached to it. Nevertheless, all the evidence is in favour of the contemporary character of these fragmentary records, by whomsoever collected together. The possibility of their having been written at that distant time is demonstrated, not only by the proved antiquity of alphabetic writing, but also by the existence of records such as the Tel el Amarna tablets.[2] It is further contained in the text itself by the casually mentioned fact that a young man of Succoth 'wrote down' (Jdg. viii. 14, R.V. mg.) a list of princes. The narratives extend over so long a period that to attribute their preservation to oral tradition would be to postulate a miracle of memory.

Archaeological research testifies to the accuracy of the geographical details and the conditions which then obtained, especially with reference to the natural obstacles encountered and

[1] E.g. Baba Bathra, fol. xiv, c, 2.
[2] See p. 157.

the distances traversed. [1] Megiddo,which guarded the pass by which Egyptian and Assyrian armies passed over the Carmel range, figures in the inscriptions of both these nations, in which Taanach also comes in for mention (i. 27, v. 19). Excavations at Hebron, Shechem and Bethshean have also proved the accuracy of the Bible text even in small details. [2] Extensive remains of iron instruments have been found at Megiddo, Taanach and elsewhere belonging to this period (see i. 19, iv. 3; cf. Jos. viii. 31; 1 Sa. xiii. 20), thus rendering untenable the opinion that the first appearance of iron was much later.

Another indication of early date is that 'the frequent recurrence in the book of passages in which we are told that the Israelites forsook Jehovah and followed after Baal and Astarte (ii. 13), or that they intermingled with the Canaanites and served the gods of their wives or of their sons-in-law (iii. 6), harmonizes in every way with the conclusions to be drawn from a study of the personal names'. [3]

The last five chapters, which appear detached from the main narrative, tell the strange story of the erratic religion of Micah, a grandson of Moses (xviii. 30, R.V.) and the story of the horrible and inhuman conduct of the men of Gibeah, at a time when Phinehas was still living. Their very detachment bears witness to the fact that the sacred writers felt that their content spoke of actions highly irregular and unlawful. Josephus transferred these chapters to precede chapter i., presumably because the incidents belong to the beginning of the period (*Antiq.* v., ii. 8-12). Their rugged and honest character is evidence of their truth, nor would a writer at a later date have been likely to invent such a story about the city where Saul made his home.

The repeated statement that 'there was no king in Israel' (xviii. 1, xxi. 25) points to a date not earlier than the reign of Saul, whilst that in i. 21 (cf. Jos. xv. 63 and Jdg. xix. 11, 'Jebus') implies that it was before the events related in 2 Sa. v. [4]

The words in xviii. 30, 31 (cf. Ps. lxxviii. 60, 61) suggest that the book may have been compiled at the time that the sanctuary of Shiloh was dissolved, probably as a result of a Philistine cam-

---

[1] See Chapter VII.
[2] Garstang, *Joshua and Judges*, pp. 76, 198.
[3] Hommel, *Ancient Hebrew Tradition*, p. 384.
[4] There is no reason to think that Benjamin is here a mistake for Judah; the explanation of the apparent discrepancy between i. 8 and i. 21 being that the former refers to the city itself and the latter to the district inhabited by the Jebusites, of which the city was the centre, and which extended beyond the borders of the tribe of Benjamin.

paign. (See also Je. vii. 14, xxvi. 6.) The number of references to
Ephraim and the greater minuteness of the stories connected with
that tribe would accord with a surmise that it was from documents
kept at this sanctuary that the compilation was made.

In this book we learn of the rise of the Nazirites, whom Amos,
looking back upon this period (ii. 11), classes with the prophets as
'raised up' of God. The references to this order in Judges (xiii. 5-7,
xvi. 17) form a connecting link between, and explain, those in
Numbers and Am. ii., which otherwise would hang in the air.
Like the Rechabites of later times (2 Ki. x.), they represent the
faithful nucleus who kept alive the spiritual ideals of religion
enshrined in the Mosaic law. Vows were made unto Jehovah in
many places, and it is important to note that there was no
restriction of family or tribe; Jephthah was a Gileadite, Samson a
Danite, and Samuel an Ephraimite. The spirit of separation
(*nazar*, to separate) characterized those who were to be the
divinely inspired leaders and saviours of the people. Upon them
came the Spirit of Jehovah (iii. 10), who 'clothed Himself' with
Gideon (vi. 34, R.V. mg.) and 'came mightily' upon Samson
(xiv. 6). The prophetic author never once loses sight of God.

ANALYSIS

CONTENTS

The title of the book in the Hebrew Bible (*Shophetim*, cf. *Mishpat*, 'judgment') is a word of special meaning, 'Judges' being a near equivalent. Signifying 'deliverer', 'ruler', or 'magistrate', it is used to denote a man raised up to bring the life of the people into line with the divine law (Ex. xviii. 16; Jdg. ii. 18, iii. 9). Only in this sense can we understand the 'judge' as having his rightful place in the long history of the people of God. They were thus 'saved to serve' Him, a belief that we find showing itself in the New Testament (Lk. i. 74; Heb. xi. 32-34).

In general the space allotted to each judge is in proportion to the influence upon the nation of his life and work. The greater detail of Samson's exploits may be due to their relative closeness to the time of the author. The momentum of Joshua's conquering progress is reflected in chapters i., ii., and the character of the ensuing period in ii. 6-iii. 6. Two reasons are given by the Lord (ii. 20-23) for the experiences through which Israel had to pass, one moral, to punish the people for their disobedience, and the other spiritual, to prove their fidelity. The author adds a third, and political, reason (iii. 1-4) that their generations might be taught to war, so giving them a place among the nations.

The central portion of the book (iii.-xvi.) is devoted to the accounts of the various 'judges' and covers a period of about three centuries from the time of Othniel to that of Eli.[1] The 300 years of Jdg. xi. 26 would be 1400-1100 B.C. It was a period of declension from the high ideals and great moral principles inculcated by Moses and Joshua. Signs of anarchy, violence, disorder, moral corruption and tribal division constantly re-appear. There was a loss of national consciousness until the people were recalled to it by some great leader and then what was gained in the subjugation of their enemies and the assertion of their moral ascendancy in one generation was too often lost by the defection of the next. The long story exhibits the recurring cycles of retrogression, recall, repentance, renewal and rest.

Yet the sense of national unity and the call to 'walk in the way of Jehovah' was never altogether lost, as is testified in Deborah's song. She is 'a mother in Israel' and they are 'the people of the Lord' (v. 7, 11). The real significance of this poem is even now too often overlooked. Not only does it refute the theory that the tribes arrived in Canaan at different epochs from different

---

[1] See Chapter VII, *Historical Background*, p. 93.

directions and with different origins, but it proves (by its very assumption that even the most distant must rally to the divine summons) that the nation was already serving Jehovah as a united whole, long before it entered the land of promise.[1] The relation to Egypt is discussed in Chapter VII. The passage of Egyptian armies along the coast corridor route from Askelon to Mount Carmel would add to the 'thorns' in the side of Israel occasioned by the unsubdued Amorite nations (ii. 3, vi. 9, x. 11, 12). The stele of Merneptah (c. 1220 B.C.) in the British Museum records that:

'The Hittite land is at peace—plundered is Canaan—with every evil—Askelon is carried off—Gezer is seized—Yenoam is made as though non-existent—Israel is desolated, her seed is not. . . .'[2]

The juxtaposition of Israel to Yenoam, in the region of Deborah's victory, which took place soon afterwards (1200 B.C.) is interesting.

There is a wild barbarity about the stories in this book which, while they vividly depict the rude age to which it belongs, cause us to ask what place these chronicles have in the story of redemption. Apart from the part played by the judges in the historical development of Israel, and the function of the written word in the achievement of the purposes of God (see Ps. cii. 18) the answer is perhaps to be found in the very bareness of the history, in that it reveals Jehovah in His work. The long periods of 'rest' are passed over in a comparative silence which is broken only when God intervenes to visit for sin, or to raise up saviours in answer to the cry of His people. His acts reveal Him as the God of mercy and judgment 'forgiving iniquity and transgression and sin, and that will by no means clear the guilty' (Ex. xxxiv. 7). His wrath falls upon the children of disobedience (Eph. v. 6, see Jdg. ii. 14, 20, iii. 8, x. 7), but when they cry to Him in their trouble, He raises up deliverers, forerunners and types of the Saviour, to overthrow their enemies and to give rest to the people of God.

THEMES FOR STUDY

1. Examine the teaching of the book on the working of God's Providence, especially in regard to the strange instruments He can use in effecting His holy purposes.

[1] Phythian Adams, *Call of Israel*, p. 42.
[2] Marston, *New Knowledge About the Old Testament*, p. 159.

2. Note the reasons for failure. What are the corresponding dangers in the spiritual life (ii. 11-19; cf. Mt. ix. 29)?

3. What spiritual meaning lies behind the reduction of Gideon's army? (See Dt. xx. 8; 1 Sa. xiv. 6; Mk. vi. 7; 1 Cor. i. 26.)

4. Study the angelic appearances in Joshua and Judges and their relation to the incarnation (cf. Ex. xxxiv. 5).

5. Note the selection in Heb. xi. 32-34 of instances of 'faith', and study how this faith was displayed.

RUTH

AUTHORSHIP, DATE AND CIRCUMSTANCES

IN the Hebrew Bible the book of Ruth is placed among the *Writings*, the third section of the Old Testament Scriptures. The Septuagint and Vulgate rightly advance it to its present position following Judges, which it may well have occupied in the MSS. which those translators followed. With that book, as the numerous marginal references show, it has close affinities, in spite of the contrast in subject matter. Origen records[1] that the Hebrews (i.e. the Hellenistic Hebrews) 'join together Judges and Ruth in one book'.

It is a masterpiece of descriptive writing with a wonderful economy of language. Only one acquainted with the customs of the age and steeped in its lore could have produced so vivid a picture of Israelitish life. 'The author is describing a life with which he was familiar.'[2] It is not without significance that the three stories in Jdg. xvii. ff. and Ruth portray incidents that took place in northern (Dan), central (Shiloh) and southern (Bethlehem) Canaan respectively, thus giving us a cross-section of country life and manners in those far-off days. The relationship to Judges is apparent from the following references, many of which have all the greater force in that they are implied rather than direct: i. 1 (Jdg. ii. 16 and xvii. 7); i. 8 (i. 24); i. 13 (ii. 15); i. 15 (xi. 24); ii. 1 (vi. 12 and xi. 1); ii. 4 (vi. 12); ii. 13 (xix. 3); ii. 17 (vi. 11); ii. 20 (xvii. 2); iii. 1 (xiv. 2 ff.); iii. 7 (xvi. 19, xix. 6); iii. 13 (viii. 19). It is to be noted that in iii. 1 the marriage was arranged by the parents (Jdg. xiv. 2 ff.).

The authorship is traditionally assigned to Samuel, and on the whole, the evidence favours a date in the early days of the

---

[1] Euseb., *Eccl. Hist.*, VI., 25.
[2] Cooke, *Camb. Bible.*

monarchy. The genealogy proceeds no further than David, and the minuteness of the description of the incidents is against a later period. On the other hand, the description of 'pulling off the shoe' as obsolete (iv. 7, cf. Dt. xxv. 8, 9) precludes a very early date. The famine (i. 1) must have been widespread and vividly held in recollection, and, in fact, may well have been the result of the Midianite incursions (Jdg. vi. 2-6). The so-called Aramaisms in the language, few enough in number, may have been acquired in transmission. They are more than counter-balanced by the purity of the classical style, which is palpably different from that of Esther and Chronicles. As for the personal names, Ruth and Orpah are Moabitish, whilst Elimelech occurs as Ilumilki in the Tel el Amarna tablets. Naomi means 'amiable one'. The absence of any reference to 'the shield, the sword and the battle', the atmosphere of simple piety that pervades the story, the sense throughout of an over-ruling providence, and the setting in that quiet corner of Judah all conspire to remind us that the story comes straight from the heart of that Hebrew consciousness of divine destiny which was later to reach so glorious a fulfilment.

ANALYSIS

The book seems to lend itself readily to dramatic treatment. It is in four scenes:

i. In the country of Moab. Ruth's affection ripens into admiration of Naomi; she follows *religiously*—'Thy God, my God'.

ii. In the field of Bethlehem. Naomi's wretchedness. The generous kinsman (Heb. *goel*) Boaz befriends the stranger.

iii. At the threshing-floor. Boaz shows his nobility and makes a promise.

iv. At the gate of the city. Before witnesses the nearer kinsman withdraws. Boaz implements his promise by marrying Ruth. The genealogy of David.

CONTENTS

The author's purpose was to show that the rise of David was not fortuitous, but providential; it was the 'hand of the Lord' (i. 13). Here fact becomes stranger than fiction. The genealogy, so far from being an addendum, is basal and primary and gives meaning to the story, the beauty and simplicity of which is a sufficient refutation of the theory that it was a propaganda story written to oppose the marriage reforms of Ezra and Nehemiah. In the fact that Ruth, an alien, impressed by the character of Naomi, professes undying devotion to her mother-in-law, and to her God, we see the truly *missionary* spirit of the book manifested. Ruth rightly infers that Naomi's amiability is traceable to her faith in the loving-kindness of Jehovah (i. 8, ii. 20, iii. 10). Here is an adumbration of the new covenant (2 Cor. iii. 6) which embraces strangers (Eph. ii. 12) who were debarred under the law (Dt. xxiii. 3) and bestows on them the blessing of full fellowship (Ru. ii. 14). In the providential government of the world true *piety* is the greatest power for good for all its apparent frailty. Truly 'the meek shall inherit the earth'. It is more than a coincidence that the greatest drama of all time opens on the same spot and in a similar setting of circumstances.

THEMES FOR STUDY

1. Compare the circumstances of Rebekah, Rahab and Ruth, all of whom were included in the line of messianic promise. Compare Acts x. 34, 35 and Heb. xi. 31.

2. Note the parallels between the Magnificat (Lk. i. 46-55) and the story of Ruth.

3. Note the references to the 'kinsman' and his right to 're-deem' (cf. Lv. xxv. 25-31, 47-55; Dt. xxv. 5-10; and Jb. xix. 25), and see in these a foreshadowing of Christ, our Kinsman and Redeemer.

I and II SAMUEL

AUTHORSHIP, DATE AND CIRCUMSTANCES

IN the Hebrew text the two books of Samuel were not separated; the division originated with the Septuagint and was carried over into the Vulgate. The whole book was known from the earliest times as the 'book' of Samuel (Talmud, Origen) but this does not necessarily imply that Samuel was the author. Similarly the title 'Ruth' or 'Esther' does not imply that the heroine of the story wrote the book that bears her name.

Certain of the Davidic Psalms (see R.V. headings) portray

situations identical with those which it describes. For example, Kirkpatrick[1] writes of Ps. xviii. (2 Sa. xxii.) as being 'at once the best illustration of David's life and character, and the noblest specimen of his poetry'.

There are various references made in the book to contemporary writing. Samuel wrote the 'law of the kingdom' (1 Sa. x. 25), and Jehoshaphat was David's 'recorder', whilst Seraiah was 'scribe' or 'writer' (2 Sa. viii. 16, 17). The chronicler had before him 'histories' of Samuel, Nathan and Gad (1 Ch. xxix. 29, mg. 'words'). It cannot be asserted that the first of these was our book of Samuel, but he probably knew of its existence. If we can trust the statement in 2 Macc. ii. 13 that 'Nehemiah, founding a library, gathered together the books about the kings and prophets and the books of David', these would probably include Samuel, which would therefore have taken its place in the canon before the time of the Maccabees.

The book contains a picture so primitive, vivid and detailed as to force the conclusion that the author lived near to the events. The geographical facts are scrupulously exact, and Professor Hommel has pointed out that the absence of names compounded with Baal is consistent with the influence exercised by Samuel.[2] The ancient belief that Samuel wrote 1 Sa. i.-xxiv. and that the rest was compiled by Nathan and Gad is accepted by Kirkpatrick as substantially correct. He adds, 'If, then, the book of Samuel was compiled largely from the chronicles of Samuel, Nathan and Gad, supplemented by other records kept in the schools of the prophets, it follows that it rests on the best possible authority.'[3]

Some critics analyse the book into two main documents due to J and E, and said to contain divergent views of Samuel (as an unknown seer on the one hand, and a great national figure on the other) with various additions. Others divide it still further. They discern two differing accounts of (1) David's introduction to Saul (1 Sa. xvi. 17; xvii. 55); (2) the way in which Saul met his death (2 Sa. i. and 1 Sa. xxxi.); and (3) the origin of the proverb, 'Is Saul also among the prophets?' (1 Sa. x. 11, xix. 24), and of some other incidents. Of the latter, most are more easily understood as different events (e.g. the sparing of Saul's life in 1 Sa. xxiv. 3 ff., xxvi. 9). The account of Saul's meeting with David in 1 Sa. xvii. 55 presents a real difficulty, but the battle with Goliath presumably took place earlier (cf. 1 Sa. xvii. 15 with xvi. 19)

---

[1] *Camb. Bible*, p. 84.
[2] *Ancient Hebrew Tradition*, p. 305.
[3] *Camb. Bible*, 2 Sa., p. 11.

and may have been inserted here to complete the picture. In any case, some such exhibition of youthful prowess must have taken place to arouse Saul's jealousy, and he may have felt it necessary to make further enquiries about David's identity. On the other hand his ignorance may have been feigned. The Amalekite's story of Saul's death may have been an invention, and a proverb may as well rest upon two incidents as upon one. Such considerations are of little weight against the unity of plan and style, the book affording one of the best examples of Hebrew prose, and that from the golden age of Hebrew literature. It is also marked as different from the succeeding books by the absence of any reference to the 'law of Moses' (cf. 1 Ki. ii. 3 and elsewhere in Kings) and by its use of the title 'the Lord of Hosts'.

The problem of the two attitudes towards the monarchy is created by assigning to two different authors passages in which the kingdom is seen from different points of view, the human and divine. The people clamoured for a king in the political sense, like the nations around (see also Jdg. viii. 23; Jn. vi. 15). When Samuel, under the direction of Jehovah, acceded to their request, he was pointed to Saul and told to anoint him captain (R.V. prince, Heb. *nagid*, i.e. leader) to save the people from their enemies (1 Sa. ix. 16). This word is used of David (1 Sa. xiii. 14) on an occasion earlier than his official installation as *king* in the political sense. The interplay of these two currents, the worldly desire of the people on the one hand, the divine and spiritual purpose on the other, personified in Saul and David, runs through the whole book.[1]

The book covers a period of about a century and thus links up with the events of Jdg. xiii.-xiv. The accuracy and vividness of both histories lead us to infer that no great interval followed before the recording of the events they contain. For instance, Eli is introduced in 1 Sa. i. 3 without comment, as one still vividly remembered. A close study of 2 Sa. ix.-xx. also compels us to see in its author either an eyewitness or one who possessed first-hand information.

The time was one of transition, both politically and spiritually. The theocracy under Moses and Joshua had been replaced by the conflicts recorded in Judges, and the way was now being prepared for the establishment of the monarchy. The spiritual history of these centuries is told in Ps. lxxviii. 65-72. God was leading up to the choice of a 'man after His own heart' to be the type and fore-runner of the messianic King. The ancient and less definite

[1] See E. Robertson, *Samuel and Saul*.

order of seers was giving way to the new and more regular order of prophets.

King David's reminiscences of his life as an outlaw, in particular, must have been supplied either by the king himself or by a close companion (1 Sa. xxiv. 3, 7, 22, xxvi. 6). This necessitates a date somewhere in the first quarter of the tenth century B.C.

ANALYSIS

1 Samuel

i.-iii.	Birth, novitiate and call of Samuel.
iv.-vii.	Conflict with Philistines; loss and return of the ark.
viii.-x.	Samuel judges Israel. Saul anointed as 'prince'.
xi.-xiv.	Saul's kingship confirmed. Victories over the Philistines.
xv.	Battle with Amalek. Saul's disobedience.
xvi.-xviii.	David anointed; his victory over Goliath and 'wise behaviour'.
xix.-xxiv.	David and Jonathan. David an outlaw.
xxv. 1.	Passing of Samuel.
xxv. 2-xxx.	David and Abigail. Retirement to Gath. Gradual eclipse of Saul.
xxxi.	Defeat and death of Saul and Jonathan.

2 Samuel

i.	David's lament over Saul and Jonathan.
ii.-v.	David proclaimed king at Hebron, and reigns in Jerusalem over all Israel.
vi.-x.	The ark brought to Zion. David's victories and magnanimity towards the house of Saul.
xi.-xiii.	David's sin and Nathan's rebuke. Flight of Absalom.
xiv.-xviii.	Absalom's revolt. David's flight. Death of Absalom.
xix.-xxi.	David's return and treatment of various persons.
xxii., xxiii.	Songs and deeds of triumph.
xxiv.	The census and the plague. The altar erected on the threshing-floor of Araunah.

CONTENTS

The book contains the chief incidents in the lives of Samuel, Saul and David, but passes over everything not related to the divine purpose. Each of these three men passes through a time of early training. Their three careers overlap one another. The story is told in just sufficient detail to enable us to trace the course of events that led to the final triumph. First come Samuel's early days (1 Sa. i.-vii.); then his prophetic work (viii.-xxv.). At the outset of this is the anointing of Saul and the events preceding his proclamation as king (viii.-x.). In the early days of Saul's reign comes the private anointing of David (xvi.). Then after the death, first of Samuel and then of Saul, the second book follows the story of David's reign (2 Sa. ii.-xxi.).

As the book opens we see Shiloh as the focal point of the national religion from which went forth the teaching of the law (see Ps. cv. 45) and to which the people came to sacrifice. Here was located the traditional priesthood, the tabernacle and the ark of God. Here the pious Elkanah and Hannah dedicated Samuel, if not as a Nazirite,[1] yet to be 'separated' to God. Such separation helped to recall the people to the simplicity of the Mosaic order of Israel's early days, with its clear-cut distinctiveness from the heathenism of the surrounding nations.

Under Samuel's leadership we see the growth of the prophetic order as he went 'in circuit' to judge the people (1 Sa. vii. 16, 17), and presided over the school of the prophets (xix. 18-24), in which men of God were kept in touch with Jehovah. It was Samuel who wrote down for the people the 'law of the kingdom' which he laid 'before the Lord' in Mizpah (1 Sa. x. 25 and cf. Dt. xvii. 14-20), so paving the way for the transition from the theocracy to the kingdom.

The establishment of David in the kingdom was accompanied (2 Sa. vii.) by the prophetic announcement of a line of kings to succeed him and of One whose dominion should be for ever, thus linking the patriarchal promise to Judah (Gn. xlix. 10) and the fulfilment on the first Christmas day (Lk. i. 69, ii. 11).

There are manifold signs throughout this book that the law of Moses, though never mentioned by this title, and though in partial abeyance, was in existence and not altogether forgotten. The day to which Dt. xviii. 18 looked forward had not yet come, but was approaching.

Thus we read of burnt offerings and peace offerings, and we can

[1] See under *Judges*, p. 162.

trace references to the laws of sacrifice (1 Sa. ii. 12-17, ix. 24, xv. 15, 22; 2 Sa. xxiv. 25). We read of the tabernacle, the ark between the cherubim, the incense and the shew-bread (1 Sa. ii. 22, 28, iv. 4, xxi. 4). There are references to Aaron and to the Levites (1 Sa. ii. 27, vi. 25; 2 Sa. xv. 24); to the laws of abstention from blood (1 Sa. xiv. 32) and fourfold reparation (2 Sa. xii. 6). The incidental nature of these references adds to their evidential value.

God is revealed as the prime author and originator of events, especially as concerns His servants, in the accomplishment of His purpose. As in Jdg. ii. 18, 'the Lord raised them up' (i.e. caused them to rise), so in 1 Sa. ii. 35, 'I will raise me up a faithful priest'; 1 Sa. ii. 8, 'He raiseth up the poor' (cf. Am. ii. 11). In each instance it is the same causative form of the verb that is used; the same word spoken so authoritatively by our Lord in the 'raising' of Jairus' daughter (Mk. v. 41).

The three basic attributes of justice, mercy and holiness are clearly illustrated in the book; 'kindness like that of God' (2 Sa. ix. 3, x. 2, iii. 8, ix. 1, 7; cf. 1 Sa. xx. 8); 'holiness' (1 Sa. ii. 2, xxi. 5); 'justice' (2 Sa. xxiii. 3).

It was for the moral law as representing the eternal verities in action that Samuel (and David) stood, and in the final break with Saul (1 Sa. xv.) is expressed in classic phrases the evangelical principle of obedience to that moral law as superior to a mere gesture of subservience in 'sacrifice'. Veneration for the ark as a sacred thing was no substitute for the moral law that it symbolized (1 Sa. iv. 5; 2 Sa. vi. 21).

THEMES FOR STUDY

1. Study the prayers here recorded and their answers.

2. See how the office of Christ as Prophet, Priest and King is foreshadowed and illustrated in these books.

3. Study how David was a type of Christ in his person, office, and life.

4. Note the following Psalms as illustrating various events in David's life: (a) xxiv., ci.; (b) xx., xxi., lx.; (c) xxxii., li.; (d) iii., iv., xxvi.-xxviii.

I and II KINGS

AUTHORSHIP, DATE AND CIRCUMSTANCES

JEWISH tradition claimed that Jeremiah was the author of 1 and 2 Kings, but of this there is no other evidence, and the second book goes on to a date too late for him to have been the author of the whole of it. The two books are treated as one in the Hebrew text, but divided in the LXX. There is a unity of treatment about them that suggests their having been compiled from various sources by one hand.

The sources named in the book of Kings, and to which the reader is referred for further information, are the books of the Acts of Solomon, the book of the Chronicles of the Kings of Israel (seventeen times), and the book of the Chronicles of the Kings of Judah (fifteen times). They appear to have related to buildings, wars, and political events, like the monuments which have been recovered belonging to Assyria and other nations. Many critics postulate also a collection of Elijah and Elisha narratives that was used as a separate source, but this can only be regarded as doubtful. Some, still more doubtfully, claim to be able to trace a separate source for each of these two prophets, as well as a book that may be called the 'Acts of Ahab'.

Most modern scholars give the end of the seventh century as the most probable date for the compiling of the books of Kings because the conduct of the kings appears to them to be judged in the light of the reforms carried out under Josiah. There are passages (e.g. 1 Ki. viii. 8) that imply that the temple, and perhaps the rest of Jerusalem, were still standing when the books were compiled, and this requires a date before the fall of Jerusalem in 586. The history of the southern kingdom, however, is taken beyond this time, down to the year 560, so that the last part of the second book may have been added a little later.

The books of Kings are closely linked with the books of Samuel, and continue the record that had been begun there, and complete the story of the Hebrew kingdoms.

ANALYSIS

1 Kings

i.-xi.	The accession and reign of Solomon.
xii.-xvi.	The divided kingdom and the accession of Ahab.
xvii.-xxii.	Elijah.

2 Kings

i.-ii. 11.	Elijah (continued).
ii. 12-xiii.	Elisha.
xiv.-xvii.	Decline and fall of the northern kingdom.
xviii.-xxiii.	Hezekiah to Josiah.
xxiv., xxv.	Last days of the kingdom of Judah.

CONTENTS

The writer solves skilfully the problem of writing the parallel
history of the northern and southern kingdoms. He begins with
the first king of Israel and continues to the end of his reign, then
begins the history of Judah and continues it to the end of the reign
of the last king who overlapped the reign of the first king of Israel.
So he turns from one to the other, giving all the time careful
time-notes indicating in what year of the reign of each northern
king the next king in the south began his reign, and vice versa.
He also gives details of the king's age when his reign began and
the name of his mother. All are agreed that we have here careful
and accurate history.

One of the most interesting characteristics of the books of Kings
is the writer's practice of giving at the end of most of the reigns a
verdict on them from a religious point of view. Sometimes it is a
wholly unfavourable verdict (e.g. 1 Ki. xv. 34), sometimes, but
not often, it is a wholly favourable one (e.g. 2 Ki. xviii. 4-7).
More often it is a favourable one with a saving clause (e.g.
2 Ki. xii. 2, 3). The faults that he most condemned were such
things as failure to abolish the high places and to conform to the
rules of right worship. Again and again of the evil kings of Israel
he says that they walked in the ways of Jeroboam the son of Nebat,
who made Israel to sin; whilst righteous kings of Judah are said
to follow in the steps of David (e.g. 1 Ki. xv. 11), so emphasizing
the theocratic character of David's line.

From the above it will be seen that although 1 and 2 Kings give
us accurate history, it is history written from the religious point of
view. It is noteworthy, for example, that whereas it appears from
external history that Omri was one of the most important of all
Israel's kings, he is dismissed here in half a chapter. This is not
because of a mistaken historical perspective, but because his reign
was of no great significance from the religious view-point of the
author. It is not his business to give an exact and complete
record of all that had taken place in Israel and Judah. The books
he used as his sources had set out to do that; but he makes his
selections from the point of view from which he writes.

The two books of Kings cover about four centuries, whereas the
two books of Samuel had covered only one. It follows that the
ground is covered much more quickly and less detail is given.
Yet there is little sense of haste, and clearly portrayed characters
emerge. There is a real sense of conflict between good and evil,
which comes to a head in the two crises, one in the north, when, on

Carmel, Elijah challenges the prophets of the Tyrian Baal, and one in the south, when Jehoiada preserves the life of the boy king Joash and overcomes Athaliah who has tried to introduce the Tyrian worship.

The period thus covered was one of great religious activity on the part of the godly minority of the nation, and these books give us the historical background of the work of the great eighth-century prophets and of Jeremiah. During this time prophecy became not only a matter of action on behalf of God, but a matter of detailed teaching and proclamation of His will. The appeal is now made to written documents to recall the people to God (2 Ki. xxii., xxiii.). During this period men like Amos, Hosea and Jeremiah, who are not even mentioned in these books, were doing their tremendous work of preaching the righteousness and love of God and His willingness to enter into a new covenant relationship with His people who had so repeatedly broken His old covenant. Were it not for these books of Kings, we should know almost nothing of the immediate background of the great religious revelations of those days.

THEMES FOR STUDY

1. Note carefully the prayers recorded in these books, their occasions, contents and the answers vouchsafed.

2. What warnings do the careers of the different kings afford as to the evil results which follow from friendship with the world and from compromise with false religion?

3. Compare and contrast the careers of Elijah and Elisha. What lessons do they teach as to our witness? Note the references to both in the Gospels.

4. What lessons are there for the church and nation in the reforms of Elijah, Joash, and Josiah?

5. What place had the building and worship of the temple as a preparation for the coming of Christ? Note Acts vii.; 1 Cor. iii. 16; 2 Cor. vi. 16; Rev. xi. 19, xv. 5, xxi. 22.

I and II CHRONICLES

AUTHORSHIP, DATE AND CIRCUMSTANCES

In the Hebrew Bible the books of Chronicles are one, and with Ezra-Nehemiah stand apart from the other historical books (or Former Prophets), and form a part of the Kethubim (Writings) or *Hagiographa*, the last section of the Hebrew canon, being placed at the end of these as the last book of the Hebrew Bible. The Hebrew title for them, the 'Words of Days', or 'Journals', is an allusion to their annalistic character, whilst the LXX description as 'Omissions' (*paraleipomena*) suggests the thought that they supplement Samuel and Kings. The name of 'Chronicles' was given to them by Jerome.

Their place in the *Hagiographa*, or 'sacred writings', is an indication that the point of view is religious rather than merely historical. The writer does not continue the history from the point at which it is left in 2 Kings, but covers the same historical period as 2 Samuel and 1 and 2 Kings. He does not, however, attempt to cover all the ground of these books, but selects those incidents that are of significance from a religious, and particularly from a priestly, point of view, and concentrates on the southern kingdom. In more than one way his book may be said to bear a relationship to the earlier historical books akin to the relationship of the 'spiritual' fourth Gospel, centred in Jerusalem, to the Synoptic Gospels.

The questions of authorship and date are wrapped up with the question of the unity of the books of Chronicles and Ezra-Nehemiah. It is thought that these books were originally a single work. The chief reasons for this view are as follows:

1. The last verses of 2 Chronicles are the same as the first verses of Ezra.

2. The point of view of the writer in both is priestly and shows great interest in the worship and ritual of the temple, in the Levites, and in the observance of the law.

3. The literary style of all these books is the same, and they all contain various genealogies and lists of names.

4. Hebrew tradition assigns this common authorship to Ezra.

None of these facts proves conclusively that Chronicles and Ezra-Nehemiah were compiled by the same writer, but taken together they do at least suggest that they come from the same period. The most we can say is that they were compiled by Ezra or some other writer, whose interests were more priestly than prophetic.

Chronicles and Ezra-Nehemiah have been variously dated. It has been urged that they bear traces of having been compiled in the Greek period (332 B.C. onwards), but the evidence for a date as late as this is slender. The verses (1 Ch. iii. 17-24) which carry on the pedigree of the descendants of David to the sixth generation after Zerubbabel, may be a later addition.

The sources used by the Chronicler appear to have been the Pentateuch, possibly the books of Samuel and Kings, Isaiah (2 Ch. xxvi. 22) the *Midrash* (R.V., 'commentary') on Kings (2 Ch. xxiv. 27) and on the prophet Iddo, and a number of collections of 'words' of various prophets to which he refers (1 Ch. xxix. 29; 2 Ch. ix. 29, etc.). These prophetic writings may also have been sources used in the compilation of the earlier historical books. The chronicler frequently mentions them by name, and refers the reader to them for further information.

The canonical sources, the only ones available for us to compare with the chronicler's work, are sometimes quoted word for word. There are notable omissions, and in general the chronicler confines himself to the history of the southern kingdom. He does this partly, no doubt, because the northern kingdom had ceased to exist many years before he wrote, partly because it was in the south that were found all those things in which he was most interested, centred on the temple and its ritual. Kittel claimed to have found traces of four stages in the compilation of the Chronicles, but there is an essential unity of outlook in them which makes this improbable.

Comparison of the books of Kings and Chronicles reveals a number of apparent discrepancies which, together with the later date of Chronicles, has led scholars to regard the books of Kings as the only really reliable historical source for the period. Many of these discrepancies are in figures and dates, and may be due to different modes of reckoning or to errors in copying manuscripts, for all who have had much transcribing to do know how much easier it is for mistakes in numbers to creep in than mistakes in words. Other differences appear to be due to a difference of aim, or to the fact that the chronicler has used at those points different sources. As is the case with the Gospels, the twofold account enlarges our understanding of the facts and confirms their historical character. A detailed account of these differences will be found in Keil's commentaries on Kings and Chronicles.

ANALYSIS

1 Chronicles

i.-ix. Genealogical summary.

x. Death of Saul.

xi.-xvi. David's accession, his mighty men, and the restoration of the ark.

xvii.-xxi. God's promise to David, his victories, and the numbering of the people.

CONTENTS

The books of Chronicles are in four main parts:

1. 1 Ch. i.-ix. Here we have a series of genealogies from the time of Adam, with historical notes interspersed. It may be noted that only the Davidic and high priestly lines are carried beyond the exile, to about the time of Ezra, and that the most copious registers belong to the three tribes of Judah, Levi, and Benjamin which formed the bulk of the returning exiles.

2. 1 Ch. x.-xxix. Chapter x. deals briefly with the death of Saul, and all the rest of this section deals with the reign of David. Many lists of names are included that are not found in 2 Samuel, and many of the interesting stories there told are omitted by the chronicler, who characteristically records those which show the strength of David's kingdom and those of interest from a priestly point of view.

3. 2 Ch. i.-ix. These chapters cover the reign of Solomon, and are largely concerned with the temple and its ritual.

4. 2 Ch. x.-xxxvi. These chapters deal with the history of the southern kingdom from the time of the disruption to the exile. No attempt is made to record the history of the northern kingdom, except where it touches the life of the southern kingdom, and even Elijah and Elisha are passed over except for one reference to Elijah (xxi. 12-15).

The chronicler brings out the consequence of the wavering devotion to the pure worship of Jehovah shown by the kings of Judah. He could have found many illustrations of this in the story of Israel, but he finds enough material in the history of Judah. Some kings have been faithful to Jehovah and some unfaithful. Unfaithfulness was followed by judgment, and faithfulness by blessing. Evil kings are denounced for their idolatry and offences against the law; the good kings are praised for walking in God's ways and turning the people's hearts to Him (2 Ch. xiv. 2-4, xxxiii. 3, 4).

The chronicler emphasizes the transcendence of God (1 Ch. xxix. 11-13). Yet this transcendent God is not detached from the world, but active in it. His eyes 'run to and fro throughout the whole earth, to shew Himself strong in the behalf of them whose heart is perfect toward him' (2 Ch. xvi. 9). Whatever kind of evil overtakes them, 'sword, judgment, or pestilence or famine', if they repent, repair to the house of God, and pray, God will hear and save them (2 Ch. vi. 24-31, xx. 9).

THEMES FOR STUDY

1. If you had to continue the list of the heroes of faith given in Heb. xi. into the days of the monarchy, which of the names would you single out from this book, and for what actions?

2. What do these books tell of the value and importance of worship and praise?

3. How was love for the house of God manifested by David and his successors?

4. What virtues and sins of leaders and people called forth God's blessing or punishment?

EZRA—NEHEMIAH

AUTHORSHIP, DATE AND CIRCUMSTANCES

THE books of Ezra and Nehemiah are a continuation of the books of Chronicles. In the Hebrew canon, Ezra and Nehemiah appear as one book, and they are treated as such here. The questions of authorship and date of all these books was discussed under 1 and 2 Chronicles (q.v.). The conclusion there was that Chronicles and Ezra-Nehemiah both came from the same school of thought and period, and were probably the work of the same compiler.

The author appears to have used the following sources:

1. *The Memoirs of Ezra.* Ezr. vii. 27-ix. 15 is in the first person, and other passages in the third person may be assumed to have been taken in the main from the same source.

2. *The Memoirs of Nehemiah.* The first seven chapters of Nehemiah and xiii. 4-31 are in the first person, and other parts of the book, while not in the first person, appear to be based on the personal memoirs of Nehemiah.

3. *Aramaic Documents.* Ezr. iv. 7b-vi. 18 and vii. 12-26 are in Aramaic. These passages are made up chiefly of official documents, correspondence with the Persian kings, and decrees issued by them. We know from the Elephantine Papyri that, under the Persian Empire, Aramaic was a language used for international correspondence. The compiler writes in Aramaic himself in these sections, even when he is not quoting from the official documents.

4. *Official Lists.* These include a list of the exiles who returned under Zerubbabel, which appears in Ezr. ii. 1-61 and, with some variations, in Ne. vii. 6-63. Other lists of names are in Ezr. x. 18-44 and in Ne. x. 1-27, xi. 4-xii. 26, xii. 32-42. Some of these lists appear to have formed part of the memoirs of Ezra and Nehemiah, others to have been incorporated separately by the compiler.

Some critics have raised the question whether the return from exile recorded in Ezr. i.-iv. really took place. They have urged that Cyrus' decree (Ezr. i. 2-4) is not likely to have been issued in that form by a Persian king, that Haggai and Zechariah mention no return, and that it was probably the Jews left in the land who rebuilt the temple, the chronicler having reconstructed the history from insufficient data according to his own ideas of what happened. This view does not find favour with a majority of scholars to-day. It is known that the Persian kings were tolerant of other religions, and one of the Elephantine Papyri written in 419 B.C. records that Darius II actually commanded the Jewish community at Yeb to celebrate certain Jewish feasts. It is also extremely unlikely that the Jews left in the land by Nebuchadnezzar would have been capable of rebuilding the temple, as they were the poorest of the nation, and, according to Ezk. xxxiii. 25 f., lacking in devotion to Jehovah. There is no real reason to deny that there was a return from exile in 537, as recorded in Ezra.

Another critical problem raised is as to which of the two central figures did his work first. The book as it stands speaks of the return of a large number of exiles under Ezra in 458 B.C. in the reign of Artaxerxes I, and of the appointment of Nehemiah as governor in 444 under the same king; a year or two later Ezra and Nehemiah appear together. In recent years some scholars have rejected the Biblical order of events, and claimed that Ezra did his work not before, but after, Nehemiah, and that the compiler put the work of Ezra and Nehemiah in the wrong order. None of the arguments used for this view has much weight.

1. The fact that Ezra does not appear in Nehemiah until viii. 1 may be due to his absence from Jerusalem during that time, or to his not having taken any part in the events described.

2. The reference in Ezr. ix. 9 to God's having given the people 'a wall in Judah and in Jerusalem' cannot be pressed to mean that the city wall had already been rebuilt. The word used may mean 'fence' or protection (see R.V. mg.).

3. It is said that the small numbers referred to in Ne. vii. 4 indicate a state of affairs likely to have preceded that described in Ezr. x. 1; but examination shows plainly that the latter passage does not refer to the normal state of affairs in Jerusalem, but to a congregation 'assembled out of Israel', when 'all the children of the captivity' had been commanded, on pain of forfeiting their property, to come to Jerusalem (Ezr. x. 1, 7 f., 13).

4. Finally, it is urged that, whereas Nehemiah was a contemporary of Eliashib the high priest, Ezra was a contemporary of his grandson Jehohanan (Ne. iii. 1, xii. 10 f., Ezr. x. 6). Ezra does not say, however, that Jehohanan was high priest at the time, but simply that Ezra 'went into the chamber of Jehohanan the son of Eliashib'. According to the Elephantine Papyri Jehohanan was high priest in 408 B.C., but he may have had a room at the temple as a young man, and have been sympathetic to the cause of Ezra in 458 B.C. His name would then be mentioned because of the interest of his having later become high priest.

It is in any event unlikely that one writing even a hundred years after the event, and having careful records as his sources, should make a mistake in a major matter of chronology of that kind.[1]

ANALYSIS

Ezra

i., ii. The return of exiles to rebuild the temple.
iii. The altar erected and the temple foundations laid.
iv. The work opposed and made to cease.
v. The work resumed.
vi. The temple completed.
vii., viii. Ezra's journey to Jerusalem.
ix., x. Reforms promoted by Ezra.

[1] For a fuller treatment of the whole problem see J. S. Wright, *The Date of Ezra's Coming to Jerusalem* (Tyndale Press).

G

Nehemiah

CONTENTS

There are three chief series of events recorded in Ezra-Nehemiah.

1. Ezr. i.-vi. tells of the return of a large party of exiles under Zerubbabel and Jeshua, and the rebuilding of the temple.

2. Ezr. vii.-x. tells of the return of a second large party under Ezra, and the promulgation of the law.

3. Nehemiah tells of the appointment of Nehemiah as governor, and his work of rebuilding the wall of Jerusalem, restoring the temple worship, and enforcing the law.

The books of Haggai and Zechariah should be read in conjunction with Ezra, and Malachi in conjunction with Nehemiah.

There are found in Ezra-Nehemiah as in Chronicles, the same love for the city of Jerusalem and interest in the worship and ritual of the temple and in the observance of the law. There are no miracles in these books, and little of the direct voice of God that we have become used to in earlier historical books ('the Lord said unto . . .'), yet they are no less religious. Ezra and Nehemiah are both conscious of 'the good hand of God' upon them (Ezr. vii. 6, 9, 28, viii. 18, 22, 31; Ne. ii. 8, 18). If they do not state that they hear the voice of God, they are conscious that it is He who has put into the hearts of men to do His will (Ezr. vii. 27; Ne. ii.

(2, vii. 5). There is throughout a sense of the vital importance
of the events recorded for the survival of the Jews and all that the
temple and the law stood for in the purpose of God, and it is with
evident joy and thankfulness that the writer tells his tale of
restoration and reform.

THEMES FOR STUDY

1. Study Ezra's love for the law and the house of God in
connection with Pss. cxix. and cxxii.

2. What principles of holiness and separation from the world
can be learned from these books?

3. Study Nehemiah as the man of action, the good man and
the man of prayer.

4. What principles found here will be of value for the work of
reconstruction to-day?

ESTHER

AUTHORSHIP, DATE AND CIRCUMSTANCES

THERE is no internal or external evidence as to who was the
author of the book of Esther, and little indication of its date.
The Ahasuerus of the story is Xerxes,[1] who was King of Persia
from 486 to 464 B.C. It is in the third year of his reign that the
story begins (i. 3), and in the seventh that he marries Esther
(ii. 16). When the book as we have it now was written we cannot
tell. Some have dated it as late as 130 B.C., thinking that its
intensely nationalistic point of view reflects the temper of the
Maccabean period. There is plenty of evidence, however, that
there was a strong nationalistic spirit among the Jews long before
the persecution under Antiochus Epiphanes fanned it into a
flame.

The language of the book of Esther (i. 2) suggests that it was
written some considerable time after the period it describes, but,
at the same time there is so much detail that would be of little
interest to succeeding centuries, particularly the notes of time and
detailed names of Mordecai's ancestors, Ahasuerus' ministers, and
Haman's sons, that we may be suspicious of any attempt to date it
very late. The writer is so skilled in composition and in the

---

[1] But see below.

economical use of words that he would have been unlikely to have introduced details that had no immediate bearing on the story itself unless they were of interest and importance to those for whom he wrote. The language of the book has affinities with that of the chronicler, and they probably belong to the same period.

The book of Esther, although the name of God is conspicuously absent, tells the story of a providential deliverance and provides the explanation of the annual celebration of the feast of Purim as observed by the Jews (ix. 26-32). The writer reassures the Jews that those who plot and work against them will not prosper, and tells his story with great dramatic skill. Attempts by some scholars to find the origin of the feast of Purim either in (1) Babylonian new year customs, (2) a Persian spring festival, or (3) a Zoroastrian feast for the dead, are indefensible on philological and historical grounds.

ANALYSIS

i.	Ahasuerus' feast. Divorce of Vashti.
ii.	Esther made queen. Mordecai detects a plot.
iii., iv.	Haman's promotion, and plan to destroy the Jews.
v.-vii.	Esther's intercession defeats the plot. Mordecai honoured. Haman executed.
viii.-x.	Advancement of Mordecai and deliverance of the Jews. The feast of Purim.

CONTENTS

The book of Esther is one continuous whole, a story that moves steadily to its dramatic climax. It begins with a description of a feast given by the King of Persia to his provincial nobles, which leads to the banishment of Queen Vashti, tells how Esther, a young Jewess, is chosen to be queen in her place, how Haman persuades the king to order the extermination of the Jews, and how the king, on Esther's intercession, reverses his decree against the Jews, so that the Jews are at last allowed to live in peace. The statement that Esther was made 'queen' must be taken to mean a queen. The chief, or legal queen, of Xerxes was Amestris, the daughter of a Persian general. Herodotus records that at this period Xerxes consoled himself for the defeats which his armies were suffering in Greece with the delights of his harem, and gives an account of his character and the extent of his kingdom which harmonizes with what we read in the book of Esther.

Olmstead, however, follows the LXX in identifying Ahasuerus with Artaxerxes II (404-355 B.C.), and adduces many facts from Gentile authors concerning his reign which fit in well with the Bible story.[1]

It is a remarkable fact that there is no mention of the name of God in the book of Esther, but it is remarkable also how effectively the idea of the providence of God is conveyed in the story without the name being mentioned. Various explanations of this have been offered, e.g. that the book was taken substantially from official records of the Persian kingdom (ii. 23, vi. 1), that it was omitted to avoid giving offence to Persian readers, or lest the sacred name should be profaned by being read by the heathen. Whatever the reason, the beauty of the writing and the value of its lessons remain. Some have condemned what they call the narrow nationalism of the book, but we must remember that the Jew had a philosophy of history founded upon his belief in the sovereignty of God, and the certainty that Israel was His chosen people. If that were so, then their survival was of more than national importance. Israel could not fulfil her divinely appointed mission in the world unless she received divine protection from her enemies in fulfilment of Isaiah's prophecy, 'No weapon that is formed against thee shall prosper' (Is. liv. 17). The tragic events of the second world war afford a modern illustration of this book, and remove the critical objection once raised that such wholesale murder of the Jews was 'improbable'.

THEMES FOR STUDY

1. Study the book of Esther as an illustration of two New Testament principles:

(i.) 'Whosoever exalteth himself shall be abased, and he that humbleth himself shall be exalted' (Lk. xiv. 11).

(ii.) 'We know that to them that love God all things work together for good, even to them that are called according to His purpose' (Rom. viii. 28, R.V.).

2. How can the message of the book of Esther on the treatment of minorities be applied to the present day?

3. What parallels to the life of Mordecai can be found in those of Joseph in Egypt and Daniel in Babylon?

[1] *History of Palestine and Syria*, pp. 611 ff.

CHAPTER XI

HEBREW POETRY

POETRY is the natural vehicle of thought when the emotions are stirred, and among the Hebrews it goes back to the earliest days (Gn. iv. 23, 24, ix. 25-27). So we find a song for the digging of a well (Nu. xxi. 17), songs of victory (Nu. xxi 27; Jdg. v.) and laments over loss (2 Sa. i. 17). The Psalms are *par excellence* the religious poetry of Israel, but Job, Proverbs, Canticles and Lamentations are also, in the main, poetical in form.

Hebrew poetry knows no rhyme, but is distinguished from prose by rhythm and metrical arrangement, by its special vocabulary and style, and by a characteristic feature known as *parallelism* which may be of three kinds.

1. *Synonymous*, where the second half of a verse repeats the content of the first, or nearly so, in different words (e.g. Nu. xxiii. 8 Ps. xxxvii. 2, 6, 10, 12).

2. *Antithetic*, where a contrast, or antithesis, is set out in the second clause (e.g. Ps. xxxvii. 9).

3. *Synthetic*, where the second part develops the thought in the first, either as a consequence or as an expansion (e.g. Pss. ii. 6 xxxvii. 4, 5, 13; Pr. xvi. 3, 5).

It is common to find just three main words making up the sense of one line, so giving a peculiar terseness of expression.[1]

Some poems take on an acrostic or alphabetical form, i.e. the lines (or sets of lines) begin with the successive letters of the Hebrew alphabet. The interval is one line in Pss. cxi., cxii.; two lines in Pss. xxv., xxxiv., cxlx.; Pr. xxxi. 10-31; La. iv.; three lines in La. i., ii., iii.; four lines in Pss. ix., x., xxxvii.; and sixteen lines in Ps. cxix. In the last named each couplet in the octrain begins with the characteristic letter.

There is a vigour and appropriateness in the original Hebrew which is not easily reproduced in translation; for example, the language in Ps. ii., which is rough and tumultuous in verses 1-3 becomes calm and majestic in the verses which follow.

The 'songs of Zion' were far-famed (Ps. cxxxvii. 3). The title

---

[1] C. F. Burney, *The Poetry of Our Lord*, has pointed out several instances where the sayings of Christ rendered into the original Aramaic exhibit this feature of poetic parallelism.

to the Psalms (q.v.) bear witness to the fact that they were sung to well-known tunes and musical accompaniment. The poetical form of the proverbs rendered them easy to memorize, and the poetry of Job and of the Song of Solomon are well adapted to their dramatic setting.

JOB

AUTHORSHIP, DATE AND CIRCUMSTANCES

THE question of authorship depends upon whether the book is to be regarded as a record of fact, as a dramatic parable, or as something between. Ancient tradition, though not without exception, accepted it as history and ascribed its authorship in the main to Moses.[1] In the Syriac Version the book of Job is placed between Deuteronomy and Joshua.

Luther reckoned it as 'real history', but thought that it owed the form of its composition to 'some pious, learned man'; Grotius said 'these things really happened, but are poetically expressed'. The symbolical numbers, the nature of the debate and the dramatic form, combine to confirm this opinion, that it is a didactic poem with a historical basis.

Some critics regard the speeches of Elihu as reflecting a later date than the remainder, but the language used does not suggest this. The speeches provide new elements, and 'prepare the way, by his description of God's majesty, for Jehovah's speech from the storm'.[2]

Luther and Delitzsch argued for the authorship of Solomon or of one of his contemporaries. In support of this contention J. H. Raven says:[3] 'The masterly and original way in which the questions of "wisdom" are dealt with in the book of Job precludes the idea of a late date when the Wisdom Literature had become formal and imitative.'

In all discussions of authorship and date it is important to distinguish between the age when it was written and the age when events described took place. That Job is an historical figure is implied in his description as being 'a man in the land of Uz' and in the references to him in Ezk. xiv. 14 and Jas. v. 11; and it is to be noted that none of the names in the book is symbolic. On the other hand, the author may well have lived centuries later and

---

[1] *Talmud, Ephrem Syrus* (fourth century A.D.).
[2] J. H. Raven, *Old Testament Introduction* (Fleming Revell).
[3] *Op. cit.*, p. 276.

may have clothed the original story in a poetical form to make it the occasion of a profound discussion on the problem of suffering. The patriarchal way of life presupposed in the book (e.g. wealth computed in cattle, Job sacrificing without a priest, etc.) persisted for many centuries alongside the development of higher forms of civilization, so that the times of the author and of the hero of the poems may be closer than some imagine.

The setting of the poem lies outside the borders of Israel. The location of Uz is generally believed to be in Edom (see 1 Ch. i. 42, and La. iv. 21). The characters are non-Israelites, but the problems are discussed from the Jewish standpoint. The Covenant-Name *Jehovah* is used only in the prose narratives at the beginning and ending of the book; Job himself, the three friends, and Elihu speak of God as *El, Eloah, Shaddai* and *Elohim,* names used in the patriarchal age, and indicative of an early origin.

The subject of the book is the perennial problem of the workings of the divine justice. This, in the author's day, was complicated by:

1. The doctrine that God metes out proportionate rewards and punishments in this life (cf. Pss. lxiv., lxxiii. 1-20, xxxvii. 25).

2. A purely negative conception of Sheol, the place of departed spirits (cf. Jb. xxx. 23; Pss. vi. 5, xxx. 9, lxxxviii. 11, 12).

3. A developed sense of the value and accountability of the individual with its demand for a more searching investigation of the facts of life.

The problem is stated elsewhere in Ec. viii. 14 and Je. xii. 1-3. The book of Job exposes the naïveté of the traditional solution and indicates a resolution of the problem at a deeper level.

ANALYSIS

i., ii.	Prologue. Two heavenly scenes, and the arrival of three friends.
iii.-xxxi.	Dialogue.

First Cycle, iii.-xiv.: Job—Eliphaz—Job—Bildad—Job—Zophar—Job. Conventional theories criticized.

Second Cycle, xv.-xxi.: Eliphaz—Job—Bildad—Job—Zophar—Job.

Third Cycle, xxii.-xxxi.: Eliphaz—Job—Bildad—Job.

CONTENTS

The book consists of a dialogue in verse with a prologue and epilogue in prose.

In the prologue (i., ii.) the combination of uprightness and material prosperity in the person of Job is seen to be an offence to Satan, the adversary of mankind, who, with the taunt on his lips, 'Doth Job fear God for nought?' (i. 9), is allowed by the Almighty to touch, first Job's property and then his person, thereby testing his adherence to God. Thus, as in Greek tragedy, the reader is shown the reason of Job's sufferings at the very beginning of the drama, and this gives particular poignancy to the subsequent attempts of Job's three friends, Elihu, and Job himself, to wrestle with the problem as to whether his sufferings were 'merited' or not.

In the dialogue (iii.-xxxi.) the three friends, Eliphaz the Temanite, Bildad the Shuhite, and Zophar the Naamathite, all starting from the same premiss, that great suffering presupposes great sin, try again and again to bring Job to a conviction of his guilt (e.g. Eliphaz, iv. 7, 8; Bildad, viii. 3; Zophar, xi. 20). But although Job at first accepts their premiss (he rejects it in xxi. 7-15), he cannot let go his integrity (see vi. 24, 25, 29, vii. 20, 21, xxiii. 11, 12, xxvii. 6, xxxi.). Even if he had sinned unwittingly (see Nu. xv. 22-31 for the distinction between sins of ignorance and sins done 'with a high hand', i.e. deliberately), a sin which merited such dire punishment as this could hardly have been committed in ignorance.

Here then is Job's dilemma. Either his good conscience must go, or else the goodness of God must go. Is Job more just than God? Is God Job's enemy? (xvi.). Why are there no courts of justice where Job can plead his cause before the Almighty? (xxiii. 3, 4). Why is there no arbiter ('daysman', ix. 33) who can lay his hands on both parties and bring about an understanding?

Meanwhile another thought has found a place in the discussion. It is that Job's sufferings are not punitive, but a means of testing his character, an echo from the heavenly scenes in the prologue.

This thought comes in the first speech of Eliphaz (v. 17). It re-appears in the speeches of Elihu (xxxiii. 15-18, xxxv. 9-11, xxxvi. 15). Job himself can never let go the conviction that God is his friend. Somehow, somewhere, somewhen, God will inter-vene and vindicate his servant. Faith pierces the clouds and the climax is reached in the matchless words of xix. 25, R.V.: 'I know that my Redeemer (avenger) liveth and that he shall stand up (for me) at the last. . . .'

The speeches of Jehovah (xxxviii.-xli.) confirm Job's insight into the goodness and greatness of God. He who created and sustains the world with all its wonders has not lost sight of suffering Job. He who made strong the hippopotamus (*behemoth*, xl. 15) and the crocodile (*leviathan*, xli. 1) is Himself strong in the behalf of a man who trusts Him in sincerity.

No direct answer is given to the problem of Job's sufferings. But the right attitude is shown, that of complete trust in God in spite of all incentives to the contrary (see xiii. 15a). Job has 'found Jehovah on his side, no more estranged from him than in the days of his former prosperity, but more intimately known' (Gray). And the way is prepared for the fuller revelation, viz., 'that the true reward of the just is not material prosperity, but eternal life in the presence of God' (Kissane).

In the epilogue, Job is restored to twice his former affluence, the double restoration of his goods being an indication of the overplus of God's goodness.

The book of Job is one of the Poetical Books, and here the mind of God in relation to individual human suffering is more clearly revealed than anywhere else in the Old Testament. 'It is our first, oldest statement of the never-ending problems of man's destiny and God's ways with him here in this earth. It is grand in its sincerity, in its simplicity, in its epic melody, and repose of reconcilement. There is nothing written, I think, in the Bible or out of it, of equal literary merit' (Carlyle). And as a *præparatio evangelica* the following words of J. B. Mozley[1] are in point: 'If the Jew was to accept a Messiah who was to lead a life of sorrow and abasement and to be crucified between thieves, it was necessary that it should be somewhere or other distinctly taught that virtue was not always rewarded here, and that therefore no argument could be drawn from affliction and ignominy against the person who suffered it.' It is but a step from this to the idea of vicarious suffering which is a feature of Is. liii. and to its fulfilment in Jesus Christ.

[1] *Essays*, II, 27.

The most striking verbal parallels with other Old Testament passages occur in vii. 17 (Ps. viii. 4); iii. 3-10 (Je. xx. 14-18); and xxviii. 28 (Pr. ix. 10). Scholars argue for dependence either way. In the New Testament 'the patience of Job' is referred to in Jas. v. 11, and v. 13 is quoted in 1 Cor. iii. 19. There are no other explicit references.

THEMES FOR STUDY

1. Trace the development of Job's thought, as given in his speeches, with special reference to his attitude to (a) God, (b) himself, (c) conventional theories about sin and suffering.

2. Contrast xxxviii. 2 with xlii. 7. What is referred to in each case and how can these statements be reconciled?

3. Paul (1 Cor. iii. 19) quotes Job v. 13 to illustrate the variety of human wisdom, and James (v. 11) uses the story of Job to illustrate the purpose and mercy of God. Study the book from these aspects.

4. Find quotations which show that suffering may be viewed as (a) retributive, (b) disciplinary, (c) a probation, and (d) leading to a deeper experience of God's mercy. In this connection look up any marginal references to the New Testament which may be given.

PSALMS

AUTHORSHIP, DATE AND CIRCUMSTANCES

The titles

1. *Names of authors.* Two-thirds of the Psalms have ascriptions of authorship prefixed to them. As these are reproduced in the LXX they must at least be older than 150 B.C., and as they are mainly found attached to the earlier (pre-exilic) Psalms, they are probably very ancient. They are as follows:

Moses, one (Ps. xc.); *David*, seventy-three (chiefly in Books I and II, see R.V.); *Solomon*, two (lxxii., cxxvii.); *Asaph*, twelve (l., lxxiii.-lxxxiii.); *the sons of Korah*, eleven (xlii.-xlix., lxxxiv., lxxxv., lxxxvii.); *Heman the Ezrahite*, one (lxxxviii.); *Ethan the Ezrahite*, one (lxxxix.).

Half of the Psalter is thus associated with David, and his name is often given to the whole collection. Radical critics, therefore, who deny that David wrote any Psalms at all, or who place them all in the post-exilic period (e.g. Duhm) are failing to recognize the strength of a very early tradition. In support of the antiquity of the greater part of the Psalter the following reasons can be urged.

(i.) Religious, or semi-religious poetry existed long before the time of David. Hymns are found in Egypt and Babylonia as early as the fifteenth century B.C., and in the Bible itself there are *the Song of the Well* (Nu. xxi. 17, 18), *the Song of Deborah* (Jdg. v.), and the *Oracles of Balaam* (Nu. xxiv.).

(ii.) David himself was well suited to be a Psalmist. See 1 Sa. xvi. 15-23; 2 Sa. i. 19-26 (the lament over Saul and Jonathan), and 2 Sa. iii. 33, 34. That he was a 'man of war' (1 Sa. xvi. 18) and guilty of grievous sins, in no way renders him unimaginative or incapable of deep feeling. 'The habit of refusing to admit complexity in the capacities of Bible characters is exceedingly hazardous and unsafe when history is so full of instances of the combination in one person of qualities the most diverse' (J. Robertson). In regard to the phrase 'the sweet psalmist of Israel' in 2 Sa. xxiii. 1, the R.V. margin should be noted.

(iii.) The early monarchy was a time of national revival like the Elizabethan age in England. The nation had withstood her enemies; trade was developing; the ark had now been brought to Jerusalem, and worship established there; the temple was about to be built. It would be surprising if no trace of this period were left in lyrical production.

(iv.) Many prophetic oracles are like the Psalms in form. 'These imitations of Psalmody by the prophets presuppose the existence of genuine Psalms at the time of their compositions' (Gressmann).

While not under obligation to accept every ascription, Davidic or otherwise, as authentic, we are not in a position to reject their evidence to the antiquity of those to which they are attached. In Hebrew the phrase 'of David' can mean 'belonging to' or 'for' David, and need not necessarily imply authorship, although this is generally the most satisfactory interpretation. Earlier Psalms seem in some cases to have been adapted and rearranged by later hands.

2. *History and description.* Together with the ascription of authorship, the titles often contain historical, descriptive, musical or liturgical notes. The accounts of the occasion of writing are sometimes illuminating (e.g. iii., xviii., li.); but sometimes they seem to throw little light on the composition. This latter fact, with

the obscurity of the reference, testifies to their age and genuineness.[1]

Of the descriptive words, 'Song' (e.g. xlv.) seems to be distinguished from 'Psalm' (e.g. xix.) as being *sung* without the aid of music. Some are described as 'Prayer' (e.g. xvii.) and one (cxlv.) as 'Praise'. *Maschil* implies meditation or instruction, *Michtam* a proclamation or epigram. (See also Pss. xxxviii., lxx., c.).

3. *Musical directions.* For *Selah* the LXX has *diapsalma*, i.e. a musical interlude, which is probably its right meaning. Some titles refer to musical instruments. *Neginoth* (e.g. iv.) means stringed instruments (cf. 1 Sa. xvi. 16, *play*), and *Nehiloth* (e.g. v.) wind instruments. *Alamoth* (Ps. xlvi.) probably means female voices, and *Sheminith* (octave) perhaps refers to men's voices. *Jeduthun* (see xxxix.) was the name of a choir leader in the time of David (1 Ch. xvi. 41), and several Psalms are dedicated to the 'chief musician'. Some of the directions are supposed to refer to well-known melodies (e.g. ix., lvi., lvii., Note A.V. and R.V. margins).[2]

Dates of compilation

The Psalms belong to the third section of the Hebrew Bible known as 'the Writings'. Because they stood first, the name 'Psalms' is often applied to the whole section (cf. Luke xxiv. 44, where the three sections of the Old Testament appear as 'The Law, the Prophets, and the Psalms'). The Psalter formed the hymn book of the Jewish people. Ps. xc., if Mosaic, may well be the oldest; cxxxvii. certainly dates from the period of the exile; lxxiv. and lxxix. are generally thought to be post-exilic. Behind their present arrangement may be discerned still older collections. The colophon at the end of lxxii. clearly refers to more than one Psalm.

The Jews divided the whole Psalter into five Books, viz., Book I, i.-xli.; Book II, xlii.-lxxii.; Book III, lxxiii.-lxxxix.; Book IV, xc.-cvi.; Book V, cvii.-cl. (see R.V.). Each of them ends with a doxology. Pss. i. and cl. form a fitting introduction and conclusion to the whole collection.

[1] See Kirkpatrick on Ps. vii.
[2] Some scholars think that these directions should form a postscript to the Psalm which *precedes*, and not the one which they now introduce (cf. Hab. iii. 19). In many cases this seems more apposite, e.g. the title of lvi. fits well verses 6, 7 of lv.

A recent commentator has suggested the following groups:

(i.) *The Davidic collection* (iii.-xli.). God is here, with a few exceptions, addressed as *Jehovah* (LORD).[1]

(ii.) *The mixed collection* (xlii.-lxxxix.). God is addressed more often as *Elohim* (God). The ascriptions 'of the sons of Korah', 'of David', 'of Asaph' may indicate still older collections (Pss. lxxxiv.-lxxxix. use chiefly *Jehovah*).

(iii.) *The Anonymous collection* (xc.-cl.). Uses *Jehovah*. Mostly liturgical Psalms for use in temple worship.[2]

Psalms i. and ii. are introductory and one Psalm is found in more than one collection and appears as xiv. and liii., with a change in the divine name.

Occasion and setting

Not all the Psalms were originally composed for use in public worship. They include meditations, didactic poems and historical recitals; in fact they have been called forth by a variety of circumstances, both personal and national.

It is not always clear whether the 'I' of the Psalmist is an individual or simply the spokesman of the worshipping community. The attempt to regard all Psalms as 'corporate' has not succeeded, but 'the community is never far off' (Montefiore).

Recent scholarship tends to regard the historical setting as being subsidiary to the liturgical expression of recurrent needs. In Dt. xxvi. a set form of words is prescribed for the Israelite who comes to offer the firstfruits to the Lord. Another such formula occurs in Dt. xxi. 7, 8. In the same way Ps. cxvi. may have been used by a man who, at one of the great festivals (see verse 14) had come to pay a vow after recovery from sickness, and Ps. cvii. by a number of people joining together in a comprehensive form of thanksgiving. Pss. cxiii.-cxviii., known as *The Great Hallel*, were sung at the three annual festivals of Passover, Tabernacles, and Pentecost, and constitute the 'hymn' referred to in Mt. xxvi. 30.

While welcoming the added light which this idea throws upon the growth of some of the Psalms, we need to remember that it is capable of only limited application. The Psalms display a freshness and originality which does not belong to stereotyped formulas. It seems evident that a large number originated in a personal setting and were subsequently gathered together for public use in the sanctuary and in the homes of the people.

[1] It is impossible to determine how far the use of the divine names is due to later editors.

[2] See Kirkpatrick, *Psalms*, pp. lv-lix.

In addition to the internal signs of previous collections already noticed there are suggestions of the formation of such collections in the time of David (1 Ch. xv. 16), Hezekiah (cf. Pr. xxv. 1), Ezra and Nehemiah (Ne. viii., ix.).

CONTENTS

The Psalms are a treasury of prayer and confession for private and public devotion. Through them countless thousands of God's saints, both Hebrew and Christian, have delighted to come into God's presence. God's people in times of emergency are drawn instinctively to Ps. xlvi. with its assurance that 'God is our refuge and strength'; their penitence is expressed in the words of Ps. li., their confidence in God's loving care in Ps. xxiii. It was in the language of the Psalms that Edward Wilson of the Antarctic expedition found the truest expression of his sense of awe amidst these scenes of desolate grandeur.

It may be asked why the Psalter, the official hymn book of one of the most exclusive communities in the world, has so lent itself to universal application. Lord Ernle (R. E. Prothero) supplies the answer in his fascinating book, *The Psalms in Human Life*. Here, he says, 'is painted for all time in fresh and unfading colours, the picture of the moral warfare of man . . . the revelation of a soul, deeply conscious of sin, seeking, in broken accents of shame and penitence and hope, to renew personal communion with God. It is this which gives to the Psalms their eternal truth'.

(a) The nature of God

God is approached indeed with reverence, but with a holy boldness which foreshadows the 'access' of New Testament times (Eph. iii. 12). His Name 'Jehovah' is known and loved; His character is proved and sure. 'Thy word is tried to the uttermost; therefore Thy servant loveth it' (cxix. 140, P.B.V.).

God is always a Person, and stands without a rival. 'The recurring phrase "the gods" is most probably only poetical language, only a concession to a usage of common speech' (W. E. Barnes). He is the sovereign Creator of the universe and acts directly on His creatures. There are for the Psalmist no 'laws of nature' possessing independent authority: God Himself controls directly the storm and the rain.

(b) God and man

To man God is the supreme Lord and King. He makes an ethical demand upon His people (cf. Ps. xv.). Morality is more important

than ritual (l.). At the same time He is a loving Father (ciii.).
Great emphasis is laid on His faithfulness (lxxxix. 1), His truth
(xxxi. 5), and His lovingkindness (xxxvi. 7). He may be approached without a mediator and intimately known—'my God'.
Sins are confessed with moving intensity (e.g. li. 4) and a deep
humility is in evidence throughout (e.g. viii. 4). Phrases implying
what may seem to us to be undue self-righteousness (e.g. xviii. 23)
are to be understood in a relative sense and as conveying the idea
of faithfulness rather than of perfection.

(c) God and Israel

With Israel Jehovah has entered into a covenant bond and many
Psalms are full of the mighty acts of the Lord on behalf of His
chosen people (xlviii., lxxvi., lxxviii., lxxxi., cv., cvi., cxiv.).
They are called to be witnesses of His power and goodness, but the
service of God is not to be confined to Israel alone (see lxvii. and
lxxxvii.). Egypt and Ethiopa shall stretch out their hands to Him,
Babylon, Philistia and Tyre shall acknowledge His sway.

(d) Rewards and punishments

Sin must be punished and virtue brings its own reward. But the
Psalmist is often acutely conscious of apparent injustices. Sometimes, as in Ps. xxxvii., he finds the solution in God's judgments
exercised in this life, but in Ps. lxxiii. he points towards a doctrine
of rewards and punishments after death (see especially verses
23-26), and to a fellowship with God which death cannot touch.
The doctrine of immortality is as yet a hope, rather than an
assured belief; nearness to God now enables the Psalmist to meet
all life's vicissitudes in the certainty that God will not forsake His
child (see xxxi., lxxvii., cxvi., cxxiv.).

(e) The imprecatory Psalms

With regard to those Psalms (e.g. lxix., cix.) which invoke God's
judgments upon the enemies of the writer or of his people the
following points should be noted.

1. The Psalmists are convinced of 'the absolute antithesis
between that which chooses for and against God' (A. Kuyper),
and speak out as God's champions in a world that has rebelled
against Him. Their plea for judgment is based upon God's
promises of protection and upon the righteousness of their cause
(Ps. lxxxiii., cxxxvii. 8); they abstain from avenging themselves,
and commit their cause to God.

2. They are clothed in the thought-forms of the people and the

age to which they belong. To the Hebrew mind all was personal, the sinner was identified with the sin, the man with his family, and the only way to purge a city from iniquity was to destroy the wicked.

3. Woes and imprecations are found in the New Testament as well as in the Old (Mt. xiii. 49, 50, xvi. 27, xxiii. 13-33; Jn. v. 29; Rom. vi. 23; Rev. vi. 10; xviii. 6). But in the old dispensation there was no clear light as to the future life or the gospel of redeeming love, and the justice demanded seemed to belong to this life. Our Lord sanctions the principle that a higher standard is required for Christians with this fuller light (Mt. v. 43, 44; cf. xix. 8).

(f) The Psalms in the New Testament

The Psalms were especially dear to the Lord Jesus. Their moving phrases were in His mind even on the Cross, for His last words come from xxxi. 5, and the cry, 'My God, why hast Thou forsaken Me?' is the opening phrase of xxii. The rest of that Psalm is as detailed a description of the sufferings of Calvary as may be found any where in Scripture. The Psalmists spake 'wiser than they knew' in this and similar passages (1 Pet. i. 10-14), the Holy Ghost, the real author of Scripture, illuminating their minds.

The messianic hope burns brightly in ii., xlv., lxxii. and cx. The Messiah is described as a mighty King enjoying the support of Israel's God. Other Psalms (xcvi.-c.) speak of His growing kingdom which reaches universal dimensions in xlvii.

(g) Subject classification

This is not exhaustive, and all such attempts at general classification must leave out of account the great diversity of interest and breadth of thought characteristic of so many of the Psalms.

1. *Prayer:* xvii., lxxxvi., xc., cii., cxlii.
2. *Praise:* viii., xix., lxxxi., xcii., xcv.-c., cxlv.-cl.
3. *Petition for deliverance:* vi., xvi., xxxviii., xxxix., xli.
4. *Confession of faith:* viii., xxxiii., xciv., civ.
5. *Confession of sin:* vi., xxxii., xxxviii., li., cii., cxxx., cxliii. (the penitential Psalms).
6. *Intercession:*
   For the King: xx., xxi., lxi.
   For Israel and the nations: lxvii.
   For the House of David: lxxxix.
   For Zion: cxxi., cxxii., cxxxii.

7. *Deprecation:* xxxv., lix., lxix., cix.

8. *Instruction:* xxxvii., xlv., xlix., lxxviii., ciii.-cvii.

9. *Meditation:* xlix., lxxiii., xciv.

10. *Exaltation of the Law:* xix., cxix.

11. *Expectation of the Messiah:* xvi., xxii., xxiv., xl., lxviii., lxix., cx., cxviii.

There are frequent quotations in the New Testament, both direct and indirect. Of the former the most important are:

Ps. ii. 7 (Acts xiii. 33, Heb. i. 5, Heb. v. 5); viii. 2 (Mt. xxi. 16); viii. 4, 5 (Heb. ii. 6, 7); xxii. 7, 8, 18 (Mt. xxvii. 35, 39-48); xxxi. 5 (Lk. xxiii. 46); xxxii. 1, 2 (Rom. iv. 6-8); xl. 6 (Heb. x. 5 ff.); xlv. 6 (Heb. i. 8, 9); cx. 1 (Mt. xxii. 44, Acts ii. 34, Heb. i. 13).

All these are associated with Christ as the fulfiller of Old Testament prophecy.

THEMES FOR STUDY

1. Using the subject classification above, draw out the teaching contained in the Psalms, subject by subject.

2. Study the teaching in the 'proper' Psalms for *Christmas* (xix., xlv., lxxxv., lxxxix., cx., cxxxii.), *Good Friday* (xxii., xl., liv., lxix., lxxxviii.), *Easter* (ii., lvii., cxl., cxiii., cxiv., cxviii.), *Ascension Day* (viii., xv., cviii., xxiv., xlvii.), and *Whitsunday* (xlviii., lxviii., civ., cxlv.) as prophetic of the events which these festivals commemorate.

3. Draw up a summary of the Christian faith as it is contained in the verses of the Psalms quoted in the New Testament (see above) as these are used by those who quote them.

4. Make a brief selection of verses which could be used for (1) prayer, (2) thanksgiving, (3) praise.

5. Show how each separate phrase in Lk. xxiv. 46-48 can be found predicted in the Psalms.

PROVERBS

AUTHORSHIP, DATE AND CIRCUMSTANCES

THE book of Proverbs consists of an introduction (i.-ix.) devoted to the praise of wisdom and exhortations to seek it, followed by a series of proverbs (x. 1, xxv. 1) and 'words of the wise' (xxii. 17, xxiv. 23).

It would appear from xxv. 1 that the men of Hezekiah, among whom Isaiah and Micah may have been included, had before them the collections contained in x. 1-xxiv. 34 to which they added xxv. 1-xxix. 27 at least. Whether the two last chapters were included then, or later, cannot be determined, nor is anything known of Agur and Lemuel who wrote or collected them. Neither can it be settled from i. 1 whether chapters i.-ix. are the work of Solomon, or of those who later completed the whole book. Keil asserts that chapters i.-xxix. display throughout one and the same historical background corresponding in every respect to the conditions of Solomon's reign, and so regards all as proceeding from Solomon himself.

In any case there is no reason to doubt that Solomon's name is rightly attached to the main body of proverbs, a selection which he may have been inspired to make from the three thousand mentioned in 1 Ki. iv. 32; though the possibility of their having been added to by the men of Hezekiah must not be ruled out. Proverbs existed long before Solomon's time (Nu. xxi. 27; 1 Sa. xiv. 13), and many of these in the book may have been words of ancient wisdom which he cast into this form.

It is evident that the book was not completed as we have it before the time of Hezekiah. Davidson regards the Hebrew style of the early chapters as that of the ninth century B.C., but linguistic arguments have led critics to such contradictory results,[1] that little reliance can be placed upon them.

ANALYSIS

i.-ix.	The value and attainment of true wisdom.
x.-xxii. 16.	'The proverbs of Solomon'.
xii. 17-xxiv.	'Words of the wise'.
xxv.-xxix.	Collection by the men of Hezekiah.
xxx.	Proverbs of Agur.
xxxi.	Proverbs of Lemuel. The virtuous woman.

CONTENTS

The Hebrew word for proverb (*mashal*) means a comparison or generalization. The proverbs in chapters x.-xxiv. are mainly couplets in antithetic form, terse maxims of one verse only, containing a moral truth or piece of practical wisdom illustrated by

---

[1] Eichhorn ascribes the book to the tenth, Hitzig to the ninth, Ewald to the sixth century B.C.

a simile. The word could also be applied to a parable (Nu. xxiii. 7; Ps. xlix. 4; Ezk. xvii. 2) in which the lesson to be drawn from the simile was left unexplained. In the later chapters many of the proverbs extend to two or four verses. In chapter xxxi. the last twenty-two verses are in the form of an acrostic (like Ps. cxix.) the verses beginning with the letters of the Hebrew alphabet in order.

The praise of wisdom in chapters i.-ix. might also be regarded as an extension of the 'proverb'. It rises to wonderful heights and the Christian reader feels that the author was inspired to give expression to thoughts which would find their fulfilment in Him who is both the wisdom and power of God (cf. Pr. viii. 22-31 with Jn. i. 1-5, xvii. 5; Col. i. 15-17).

The author declares that his aim is to give knowledge and discretion (i. 4). As the Psalms are a handbook of devotion, the proverbs afford a guide to practical ethics. In applying them it should be remembered:

1. That 'the fear of the Lord' must come first (i. 7, xiv. 27 xxiii. 17); only in the strength that He gives can they be put into practice;

2. That they are not unlimited in range, and rules may have exceptions; and

3. That they are best illustrated by examples drawn from the abundant biographical material which the Bible supplies.

There are some notable quotations from this book in the New Testament (see Rom. iii. 15, xii. 16, 20; Ja. iv. 6; 1 Pet. iv. 18 2 Pet. ii. 22).

THEMES FOR STUDY

1. What guidance for his work with the young can the modern teacher derive from this book?

2. Study the passages in which 'the Lord' is mentioned, and collect their teaching.

3. Collect passages which speak of (i.) wisdom and the wise man, (ii.) the fool and scorner, (iii.) the sluggard. Summarize the teaching.

4. Collect passages, especially from chapters i.-ix., which seem to foreshadow the wisdom incarnate in Christ.

5. What light do the life and character of king Solomon throw on this book?

ECCLESIASTES

AUTHORSHIP, DATE AND CIRCUMSTANCES

THE Hebrew name of the book is *Qoheleth,* which means the con-
vener of, or a speaker at, an 'assembly'. *Ecclesiastes* is the Greek
equivalent of this, and 'The Preacher', though not quite the same,
sufficiently gives the sense. In the introductory section the author
speaks through the mouth of Solomon, who though not named is
clearly intended (i. 1), but further examination leaves it doubtful
whether Solomon claims to be the author of the whole book, and
makes it appear rather that the opening section is an ideal
presentation of Solomon's outlook used to introduce what follows.

The expression 'I was king' (i. 12) implies a backward look, the
added words 'in Jerusalem' and some other phrases (e.g. i. 16)
might point to a knowledge of the divided kingdom; and some of
the references to kings, princes, and oppressive rulers would be
more natural after the monarchy had run its course (iv. 13, 14,
v. 16, 17). It lacks such personal notes as might be expected if it
had been written by King Solomon in his old age and in the spirit
of repentance, as some have maintained. Nevertheless, the two
opening chapters may be based on some ancient memoirs such as
the 'book of the Acts of Solomon' (1 Ki. xi. 41), or the writings
of contemporary prophets (2 Ch. ix. 29). A curious Talmudic
tradition includes Proverbs, Ecclesiastes and Canticles among
books written by 'Hezekiah and his company'. (See Pr. xxv. 1.)

If, then, with Hengstenberg, C. H. H. Wright, and other conservative scholars, we look for an author other than Solomon, the
date becomes a matter of conjecture. It must be earlier than
200 B.C. because it was included in the canon and mentioned in
Ecclesiasticus. The style of the Hebrew is similar to that of the
post-exilic writings, and the strain of pessimism which runs through
the book would fit in with the time of the return.

ANALYSIS

i., ii.   The vanity of all things 'under the sun', novelty,
          pleasure or the results of labour; yet God grants the
          good man wisdom, knowledge and joy.

iii.-vi. Vanity is increased by oppression and envy, and by the
          shadow of death over all. God's gifts should be
          enjoyed, but not be made the aim of life.

vii.-x. Wisdom is better than folly, and the fear of God brings a sure reward. God's works are unsearchable.

xi., xii. Childhood and youth end in old age and death. The ultimate conclusion: Fear God and keep His commandments.

CONTENTS

In order to understand the message of this profoundly illuminating book, the writer's outlook and method must be clearly envisaged. These can be found in the preface (cf. Rom. viii. 20), in the conclusion (xii. 13, 14; cf. Mt. xix. 17), and in the refrains which run through the book; the 'vanity' of all things 'under the sun', the lessons of experience 'perceived', and the ways of God past 'finding out'. The author sets himself to consider one after another the objects of desire which man sets before himself namely, mirth, pleasure, labour, the acquisition of wealth or learning; and he finds that all that is 'under the sun', even things good and wise in themselves, end in 'vanity and vexation of spirit'. By 'under the sun' he means all that the man of the world seeks in this present life here below, regardless of its end in death, and of God above.

In the course of his spiritual explorations he notes many things which are 'better', and of value in their place, even in this life: the moderate enjoyment of God's good gifts (iii. 13, v. 18, 19, viii. 15, ix. 7-10), a tranquil care-free spirit (iv. 6), a righteous life (iii. 12, 22), and the wisdom, knowledge and joy which are God's reward to the good man (ii. 24-26). Like Job, he finds much in life that he cannot explain, and is often baffled in seeking to understand the ways of God, yet he is sure that God will vindicate His righteousness in the end.

Side by side with pithy sentences of wordly wisdom there are recurrent references to Him who is not 'under the sun', but God over all, seated in His high and holy place.

So by an experimental method of induction, illuminated by upward glances of faith, he reaches his grand conclusion that no mundane object can secure happiness, and that the whole duty of man is to fear God and keep His commandments, remembering man's responsibility to Him.[1]

It is only a shallow criticism that would see in its contrasts a variety of authors, one extolling sensual pleasure, another

[1] See article, 'Interpretation of Ecclesiastes', by the Rev. J. S. Wright in Evangelical Quarterly, XVIII (1946) for a fuller treatment of the contents of this book.

wisdom, and a third piety. It is all of a piece, one grand, if enigmatic, whole; and life itself contains contradictions, puzzles and disappointments in plenty when the 'fear of God' is left out. Whether Solomon be author or not, his life and that of his son Rehoboam taken together afford a striking commentary on this unique book, and another can be found in Bunyan's picture of Vanity Fair in *Pilgrim's Progress*. When read in its true light it affords a grand arraignment of the materialistic outlook which dominates so much of modern life and literature, and contains a much needed lesson for the Christian who is tempted to seek satisfaction in the things which this world can offer, rather than in the fulness of life which Christ alone can bestow.

In the parable of the Rich Fool, Christ teaches the same lesson of the need of being 'rich towards God', and almost in the very words of the Preacher (Ec. vi. 2, viii. 15, xii. 14), while Paul develops further the same theme in Rom. viii. 18-25.

THEMES FOR STUDY

1. Make a list of all the 'better' things which are here detailed. How do you interpret the still better things of Heb. xi. 40?

2. Supposing the book to be addressed by an old man to a young one, how relevant do you consider it to be for modern youth?

3. Note all the references to God, and see how they form a commentary on Rom. xi. 33, 34, xii. 1, 2.

4. Find parallels between Ecclesiastes and the Sermon on the Mount.

5. Summarize the main teaching of this book and compare it with the fuller revelation in the New Testament of the Christian outlook on life.

THE SONG OF SOLOMON

AUTHORSHIP, DATE AND CIRCUMSTANCES

THE heading and uniform ancient tradition attribute the authorship to Solomon, the title 'Song of Songs' (R.V.) meaning that of all the songs he wrote (1 Ki. iv. 32) this was the most excellent.

There is good reason to believe that it belongs to the Solomonic period. Its poetry is acknowledged to be exquisite, and competent scholars regard the language and style as that of the golden age of Hebrew literature. Of the many rare words found in it some are

the names of choice plants or articles of commerce which may have
been introduced by the intercourse with foreign nations under the
great king. Others may be northern provincialisms, for the place-
names show that the author was well acquainted with the northern
regions and especially the Lebanon district. The references to the
shields in the tower of David (iv. 4) to Heshbon (vii. 4), which
later came under the power of Moab (Is. xv. 4), and Tirzah
(vi. 4), which lost its glory in the time of Omri,[1] all favour an
early date.

The view of some critics that it is a collection of ballads may be
dismissed as sufficiently met by that of others who emphasize its
unity of plan as evidenced, for example, by its recurrent phrases
(ii. 7, iii. 5, viii. 4; ii. 16, vi. 3, vii. 10; ii. 6, vi. 10, viii. 5) and
by its well marked sections. In the Hebrew canon its place is
among the *Kethubim* or *Writings*, where it is preceded by Psalms,
Proverbs and Job, and followed by Ruth; which indicates that it
was then regarded as among the earlier books.

As one reads the song, Solomon appears to be rather subject
than author, and an ingenious conjecture[2] is that it was composed
by a prophet in Solomon's reign and presented to the erring king
in the hope of winning him back to a pure life. On the other hand,
the love of flowers and spices, the marked resemblance in thought
and diction to the book of Proverbs, and some of the characteristics noted above point in the direction of Solomon's authorship.
The Jews believed that he wrote the Song in his early youth,
Proverbs in middle life, and Ecclesiastes in old age.

ANALYSIS

i. 2-ii. 7.	In Solomon's garden. The bride searches for and finds the king.
ii. 8-iii. 5.	The bride alone recalling two past experiences.
iii. 6-v. 1.	Jerusalem. The royal pageant approaches, the espousals and banquet.
v. 2-vi. 9.	The palace. The bride describes how (? in a dream) the bridegroom was lost and returned.
vi. 10-viii. 4.	Solomon's park at Etam. The lovely but modest bride is admired by her companions, and visited by the king.
viii. 5-14.	The bride's rustic home. The bridal pair together.

[1] The discovery of the site of Tirzah by the French Biblical School of
Archeology in Palestine was reported in the daily Press of October 18th, 1946
[2] See article in Smith's *Dictionary of the Bible*.

CONTENTS

(a) Plan

The book is cast in the form of an idyllic drama, and can be understood only as this is borne in mind. It consists entirely of the speeches of the various speakers or *dramatis personae*, of whom Solomon and the bride are the chief. There are also the 'daughters of Jerusalem', the 'brothers' of the bride, and others standing by. There is no narrative or description; the scenes and the speakers can be judged only by the words. (The Hebrew can indicate both the number and gender of the person addressed in a way which cannot easily be expressed in the English translation.)

The six sections into which the analysis divides the book show the general plan, and the headings in the A.V. indicate who are the speakers. A list of these with the verses at which their words begin is here given: (i. 2) bride, (i. 8) companions, (i. 9) Solomon, (i. 12) bride, (i. 15) Solomon, (i. 16) bride, (ii. 2) Solomon, (ii. 3) bride, (ii. 15) brothers, (iii. 6, 7, 9), three citizens, (iv. 1) Solomon, (iv. 16) bride, (v. 1) Solomon, (v. 2) bride, (v. 9) companions, (v. 10) bride, (vi. 1) companions, (vi. 2) bride, (vi. 4) Solomon, (vi. 10) companions, (vi. 11) bride, (vi. 13a) companions, (vi. 13b) bride, (vii. 1) Solomon, (vii. 10) bride, (viii. 5a) villager, (viii. 5b) Solomon, (viii. 6) bride, (viii. 8) brothers, (viii. 10) bride, (viii. 13) Solomon, (viii. 14) bride.

(b) Interpretation

The bride is called Shulamith, which may mean 'daughter of peace' corresponding to Solomon the 'prince of peace', or may mean the 'Shulamite', denoting her place of origin. The idyllic form of the book is against too literal an interpretation. From early times the Jews saw in it a picture of Jehovah's love for His people. Its idyllic picture of mutual love and devotion certainly affords a beautiful picture of human love; but also of the divine. In the Old Testament God condescended to appear as a bridegroom (Is. lxii. 5; Je. iii. 1; Ezk. xvi. 8), and Jesus Christ adopted the same figure (Mt. ix. 15, xxii. 2, xxv. 1), which was elaborated in the apostolic teaching to denote the relationship between Christ and the church (Eph. v. 23-32; Rev. xxi. 9).

We therefore cannot but apply this book in a similar sense. Origen said that the contents of Ecclesiastes had a natural application, Proverbs a moral, and Solomon's Song a mystical; and Christians since have delighted in the thoughts here suggested of the church as the garden of the Lord, and as the bride seeking and finding Him whom her soul loveth, and delighting in His presence. 'The experimental knowledge of Christ's loveliness and the believer's love, is the best commentary on the whole of this allegorical song' (Archbishop Leighton).

THEMES FOR STUDY

1. Work out the application of the message interpreted as referring to the love of Jehovah for Israel, its condescension, constancy and completeness.

2. Having in mind Rev. xxii. 17, 20, note all the invitations to 'come', and apply to Christ and the church.

3. Find parallels in this book to Ps. xlv. and Eph. v. 23-32.

HEBREW PROPHECY, I: ISAIAH TO DANIEL

THE PROPHETS

PROPHECY was an element in Sumerian and Accadian religion, and prophetic ecstasy among them may have possessed some external features akin to its manifestation among the prophets of Israel. But the latter presented a phenomenon unique in the history of the world in the religious and moral content of their messages, and in the uprightness and fearlessness of their characters.

(a) The men

The Hebrew name for prophet, *nabi* (Gk. *prophetes*), is thought to be connected with a root meaning 'to announce', and Augustine calls the prophet 'the announcer to men of the words of God'. They were also called 'seers' (*roeh*, 1 Sa. ix. 9), as being endowed with divine powers of insight and foresight, and 'men of God' (2 Ki. iv., viii.). Conscious of weakness and sinfulness in themselves (Ex. iv. 13; Is. vi. 5; Je. i. 6; Am. vii. 14), they stand as men coming from the immediate presence of God, 'charged with strict and definite orders from Him' as to the word they should proclaim. They are impelled by an irresistible power to undertake a 'strange, intense, uncertain and yet mysteriously well-planned service' (Barth). No less than the apostles who succeeded them, they were 'sent forth' by God (cf. Mt. xxiii. 34; Lk. xi. 49; Rev. xix. 10, xxii. 6). In the Old Testament the expression 'to prophesy' is used in a wide sense, being applied also to the elders appointed by Moses (Nu. xi.) and to the singers under Asaph (1 Ch. xxv. 1). Samuel instituted a 'company' of prophets (1 Sa. x. 5, xix. 20) where the 'sons of the prophets' seem to have been taught in the law and in psalmody, their singing being accompanied by ecstatic exercises. These exercises occasionally took strange forms (see 1 Sa. xix. 23 f. and cf. Je. xxix. 26), but it would be wrong to infer from a few instances that frenzied excitement was a necessary, or even the usual, accompaniment of Jewish prophecy in its earliest form.

[1] See also Chapter XIV, *The Messianic Hope.*

(b) The function

The function of the prophets was two-fold; to the men of their own day they were 'impassioned seers of spiritual truth and preachers of religion' (Sanday); to succeeding generations their writings became the medium of God's revelation. They boldly rebuked vice, denounced idolatry and superstition, and exposed the hollowness of ceremonial when divorced from 'judgment and mercy', and their predictions came to pass. Our Lord summed up their teaching in the golden rule (Mt. vii. 12) and in love to God and man (Mt. xxii. 40). They stand in sharp contrast with the prophets of Baal and the 'false prophets' (Dt. xiii. 1-5; 1 Ki. xviii.; Je. xxiii., xxviii.; Mi. iii. 5; Zc. xiii. 2) who preached peace when there was no peace, and whose predictions failed.

Mingled with their ethical teaching are found predictions of future events which they were commissioned to proclaim. These do not take the form of magical acts of second sight, but are put forward as part of the divine plan and purpose, the necessary consequence of God's character and moral government of the world. Frequently they are framed in general terms of blessing or of judgment, as in the oft-repeated statement that God will deliver rebellious Israel into the hands of their enemies, and that, for His name's sake, He will gather again a faithful remnant (Dt. xxx.; Is. vi. 9-13). At other times they are startlingly definite; for example, the prediction of the seventy years' captivity (Je. xxv. 8-14; Mi. iii. 12, iv. 10), and that of the sufferings of the Messiah (Is. liii.).

Some predictions are *conditional* upon the future conduct of those whom they concern, and may be taken rather as warnings leading men to repentance (Jon. iii.). Other prophecies have a *double reference*, first to an immediate fulfilment in the prophet's own time, as is apparent in the case of Is. vii. 3-9, and then to an event far beyond the prophet's own ken, yet seeming to rise out of the present circumstances, as when, in a landscape, ranges of distant hills constitute one picture with the foreground. (See Is. vii. 1-14 and Mt. i. 23; Is. xl. 3 and Mk. i. 2; Dn. vii. 13 and Mk. xiv. 62).

THE PROPHETIC WRITINGS

The book of Jeremiah contains some account of how the prophecies were committed to writing, and how the prophet himself was led to arrange them.[1] Whilst some allowance may be made for

---

[1] See p. 222.

revision by other hands, it will be safe to assume that, in general, the Scriptures as we have them came substantially from those whose names they bear. When we bear in mind the references in the New Testament, which all rest upon the *written* word (Acts iii. 18-22, xiii. 32-43; 2 Pet. i. 19-21) we are justified in believing that the Holy Spirit not only 'spake by the prophets', but guided them in the selection of what they recorded.

In the Old Testament, history and prophecy are very closely interwoven[1] as becomes a revelation from the Living God. The great events of Israel's history, the call of Abraham, the Exodus, the Davidic kingdom, the building of the temple, the sufferings of the exile and the experiences of the return, were as much a divine preparation for the coming of the Son of God, as were the teaching of the prophets and their messianic predictions. From early times the historical records were kept by prophets (1 Ch. xxix. 29), and, when the Jewish canon came to be formed, the historical books were placed before the prophetical and termed the *Former Prophets*.

THE PROPHETIC TEACHING

From the first, prophets and priests like Moses and Aaron existed side by side, distinct in function but united in their teaching. It was the part of the priest to teach the holiness of God dwelling in the midst of His people by the lessons of ceremonial cleanness, and to emphasize His claims upon their lives and His grace towards their trespasses through the offering of the sacrifices ordained by the law. The prophets equally declared the holiness of God, and proclaimed Him as ruler and judge, teaching the same lessons of His mercy and truth by direct precept, by the lessons of past and present history, and by warnings and promises regarding the future.

These two streams of thought, both issuing from a fountain as high up as the very origin of the nation, ran side by side down the whole history of the people.[2] It is therefore a mistake to speak of 'prophetic' and 'priestly' religion either as in contrast, or in succession the one to the other. True, the prophets find fault with the priests, but it is for abusing or neglecting their functions, not for fulfilling them (1 Sa. ii. 28, 29; Ho. iv. 6). When Isaiah lifts up his voice against empty ceremonial it is not against the oblation itself, but the *vanity* of it that he inveighs (i. 13), as also

[1] See p. 154.
[2] Davidson, *Ezekiel*, p. liv.

in regard to the sabbath, the appointed feasts, and prayer
(i. 13-15). So Jeremiah, himself a priest, honoured the sabbath,
the temple and its sacrifices (xvii. 24-27), and for that very reason
could not bear to see it made a place for commerce and idolatry
(vii. 11; cf. Mk. xi. 17).

Their complaint against the priests is not for innovations
regarding the temple worship, but that they had been given a law
which they had failed to study or to keep (Ho. iv. 6, viii. 12;
Is. i. 10); they rejected the law of Jehovah and despised His word
(Is. v. 24). It is evident from the prophetic teaching that the 'law
of Jehovah' was regarded as an ancient law, once kept but now
too often neglected. They do not call the people to enter on new
paths, but they re-call them to walk in the old ones (Je. vi. 16).
They plead with them to 'return' to the Lord (Ho. xiv. 1; cf
Am. iv. 6-13) from whom they have 'backslidden' (Ho. xiv. 4;
Je. ii. 5-7), and whom together with His law, they have 'forsaken'
(1 Ki. xi. 33; Is. i. 4; Je. ix. 13).

The prophets, true to the historic sense of God's revelation,
constantly make their appeal to the past (1 Sa. xii. 6-11; Am. ii.
9-11; Mi. vi. 3-5; Ho. xii. 2-5); and far from seeing in it a degraded
religious state which they have now outgrown, they look back upon
it as a time of righteous judgment and God's favour (Is. i. 26,
v. 2; Je. ii. 2, 3).

They do not profess to proclaim, as some suggest, any new truth
about Jehovah, but that He is the same from the beginning of their
race, the God of Abraham, Isaac, and Jacob (Is. xxix. 22; Mi.
vii. 20), whose covenant-love (*chesed*)[1] began with them (Gn.
xxiv. 27, xlvii. 29, *kindly*), was revealed afresh to Moses (Ex.
xxxiv. 6), praised by David (Pss. xxv. 6, 10, xl. 11) and Solomon
(1 Ki. viii. 23), and recorded by the earlier and later prophets
(Ho. ii. 19; Is. iv. 2; Mi. vii. 20; Is. xvi. 5, lv. 3; Je. ix. 24; Dn. ix.
4; Ne. ix. 7 ff.). This Jehovah, whom they served from time im-
memorial, rules the nations (Am. ix. 7), guides the stars in their
courses (Am. v. 8), and displayed His power by the deliverance
of His people from Egypt (Ho. xi. 1, xii. 9; Hg. ii. 5).

In order to appreciate to the full the teaching of the prophets
each should be read in the light of contemporary writings and
events, and of New Testament references. We may distinguish the
following stages:

1. Prophecy first appears in the Pentateuch (Gn. xlix., Nu.

---

[1] On the close connection of this word, rendered in A.V. 'mercy', 'kindness'
and 'lovingkindness', with the covenant, see Snaith, *Distinctive Ideas of the Old
Testament*, Ch. V.

xxii.), and Deuteronomy in particular contains those features of exhortation and prediction which appear in the latter prophets.

2. In the early days of the monarchy the revelation of truth and the historical manifestation of God's purposes were communicated through Samuel, Nathan, Gad, Elijah and Elisha, with others (see 1 and 2 Sa.; 1 Ki. i.-xi.; 1 Ch., 2 Ch. i.-xi.).

3. The Assyrian period[1] produced the books of Joel, Isaiah, Micah, and Nahum, in relation to Judah, and Jonah, Amos and Hosea in Israel. (See 1 Ki. xii.-2 Ki. xix.; 2 Ch. xii.-xxx.)

4. In the Babylonian period[2] come Zephaniah, Habakkuk, Jeremiah, Obadiah, and Ezekiel (2 Ki. xx.-xxv.; 2 Ch. xxxii.-xxxvi.).

5. From the captivity to the end of the Old Testament we have Daniel, Haggai, Zechariah, and Malachi.[3]

When, after patient study, it is possible to survey the whole field of Old Testament history and prophecy in the light thrown back upon it by the Christian revelation, the grandeur of God's redemptive scheme becomes visible. The calling and election of Israel is seen, from the earliest days, against the background of Jehovah's universal rule. The true, spiritual meaning of the ancient law is constantly reasserted, and the inward and spiritual nature of the covenant becomes clearer, till, finally, the coming of Messiah, His sufferings and victory, are plainly foretold. It is evident that these prophecies came not by the will of men, but as the writers were borne along by the Holy Ghost (2 Pet. i. 21).

ISAIAH

AUTHORSHIP, DATE AND CIRCUMSTANCES

ABOUT no book in the Bible have more diverse views been expressed, or with greater assurance, than concerning Isaiah. All critics agree that Isaiah wrote some of the book, and some assert that he wrote all of it; some divide it among two, others among three, and others among many authors.

Dr. Driver assigns chapters xl.-lxvi. to one great prophet of the exile, giving as reasons:

1. The different standpoint adopted;
2. The difference of style; and
3. The difference of the theological outlook.

---

[1] See p. 98.
[2] See p. 100.
[3] See Chapter X under *Ezra* and *Nehemiah*.

Others (from Duhm onwards) divide the book into three, giving xl-lv. (Deutero-Isaiah) to an exilic, and lvi.-lxvi. (Trito-Isaiah) to a post-exilic writer, and this is to-day the more popular hypothesis. The reasons given are conflicting and sometimes contradictory, but have in common an unwillingness to admit the predictive character of the later chapters. The following considerations will show that, whereas some of the arguments in favour of more than one author may be strong, those in favour of the unity of the whole book are stronger.

External evidence

1. The tradition that Isaiah is the author of the whole book is early, uniform and unchallenged. Josephus preserves a tradition that Cyrus was influenced by reading chapter xlv.

2. Some great scholars have concluded from the evidence that Zephaniah and Jeremiah possessed the whole book, and copied and made extracts from it.

3. The grandeur of the last twenty-seven chapters is undisputed. If, therefore, they were by one 'great prophet of the exile' (so Ewald), is it likely that his name was utterly unknown? If they were by two or more, is it likely that whereas the minor prophets, some very brief, were collected into the 'book of the Twelve' each bearing its own name, the writers of these should be unrecorded and forgotten?

4. In the New Testament its unity is taken for granted (Mt. xii. 17, 18; Jn. xii. 38-41; Rom. x. 16, 20).

Internal evidence

1. The argument based upon the standpoint taken by the writer can be met with the fact that Jeremiah, and Ezekiel also, speak at times of the future as if it were the present. A striking example of the same feature is our Lord's prophetic discourse (Mk. xiii.), where His standpoint is at one time in the immediate present, then in the near, and then in the more distant future.

2. The argument from difference of style is two-edged. Delitzsch, a great student of Isaiah, could say, 'It is Isaiah's spirit which animates the whole, Isaiah's heart which beats, and Isaiah's fiery tongue which speaks in both the substance and the form'. Some critics (e.g. Klostermann) have attributed sections of the latter part to Isaiah, or to pupils who wrote in his style.[1] Professor Margoliouth points out certain words, 'only known otherwise to the first Isaiah, of which the meaning was lost in Jeremiah's

[1] G. A. Smith, *Isaiah*, II, p. 23.

time', and even the English reader can observe how the name of God as the 'Holy One of Israel' recurs throughout the whole.

The difference of treatment can be fully accounted for by the change of subject, particularly if the closing chapters belong to the closing years of the prophet's life. Readers of Plato or Milton will not need to be told how a great writer can adapt his style to his subject.

3. On the positive side the book displays a consistent plan, and orderly development such as would be scarcely possible in a collection of fragments.

4. The portions which are regarded as insertions or additions are mainly those which contain distinct predictions of the future. No adequate reason is given as to why these should have been composed *after* the events predicted, nor *why* they should have been wrongly attributed to Isaiah and inserted where they stand.

5. The mention of Cyrus by name in chapter xlv. is admittedly unusual, although 1 Ki. xiii. 2 affords a parallel; and it is possible that the actual names were inserted later. But the repeated claim that God is able to reveal the future (xli. 22, xliii. 9, xliv. 7, xlvi. 10, xlviii. 3) may point to these very predictions revealed to Isaiah and recorded as a proof designed expressly to strengthen the faith of the exiles who should afterwards read them (cf. Mt. xxiv. 25).

6. There is much conflict of opinion as to the background of the later chapters. The absence of Babylonian colouring made Ewald think they were written in Egypt. Healing,[1] on the other hand, sees many signs of a Babylonian background and adds that 'Egypt almost disappears from view'. The imagery of chapter lvii. is generally admitted to be Palestinian. The older critics attributed it to Isaiah, modern ones are divided between a pre-exilic and a post-exilic author; and so with chapters lxiii.-lxvi. which are variously assigned to a pre-exilic, an exilic, and a post-exilic date.[1] To believe that Isaiah wrote them all is at once more simple and more natural.

Isaiah the son of Amoz was born in the time of Uzziah (Is. vi. 1), of whose reign he wrote a chronicle (2 Ch. xxvi. 22); he dwelt in Jerusalem and had easy access to the court (vii.). According to tradition he lived on until the days of Manasseh, when he was sawn asunder (*Talmud*, cf. 2 Ki. xxi. 16).

[1] *The Old Testament*, p. 192.
[1] See G. A. Smith, *Isaiah*, II. *In loc.*

H

Turning points in Isaiah's life

The dating of certain events of his life enables us to divide it into periods, and affords much help in understanding the progressive unfolding of his prophecy.

1. Since his son (vii. 3) must have been a growing boy when he went to Ahaz in 734 B.C., Isaiah must have been born about 760 B.C. His early years were therefore spent in the prosperous, luxurious and careless days of king Uzziah, the conditions of which are reflected in chapters ii., iii.

2. Soon after Ahaz came to the throne, Ephraim joined hands with Syria to declare war on Judah (734-732 B.C.), the time represented in chapters vii.-ix.

3. In chapter x. we hear the echo of Assyrian campaigns which led to the fall of Samaria in 721 B.C.

4. In chapter xx. there is a brief account of Sargon's invasion in 711 B.C.

5. In chapters xxxvi., xxxvii. the invasion of Sennacherib is recorded which may be dated about 700 B.C., followed by the embassy from Merodach-Baladan in chapter xxxix.

ANALYSIS

i.-xii.	Prologue (i.), denunciations and appeals (ii.-v.), Isaiah's call (vi.), the 'book of Emmanuel' (vii.-viii.), messianic and other prophecies (ix.-xii.).
xiii.-xxvii.	Oracles of judgment and mercy on the nations, including Babylon, Egypt and Tyre (xiii.-xxiii.); concluding with an apocalyptic vision of 'the day of Jehovah' (xxiv.-xxvii.).
xxviii.-xxxv.	Israel's revolt from Assyria and its consequences, with reproofs and promises (xxviii.-xxxiii.), merging into a declaration of God's judgment on Israel's enemies and the return of His redeemed and ransomed people (xxxiv., xxxv.).
xxxvi.-xxxix.	The siege of Jerusalem by Sennacherib, and its deliverance (xxxvi., xxxvii.). Hezekiah's sickness, recovery and song (xxxviii.). Embassy from the king of Babylon, and prophecy of the Babylonian captivity (xxxix.).

xl.-xlviii.	Words of comfort for God's people suffering punish-ment. God is the Creator of the ends of the earth; the nations and their rulers are but His instru-ments. Cyrus shall open the way to the return. Scorn thrown at the idols who cannot save. Blessings on God's people, 'but no peace unto the wicked'.
xlix.-lvii.	The servant of Jehovah, 'a light to the Gentiles' (xlix.), appeals to the people to awake and hearken; the vicarious sufferings of the Messiah (lii. 13-liii.); the free offer of grace (liv., lv.), and further appeals and promises, again ending in 'no peace unto the wicked'.
lviii.-lxvi.	Rebukes and promises to Israel (lviii., lix.); the gathering of the Gentiles to Zion (lx.-lxii.), the Saviour coming from Edom (lxiii.), the glory of the church of the future merging into the vision of new heavens and a new earth, ending with a final warning (lxiv.-lxvi.).

CONTENTS

Arrangement of the prophecies

The fixed points in Isaiah's life mentioned above suggest the plan on which the various parts of the book are arranged.

1. Chapter i. appears to be a general preface, and is followed by prophecies (ii.-v.), and the account of Isaiah's consecration (vi.), all belonging to the first peaceful period of his life.

2. Chapters vii.-ix. belong to the second period which is over-shadowed by the cloud of the Syro-Ephraimite invasion recorded in 2 Ki. xvi., and Ahaz's folly in calling in Assyria to help, so bringing nearer the power which was to call down calamity both on Israel and Judah. This is followed by chapters x.-xii. corres-ponding to the events of 2 Ki. xvii.

3. The 'oracles' (xiii.-xxiii.) were doubtless delivered at various times prior to the events recorded in chapters xxxvi.-xxxix., and are here collected together owing to similarity of subject.

4. The next group of chapters, xxiv.-xxxv., carry little sign of date. The rebukes in xxx. 1-5, xxxi. 1-5, suggest that Hezekiah was seeking the help of Egypt against the Assyrians (cf. 2 Ki. xviii. 21).

5. Chapters xxxvi.-xxxix. include, within a historical framework nearly identical with 2 Ki. xviii. 18-xx. 19, Isaiah's predictions concerning the period of the Assyrian siege. This section helps to connect and to explain those which precede and follow it.

6. The final twenty-seven chapters follow xxxix. 6, 7 naturally and belong to the last period of Isaiah's life.

The prophecies of the captivity

It is now possible to see the stages by which Isaiah realized the approaching captivity.

1. At the very outset of his prophetic ministry he knew that the sins of his nation must bring down God's judgment and it was revealed to him that they should be carried into captivity (vi. 11-13). Nevertheless a remnant should return, and these facts were impressed upon him by the gift of two sons with divinely appointed names (vii. 3, viii. 1, 18; cf. Heb. ii. 13). Assyria and Egypt are seen as the conquering nations, and the place of captivity is yet undetermined.

2. The first mention of Babylon comes in xi. 11 when he sees Israel and Judah scattered among the nations, of which Assyria stands first, but in which Shinar (Babylon) and Elam (Persia) also appear. Every nation there mentioned received its quota of captive Jews before the Bible was complete.

3. It may have been much later, and possibly at the time of Merodach-Baladan's embassy (xxxix. 1) when the oracles in chapters xiii., xiv. and xxi. were delivered, which now plainly declare Babylon as the land of Judah's captivity (cf. Mi. iv. 10) and proclaim the national fall, and the return of the 'remnant'. Elam and Media are given as the instruments to bring this about (xiii. 17, xxi. 2). It may be noted that there is no mention of Persia such as a later writer would have made.

4. We can picture Isaiah in the last years of Hezekiah, and towards the close of his own life, now fully convinced that all these predictions had been divinely inspired and would surely be fulfilled, receiving like John in Patmos the vivid revelation of the future contained in chapters xl.-lxvi. Isaiah now sees the judgment as having already fallen (xl. 2); but God's righteousness is near, and His salvation has gone forth (li. 5); and on the far horizon there dawns on him the vision of a new heaven and a new earth (lxv. 17).

Message and ruling ideas

To get at the heart of Isaiah's message we should first visualize the conditions as they appear to man, and then in contrast listen to the words of God. In his early days man saw a golden age of peace and plenty, but in the sight of God the whole head was sick and the whole heart faint (i. 5); where man saw security God saw approaching desolation (i. 7); where man saw ceremonial solemnities God saw iniquity (i. 13), and in the forms of justice God saw not silver but the dross of corruption (i. 22).

Ahaz saw in Assyria the great power who could give him help, but Isaiah taught that this was folly, for his help was in Jehovah, in whose hand Assyria was but an instrument. Then, when man saw only calamity, and ruin, the prophet saw divine judgment and prophesied redemption (i. 7-9). Similarly, at the very summit of the prophecy, where man sees the Servant of Jehovah despised and afflicted, God sees Him offering the great sacrifice for sins for ever, and justifying those for whom He died (liii. 3, 4, 10, 11).

In the course of the book various themes are introduced, which can be followed through.

1. In chapter i. we have sin, righteousness and judgment, not as three separate items of spiritual experience, but as three intertwining strands of man's relationship to God. Etymologically the Hebrew word *tsedeq*, like our English 'right-eous', means 'straight'. As used by Isaiah it denotes the goodness of God, in which justice and mercy unite, but with mercy rejoicing against judgment (liv. 8). God is right, and puts all things right (cf. Rom. iii. 26). God's righteousness is so much higher than any human conception of it, as His thoughts are higher than ours (lv. 8, 9). Those who have caught the shining vision of God's righteousness see by contrast how sordid are the best efforts of man (lxiv. 6) and how deep is his need of 'justification' (liii. 11; see also i. 26, 27, v. 7, xi. 4, xxxii. 17, xlii. 6, li. 5, lix. 17, lxiv. 6).

2. In chapter vi. we have the vision of the *holiness* of God, and closely connected with this, Isaiah's own special title for Jehovah, the 'Holy One of Israel', a title recurring eleven times in the first thirty-nine chapters, and thirteen times in the remainder. Isaiah from this first experience becomes the distinctive messenger of the 'holiness' (*qodesh*) and the 'glory' (*kabod*) of Jehovah, the transcendent purity, goodness and majesty of God, in face of which He is to be feared, honoured, and rendered loving obedience.

3. The doctrine of the *elect remnant* which is set forth at the outset (i. 9) as the one source of hope is pursued and developed. This

remnant must be refined by the fires of punishment (xxx. 27, 30, xl. 1) which will burn up the dross, but purify God's chosen (iv. 3, 4). Light shall break upon them out of darkness (ix. 2-5), and after being scattered among the nations, they shall be gathered (xi. 11, xxvii. 12, xliii. 5, lxv. 8-10); sorrow and sighing shall flee away, and the wilderness blossom as the rose (xxxv.).

4. Isaiah has justly been called the *evangelical* prophet. He brings the 'good tidings' of 'salvation' (xii. 1, 2, xl. 10, lii. 7, lxi. 1); of pardon (vi. 7, xl. 2, liii. 5, lv. 7); of cleansing (i. 18, 25, xxvii. 9, lii. 15); and of peace (ix. 6, xxvi. 12, xxxii. 17, liii. 5). These blessings will not be confined to Israel, but extended to all nations (xi. 10, xlii. 6, xlv. 22). This wonderful salvation is linked with the coming of Immanuel, the virgin's Son, the Prince with the wonderful name, the Son of David, the Conqueror, God's chosen and well beloved Servant (vii. 14, ix. 6, 7, xi. 10, lv. 3, lxiii. 1).

Chapter xlii. (1-7) contains the first of the great 'servant' passages, in which the gospel messages of Isaiah find their clearest and deepest note (xliii. 5-10, xlix. 1-9, lii. 13-liii; see also xli. 8, l. 10). At first the servant is seen as the whole nation personified in Jacob its ancestor, then in the faithful remnant, and finally in the person in whom even rabbinic tradition recognized the Messiah.

Thus the prophecies of Isaiah correspond point by point in a remarkable way with the words spoken by the risen Lord: 'Thus it is written, and thus it behoved Christ to suffer, and to rise from the dead the third day, and that repentance and the remission of sins should be preached in His name among all nations, beginning at Jerusalem' (Lk. xxiv. 46, 47).

THEMES FOR STUDY

1. Study Isaiah's teaching regarding human sin and divine pardon. Could a doctrine of the atonement be derived from this prophecy?

2. The gospel message should include the following elements (see Lk. xxiv. 46-48): (i.) the sufferings and exaltation of Christ; (ii.) the preaching of repentance and the remission of sins; (iii.) the witness to be borne; (iv.) to all nations. How are all these foreshadowed by Isaiah?

3. What various aspects of Christ's person and work are to be found in the following chapters (vii., ix., xi., xxxv., xli.-xliv., xlix., lii., liii., lxiii.)?

4. Study God's purposes for Israel as revealed in this book, and compare its teaching with that found in Rom. ix.-xi.

5. Collect and summarize Isaiah's teaching on the attributes of God, especially His majesty, His holiness, and His mercy.

JEREMIAH

AUTHORSHIP, DATE AND CIRCUMSTANCES

THE book of Jeremiah is of outstanding interest and fascination, both in itself and because of the way in which it reveals the life and character of the writer. The prophecies are interleaved with vivid, personal narratives and soliloquies, so that the reader seems to stand at Jeremiah's side, sharing the strange vicissitudes of his fortune and his inner conflicts, admiring and profiting by his earnest entreaties and the deep-seated faith which rises victorious over his successive disappointments.

It has never been seriously doubted that Jeremiah was the author, although some critics would eliminate the more definite of his predictions and ascribe them to a later date. In the LXX version the prophecies are somewhat differently arranged, chapters xlvi.-li. in particular being placed between xxv. 13 and 14, and there are a few omissions (probably due to the translator's tendency to abridge).

Jeremiah's career may be divided into three periods separated by two great events which profoundly affected the life of the nation. These were the defeat of Egypt by Babylon at Carchemish in the fourth year of Jehoiakim (605 B.C.), and the fall of Jerusalem in 586 B.C. (see 2 Ki. xxii.-xxv.; 2 Ch. xxiv. -xxxvi.).[1]

1. Five years before Jeremiah's call, which was in the thirteenth year of Josiah (625 B.C.), the king had led a successful raid against the outward manifestations of idolatry. Soon afterwards, the discovery of the 'book of the law' in the temple led to a national reformation in which no doubt Jeremiah played his part (xi., xii.). Meantime great commotions were seething in the north, from which direction came threats of invasion by Assyria and by bands of Scythian marauders (i. 13, iii. 12, iv. 6, vi. 1, 22,

[1] See also p. 98.

x. 22). At this time the royal house was on the side of righteousness, though too prone to rely upon the help of foreign powers (ii. 18, 36).

When, after Josiah's death, Pharaoh made Jehoiakim king, all was changed. Several years earlier Babylon had thrown off the Assyrian yoke, and after the battle of Carchemish became mistress of the destinies of the surrounding world. Jeremiah's warnings and earnest appeals received a friendly hearing from some of the princes (xxvi. 16, 24; cf. xxxix. 14), but met with opposition from the priests, the false prophets and the king. This culminated in his arrest and release in the temple court (xx. 1-6, xxvi. 7-24), and soon after in the burning of the roll (xxxvi. 5-25) and Jeremiah's escape (v. 26). (The consecutive narrative of this time may be read in i., xiii. 1-7, xiv. 1-6, xxxv., xviii. 1-4, xix. 1, 2, 14, 15, xx. 1-6, xxv. 1-4, xxvi., xxvii., xxxvi., xlv., xlvi.).

2. The *second period* of Jeremiah's life was one of constant struggle, for Jehoiakim, his brother Jehoahaz (or Shallum), Jehoiachin (Coniah), and finally Zedekiah all 'did evil in the sight of the Lord'. The people were delivered from fear of Assyria only to come under the yoke of Babylon, and were governed by weak and sinful kings who sometimes submitted to, and sometimes revolted from, the suzerain power, until Nebuchadnezzar carried Jehoiachin into captivity and placed Zedekiah on the throne (597 B.C.).

Jeremiah constantly urged fidelity to the treaties of submission which had been made with Babylon (cf. Rom. xiii. 1). Zedekiah was on the whole friendly but weak, and as the priests and princes refused to listen to the prophet's good advice, the fortunes of Judah steadily waned. Arrested a second time and imprisoned, first in a dungeon and then in the prison court, Jeremiah's faith in God and his love for the nation shines forth in his prison utterances (xxxi.-xxxiii.), but his predictions of the captivity become now more distinct, and his vision is directed to the faithful remnant who might return to their land, and to the more distant future of Messiah's reign. (For the narrative read xxi. 1-3, xxiv. 1-8, xxviii., xxix. 1-3, 30-32, xxxii. 1-6, xxxvii.-xxxix.)

3. The *third period* begins with the fall of Jerusalem, after which Jeremiah, faithful to the end and now in favour with the Babylonian rulers, stayed with the remnant of the people and continued to give them wise counsel and messages of hope. To these once

again they turned a deaf ear, raised the standard of revolt, and after the murder of Gedaliah, fled to Tahpanhes in Egypt, taking Jeremiah with them, where he delivered his last recorded message (xliii. 9-11, xliv. 30). Tradition says that he met his death by stoning, and an ancient Jewish synagogue in Cairo, pre-Christian in origin, claims to possess his tomb.

Archaeological confirmation

The present century has seen the contents of this book confirmed by two discoveries. At Tahpanhes Professor Petrie discovered the ruins of 'Pharaoh's house' (xliii. 9), to which there was only one entry, in front of which was a wide paved area 'exactly corresponding to Jeremiah's detailed account'.[1] In 1935, among the debris in a gate tower in Lachish were found some fragments of correspondence, written upon ostraka, which have come to be known as 'The Lachish Letters', and to these others were added in 1938. All authorities agree that these ostraka, which contain some ninety lines of readable Hebrew, belong to the closing years of Zedekiah's reign, and so are contemporaneous with Jeremiah. Reference is made in them at least once to a prophet whose name appears to have ended in . . . iah, and in one place the words occur, 'the words of the prophet are not good . . . liable to weaken the hands of . . .' (cf. xxxviii. 4). Professor Torczyner, who first deciphered the writing, identified the prophet with Urijah (see xxvi. 20), which is scarcely possible; and Dr. J. W. Jack with Jeremiah, for which there cannot be said to be anything approaching proof. What is certain is that the letters reflect a condition of things which in many respects is identical with that described in the book of Jeremiah.[2]

ANALYSIS

In order to help the student to arrange the chapters in chronological order the approximate dates of the various events are given in brackets.

i.	Jeremiah's call (625).
ii.-vi.	Calls to repentance (625-615).
vii.-x.	In the temple gate, against idolatry (610).
xi.-xii.	The broken covenant (607).
xiii.-xv.	The linen girdle, the dearth, Jeremiah's prayer (607).

[1] Petrie, *Egypt and Israel*, p. 92.
[2] See Prof. D. Winton Thomas, '*The Prophet*' *in the Lachish Ostraka* (Tyndale Press).

CONTENTS

The *arrangement* of the various sections, which are liberally supplied with headings (i. 1, ii. 1, iii. 6, etc.), is at first very puzzling. Some are dated, others not. Of the narratives, some are in the first person, some in the third. The *key* is to be found in xxxvi. 27, 28, 32, by the help of which the prophecy may be divided into four parts, beginning at chapters i., xxv., xxxvi., xlvi. Apart from two chapters each of these is in chronological order within itself, although the periods overlap one another.

The 'first roll' seems to consist of chapters i.-xx. to which xxi.-xxiv. were appended at a later time. The 'added words' commenced in xxv. and continued to xxxiv., with xxxv. as an appendix. A third part (xxxvi.-xliv.) is made up of narrative to which is added the 'word of Baruch' in xlv. Finally, chapters xlvi.-li. contain oracles of doom on the surrounding nations (originally placed earlier in the book); and lii. is thought to have been copied at a later date from 2 Ki. xxiv. 18-xxv.

Jeremiah as prophet

In the prophetic succession Jeremiah came seventy years after Isaiah, whom he was like in his world vision, his intense patriotism, and his love of Jehovah. In his early years Nahum and Zephaniah foretold the fall of Nineveh, and he saw their prediction fulfilled; he took up also the promises to 'the remnant' made by Isaiah (i. 9, vii. 3, xlvi. 3), and Zephaniah (ii. 9, iii. 13; Je. xxiii. 3, xxxi. 7).

In the days of Zedekiah, Habakkuk (i. 6) saw the hand of God in the aggression of Babylon, into which country Daniel and Ezekiel had been carried captive as young men to carry on the prophetic role, telling of the coming of Messiah and looking beyond into the far future.

The book of Jeremiah, like the Epistles of Paul, affords a wonderful picture of its author. We see a man, by nature sensitive and retiring, made strong and courageous by the grace of God. Opposed and ill-treated by priests and people, he was unwearying and unwavering in his efforts on their behalf, ever giving wise and practical counsel, with a heroic patience and utter unselfishness which must stir the coldest heart. In him we see a type of the Man of Sorrows, despised and rejected of men, proclaiming God's invitation with unfailing love to a disobedient and gainsaying people.

His message

1. *National.*—Jeremiah was called to deal with kings and nations (i. 10, 18), and his words have as their background the events of that period, but contain lessons very relevant to to-day. He saw the great powers as instruments of judgment in the hands of God: their rise and fall, equally with the fate of the smaller states, were subject to His sovereign will.

2. *Religious.*—He saw that the prosperity of his people depended

upon righteousness, justice and morality in their daily life; and that these in turn depended upon spiritual religion, a forsaking of the broken cisterns and a return to the fountain of living waters (ii. 13).

Let the people ask again for the old paths (vi. 16) and walk according to the law (xxvi. 4, xliv. 10) in security and truth; unless they do this neither ark, nor temple, nor sacrifices shall profit them (iii. 16, vi. 20, vii. 10, 21). In the perils that threaten, the arm of the flesh cannot save them. Their one hope is to trust in the Lord who brought them out of Egypt. He is their Saviour and Redeemer (ii. 18, xviii. 6, xxiii. 7, l. 34).

3. *Individual.*—Jeremiah was especially a preacher of individual religion, the religion of the heart (the word 'heart' occurs seventy-one times). This was the spiritual accompaniment of Josiah's reformation (iii. 6-10, vii. 8-11, ix. 2-6, xi. 20).

As with sorrow he saw his message rejected by the many and received by the few, he came to realize that God's purpose of grace was not to be fulfilled in the nation as a whole, but in a people gathered out one by one in whose hearts the law of God should be written in a new covenant of grace (xxxi. 31-34, l. 5).

4. *The future.*—Of Jeremiah's predictions some came to pass in his own day, and some (e.g. Je. xliv. 30) soon after, but many received their fulfilment only in the New Testament dispensation. Jeremiah saw Rachel, the mother of Israel, weeping for her children about to be carried into captivity (xxxi. 15); and Matthew saw a further fulfilment of this in the massacre of the innocents (Mt. ii. 17, 18). His prophecy of the Branch (LXX 'Dayspring', xxiii. 5) is referred by Zacharias to the birth of Christ (Lk. i. 78). His prophecy of the new covenant (xxxi. 31-34) is the subject of Heb. viii. 8-13 and x. 15-17, and appears to have been in our Lord's mind in His words at the last Passover (Lk. xxii. 20).

Our Lord made use of Jeremiah's words when cleansing the temple (vii. 9-11; Mk. xi. 17). The book of Revelation quotes or reflects him in various places, notably in regard to the overthrow of 'Babylon' (Je. xvii. 10, Rev. ii. 23; Je. xxv. 10, Rev. xviii. 22, 23; Je. li. 7-9, 45, 63, 64, Rev. xiv. 8, xvii. 2-4, xviii. 2-5, 21).

THEMES FOR STUDY

1. Jeremiah was called to prophesy before rulers, priests, and people. Observe his attitude towards each of these classes and compare it with that of Christ in His day.

2. Study Jeremiah's prayers, their occasions, their content, and the answers received to them, taking them as a model and encouragement.

3. Collect passages showing the stress laid by Jeremiah upon (i) personal righteousness, (ii) social justice, (iii) trust in God alone.

4. Study the teaching regarding God's covenant in chapters xi., xxix., xxxi. How does it bear upon the new covenant in Christ (Heb. viii., x.)?

5. Note Jeremiah's attitude to Babylon (i) as a sovereign and protecting power, and (ii) as a pagan nation that must come under the judgment of God. Compare this with the attitude of Paul and John in the New Testament towards Rome, and draw lessons for the nations of our time.

6. Of the evils against which Jeremiah raised his voice, which are the most prevalent to-day? What can we learn from his teaching as to our own attitude towards them?

LAMENTATIONS

AUTHORSHIP, DATE AND CIRCUMSTANCES

IN the Hebrew text the book is anonymous, but in the LXX it is assigned to Jeremiah, as it is by unanimous tradition; and 'Jeremiah's grotto', in which he is said to have composed it, is pointed out in a hill overlooking the walls of Jerusalem. In the Hebrew it is found among the *Megilloth*,[1] between Ruth and Ecclesiastes. It owes its present position to the LXX.

It consists of five poems, and the *qinah* metre in which it is written is common in Jeremiah. The internal evidence is indecisive. The reference to the king in iv. 20 is in contrast with Jeremiah's general attitude to Zedekiah, but corresponds closely with David's lament over Saul. Zedekiah was, after all, the Lord's anointed (see 2 Sa. i. 14, 21). It is evidently contemporaneous, and some have suggested Baruch as the author. The lament referred to in 2 Ch. xxxv. 25 has apparently been lost.

The whole book breathes the atmosphere of a patriot who had himself passed through the siege of Jerusalem, whilst the artificial form suggests that some time had since elapsed. An emotional rather than a logical unity runs through the whole.

[1] See p. 31.

ANALYSIS

i. The prophet laments the misery of the city, and Zion confesses her sin.

ii. The ruin of Jerusalem and the cause of God's anger.

iii. The prophet, speaking for the people, profits from the discipline, and stays himself upon God's compassion and faithfulness.

iv. The days of prosperity contrasted with the horrors of famine.

v. The nation appeals for forgiveness and deliverance.

CONTENTS

The first four chapters are in acrostic form like several of the Psalms.[1] In the third chapter every three verses begin with the same letter.

The poignant sorrow of the prophet is no less for the sin than for the misery of his people, and inevitably reminds us of our Lord's own laments (Lk. xiii. 34 f., xxi. 41-44; cf. La. iv. 13); as the sorrows of Jerusalem remind us of His sorrows (i. 12, ii. 15, iii. 19, 30). The book speaks of the inevitable consequences of human sin, the need of humiliation and penitence, the discipline of divine chastisement, and the hope that remains for those who make the Lord their portion (iii. 22-23).

It is recited by pious Jews at 'the wailing place' outside the wall of Jerusalem every Friday.

THEMES FOR STUDY

1. What grounds does this book afford for hope of restoration to nations and individuals who suffer for their own sin and folly?

2. What parallels exist between 2 Sa. i., the laments in this book, and those of our Lord in Lk. xiii. 34 ff., and xix. 41 ff., and what lessons do they teach?

EZEKIEL

AUTHORSHIP, DATE AND CIRCUMSTANCES

EZEKIEL's authorship of the book that bears his name is acknowledged by the great majority of scholars. Theories of multiple authorship have been advanced by Hölscher and others, and

---

[1] See Chapter XI, p. 186.

C. C. Torrey would relegate the whole book to about 320 B.C., but these views have obtained little acceptance. The unity of style and plan, the personal details and dating, all testify to the book being the authentic work of Ezekiel. The careful arrangement in chronological order, closing with a vision of the future, suggests that the prophecies were thus collected and put together during his later years.

Like Jeremiah, Ezekiel was a priest, but whereas the former sprang from the lower, the latter belonged to the higher ranks of the priesthood. He was personally acquainted with the princes (xi. 1), and having been carried into captivity with Jehoiachin and the flower of the nobility (2 Ki. xxiv. 15) he dwelt there in his own house, where the elders came to seek his counsel (iii. 24, viii. 1, xiv. 1, xx. 1).

If the 'thirtieth year' of i. 1 be the year of his age, his babyhood would correspond with Josiah's reformation, and his early manhood be spent under the influence of Jeremiah's preaching.

The dated prophecies extend from 592 B.C., the fifth year of Jehoiachin's captivity (i. 2), to 570 B.C. (xxix. 17); that is, from six years before to sixteen years after the fall of Jerusalem. He was thus a younger contemporary of Jeremiah, some of whose earlier prophecies he had probably heard, and with whose later messages to Babylon (Je. xxix., li. 59) he would be acquainted. The conditions of the exile evidently allowed much freedom of movement, and frequent communication took place between the exiles and their fellow-countrymen in Jerusalem (see Je. xxix). Jerome thought that Jeremiah and Ezekiel must have exchanged prophecies, and likened them to two singers chanting in responsive strains.

Ezekiel's prophecies were delivered in Babylon and a likeness can be traced in his imagery to the sculptures recovered from that great city of Nebuchadnezzar (Dan. iv. 30). From that metropolis his thoughts often turned to his beloved Jerusalem. The 'house of Israel' (ii. 3, iii. 17) to whom he was sent had declined in faith, and instead of putting their trust in Jehovah sought alliances with the heathen, by which they were led into idolatry, and into the immorality and bloodshed associated with it (viii., xvi., xxiii.).

Those who partake of the sins of the heathen must share in their judgment. Ezekiel saw this, and, in opposition to the seductive voice of the false prophets (xiii. 9), prophesied the destruction of Jerusalem and the captivity of its inhabitants.

Jerusalem fell; and the later prophecies tell of a remnant to be gathered out and redeemed (xxxiv. 12-16, xxxvi. 24) and though the house of David had rebelled, yet a representative of David should be their shepherd (xxxiv. 23), and reign as their prince for ever (xxxvii. 25).

ANALYSIS

Part I: i.-xxiv. (Before the fall of Jerusalem.) God's inevitable judgment leading to national disaster

i.-iii.   Ezekiel's call and commission.

iv.-xi.   Visions and discourses, prophecies and types, of the siege and destruction of the city, and of Jehovah's abandonment of the temple.

xii.-xxiv.   The people's unbelief, delusion by false prophets, and infidelity. The equity of God's dealings, His mercy on a remnant, but the certainty of judgment.

Part II: xxv.-xxxix. Leading to Israel's restoration

xxv.-xxxii.   Judgment of the nations, in particular Tyre and Egypt, for their pride and blasphemy.

xxxiii.-xxxvii.   The restoration of Israel. The watchman, David the prince, blessing on the land, cleansing and resurrection promised to the people.

xxxviii., xxxix.   Gog and Magog overthrown, and Israel finally redeemed.

Part III: xl.-xlviii. (After the fall of Jerusalem.) The temple ideally restored and sanctified. God's return to dwell in the midst of His people

xl.-xliii.   Measurements of God's holy temple.

xliv.-xlvi.   Ordinances for a purified priesthood.

xlvii.   The land revived with streams of living water.

xlviii.   The inheritance of God's redeemed people.

CONTENTS

Ezekiel's prophecy, like that of his great predecessor Isaiah, moves forward in ordered stages, starting from the immediate present, then passing to threatening judgments impending in the near future, with their corresponding mercies, and finally looking forward to the end of the age.

Ezekiel receives his call and commission after an awe-inspiring vision of God upon the throne in the midst of the whirlwind and the fire, the whole creation being at His service to do His bidding. Following on this is a record of addresses containing rebukes and warnings which culminate in a vision of the 'glory of Jehovah' departing from the temple (x. 18) and the city (xi. 23) now destined for destruction. The section closes with further warnings, reasonings on the equity of God's dealings, and lamentations over the people's obduracy.

The second section is occupied with the complementary theme of God's judgments about to fall on the surrounding nations. It closes with a declaration of His mercy towards those who repent, foreshadowing the blessings of the gospel with descriptions of the good shepherd, the covenant of peace, the cleansed and regenerated heart, the resurrection, and the outpouring of the Spirit.

Thus the way is prepared for the final section, which sees the 'glory of Jehovah' return to a newly designed and sanctified temple and city, with an elect and purified priesthood. To his contemporaries the combination of symbol and reality in these closing chapters would indicate the return of a remnant to Jerusalem, partly revealing and partly concealing the future. But read in the light of the last book of the Bible, the Christian sees their application to the eternal city of God. For John also is taken up to a high mountain, and is told of the measuring of a temple and a city, which lies foursquare and has four gates, with the river of life flowing from it and the fruitful tree of life near by, where all is pure and undefiled, and its holy character guaranteed by the 'glory of God' and His eternal presence.

Wellhausen used chapters xl.-xlviii. to support his hypothesis that the Priestly Code[1] was post-exilic.[2] He argued: (1) that Ezekiel meant these chapters to be taken literally, (2) that, in fact, the post-exilic scribes took them as the basis for their legislation as described in Leviticus, and (3) that the distinction between priests and Levites cannot be found before the time of Ezekiel, but had its origin in the action described in chapter xliv. As the critical theory largely rests on these contentions they deserve careful examination.

1. The *ideal* character of Ezk. xl.-xlviii. could be deduced from its symbolism and from the size and symmetry of its numbers; to take it literally leads only to geographical impossibilities and

---

[1] See Chapter IV and Introduction to Chapter IX.

[2] See E. Robertson, *The Priestly Code*; Orr, *Problem of the Old Testament*, p. 306.

absurdities. Its ideal form fits its purpose, namely, to picture the
future when God shall dwell in holiness with His people. There
is, consequently, a notable absence of rebukes and appeals for
repentance.

There is no hint, either in Leviticus, or in the post-exilic books
that it was ever taken literally, and no proof of any attempt to
put it into practice in any shape or form.

2. The parallels to the Levitical code are such as to indicate
the priority of the former. The references to Lv. xvii.-xxvi. (e.g.
v. 16, 17, xxxiv. 25-27) are so distinct that many critics admit
Ezekiel's acquaintance with them. He is 'familiar not only with
burnt, peace, and meat offerings, but with sin and trespass
offerings (xlv. 17). All those are spoken of as things customary and
well understood (xliii. 13, xliv. 29-31, xlvi. 20)'.[1]

That some features in Leviticus are not mentioned is natural,
particularly in view of the prevailing neglect (v. 7, xl. 45, R.V.
mg.). The differences are accounted for by the new and ideal
conditions. 'The plain fact, as one day will be generally recognized', writes C. C. Torrey, 'is that the author of the book (of
Ezekiel) had before him the complete Pentateuch in the very
form in which it lies before us at the present day.'[2]

3. If the Levites had been descendants of the 'degraded priests'
of Ezk. xliv. they must have known it, and would surely have
struggled for re-instatement, nor would their status have been
represented in Leviticus as sacred and honourable. On the other
hand, if the priesthood had been actually limited to the Zadokites
for some years, would they have tamely submitted to its being
opened to all the sons of Aaron?

Ezekiel's action, in fact, relates to something quite different,
the removal of uncircumcised strangers (xliv. 9) and the purging
of the Levites from idolatry. In the books of Ezra and Nehemiah
the distinction between priests and Levites appears as something
of long standing. On all these grounds Wellhausen's conjecture
must be dismissed.

Characteristic features

Ezekiel has been called 'the prophet of grace and glory'. Like
Jeremiah, having learned that the longsuffering of God with the
nation had approached its end (vii. 2, 6; Je. v. 29), his thoughts
turn to the individual (xviii. 2, 3; Je. xxxi. 27-39), and to the
remnant which God will gather and regenerate (xi. 17, xviii. 30).

[1] A. B. Davidson, *Camb. Bible*, p. liii.
[2] *Pseudo-Ezekiel*, p. 91.

To them shall be granted a clean heart and a new spirit (xxxvi. 26; Je. xxxii. 37-39). There is a Pentecostal ring in the constant references to the Spirit of God, the whirlwind and the fire (i. 4, 20); who guides and directs the revelation (ii. 2, iii. 14, 24, xi. 1, 5, xxxvii. 1, xlii. 5; cf. Jn. xvi. 13; Rev. i. 10, ii. 7, iv. 2). It is He who regenerates the individual (xxxvi. 26) and revives the nation (xxxvii. 5, 9, 14, R.V. mg.), and whose refreshing and vivifying power is pictured in the rivers of living water (xlvii. 1-12; cf. Jn. vii. 38, 39; Rev. xxii. 1, 2).

The 'glory of Jehovah' is an expression which signifies, as in the days of Moses, the immediate presence of God in the midst of His people (i. 28, iii. 23, viii. 4; cf. Ex. xvi. 7, 10, xxiv. 16, 17; also Is. vi; Rev. iv.); a glory which is closely associated with the divine holiness (cf. Ex. xxix. 43; Lv. x. 3; Is. vi. 3; Jn. i. 14). The sin which polluted the holy things and places (vii. 24, xx. 40, xxii. 26) caused the glory to depart from the temple (viii. 4, ix. 3, x. 4, 18, 19), and from the city (xi. 23); but when the new temple had been sanctified the glory of Jehovah returned and filled the house (xliii. 2-5; xliv. 4; cf. Rev. xxi. 22, 23).

Ninety times Ezekiel is addressed as 'son of man'; he is thereby identified with those to whom he was sent, and distinguished from the other agencies of the divine Being. So when our Lord applied to Himself the title '*the* Son of man', He made Himself one with the sinful race He came to redeem; and by using it in reference to His second advent, He identified Himself with the 'Son of man' in Daniel's vision (Dn. vii. 13).

The imagery and symbolism used in the apocalypse have much in common with those in Ezekiel, and each should be used as a commentary upon the other. The following ought to be noted: Ezk. i. 1 (Rev. xix. 11), i. 5 (Rev. iv. 6), i. 10 (Rev. iv. 7), i. 22 (Rev. iv. 6), i. 24 (Rev. i. 15), i. 28 (Rev. iv. 3), ii. 9 (Rev. v. 1), iii. 1, 3 (Rev. x. 10), vii. 2 (Rev. vii. 1), ix. 4 (Rev. vii. 3), ix. 11 (Rev. i. 13), x. 2 (Rev. viii. 5), xiv. 21 (Rev. vi. 8), xxvi. 13 (Rev. xviii. 22), xxvii. 28-30 (Rev. xviii. 17-19), xxxvii. 10 (Rev. xi. 11), xxxvii. 27 (Rev. xxi. 3), xxxviii. 2, 3 (Rev. xx. 8), xl. 2 (Rev. xxi. 10), xl. 3 (Rev. xi. 1), xliii. 2 (Rev. i. 15), xliii. 16 (Rev. xxi. 16), xlvii. 1, 12 (Rev. xxii. 1, 2), xlviii. 31 (Rev. xxi. 12).

THEMES FOR STUDY

1. Study the parallels between Ezekiel and Revelation and deduce lessons concerning the glory of God, heaven, and other subjects.

2. What does this book contain which foreshadows Christ's Person and His teaching?

3. Find illustrations of God's justice and mercy from these prophecies.

4. What missionary lessons can be drawn from (i) Ezekiel's calling, and (ii) his prophecies in xxv.-xxxix?

DANIEL

AUTHORSHIP, DATE AND CIRCUMSTANCES

In our Bibles the book of Daniel is found between Ezekiel and the Minor Prophets, which is the place given it in the LXX. In the Hebrew Bible it is placed among the *Kethubim* (or *Writings*) between Esther and Ezra-Nehemiah. The reason for this is that Daniel is not 'prophecy' in the ordinary Hebrew sense; that is, a delivery of God's messages to Israel. It is rather 'apocalyptic', i.e. 'revelation' of the future in figure and symbol, a kind of literature that increased among the Jews after the exile. The Jewish prophetical books are national in character, and though they contain predictions, these are closely connected with the message of the prophet to his contemporaries. The book of Daniel, with its series of visions of world-history and its view of spiritual forces behind the veil, together with the more intimate and personal nature of its narratives, was classed, therefore, among the *Writings*. No argument concerning *date* enters in here, since classification (as with the Psalms and Proverbs) is determined not by date but by subject.

It claims in places (e.g. viii. 1, ix. 2) to have been written by the prophet Daniel, of whose life it reveals so much, at a period contemporary with, or soon after, the events it relates; that is to say, about the time of the conquest of the Babylonian Empire by the Persians in the sixth century B.C. The visions claim to be prophecies of the future of world history given at that time, those in chapters ii. and vii. covering the whole period of Gentile dominion in a series of world empires up to the end of the age, and those in chapters viii. to xi. a period of Jewish history that falls between the close of the Old Testament and the advent of Jesus Christ. The earlier narrative chapters (i.-vi.) are in the third person, and in places (i. 19, vi. 3, 28) may indicate another writer, but the historical trustworthiness and prophetic character of the book are not dependent upon the condition that Daniel wrote the whole with his own hand.

That it is intended as prophecy is the impression given by the book itself, and is the view of its authorship and character which has been held by the church generally, and is still held by many competent scholars of recent years.[1]

It was to be expected that a book bearing such testimony to supernatural events would be subject to criticism and opposition. In the third century A.D. it was attacked by Porphyry, who suggested that it was not written till 165 B.C., the time of the main events in Jewish history which it professed to predict. This theory was revived in the seventeenth and eighteenth centuries by the rationalistic school and is maintained to-day by the majority of critics. Recently it has been modified as a result of archaeological discovery, and by the linguistic researches of R. D. Wilson, and others, so that the date is at the present in the process of being pushed by the critics further and further back in time.[2]

Evidently the genuineness and value of the book, as well as its interpretation, depend upon this question of date. The confidence with which the critical objections have been sometimes put forward requires that they should be carefully examined, when it will be found that, apart from the objection to the supernatural which underlies them, they are by no means as substantial as they are made to appear.

The book consists partly of narratives, and partly of dreams and visions and their interpretations. It is also bilingual, chapters ii.4-vii. 28 being in Aramaic and the remainder in Hebrew. The critical objections brought forward are of two kinds, historical and linguistic.

The omission of Daniel from the list of worthies in Ecclesiasticus cannot be due to ignorance of Daniel's existence, in view of Ezk. xiv. 14, 20 and xxviii. 3. This, therefore, is no criterion of the date. On the other hand, an early date is suggested by the apocryphal additions. There are three of these, namely, the prayer of the three children (which includes the hymn known as the *Benedicite*) between verses 23 and 24 of chapter iii., and two appendices, the stories of Susanna, and of Bel and the Dragon. These do not appear in the original Hebrew version, but are found in the LXX

[1] Among them E. B. Pusey, C. H. H. Wright, C. Boutflower, R. D. Wilson, R. P. Dougherty, and Prof. G. Ch. Aalders.
[2] See Aalders, *Recent Trends in Old Testament Criticism*, I.V.F., p. 27.

translation. Their insertion shows that they must have existed long before in some copies from which the translation was made, and this pushes the date of the original further back still.

The critics find further support for a late date from historical difficulties and supposed inaccuracies. The mention in Dn. i. 1 of an expedition in the *third* year of Jehoiakim is asserted to be inaccurate as no expedition is known in that year. But one in the fourth year is mentioned in 2 Ki. xxiv. 1, 2 and 2 Ch. xxxvi. 6, 7, which might well be the same on a different mode of reckoning, or there may have been an earlier one of which no record remains. The kingship and even existence of Belshazzar was at one time confidently denied, but his name, and facts concerning him, have since been discovered which have led to a complete confirmation of the Bible story of his death. Prof. R. P. Dougherty has given it as his opinion that chapter v. may reasonably be regarded as accurate history.[1]

The identity of Darius the Mede (v. 31) is still an unsolved problem, but various solutions have been suggested, such as Cyaxares the Median king, or Gobryas, Cyrus's general. Some new discovery may one day reveal his identity.

Another objection is that in the sixth century the term 'Chaldaeans' was not used to denote a class of astrologers, but such an argument from silence is of little weight.

The arguments from the linguistic side seem at first sight more impressive. Dr. Driver says, with characteristic assurance, 'The Greek words *demand*, the Hebrew *supports*, and the Aramaic *permits*, a date after the conquest of Palestine by Alexander the Great.[2] As to the Aramaic, it was at one time thought that its use involved a late date, but recently Aramaic forms and documents have been found centuries older than Daniel's time. There is an interesting parallel to the bilingual character of the book in certain ancient Indian plays, in which the players representing the common folk use Prakrit, whereas the rest is in the classical Sanskrit. But too little is yet known on the subject to base any safe argument upon it. It is worth noting that there are appreciable resemblances in the Hebrew to that of Ezekiel (see i. 7, viii. 2, ix. 3, x. 21, xii. 3, xiii. 9, xviii. 7, xx. 6-15). The claim regarding Greek words rests on the slender foundation of the mention of three Greek musical instruments, of which no previous mention has been found in Babylon. Every year, however, brings to light fresh evidence of Babylonian enthusiasm for music, and

[1] *Nabonidus and Belshazzar* (1929). See also p. 101.
[2] *Literature of the Old Testament*, p. 476.

there is proof of a rapid development of Greek trade with the East in the seventh and sixth centuries B.C.

Nebuchadnezzar is known to have extended his rule over Egypt, Assyria and the whole Eastern world (ii. 37, 38). In other respects, also, recent discovery has shown that the picture of Babylon is strikingly true to the conditions of Daniel's time. Sir L. Woolley tells us that Nebuchadnezzar 'rebuilt his capital so thoroughly that modern excavators could scarcely find any trace of buildings older than his time', and quotes Dan. iv. 30 in illustration.[1] His excavations at Ur have laid bare a temple with a court capable of accommodating a large concourse of people, at one end of which was found the pedestal for a great image. Woolley comments on the 'striking correspondence' of this with the scene pictured in chapter iii., adding that the 'written story and the facts of the ruins . . . completely . . . explain each other'.[2]

Archaeological research has also not only removed objections to the historicity of chapter v., but has afforded positive vindication of the manner in which the stronghold of Babylon was taken. The position of Belshazzar, now known to have been vice-gerent to Nabonidus, accounts for Daniel's appointment to be the *third* ruler in the kingdom.

Summing up the evidence for and against Daniel's authorship it may be said that the weight attached to either side is dominated by the view taken of its supernatural elements, and that, but for the objection taken to these, its genuineness would probably never have been challenged. It was, in fact, uniformly received as inspired both by the Jews and by the early church.

Daniel was carried into captivity as a youth (i. 1) in the third year of Jehoiakim, and his last prophecy was delivered, more than seventy years later, in the third year of Cyrus. The book was probably written in Babylon and brought by Ezra with the other books on his return to the Holy Land.

ANALYSIS

The book falls roughly into two sections, the former consisting of narrative and the latter of vision and prophecy.

i. Daniel and his three companions appear as youths in the course of an education as court astrologers to king Nebuchadnezzar.

[1] *Ur of the Chaldees*, p. 185.
[2] *Op. cit.*, p. 138.

ii. The great king's prophetic dream of four successive world empires, under the symbol of a great image, which is interpreted to him by Daniel, whose career becomes thereby assured.

iii. Daniel's three companions are cast into a burning, fiery furnace by the infuriated king on their refusal to worship the image he had set up.

iv. Nebuchadnezzar's madness and recovery.

v. Belshazzar's feast during which appeared a mysterious writing on the wall.

vi. Daniel's delivery from the lion's den.

vii. Daniel's vision of the four beasts and its interpretation.

viii. The vision of the ram and the he-goat.

ix. Daniel's prayer of contrition and repentance on behalf of his nation, answered by the prophecy of the seventy weeks.

x., xi. The vision of the man clothed in linen, and the prediction of the kings of the north and south.

xii. Prophecy of the resurrection and 'the time of the end'.

CONTENTS

The lessons to be drawn from the narrative portions lie on the surface, and the steadfastness and deliverances of Daniel and his companions have been an inspiration to all subsequent generations (see Heb. xi. 33). God is seen as the King of kings and ruler over all. His warnings to Nebuchadnezzar and Belshazzar are a witness to His longsuffering, whilst the retribution on those who despised His word reveals Him as a God of judgment. Daniel's life shows how firmness of conviction in youth lays the foundation for a life of courageous witness and service.

The vision in chapter vii. forms a further commentary on the dream of Nebuchadnezzar. Both concern four great empires, evidently the same. There are two views. The first is that they represent Babylon, Medo-Persia, Greece and Rome. That this is the view of the prophet regarding the second and third kingdoms is evident by comparing v. 28 with ix. 1 and x. 1, showing that he regarded the kingdom of the Medes and Persians as one; and viii. 20, 21 compared with xi. 1, 2 shows that he intended to indicate the Grecian Empire as the third. This is the view held by Hippolytus, Theodoret, Jerome, Calvin, Tregelles and Pusey.

The other view, held by Hitzig, Driver, and critics of the liberal school, makes the empires to be those of Babylon, the Medes, the Persians, and the Greeks. They are forced to this interpretation, in spite of obvious objections, in order to maintain the Maccabaean date of the book and to explain away its predictions. In no case can it be denied that four world-empires are prophesied, in the last of which the Kingdom of God should be set up (ii. 44, vii. 13).

With chapter viii. the Hebrew language is resumed. The great empires recede from sight and the future of Israel is the subject, culminating (verses 9 ff., 23 ff.) in the appearance of Antiochus Epiphanes, who, as the 'Jewish anti-Christ', is a type of the 'man of sin' (cf. 2 Thes. ii. 4).

The prophecy of the seventy weeks, or heptads, in chapter ix. is in some respects the climax of the book. It is not easy to fix precisely the points at which the periods commence and terminate. The prophecy is undoubtedly messianic, and a comparison of ix. 2 and 24 indicates that true deliverance was to come, not at the end of seventy, but of seventy times seven years. That it was *about* this length of time from the edicts of Artaxerxes (Ezra vii. 1, Neh. ii. 1) to the Crucifixion no one can deny, and some measure exactly 483 (or 486½) years to that event, interpreting the last seven (or three and a half) as referring to the second advent. There can at any rate be no doubt that the six great purposes mentioned in v. 24 were accomplished at and through the death of Christ.

The last great prophecy in chapters x. to xii. is notable for its detail in plain, and apparently literal, language. It develops the theme of chapter viii. as chapter vi. does that of chapter ii. Chapter x. is a prologue setting forth the spiritual powers in the background; chapter xi. the main prophecy; chapter xii. the climax and epilogue. Whereas chapters vii., viii. leave Daniel troubled and downcast, in the four last chapters he is given understanding and encouragement.

From any point of view the interpretation of chapter xi. is difficult. There is much evidence that the kings of the north and the south were the Seleucids and the Ptolemies who ruled in Syria and Egypt after the division of the Greek kingdom into four parts, and that verses 21 ff. refer to Antiochus Epiphanes; but it is not easy to make the details fit into the history. From Jerome onwards many have adopted this interpretation. In recent years others have taken chapter xi. as relating to events accompanying Christ's second advent; and there may, as in other cases, be a nearer and a more distant fulfilment.

Christ's prophetic discourse in Mt. xxiv. (compare v. 15 with Dn. ix. 27 and xii. 11) shows that some part of Daniel's predictions were then still awaiting fulfilment. The references to the book of Daniel in the New Testament are too numerous to mention, and are best studied by the use of a Reference Bible. Our Lord identified Himself with the Son of man of Daniel's vision (vii. 13, see Mt. xvi. 13, xxvi. 64), and His words in Mt. xxv. 46 reflect those in Dn. xii. 2. The book of Revelation is full of references to the book of Daniel, and the comparison is necessary to the right interpretation of both; Babylon, the beast with horns, God's majesty and Kingdom, the numbered 'times' and 'days' and the 'sealing' of the visions may be mentioned as subjects. The difficulties of this book may well be left aside by beginners in order to concentrate on that which is clear and obvious. They will be no deterrent to those who delight in the mysteries of the Word.

THEMES FOR STUDY

1. What qualities of the true man of God are to be seen in Daniel and his three friends?

2. What purpose of God can you discern from the dreams and warnings of this book for the rulers of Babylon, for the captive Israelites, and for God's people generally?

3. Study the messianic references and predictions to be found in Daniel with their New Testament fulfilments.

4. With a reference Bible work out the parallels between Daniel and the Revelation.

5. Study the parallel as regards the rise, the pride and the fall of empires as seen in Daniel with recent convulsions in Europe.

CHAPTER XIII

HEBREW PROPHECY, II : HOSEA TO MALACHI

HOSEA

AUTHORSHIP, DATE AND CIRCUMSTANCES

THE prophecy is entitled 'The word of the LORD that came unto Hosea, the son of Beeri' (i. 1). So begins the book which in the Hebrew Bible stands first in the list of the twelve minor prophets. This verse should be compared with the opening verse of the major prophets (Is. i. 1).

Hosea's message is primarily, but not only, addressed to Israel. He may himself in later years have written the narrative of his own life which forms such a significant background (chapters i., iii.), and arranged the poems of which the greater part of the prophecy consists (chapters ii. and iv.-xiv.).

In the evil days of Jeroboam he married at Jehovah's word a wife named Gomer, who proved, as anticipated, unworthy and unfaithful. Children were born, but he was forced to conclude that they were not his own (i. 2). Yet he acknowledged them (i. 4, 6, 9), and even when Gomer forsook him his love followed her. He found her shamed and deserted, perhaps sold into slavery, and even so redeemed her and through discipline restored her to his home (chapter iii.).

These narrative chapters are now generally agreed by scholars to be a record of actual experience. History has also shown that the prophet's experience was a parable of God's treatment of His erring people. Hosea's life story was an anticipation in miniature of Israel's subsequent career. The name Jezreel typified the breaking of the northern monarchy (i. 4, 5), Lo-ruhamah, mercy taken away from it (i. 6, 7), and Lo-ammi, the calling of a fresh people (i. 9; cf. Rom. ix. 24-26). Gomer's final restoration shows God's unquenchable love to Israel in spite of all her backslidings (iii. 4, 5, cf. i. 11). Some critics consider the references to Judah and the passages of promise (e.g. ii. 14-23) to be later additions, but there is little justification for such an assumption.

[1] See also Chapter XIV, *The Messianic Hope.*

Starting his prophecies in the reigns of Uzziah of Judah and Jeroboam II of Israel, and concluding before the fall of Samaria, Hosea prophesied for at least fifty years, i.e. during the period of the decline and fall of the northern kingdom (*c.* 775-725). Attempts by the kings to save themselves by clutching at foreign help only dragged them down (v. 13, x. 6). The tottering monarchy finally collapsed (x. 15).

It is evident that Hosea knew the root of the trouble to be apostasy from the Mosaic covenant (viii. 1; cf. Ex. xxiv. 7). The details of the law were known but considered irrelevant to that age (viii. 12), whilst the original sacrificial system was corrupted with false sacrifices (viii. 13). Not only was the book of the covenant ignored, but the whole Levitical system corrupted (ix. 3-5). Hosea sensed that the predicted Deuteronomic judgments were imminent (xi. 8; cf. Dt. xxix. 23). His mind reverted to the great figure of Moses (xii. 13; cf. Dt. xviii, 15). He realized how utterly the calf worship with all its attendant idolatries had debased the purity and grandeur of the divine Mosaic original (xiii. 2).

Hosea lived and prophesied in the northern kingdom. The scene passes from Ahab and from Elijah's Jezreel (i. 4, 5) to the hot Jordan valley and Achor (ii. 15), by way of Deborah's historic Tabor (v. 1). Gibeah of Saul, in the hill country of Benjamin, is a frequent scene of prophecy (v. 8) and Hosea also visited Transjordan (vi. 8). Ephraim, the leader of Israel, figures largely in the book. Hosea knew her capital (vii. 1) and witnessed also Judah's fortifications (viii. 14). The sanctuaries of Gilgal (ix. 15) and Bethel (x. 15) heard him, where he remembered Jacob's story (xii. 12; cf. Gn. xxviii. 2), and looking north he drew inspiration from snow-capped Lebanon (xiv. 5-7).

There are also sounds from afar and rumours from neighbouring lands. Egypt is often mentioned (vii. 16) and Memphis (ix. 6), and Tyre the ravisher (ix. 13). The rumble of Assyrian politics and the tramp of her soldiers is an undertone throughout (v. 13, viii. 9, x. 6) and bursts out in Samaria's destruction (xi. 5, xiii. 16).

ANALYSIS

i., ii.   Hosea and his three children.

iii.   Hosea's later life.

iv. 1-vi. 3.   Israel and her leaders' sin and the hope of revival.

CONTENTS

The prophecy is now vividly earnest, now passionately tender. The desperate problem of dealing with backsliding (iv. 16, xi. 7, xiv. 4) runs through the whole and the following leading ideas may also be traced:

1. The sinfulness of the idolatrous Jehovah worship and of the confusion of Jehovah with Baal. The sacrifices of apostate religion were unreal (vi. 6) and unacceptable (viii. 13). Increased religious zest only sunk them deeper (xiii. 2).

2. All this led to immorality. The land was choked with the weeds of vice (i. 2, iv. 1, 2, 12-14, vi. 9, vii. 4).

3. The sinfulness of the northern kingdom (i. 4, v. 1, x. 7, 15).

4. This likewise led Israel's leaders to a sinful foreign policy (v. 13, viii. 9, x. 6, xi. 5).

5. Love remained the bond between Jehovah and Israel and individual Israelites. Hosea emphasized the holiness of God in repugnance of sin (ii. 2, 3, vi. 5, 10, ix. 9, xii. 14, etc.), but also the love of God for His people (iii. 1, xi. 1-4). 'Sin, in the last analysis, in its most terrible form, is infidelity to love. It hurts God. It destroys the sinner. He can never condone sin, but He can and does redeem the sinner.'[1]

THEMES FOR STUDY

1. To which historical incidents and personages of the past does Hosea refer, and why?

2. Describe the religious and social life of Hosea's day (see also 2 Ki. xiv. 23-27).

3. What help does this book afford towards solving the problem of God's holiness and love, His mercy and judgment?

4. What hope does Hosea hold out to those who are conscious of backsliding?

[1] Campbell Morgan, *Voices of Twelve Hebrew Prophets.*

JOEL

AUTHORSHIP, DATE AND CIRCUMSTANCES

JOEL means 'Jehovah is God' and is a common name in Scripture. All that is known of him is the statement of the opening verse that 'he was the son of Pethuel'. The book would suggest that he was a man of Judah, an inhabitant of Jerusalem, and a prophet of the southern kingdom—not a priest (i. 13, 14 and ii. 17). The style is graphic and vivacious, full of rhythm and poetry.

The unity of the book has been attacked, and the apocalyptic passages taken as interpolations, but the uniform plan and style afford a sufficient answer to this objection.

The book itself is not dated, and we must rely upon internal evidences for guidance in this respect. The date is thought to be either before the reign of Ahaz (742-726 B.C.) or after the exile, because of the absence of any mention of Syria, Assyria or Babylon among the enemies of Israel. The former of these is to be preferred for the following reasons:

1. The enemies mentioned in iii. 4, 19 (the Phœnicians, Philistines, Egypt and Edom) are those of the period preceding, and during the early years of, the reign of Joash (c. 800 B.C.: see 2 Ch. xxi. 16, 17).

2. The mention of priests and elders, without reference to the king, would fit in with this period.

3. Am. i. 1, 2 appears to be an echo of iii. 16.

4. The style and general background is like that of the earlier prophets, and in marked contrast with that of Haggai, Zechariah, and Malachi.

5. Those who urge a late date see in iii. 1, 2 a retrospect of the fall of Jerusalem. It is cast, however, in the form of a prophecy and finds a parallel in Am. ix. 14.

ANALYSIS

i. 1-ii. 17. The plague of locusts and a call to repentance.
ii. 18-32. The promised outpouring of the Holy Spirit.
iii. The day of the Lord; the judgment of the nations and blessings on Jerusalem.

CONTENTS

A dreadful plague of locusts gave the prophet occasion to warn the people of the judgment of Jehovah upon their sins. Unless they repent the punishment is certain, and the blessings which God has in store for His people can never be theirs. The thought of repentance as the gateway to rich blessing is developed in the second part of the book. The nearness of the 'day of the Lord' runs like a refrain through the prophecy.

THEMES FOR STUDY

1. Note the use of ii. 28-32 made by Peter in Acts ii. and by Paul in Rom. x. 13, and consider the relevance of these verses to the missionary enterprise.

2. Find traces of reference to this prophecy in Mt. xxiv. and Rev. ix.

AMOS

AUTHORSHIP, DATE AND CIRCUMSTANCES

THE prophecy is described as 'the words of Amos, who was among the herdmen of Tekoa'. Its genuineness is unquestionable, and is testified to by the historical incident related in vii. 10-17, by the unity pervading the whole, and by its close correspondence with the external conditions under which it was delivered.

Tekoa is situated in the barren hill-country six miles south of Bethlehem, overlooking the Dead Sea. The prophecy abounds with pastoral images derived from these surroundings (i. 2, ii. 13, iii. 4, 5, iv. 7, v. 8, vi. 12, vii. 1, viii. 1, ix. 6). Near by was the highroad leading from Jerusalem to Hebron and Beersheba, where Amos would see and meet with troops of pilgrims passing to and fro (v. 5, viii. 12). In his pages we hear repeated the rumours of the caravan and market place, how the plague was marching up from Egypt (vi. 10), ugly stories of the Phœnician slave-market (i. 9), accounts of the great festivals and fairs (v. 21 ff.), of the oppression of the poor and the careless luxury of the rich.

As a herdsman Amos would take his wool to the markets of northern Israel, whence he derived his vivid pictures of her town life, her commerce, and the ceremonial of her great sanctuaries.[1] Among these were Bethel, the chief centre of the apostate worship of Jehovah under the image of a calf, and Gilgal, seven miles further north (iv. 4, vii. 10, 13).

The judgments of God by war are abroad throughout the prophecy, soon to be fulfilled upon the surrounding nations, and finally upon Israel, by the hand of Assyria.

[1] See G. A. Smith, *The Book of the Twelve Prophets*, I, p. 79.

'The prophet writes as he spoke, preserving all the effects of pointed and dramatic delivery, with that breath of lyrical fervour which lends a special charm to the highest Hebrew oratory.'[1]

The prophecies were delivered during the forty years of the prosperous reign of Jeroboam II (i. 1, vii. 10; cf. 2 Ki. xiv. 23), and probably towards their close. The earthquake which Amos predicted (i. 1, viii. 8, ix. 5) took place soon afterwards and was for long remembered (Zc. xiv. 5). A total eclipse of the sun which occurred on June 26th, 763 B.C., may be alluded to in viii. 9.

Amos describes how God spoke to him personally (vii. 8, viii. 2) and called him (vii. 14, 15). The call came in days of material prosperity but of moral decline.[2] Amid luxury and ease the temples were crowded with worshippers, but although the worship of Baal had been suppressed by Jehu, that offered to Jehovah differed in little but the name. Superstition and immorality took the place of sincerity and faith; and although Jehovah was worshipped, His voice was disregarded and His laws were disobeyed. Within the nation were the seeds of decay, and on the distant horizon was to be seen the rising power of Assyria which would soon be God's instrument of judgment upon Israel.

In these circumstances Amos thunders out his message recalling the fundamental ideas of the Mosaic revelation, when God delivered Israel out of Egypt by His free grace, and called them to be His people (ii. 10, ix. 7), delivering to them His law and commandments (ii. 4). These they had despised, maintaining the outward form of worship (iv. 4 ff., v. 21 ff.) but with their heart far from Him. From the sanctuary of Bethel itself he sounds the note of alarm (v. 27, vi. 14, vii. 10 f.), and predicts the judgment of God.

So Amos, the last prophet to northern Israel, issued his impressive warnings a generation before the fall of Samaria, even as Christ's word of judgment (Mt. xxiii. 34-36) was fulfilled a generation later in the fall of Jerusalem.

ANALYSIS

i. 1, 2.   Amos delivers his message from Zion, the true centre of the theocracy.

i. 3-ii. 16. He describes Jehovah's judgment by the fire of war against Damascus, Gaza, Tyre, Edom, Ammon, Moab, Judah, and finally Israel.

[1] Robertson Smith, *Prophets of Israel*, p. 127.
[2] See Chapter VII.

iii., iv.   He now makes an urgent appeal for attention, addressed first to all Israel, then to the religious and the wealthy.

v., vi.   A further appeal to northern Israel is concluded with two woes upon those confident in their religious observance (v. 18, 19) and upon the utterly careless (vi. 1, 2).

vii.-ix. 10.   A series of five visions, which authenticate and illustrate his message. Of these, that of the plumb-line marks a turning point, being followed by two visions of judgment.

ix. 11-15.   The bright promise of a day when David's kingdom shall be restored and accompanied by the blessings of peace.

CONTENTS

Some critics following Wellhausen, assign the predictions of ix. 8-15 to the post-exilic period, but Dr. Driver[1] has shown that there are no adequate grounds for this, and the reverent reader will recognize in the prophecy a grand symmetrical whole, which terminates, in the true prophetic manner, with a threefold message of hope and encouragement; individuals will be spared (ix. 9), Messiah will come (ix. 11), and Israel will prosper (ix. 15).

With great fervour Amos makes his urgent appeal to Israel to turn and seek the Lord (v. 4, 6, 14). Here is the centre and heart of his message. With merciless plainness of speech he exposes and denounces the hollowness and corruption of their worship (iv. 4, v. 21) and the wickedness and social injustice which are its bitter fruit (ii. 6-8 iv. 1, v. 12, vi. 3, viii. 5). Against this dark background there flashes forth his lofty faith in Jehovah, the Creator of all things (iv. 13, v. 8), the Ruler of the nations (i. 5, v. 27, ix. 7), their merciful Deliverer in the past, who is yet calling on them to forsake their sins, to seek His face and live (v. 6).

THEMES FOR STUDY

1. What likeness, or difference, can you see between the early life, call, and mission of Moses and those of Amos?

2. Trace any references to the Pentateuch, its history or ordinances, in this prophecy.

[1] *Amos, Cambridge Bible for Schools.*

I

3. Make a list of the sins, individual and national, which Amos rebuked. Which of these have a parallel in our land to-day?

4. What are we told of the greatness and goodness of God in this book?

5. The central message of the book is found in the two imperatives in v. 4, Seek, Live (so in the Hebrew). By what means did God try to get the people to seek Him?

6. Note, and put into modern form, the passages which show the futility of seeking God through insincere ceremonial.

OBADIAH

AUTHORSHIP, DATE AND CIRCUMSTANCES

ALTHOUGH the name 'Obadiah' is quite common in the Old Testament, and means 'servant of Jehovah', the writer cannot be identified with any of those who bear this name.

The date depends upon the interpretation of the reference in verses 11-14. Some expositors see in these an allusion to events in the reign of Jehoram (2 Ch. xxi. 16, 17) or of Ahaz (2 Ch. xxviii. 17). But it is more probable that, like Je. xlix. 14-16, they refer to the evil part that Edom played in the sack of Jerusalem. In this case Obadiah and Jeremiah would be contemporaries, and the close connection of these passages would find an easy explanation; they might, for instance, have been uttered by Jeremiah and heard by, or reported to, Obadiah. It may be noted that whereas Edom is masculine, Obadiah speaks of 'her' in v. 1, perhaps following Je. xlix. 13, 14, where the reference is to Bozrah (feminine), the capital of Edom.

ANALYSIS

1-9. The doom of Edom, despite his confidence in his impregnable stronghold.

10-14. The sin for which Edom is to be punished.

15-21. The Day of Jehovah is at hand when Edom shall be punished, and Israel shall triumph.

CONTENTS

The uncharitable relationship of Edom to Israel is the burden of the prophecy. Certain punishment for Edom is predicted unless a new spirit enters into her dealings with Israel. To the latter, however, is promised the blessing of prosperity.

This short book is valuable because of its remarkable prophecy, remarkably fulfilled, as testified by many modern visitors and by the remains at Petra. Though God so judged Edom, He remembered His promise to Jacob, and spared a remnant, whereby blessing in 'salvation and sanctification' (v. 17) have come to the church.

THEME FOR STUDY

Note the parallels and contrasts between Obadiah's prophecy and Je. xlix. 7-22 and Ezk. xxxv.

JONAH

AUTHORSHIP, DATE AND CIRCUMSTANCES

THE name means 'a dove' and the only mention of Jonah elsewhere is in 2 Ki. xiv. 25, where we read that he prophesied to Jeroboam II 'that the Lord would restore the ancient boundary to Israel'. This probably occurred early in Jeroboam's reign (c. 780 B.C.). The prophecy is not dated, and was probably written soon after the return from Nineveh. Jonah was a native of Gath-hepher, a few miles north of Nazareth, and a contemporary of Amos. Although there is nothing in the book to signify that Jonah actually wrote it, this seems, in view of the title and substance, the most probable supposition.

It has been confidently affirmed, however, that Jonah was not the author, and it has been assigned by those who doubt the possibility of its miracles to the fourth century B.C. But for those who admit the miraculous element in Scripture, the following reasons will justify its historical character.

1. Its style is that of simple history, the names of places and people are not symbolical, and the theme of the power of true repentance which runs through the book testifies to its unity.

2. The magnitude of Nineveh, once denied by critics, has been proved by excavation. The circuit of the inner wall was eight miles, and there were suburbs.

3. Its historical character was accepted by the Jews, who were quite able to distinguish history from allegory, and our Lord's words seem to imply the reality of the events to which He referred (Mt. xii. 39-41).

4. Arguments to the contrary derived from Aramaisms[1] and the

---

[1] See p. 54.

supposed parallel in Jeremiah li. 34, and in some of the Psalms are of little weight.

We may therefore conclude that the book of Jonah is rightly included among the Prophets because of the prophetic character both of its substance and author.

ANALYSIS

i. Jonah's disobedience and punishment.
ii. Jonah's prayer and deliverance.
iii. Jonah's preaching and Nineveh's repentance.
iv. Jonah's repining and reproof.

CONTENTS

The contents are well known. That God's gracious purposes were wider than Israel was the lesson which was brought home through the prophet. Nineveh was, as it were, a test case, and Jonah's selfish nationalism induced him to try to escape from the task of preaching God's message there. Even Nineveh's subsequent repentance displeased the prophet, who became in himself a parable of the superabundant grace of God.

We need to be reminded constantly of the abiding lessons of this book. Not only are we taught the true implications of personal and national repentance in a story which so abundantly proves God's care for the Gentiles, and so for missionary work in general, but we have also in Jonah's miraculous deliverance a wonderful type of the resurrection of Christ.

It ought to be noted that the word translated 'whale' (Mt. xii. 40) cannot be pressed to mean anything more than the phrase used by the writers both here and in the Gospel, 'a great fish'.

THEME FOR STUDY

Compare and contrast Jonah's experience with that of Paul in Acts xxvii.

MICAH

AUTHORSHIP, DATE AND CIRCUMSTANCES

IN the LXX the prophecy entitled 'the word of the Lord that came to Micah' (i. 1) stands third of the minor prophets, following Hosea and Amos. Between these two, on the one hand, and

Isaiah's major prophecy, on the other, Micah stands as a bridge. Hosea and Amos deal with the northern kingdom, Isaiah with the southern (Is. i. 1). Micah deals with Samaria and Jerusalem, the capitals of both (i. 1).

Micah's name means 'who is like Jehovah?' being an abbreviation of Micaiah. His predecessor's last words rang in his ears (1 Ki. xxii. 28; cf. i. 2, A.V. mg.) and to his vision of judgment he added consolation (1 Ki. xxii. 17; cf. ii. 12). He seems to have had moments of inspired extravagance (i. 8), and of ebullient intensity (iii. 8), at sharp variance with spiritless conventionality (iii. 5-7). His terrible words about Samaria (i. 6), and his equally terrible judgment on Zion (iii. 12) arrested Hezekiah, influenced the chiefs and brought revival (2 Ch. xxx. 2, 6, 8-27; Je. xxvi. 16-19). Micah's isolation was painful (vii. 6, 7) but he concludes calmly confident in the God he trusted (vii. 18).

'Micah the Morasthite' was from Moresheth-gath (i. 14) in the Shephelah. The village is situated in 'the opposite exposure from the wilderness of Tekoa, some seventeen miles away across the watershed. As the home of Amos is bare and desert, so the home of Micah is fair and fertile'.[1] The district stood as a gateway to Jerusalem, either for the horse droves from Egypt (i. 13) or for the mailed ranks of Assyria (v. 5, 6).

The style is vehement, forceful, and very sharp in its contrasts and turns of thought. The prophecies are separate, evidently put together as a co-ordinated whole, possibly by Micah's own hand.

The prophecy starts with Jotham (i. 1), the period being c. 745-715 B.C. Assyria forms the political background (v. 5, 6, vii. 12) with Babylon on the distant horizon (iv. 10). Micah was vividly remembered after 120 years (Je. xxvi. 18).

As in Amos and Hosea (q.v.) knowledge of the Pentateuch is assumed. Directed mainly to Judah, the denunciation of apostasy is less pointed, but the Deuteronomic background is there (iii. 5-7; cf. Dt. xviii. 15-22) and prohibitions (v. 12; cf. Dt. xviii. 10) and penalties are recognized (vi. 15; cf. Dt. xxviii. 38). The prophet dwells on the exodus (vi. 4, vii. 15) and conquest (vi. 5), whilst the great figures of Moses (vi. 4) and the patriarchs (vii. 20) tower like peaks above. He is familiar also with later epic poetry (i. 4; cf. Jdg. v. 5, i. 10; cf. 2 Sa. i. 20), and modern history is enlisted in his service (vii. 10; cf. 2 Ki. ix. 33).

Micah had a pointed message for each of the villages in his own locality (i. 10-16). His pillories of social injustices are

[1] G. A. Smith, *The Book of the Twelve Prophets*, I, p. 376.

brilliant and destructive (ii. 1-3, iii. 1-4, vi. 10-15, vii. 1-4). He is equally at home in country and city. He refers to mountain torrents (i. 4), the flocks (ii. 12), nightfall (iii. 6), the threshing floor (iv. 13), dew and showers (v. 7), the everlasting hills (vi. 1, 2), and the serpent dust (vii. 17). He notes the idol market (i. 7), the schemes of big business (ii. 1), the callousness of the nobility (iii. 3), Jerusalem's citadels (iv. 8) and chariots (v. 10), the merchant's deceit (vi. 11), and the disruption of family life (vii. 6).

The prophet's message seems to have been reiterated all over the land, 'Hear all ye people' (i. 2; cf. Je. xxvi. 18, 'to all the people of Judah', and see also Mi. ii. 12, v. 2, vi. 1, 2, vii. 11, 12, 14).

ANALYSIS

The title is followed by three collections of prophecies, each introduced by the word 'Hear' (cf. Amos).

i. 1.   Title.

i. 2-ii. 13.   'Hear, all ye people. . . .' This includes words to Samaria (i. 5) and his own countryside (i. 10 f.), and a woe to evil doers with general condemnation of evil doings (ii. 1f.), issuing in hope (ii. 12, 13).

iii. 1-v. 15.   'Hear . . . O heads of Jacob. . . .' This deals with the princes (iii. 1) and prophets (iii. 5 f.), and the impending judgment (iii. 8); but also describes Jerusalem's coming glory (iv.) and the appearance of Messiah, the ideal ruler, and his influence on the nations (v.).

vi. 1-vii. 20.   'Hear ye, O mountains. . . .' This contains an appeal to the past (vi. 3 f.), a description of personal unworthiness (vi. 6 f.) contrasted with the people's deceits (vi. 10 f.).

'Woe is me' (vii. 1; cf. ii. 1) is the burden of the last series. The silhouette of evil is sharp cut (vii. 2-6), but the contrast so accentuated that good must prevail (vii. 7), the light must shine (vii. 8 f.). God will be bountiful (vii. 14 f.) and gracious (vii. 16-20).

CONTENTS

Some critics consider that only the first three chapters are Micah's prophecies. But G. A. Smith, after stating 'there is no book of the Bible as to the date of whose different parts there has been more discussion', concluded that the whole book mainly dated from Micah's day. Those who fully recognize v. 2 as decisively and divinely predictive will be ready to agree that Micah himself may well have uttered in addition ii. 12, 13, iv. 8-10 and vii. 8-13 in prediction of distant national deliverances. Certainly iii. 12 is a remarkable example of delayed fulfilment because of Hezekiah's repentance.[1] iv. 1-3 (cf. Is. ii. 2-4) looks like the comfort which Micah drew from the words of the earlier evangelical prophet. Parallels throughout are numerous (i. 9, Is. x. 28-32; ii. 2, Is. v. 8; iii. 6, Is. viii. 10; v. 3, 7, 8, Is. xi. 11; vi. 9, Is. x. 5; vii. 11, Is. v. 5). The co-ordination of Micah's prophecies is the work of the Spirit of truth.

Individuality rather than originality is the main contribution. The most moving passages are in the first person. In vi. 6 f. is found one of the loftiest descriptions in all Scripture of individual spiritual responsibility. God's greatness (i. 2-4) and holiness (vi. 5), man's sin in departure from the past (vi. 3, 4), in an altered message (iii. 5-7), and in social injustice (vi. 10-15)—all these are found as in Amos, Hosea and Isaiah. Thus Micah's prophecy is a link between them.

THEMES FOR STUDY

1. Compare the character and work of Elijah and Micah.

2. Note the word 'therefore' and, where possible, express in your own words the connections of thought.

3. List the main features of the national and international situation.

4. Give an inside description from this prophecy of the city life of the period, particularly that of Jerusalem.

5. Distinguish the fulfilled and unfulfilled prophecies of this book.

6. 'The enquiry of some soul in spiritual and moral trouble' (Campbell Morgan, *Voices of Twelve Hebrew Prophets*). Translate vi. 6-9 as far as possible into a letter of Christian spiritual advice.

[1] Orr, *Problem of the Old Testament*, p. 464.

NAHUM

AUTHORSHIP, DATE AND CIRCUMSTANCES

THE name means 'compassionate' and the only detail we have of
Nahum is that he is called 'the Elkoshite' (i. 1). It is uncertain
where Elkosh was, and perhaps Jerome's suggestion that it was in
northern Galilee is most probable. The reference to Judah (i. 15)
implies that he lived in the southern kingdom, and he may have
been a contemporary of Zephaniah.

The prophecy can be dated with certainty between the capture
of No-amon (or Thebes) in 664-3 B.C., and the fall of Nineveh in
612 B.C., because the former event is referred to as past (iii. 8) and
the latter foretold, probably when the attack on Nineveh was
threatened.

ANALYSIS

i.   God's majesty, long-suffering, and righteous judgment.
ii., iii.   The siege, downfall and ruin of Nineveh foretold.

CONTENTS

In a style which is perhaps second only to that of Isaiah, the
prophet describes the sins of Nineveh, capital of Assyria and
Israel's great enemy, and her consequent collapse and ruin.
G. A. Smith writes, 'His language is strong and brilliant, his
rhythm rumbles and rolls, leaps and flashes, like the horsemen and
chariots he describes'. [1]

If the tone should be thought too vindictive it must be remembered that the writer, a patriotic Jew, penned his words after
years of unparalleled cruelty and oppression. Assyrian sculptures
showing the horrors of a siege give pointed illustration to chapters
ii. and iii.

Behind all this, however, lies God's long-suffering and goodness
to those who trust Him, the background against which His final
judgment and vengeance must be seen.

THEME FOR STUDY

Compare the prophecies, given in this order, and relating to
Assyria, in Isaiah x. 24-xi. 11, Jonah, Nahum and Zephaniah
(ii. 13).

[1] *The Book of the Twelve Prophets*, II, p. 91.

HABAKKUK

AUTHORSHIP, DATE AND CIRCUMSTANCES

THE origin of the name is doubtful, and it may mean 'the embraced'. The writer prophesied in Judah during the reign of Jehoiakim (608-597 B.C.) and was a contemporary of Jeremiah. The liturgical arrangement of the Psalm in chapter iii. has led some to think that he was a Levite and a member of the temple choir.

The date may be placed at the very end of the seventh century B.C. because of its references to the Chaldeans. A few critics have doubted the genuineness of ii. 9-20, and of chapter iii., but without adequate reason, and able scholars maintain the unity of the whole. The woes of ii. 9-20 follow naturally on what precedes, and the prayer in the last chapter was apparently not occasioned by the same events as the rest of the prophecy.

ANALYSIS

i. 1-4.   The iniquity of Israel.
i. 5-ii. 4.   The coming of the Chaldeans.
ii. 5-20.   The sins and judgment of the heathen.
iii.   A prayer of faith.

CONTENTS

Although the sins of Judah impress themselves upon Habakkuk (i. 1-4), he is yet more impressed by the wickedness of the heathen. Like Nahum he teaches not only the divine mercy and long-suffering, but also the inevitability of God's judgment. It has been pointed out that Habakkuk puzzles over God's dealings with nations just as Job did over his personal afflictions.

Certain passages stand out above the rest: ii. 4 (cf. Rom. i. 17; Gal. iii. 11; Heb. x. 38), used with such force by Luther in his teaching on justification; ii. 3 (cf. Heb. x. 37 where it is applied to the second advent); and iii., a wonderful Psalm of faith in the majesty of God. Only a truly great prophet could write words which have proved themselves such an inspiration to all ages (see verses 3, 17-19).

The references in iii. 3-16 to earlier books of the Old Testament (Jdg. v. 4-5; Pss. xviii., lxviii., Dt. xxxiii.) deserve notice as bearing on the date of their composition.

THEMES FOR STUDY

1. Study in connection with ii. 4 and iii. 17-19, the New Testament references given above and the instances of faith in Heb. xi.

2. Observe the triumphant spirit of faith in God *alone* which is found in iii. 17-19, and compare it with the similar passages in Dt. xxxiii.; Pss. xviii., xxvii., and in the New Testament.

ZEPHANIAH

AUTHORSHIP, DATE AND CIRCUMSTANCES

ZEPHANIAH means 'He whom Jehovah has hidden or protected'. The 'Hizkiah (Hezekiah)' of his genealogy is thought by many to be king Hezekiah. This would throw a good deal of light on the book. Zephaniah would be a contemporary with Josiah, probably much concerned in his reforms (2 Ch. xxxiv. 3-7) and contemporary with Jeremiah and Nahum.

The superscription assigns the book to the reign of Josiah (637-608 B.C.) and many scholars place it before Josiah's reformation in 621 B.C. The allusion to the approaching foe may refer to the Scythians, who invaded western Asia about this time (according to Herodotus). Thus the prophecy may be dated 626-621 B.C.

ANALYSIS

	i.	The day of the Lord, God's judgment on sins.
ii. 1-iii. 7.		Call to repentance to the nations and Jerusalem.
iii. 8-20.		Call to rejoice in restoration, and to wait for salvation.

CONTENTS

Philistia, Moab, Ammon, Ethiopia, Assyria, and Judah are all warned as to the impending divine judgment upon their sinfulness, but especially is Judah singled out in the first chapter. Zephaniah pictures the terror of the final day of wrath as vividly as any other writer in the Old Testament. His language occasioned that great medieval hymn, *Dies Irae*. In marked contrast in style stands out the closing passage (see iii. 16, 17) depicting the blessings to restored Jerusalem.

The rebukes of Zephaniah find much point when read in the context of Josiah's reforms. Human nature is ever the same;

apathy and neglect of God are still to be condemned. Unlike Jeremiah, however, the prophet utters no tender pleadings for reform. Rather he seeks to arouse his fellow countrymen from their spiritual and moral stupor by emphasizing the great day of the Lord. This is a theme which finds a very real parallel in the New Testament (cf. i. 15-16 with Rom. ii. 5; Rev. vi. 17).

THEMES FOR STUDY

1. 'The day of the Lord is at hand' (Is. xiii. 6; Joel i. 15; Zp. i. 7; Mt. iii. 2; 2 Thes. ii. 2; Rev. i. 3). Note how this refrain runs through the Bible and study its meaning.

2. Compare the prophecies of Zephaniah and Malachi in respect of their combination of warning with promises of blessing.

HAGGAI

AUTHORSHIP, DATE AND CIRCUMSTANCES

APART from his name Haggai ('festal' or 'feast of Jehovah') nothing is known about the personal history of the author, except a tradition that he was born in Babylon and returned in Zerubbabel's company. The authenticity of the book is confirmed by the mention in Ezr. v. 1, vi. 14 of Haggai together with his contemporary, Zechariah, in circumstances which closely accord with the conditions described in these prophecies. In the LXX Pss. cxxxvii., cxliv.-cxlviii. are associated with Haggai and Zechariah.

The prophet gives the exact date of each of his four utterances (see i. 1, ii. 1, 10, 20). Darius reigned from 521-486 B.C. Haggai's prophecies were therefore given in the months corresponding to our September, October and December of 520 B.C.

The book of Ezra, particularly chapters v. and vi., should be read for the historical setting of the ministry and God-given messages of Haggai. By a decree of Cyrus in 537 B.C. the Jewish exiles had returned to Jerusalem with the set purpose of rebuilding the temple (Ezr. i). The work was begun soon after their return, but successive interruptions had brought it to a standstill. The Jews had lost interest in the Lord's house, yet were busy enough in building and ornamenting their own houses. After the accession of Darius, Haggai and Zechariah came as the messengers of God to stimulate the people to renew their labours on His temple.

ANALYSIS

i. 1-11. *First prophecy.* Rebuke for leaving the Lord's house in ruins. The dearth in the land is the direct punishment for their neglecting to honour the Lord.

i. 12-15. Zerubbabel and Joshua begin the work and receive in consequence an assurance of God's favour.

ii. 1-9. *Second prophecy.* Encouragement to the builders already growing faint-hearted. God's resources are limitless. His purposes for this, a more glorious temple, are worldwide.

ii. 10-19. *Third prophecy.* Selfishness is defiling, but blessing will begin from the day that the foundation of the Lord's house is laid.

ii. 20-23. *Fourth prophecy.* To Zerubbabel, the Lord's chosen servant, a type of the Messiah, whose reign will be established when the kingdoms of the world are overthrown.

CONTENTS

Haggai presents none of the denunciation of idolatry or rebuke of moral and social evils common to most of the prophets. His central theme is the rebuilding of the temple. The attitude of the Jews to this work reflected the attitude of their hearts toward God. Hence the prophet, moved by the Holy Spirit, insisted that the blessing of God upon their lands and labours depended on the degree to which they showed their concern for His honour in setting their hands to the erection and furnishing of the temple. This earthly temple would be glorified by the incarnate presence of the Messiah, who in the final day of the Lord, when all material things were to be shaken and all earthly powers overthrown, would remain the sure salvation of those who had sought the glory of God before their own personal interests. Herein lies the only hope of survival. Thus Haggai related the truth about life's immediate circumstances to the greater facts of the consummation of all things in the day of the Lord.

THEMES FOR STUDY

1. How far is the prosperity of God's creatures dependent on the degree to which they honour Him? See Mt. vi. 33; Acts iii. 6; Phil. iv. 11 ff.

2. What has this book to teach about the proportion of time and money which the Christian should devote to the work of the kingdom, e.g. to churches and missionary work, compared with what is devoted to personal comforts and luxuries? See 2 Cor. ix. 6-15.

3. Compare ii. 6, 7, 22, 23 with Heb. xii. 26. Created things and earthly kingdoms have a value. What place should they take in the life of a Christian?

ZECHARIAH

AUTHORSHIP, DATE AND CIRCUMSTANCES

ZECHARIAH ('he whom Jehovah remembers'), the son of Berechiah and grandson of Iddo (called 'the son of Iddo' in Ezr. v. 1 and vi. 14, passing over the intermediate generation), was the contemporary of Haggai. He probably returned to Jerusalem with the first party of released exiles, among whom his grandfather Iddo came as head of one of the twelve courses of priests (Ne. xii. 4). Zechariah later succeeded his grandfather in this priestly office (Ne. xii. 16), and we may therefore infer that he was a very young man when he uttered his first prophecies in the early years after the return (ii. 4; cf. 1 Sa. xvii. 33).

Many modern critics ascribe the last six chapters to some unknown author, judging by alleged internal evidence that (1) the circumstances are not those of Zechariah's time, (2) the style differs from that of the author who wrote chapters i.-viii. These arguments are vitiated by the following facts:

1. It is impossible from internal evidence to ascribe these chapters to any particular period. The critics themselves are almost equally divided between a pre-exilic date and one much later than Zechariah, but the prophecies are well adapted to Zechariah's own time.

2. The differences in style from the earlier chapters can be accounted for by the change of subject matter and by the lapse of years in the prophet's life. Even so, many links of comparison may be traced between the styles of the two sections. All fourteen chapters may well be the work of Zechariah.

Zechariah's first recorded prophecy was uttered two months later than that of Haggai (i. 1), followed three months after by his second (i. 7), and by the third two years later still (vii. 1). They cover therefore the period between November 520 B.C. and

December 518 B.C. The circumstances of these earlier prophecies correspond with those of Haggai, when the early zeal of the people, on their first return from captivity seventeen years before, had been replaced by coldness and indifference. Chapters ix.-xiv. were spoken probably many years later, when Zechariah was advanced in years, but we do not know under what conditions.

ANALYSIS

CONTENTS

The earthly circumstances which promote both Haggai's and Zechariah's first prophecies are the same, yet by the Spirit's leading a different theme appears in each. Haggai is concerned

almost entirely with the rebuilding of the temple and the establishment of all that of which the visible temple was the symbol;
Zechariah sees the calling of Israel in a world setting, and utters
messianic prophecies of remarkable power and distinctness.
Through the medium of visions and by direct appeal he preaches
God's call to repentance from the sins which brought the judgment
of Jehovah down upon His chosen people; His promises of
deliverance from the nations which oppress them; and the coming
of their Messiah King, who will restore, sanctify and use them as
His agent for the redemption of the Gentiles and the establishment in the last days of His kingdom upon the earth. Apart from
Isaiah, Zechariah is used by New Testament writers more than
any other prophet, so clear and frequent are his predictions
concerning Christ and His church, the Israel of faith. He
depicts in detail the sufferings and glory of the Messiah in His
acts of redemption, both at His first appearing and at His return to
earth in the final day of the Lord. Luther called this book 'the
quintessence of the prophets'.

THEMES FOR STUDY

1. Trace in detail the place Israel is to take among the nations.
How much of this applies to the spiritual church of Christ, and
how much to the Jewish nation as such?

2. By means of a reference Bible trace the echoes of this book
in the Apocalypse.

3. Collect all the messianic prophecies and the references to
their fulfilment in the Gospels.

MALACHI

AUTHORSHIP, DATE AND CIRCUMSTANCES

MALACHI signifies 'my messenger'. Expositors have been uncertain whether this was the prophet's own name or a descriptive
title defining an anonymous author's mission (iii. 1). All the other
eleven minor prophets introduce themselves by name, and it is
likely that this author follows the tradition, so that Malachi
might represent a proper name. Nothing is known about his
personal history, but expositors are agreed on the genuineness and
unity of the book.

The temple had by now been rebuilt, for to it offerings were brought (i. 7, 10, iii. 1). A 'governor' ruled the Jews under the Persian dispensation, but this was probably not Nehemiah; cf. i. 8 with Ne. v. 14, 15. Malachi denounces the same evils as prevailed in Nehemiah's time (cf. iii. 8-10 with Ne. xiii. 10-12; ii. 10-16 with Ne. xiii. 23-28; ii. 8 with Ne. xiii. 29). These prophecies may therefore have been issued while Nehemiah was away at Susa, 433-432 B.C. Malachi is the latest of the Old Testament prophets.

ANALYSIS

i. 1-5.   God's love for Israel and rejection of Edom.

i. 6-ii. 9.   The priests rebuked for blemished offerings, insincerity and neglect of the covenant.

ii. 10-17.   Against ungodly marriages.

iii. 1-12.   The coming of the incarnate Lord to refine and to judge, to rebuke and to bless.

iii. 13-iv. 1.   The coming day of judgment, the book of remembrance.

iv. 2-6.   The 'Sun of righteousness' heralded by 'Elijah'.

CONTENTS

In spite of the favour He had shown to His chosen people, God's name was despised and He was robbed of His dues by priests and people alike, who kept to the outward forms of religion prescribed in the law of Moses, but made light of the offerings and service of the temple, and profaned the sanctities of the divinely ordained family life. Malachi calls for sincerity in the service of God and purity of personal life, and foretells that God will raise up from among the Gentiles those who will 'worship Him in spirit and in truth', cf. Jn. iv. 21-24.

Under the direction of the Holy Spirit the author of the last book of the Old Testament fittingly unites the whole divine revelation both Old and New by recalling the chosen people to obedience to the eternal law, given under the hand of Moses (iv. 4) and proclaimed by the prophets (represented by Elijah, iv. 5), while pointing to the coming Messiah, who will both judge the people by the standards of His law, and save and purify those who fear the Lord. The New Testament begins where the Old leaves off. God's messenger appears in the person of John the Baptist (iii. 1; Mk. i. 2; Lk. i. 76); the true light shines and brings healing to the world (iv. 2; Jn. viii. 12, ix. 5); and on the Mount of Transfiguration Moses and Elijah are seen to testify to the fulfilment of the old dispensation on the cross of Calvary (iv. 4, 5; Lk. ix. 30, 31).

THEMES FOR STUDY

1. Study the various spheres of conduct in which human profession conflicts with the divine claims ('. . . saith the Lord. Yet ye say . . '), and compare them with features of modern society both religious and secular.

2. Apply the teaching of Malachi on offerings to its fulfilment in the 'living sacrifice' of the Christian's life. See Rom. xii. 1, 2.

3. Study the New Testament fulfilment of the messianic prophecies in this book, e.g. cf. iii. 1 with Mt. xi. 10, etc.

PART THREE

TOWARDS CHRIST'S COMING

CONTENTS OF PART THREE

CHAPTER XIV

THE MESSIANIC HOPE

THE Old Testament term 'Messiah' is the simple reproduction of the Hebrew original *Mashiach*, which means 'anointed'. The Septuagint and Greek New Testament both translate it by the term *Christos* with the same meaning. The English word 'Messiah' is found in our A.V. only twice (Dn. ix. 25, 26); 'Messias', the Greek form, also appears twice (Jn. i. 41, iv. 25). In the Old Testament the term is usually translated 'anointed', and so we have, e.g., 'the anointed of the Lord' (La. iv. 20), 'the Lord's anointed' (1 and 2 Sa.), 'Mine anointed' (1 Sa. ii. 35), 'Thine anointed' (Hab. iii. 13), 'His anointed' (Ps. ii. 2). Such might have been rendered 'The Messiah of the Lord', 'The Lord's Messiah', 'My Messiah', etc. Our New Testament prefers the Greek word 'Christ', rather than 'anointed', for the term by then had become a proper name applied to the divine-human Person, who fulfilled its perfect meaning. In early times 'Messiah' was relevant to any one specially set apart for office and, as symbol and seal thereof, anointed with holy oil. It is given to the patriarchs (Ps. cv. 15), to Cyrus (Is. xlv. 1), to the High Priest of Israel (Lv. iv. 3, 5, 16), to the messianic Prince (Dn. ix. 25), and above all to the king, who, supremely throughout the whole Hebrew history, is 'the Lord's anointed' or 'the anointed of the God o Jacob' with special reference to the Davidic line.

GENERAL CHARACTERISTICS

The messianic hope, which is born very early in the story of the human race, is presented throughout the whole of the Old Testament as something which has its source entirely in God. The hope is *given* to man. Hence the messianic references of the Old Testament Scriptures present a very wide field of divine redeeming activity. Whoever the 'anointed one' may be, a human 'seed', a patriarch, a prophet, a priest, a king, he is the agent of God the Saviour. The national hope strengthened as the revelation became more definite, guiding the aspirations of the ages to centre on a single person. Although for long the name Messiah did not belong absolutely to the King who should come,—for, as we have seen, the term is applied to Cyrus, the deliverer from the Exile,—

it is certain that before the Christian era the term was definitely associated with 'a son of David' and that the Jewish people were awaiting the coming of a particular and royal Messiah (Lk. ii. 26; Jn. iv. 25).

We are now in a position to follow the golden thread of revelation right back from Jesus Himself to the first hint of a divine Redeemer. We hold the key whereby we can unlock the mysteries of revelation, and these various Old Testament allusions to messianic deliverance can now be interpreted in the light of the end, as the seed can be named and explained when the flower appears. This is an important point to note for it affords a sound principle of exegesis, namely, that we should not deduce from any single reference more than can be made relevant to the historical circumstances of the prophecy. The messianic hope moved toward a goal, the consummation of the world's existence, the coming of the kingdom of God, and of His Messiah. In short, the messianic hope was broad-based, progressive, and historical; it was supremely of God and not of man. It grew toward the climax of God's redemptive purpose and found its resting place in Jesus Christ, the ideal and the real Messiah, the Saviour of the world.

THE MESSIANIC KINGDOM

The messianic hope was at first associated with a renewed and reconstructed Hebrew kingdom, an ideal beyond the achievements of Solomon. It was a national rather than an individual expectation, and focused upon the perfect manifestation of God to His people in His permanent abode among them. It looked forward to 'the day of the Lord', viewed as a prolonged era. In fact, it signified the golden age of Israel's aspirations, the kingdom of the victorious king, the reign of the Messiah. Judgment and salvation are its marks. The 'day of the Lord' would not bring only the condign punishment of all of Messiah's enemies, but also the just reward of all who acknowledged the Lord's anointed. The temptation of the chosen people was to hold a mechanical, and not a moral, view of this messianic kingdom, as if it would come automatically and spell salvation only for them. To this superficial and perverted idea the very first of the writing prophets set the alarm: 'Woe unto you that desire "the day of the Lord". It is darkness and not light' (Am. v. 18-20). While the hope of the golden age had to be chastened by the certainty of a righteous judgment, yet the fundamental outlook was transfused with joy. The messianic Psalms (e.g. ii., xvi., xlv., lxxii., xciii., xcvi., xcvii., xcviii., xcix., cx., cxviii.) notably evince this gladness, because of the character of God revealed in His merciful mission to men.

'O sing unto the Lord a new song; for He hath done marvellous things: His right hand, and His holy arm, hath gotten Him the victory. The Lord hath made known His salvation: His righteousness hath He openly showed in the sight of the heathen. He hath remembered His mercy and His truth toward the house of Israel: all the ends of the earth have seen the salvation of our God.' (Ps. xcviii. 1-3).

The dark vengeance of the Lord upon His enemies is brightly illuminated with His light and love.

'For the day of the Lord is near upon all the heathen: . . . But upon Mount Zion shall be deliverance, and there shall be holiness; and the house of Jacob shall possess their possessions' (Ob. 15, 17).

The messianic age or kingdom, in the view of many of the prophets, would be an era of complete transformation of society and even of the earth itself as a fitting environment.

"And many people shall go and say, Come ye, and let us go up to the mountain of the Lord, to the house of the God of Jacob; and He will teach us of His ways, and we will walk in His paths: for out of Zion shall go forth the law, and the word of the Lord from Jerusalem. And He shall judge among the nations, and shall rebuke many people: and they shall beat their swords into ploughshares, and their spears into pruning-hooks: nation shall not lift up sword against nation, neither shall they learn war any more' (Is. ii. 3, 4).

In more majestic tones still we have that memorable prophecy of the peaceable kingdom of the Branch out of the root of Jesse, wherein the realm of the beasts also falls under benediction (Is. xi. 1-9).

THE MESSIANIC KING

The general conception of a messianic age first dawned upon the Hebrew race under the discipline of divine revelation, before the idea of a messianic King was fully grasped. Yet the King and the kingdom are inseparable in the historic progress of the hope. *The King is essential to the kingdom.* He is the supreme agent in its coming and establishment. A backward glance proves that the ideas are indissolubly linked. The Messiah is portrayed also as

Prophet and Priest, but the royal aspect illuminates both these offices. In the thought of the people of God these offices were always closely associated and not infrequently combined. Moses foretells the rise of a prophet like unto himself in Dt. xviii. 15-22: 'The Lord thy God will raise up unto thee a prophet from the midst of thee, of thy brethren, like unto me; unto him ye shall hearken', and in Moses the two functions of civil ruler and spokesman for God were united as they were afterwards in Samuel. David is viewed as a prophet by the historian of New Testament times as he records Peter's sermon (Acts ii. 29-31). The portrait of the messianic King, sketched in Is. xi. 1-10, presents him as endowed with prophetic gifts by 'the Spirit of the Lord.'

As for the priestly function it was no uncommon thing, even outside the Hebrew nation, for the king of ancient days to approach the supernatural powers on behalf of his people and to engage in the ritual of sacrifice. So it follows that the priesthood of Messiah is involved in His kingship. Psalm cx. sets forth the priestly King in no uncertain colour.

'The Lord said unto my Lord, Sit thou at my right hand, until I make thine enemies thy footstool. . . . The Lord hath sworn, and will not repent, Thou art a priest for ever after the order of Melchizedek.'

The messianic King of Ps. ii. is enthroned in the temple; 'Yet have I set my king upon my holy hill of Zion.' The conclusion accordingly is that the prophetic office of Moses, the priesthood of Aaron, and the throne of David are all included in the idea and ideal of the Messiah. The Lord's anointed is the perfect Prophet-Priest-King.

THE MESSIANIC PRESENTATION

It is interesting to gather together the various types, figures, and metaphors by which the conception of the Messiah was transmitted to the chosen people and the messianic hope kept alive.

(a) Immanuel

'Behold, a virgin shall conceive, and bear a son, and shall call his name Immanuel' (Is. vii. 14). While the original word in the Hebrew 'almah means a young woman, and not necessarily a virgin, yet the Greek Septuagint translates by parthenos which is definitely the term for a maiden. This sign is given to the house of David that, although disaster shall fall upon its royal throne, yet out of it shall arise one who is 'God-with-us' (Immanuel). This royal child is further described by the same prophet:

'For unto us a child is born, unto us a son is given: and the government shall be upon his shoulder: and his name shall be called Wonderful, Counseller, The mighty God, The everlasting Father, The Prince of Peace' (Is. ix. 6).

(b) Suffering Servant

There is a series of 'Servant Poems' in the prophecy of Isaiah which reaches its climax in the familiar 'golden passional' of chapter liii. (Is. xlii. 1-4, xlix. 1-6, l. 4-9, lii. 13-liii. 12). These have all an immediate reference to the historical situation of the moment, but few deny that they find their fulfilment in the life, death, and resurrection of Jesus Christ, that they point to an ideal Servant-Son whose vicarious sufferings atoned for the sins of His people. The forefront of the vision in the prophet's mind seems to have been occupied at first by the nation personified and idealized (xlix. 3), or perhaps by that minor group, the principal remnant, 'the Israel within Israel'; but it is finally an individual figure that he sees (lii. 14), which even Jewish rabbis have identified with the Messiah. The essential point of the revelation is that the sin of man and its dire effects are laid upon Him by *God Himself*, who also prolongs His days and sees in His sufferings a means whereby many shall be justified. The insight of the Old Testament here makes its deepest penetration into the mystery of divine redemption.

(c) Branch

The Messiah is also presented as a Branch, or sprout, springing forth from the Davidic root, even when that royal house falls to its lowest level in history. The idea of a supernatural resurgence, and the hope of a miraculous rebirth became conserved in the term 'Branch' (Hebrew *tsemach*, from a root meaning 'to sprout forth').

'In those days, and at that time, will I cause the Branch of righteousness to grow up unto David; and he shall execute judgment and righteousness in the land' (Je. xxxiii. 15; cf. Is. iv. 2; Je. xxiii. 5; Zc. iii. 8, vi. 12).

(d) Son of Man

This title is employed in Ps. viii. in its purest human sense of dependence upon almighty God: 'What is man, that thou art mindful of him? and the son of man, that thou visitest him?' In this sense the words are used in the book of Ezekiel of the prophet himself. The interpretation of the phrase in Dn. vii. 13, 14 is different. Here the title is accepted as messianic. The tone of the whole book of Daniel is eschatological, and it became a decisive factor in the formation of the messianic hope previous to the Christian era. The title does not appear to have been generally used in the days of our Lord as a description of the Messiah for it is evident in the Gospels that Jesus used 'Son of Man' rather as a *veil* than as a *revelation* of His Messiahship.

(e) Son of David

'I will declare the decree: the Lord hath said unto me, Thou art my Son; this day have I begotten thee' (Ps. ii. 7). The second Psalm is recognized as one of the most definitely messianic revelations in the Old Testament. It presents the divine King and His universal kingdom; 'Ask of me, and I shall give thee the heathen for thine inheritance, and the uttermost parts of the earth for thy possession' (cf. Acts ii. 25, iv. 25, xiii. 33; Heb. i. 5, v. 5). The vision of limitless sovereignty had centred in the son of David ever since Nathan's prophecy (2 Sa. vii. 12, 13), and became a living messianic hope, though never a historical reality until Jesus became the heir of this glowing ideal.

(f) Star and Sceptre

'I shall see him, but not now: I shall behold him, but not nigh: there shall come a star out of Jacob and a sceptre shall rise out of Israel.'

Balaam, in spite of his crass materialism and sordid avarice, was overpowered by the Spirit of God and uttered this remarkable prophecy in the presence of Balak who had hired him to curse the chosen race (Nu. xxiv. 15-17). The sceptre is the emblem of royalty (see Ps. xlv. 6; cf. Gn. xlix. 10; Am. i. 5, 8). The metaphor of a star in this setting is suffused with all that belongs to kingship. The king of Babylon is described as a fallen star by the prophet Isaiah (xiv. 12). Thus the figure was not unfamiliar when the New Testament seer presented Jesus as declaring 'I am the root and the offspring of David, and the bright and morning star' (Rev. xxii. 16). The Jewish interpreters regarded the utterance of Balaam in a messianic sense for we have the Aramaic paraphrase in one of the Targums 'A King shall arise from the horn of Jacob, and a Messiah shall be anointed from the house of Israel'. There is no more suggestive metaphor of hope than that of a rising star. It may be that the Magi who followed the star to Bethlehem were conversant with Balaam's prophecy.

(g) Shiloh

'The sceptre shall not depart from Judah, nor the ruler's staff from between his feet, until Shiloh come' (Gn. xlix. 10, R.V.).

The passage is difficult, but its messianic significance has long been recognized. There are different views of the text.

1. Shiloh is a proper name and an accepted title of the Messiah, the equivalent of 'the Prince of Peace' (see A.V. and R.V.). The word is probably cognate with Babylonian *Shêlu*, 'prince'.

2. Shiloh is the name of the place where Joshua erected the tabernacle and the meaning is (as R.V. margin) 'until he (Judah) came to Shiloh', i.e. to receive special distinction there.

3. Shiloh may be taken, as in the ancient versions, as two words and rendered 'whose it is' (R.V. margin). Rabbi J. H. Hertz translates 'The sceptre shall not depart from Judah, nor the ruler's staff from between his feet, until that which is his shall come', i.e. until he comes to his own and all the tribes submit to his rule.

However translated the messianic allusion appears inescapable.

(h) Royal Bridegroom

See Ps. xlv. This nuptial song celebrates the marriage of some Hebrew monarch, probably that of Solomon with the daughter of the king of Egypt. The Psalm is generally admitted to be messianic in its deeper meaning and is interpreted as presenting the mystical marriage of the King Messiah with the church, His bride. Some of the sentences are written with golden letters, for ever applicable to the Lord's anointed (see verses 2, 6, 7, 13, 14; cf. Mt. xxii. 1-14; Eph. v. 32; Rev. xix. 6-9).

(i) Corner Stone

'Behold, I lay in Zion for a foundation a stone, a tried stone, a precious corner stone of sure foundation: he that believeth shall not make haste' (Is. xxviii. 16, R.V.).

The reference may be primarily to the messianic kingdom which, as being sure and steadfast and imperishable, is set forth in sharp contrast to the kingdoms of Assyria and Egypt and even to Judah itself, for the Davidic empire was but the shadow of the enduring kingdom of God. For this interpretation Daniel's reading of Nebuchadnezzar's dream may be accepted as confirmation (Dn. ii. 34-44). But more vitally this stone, this tried stone, this precious corner stone of sure foundation is an emblem of the Messiah Himself. It is another way of presenting His person and work. The sweet singer of Israel employs the symbol in this sense:

'The stone which the builders refused is become the head stone of the corner. This is the Lord's doing; it is marvellous in our eyes' (Ps. cxviii. 22, 23).

Our Lord takes up the metaphor and, in the parable of the Wicked Husbandmen, applies it to Himself in His rejection by the Jews (Lk. xx. 17). The idea was familiar to the early church and the apostle Peter has no diffidence in expressing it without ambig·uity, for he writes of a 'living stone, rejected indeed of men, but with God elect, precious' (1 Pet. ii. 4-7).

(j) Angel of Jehovah (Heb. mal'akh Yahweh)

There is a line of Old Testament revelation, sometimes considered apart from the messianic, which runs along a course of theophanies, or manifestations of God (Gn. xvi., xviii., xxii.; Ex. iii; Jos. v.; Jdg. vi.). It is believed that this mysterious 'angel of Jehovah' is a person like unto Jehovah but distinct from Jehovah. Dr. Charles Hodge[1] sums up the reformed view: 'the angel who appeared to Hagar, to Abraham, to Moses, to Joshua, to Gideon and to Manoah, who was called Jehovah and was worshipped as Adonai (Lord), who claimed divine homage and exercised divine power, whom Psalmists and Prophets set forth as the Son of God, as the Counsellor, the Prince of Peace and the mighty God, and whom they predicted was to be born of a virgin and to whom every knee should bow and every tongue confess of things in heaven and things in earth and things under the earth, is none other than He whom we now recognize and worship as our God and Saviour, Jesus Christ.'

THE MESSIAH'S PERSON

The messianic hope in its ultimate stages centred on a definite person. The goal is an ideal Messiah whose outlines grow more and more distinct and whose characterization becomes clearer as revelation progresses. There are three main lines in the Old Testament which may be traced.

(a) The divine line

The Messiah is heralded as Lord (Is. xl. 3; cf. Mal. iv. 5; Mt. iii. 3, xi. 10-14). He is 'mighty God' (Is. ix. 6-7). He is 'Immanuel'

---

[1] *Systematic Theology*, Vol. I, p 49c.

(Is. vii. 14). He is the eternal 'Son' (Ps. ii. 7; cf. Acts xiii. 33; Heb. i. 5; Lk. ii. 11). He is the 'eternal King' (Ps. xlv. 1, 6; cf. Heb. i. 8). He is 'changeless Creator' (Ps. cii. 25-27; Heb. i. 10-12). He is 'the divine Ruler' (Ps. cx. 1; cf. Mt. xxii. 41-45). He is the 'ascended Lord' (Ps. lxviii. 18; cf. Acts i. 9; Eph. iv. 8).

(b) The human line

In this direction it is to be observed how the revelation begins broadly and narrows down to a definite person. In no other manifestation of the Old Testament is the progress so obvious and well marked.

The Woman's seed. 'I will put enmity between thee and the woman, and between thy seed and her seed.' This is the first intimation of a deliverer and is commonly called 'the *Protevangelium*' (Gn. iii. 15; cf. Mt. i. 18; Heb. ii. 14, 15).

Abraham's seed. The Lord said unto Abram 'In thee shall all families of the earth be blessed' (Gn. xii. 1, 3, xxii. 18, xxvi. 4; cf. Mt. i. 1; Acts iii. 25-26; Gal. iii. 8, 16).

Isaac's seed. 'In Isaac shall thy seed by called' (Gn. xxi. 12; cf. Rom. ix. 7; Gal. iv. 28).

Jacob's seed. 'In thy seed shall all the families of the earth be blessed' (Gn. xxviii. 14; cf. Mt. i. 2).

Judah's seed. 'The sceptre shall not depart from Judah, nor a law-giver from between his feet, until Shiloh come; and unto him shall the gathering of the people be' (Gn. xlix. 10; cf. Heb. vii. 14; Rev. v. 5).

Jesse's seed. 'There shall come forth a rod out of the stem of Jesse, and a Branch shall grow out of his roots: and the spirit of the Lord shall rest upon him' (Is. xi. 1; cf. Mt. i. 6; Lk. iii. 32).

David's seed. 'I have made a covenant with my chosen, I have sworn unto David my servant, Thy seed will I establish for ever, and build up thy throne to all generations' (Ps. lxxxix. 3-4 and 35-37 cf. 2 Sa. vii. 12-13; Rev. iii. 7, xxii. 16; 2 Tim. ii. 8; see also 1 Ki. ix. 5.

Virgin birth. 'Behold, a virgin shall conceive, and bear a son, and shall call his name Immanuel' (Is. vii. 14).

Birth-place. 'But thou, Beth-lehem Ephratah, though thou be little among the thousands of Judah, yet out of thee shall he come forth unto me that is to be ruler in Israel; whose goings forth have been from of old, from everlasting' (Mi. v. 2; cf. Mt. ii. 1 ff.; Lk. ii. 4, 15; Jn. vii. 42).

(c)   The line of vicarious suffering

This divine-human Person is also depicted in the Old Testament
as suffering for His people and the full meaning of His passion as
an innocent and kingly sufferer comes to light only in the life and
death of Jesus Christ.   In the fulfilment alone is it possible to
grasp the messianic significance of this scarlet thread which runs
through the Scriptures of the old dispensation.

The Messiah was betrayed.   'Yea, mine own familiar friend, . . .
which did eat of my bread, hath lifted up his heel against me'
(Ps. xli. 9; cf. Jn. xiii. 18).

He maintained a dignified and accusing silence.   'He was oppressed,
and he was afflicted, yet he opened not his mouth: he is brought
as a lamb to the slaughter, and as a sheep before her shearers is
dumb, so he openeth not his mouth' (Is. liii. 7; cf. Mt. xxvii. 14;
Acts viii. 32).

He was cruelly scourged.   'With his stripes we are healed' (Is. liii.
5, l. 6; cf. Mt. xxvii. 26).

He was crowned with thorns.   'His visage was so marred more than
any man' (Is. lii. 14; cf. Mt. xxvii. 29).

He was crucified.   'They pierced my hands and my feet' (Ps. xxii.
16).   'And they shall look upon me whom they have pierced' (Zc.
xii. 10; cf. Jn. xix. 18, 37).

He was mocked.   'All they that see me laugh me to scorn: they
shoot out the lip, they shake the head.'   'He trusted on the Lord
that He would deliver him: let Him deliver him, seeing He delighted in him' (Ps. xxii. 7, 8; cf. Mt. xxvii. 39-43).

His raiment was divided.   'They parted my garments among them;
and cast lots upon my vesture' (Ps. xxii. 18; cf. Jn. xix. 23).

The cry of dereliction.   'My God, my God, why hast thou forsaken
me?' (Ps. xxii. 1; cf. Mt. xxvii. 46; Mk. xv. 34).

He cried 'I thirst'.   'They gave me also gall for my meat; and in my
thirst they gave me vinegar to drink' (Ps. lxix. 21; cf. Jn. xix. 28;
Mt. xxvii. 34).

He was accursed on the tree.   'He that is hanged is accursed of God'
(Dt. xxi. 23; Gal. iii. 13).

He was 'the Lamb of God' (Ex. xii. 3; Jn. i. 29). With His blood the
covenant was sealed (Ex. xxiv. 8; Lk. xxii. 20), and, in the offering

of His body once for all, the sacrifices of the Law were consummated (Heb. x. 4-9).

Thus the goal of the messianic hope was the Messiah Himself, the divine-human Person who was in very truth 'wounded for our transgressions, and bruised for our iniquities' on the cross of Calvary. The age-long ideal found its realization in the historic incarnation, life, death, resurrection, and ascension of Jesus of Nazareth, whose coming again is the complete fulfilment of every hope.

CHAPTER XV

FROM MALACHI TO MATTHEW

AS the reader turns from Malachi, the last book of the Old Testament, to the opening pages of St. Matthew's Gospel in the New he immediately becomes aware of an altogether different environment. It is as though a new world has been entered. This sudden change is not to be wondered at, however, when we remember that over four hundred years separate the histories of Ezra and Nehemiah and the prophecies of Haggai, Zechariah, and Malachi from 'the fulness of the time' when the Lord Jesus was born at Bethlehem.

By way of a parallel let us try to imagine the reactions of a citizen of London falling asleep towards the close of the reign of Henry VIII, and not waking again until our own day. To such a man names like Trafalgar and Waterloo, Nelson and Napoleon would be meaningless; and when he went to church he would utterly fail to understand the conduct of the service. So during the four hundred years between Malachi and Matthew decisive battles like Issus and Actium were fought, and names like Alexander and Julius Cæsar came into prominence. These years saw also the rise of the Pharisees and Sadducees, and the translation of the Septuagint Version of the Scriptures. It will be the aim of this chapter to show how far these things affected the people of Israel, and to give the origin and meaning of some of those terms which, absent from the pages of the Old Testament, appear without previous introduction in the New.

The history of the period follows in outline the sequence of the great world empires, Babylon, Medo-Persia, Greece and Rome, which were the subjects of Nebuchadnezzar's dream of the great image and of Daniel's interpretation as given in Dn. ii. 31-43. Israel inevitably came into contact with each empire in turn. A glance at a map of the Middle East will show how Palestine lay as a buffer state between the great civilizations of the Mesopotamian valley to the north-east and the valley of the Nile to the south-west. Just as in past years the smaller European states have been at the mercy of their more powerful neighbours, so we shall see, as the story is traced, how the fortunes of Palestine were bound up with those of the more powerful nations around.

THE PERSIAN EMPIRE

The end of Babylonian domination and the beginnings of the Persian period come within the pages of the Old Testament itself. But to get the necessary perspective we need to recall that Cyrus, king of Persia, having first conquered the Medes who then joined forces with him, captured Babylon in 539 B.C. A decree of Cyrus in 537 B.C. brought about the return of the first party of exiles, led by the prince Zerubbabel and the priest Jeshua. Ezra and Nehemiah followed much later, Ezra in *c.* 458 and Nehemiah in 445 B.C.[1]

The opening of the period between Malachi and Matthew is therefore concerned with the closing years of the Persian empire, roughly the hundred years from 433 to 333 B.C. The former was the date of Nehemiah's second visit to Jerusalem, and the latter the date of the break-up of the Persian empire. For the Jews these years were comparatively uneventful. There were Grecian wars away to the west and Parthian wars to the east, but the Persian emperor held undisputed sway over both Egypt and Mesopotamia so that Palestine, lying between them, remained undisturbed. Certain features of these years must, however, be noted.

After the Exile the name 'Jew', a title previously reserved for Judæans, came to be applied to all the children of Israel. And the people who returned from Babylon came back cured once and for all of the sin of idolatry. Indeed, so complete had the cure become that a new danger was soon apparent; in place of conformity to the nations around there arose an utter contempt for them. The system called *Scribism* emphasized the separateness of Jewish blood and exalted Israel's one remaining glory, the *law*. The term scribe (*Sopher*) originally meant any writer or recorder, but from the time of Ezra onwards (Ezr. vii. 10-12) became the special title of a class who devoted themselves to the guardianship, study and exposition of the law, meticulously regarding the letter, but disregarding its spirit (Lk. xi. 42). Doubtless this exaggerated sense of national distinctiveness had its part to play in the divine plan to complete the messianic preparation, but it is easy to see how separation, founded upon a false sense of race-pride, began to sow the seeds of the worst features of Pharisaism.

During the exile, away from their temple and its services, the Jews had gradually developed the simpler form of worship, with

---

[1] See p. 180, and also J. S. Wright, *The Date of Ezra's Coming to Jerusalem* (Tyndale Press).

K

its stress on the reading of the Law, which came to be so associated with the *synagogue*. When we remember the debt the Christian church owes to the synagogue, so far as worship and order are concerned, we must not overlook the importance of this new development. A further change during the Persian period was in the political importance attached to the position of High Priest. Although the palace-fortress of the Persian governor overlooked the Temple area, the Persians were quite content to leave home rule largely in the High Priest's hands. The nation found in him its rallying-point; the conquerors found him a useful political instrument. Thus both Persian statesmanship and Jewish nationalism were satisfied.

Mention must also be made of the beginnings of the *Sanhedrin*, a word later to become a term of infamy in connection with the trials of the Lord Jesus. The Sanhedrin was organized (it may even have originated) about this time. It possibly arose out of Ezra's 'Great Synagogue', appointed as an advisory court of seventy of the Jewish elders.

In view of what has already been said about blood-purity and racial pride, it is a little surprising to note another change which also took place at this time. The exiles brought back with them the speech of their conquerors, *Chaldee* or *Aramaic*, a language akin to Hebrew and which had already filtered into Palestine through the influence of Assyrian and Babylonian colonists. Hebrew remained the language of worship and revelation, but Aramaic became henceforward the speech of the people; and we remember that our Lord Himself spoke in Aramaic, some of His actual expressions being preserved for us in the Gospels (e.g. Mk. v. 41, xv. 34).

THE GRECIAN EMPIRE

The Persians had never been successful in their efforts to extend westwards into Europe. The battles of Marathon (490), Salamis (480) and Platæa (479) are remembered for their decisive results in barring the Persian advance as well as for the heroic resistance of the city states of Greece. By the year 336 B.C. Greece herself was ready for world conquest and found her unifying inspiration in the genius and generalship of Alexander, who succeeded to the throne of his father, Philip of Macedon, in that year. He first gained control of the Greek city states and then attacked the Persians, defeating them at the battle of Issus in 333 B.C. By 330 B.C. the Persian empire was completely under his control.

Alexander's treatment of the Jews was not unfavourable. It has been suggested that, as a pupil of Aristotle, he was able to appreciate the worth of this people with their ancient literature and distinctive culture. One of his first acts on conquering Egypt had been to plan the city of Alexandria which soon became a place where Jews were made welcome. Two out of its five quarters eventually became Jewish, and it was not long before the number of Jews in Egypt was greater than the number in Palestine itself.

It is at this point that reference must be made to the *Dispersion*. Already a large body of the people had remained in Babylon at the time when the patriots were returning from exile. Now an even larger colony was establishing itself in the 'greater Palestine' in Egypt. With the development of intercourse between Europe, Africa, and Asia as a result of Alexander's conquests, the Jewish dispersion increased throughout North Africa and Asia Minor. This was one of the ways in which God was making ready the Mediterranean world for the missionary activities of the first century of the Christian era, so that James in Acts xv. 21 could report, 'Moses of old time hath in every city them that preach him'. These Jewish colonies became strategic bases for the Christian missionaries.

We return to the history of the Grecian empire. Alexander died in 323 B.C., before he had reached the end of his thirty-third year. After his death the empire was rent by the quarrels of his generals, the Diadochi (or 'Successors'), until eventually, by 315 B.C., four kingdoms had emerged: (1) Macedonia, (2) Thrace, (3) Syria with Mesopotamia, and (4) Egypt with southern Syria (see Dn. viii. 21, 22). For over one hundred years Palestine was ruled from the south by the dynasty of the Ptolemies in Egypt, a rule which, except for two brief periods, continued up to 198 B.C., when a powerful king of Syria, of the Seleucid dynasty, Antiochus III ('the Great'), gained control of the land from the north. Jewish records of this century, the third century before Christ, are scanty, but it seems to have been on the whole a time of peace. Jews continued to settle in Egypt, encouraged by the Ptolemies; while the Seleucids, anxious to maintain friendly relations with the people on their borders, welcomed them to settle at Antioch and the cities of Syria and Asia Minor.

To this century of Ptolemaic rule belongs the commencement of a work of far-reaching importance. Ptolemy Philadelphus (285-247 B.C.), a ruler of particular culture and enlightenment, encouraged the translation of a Greek version of the Old Testament, which is still known as the *Septuagint* after the seventy Jewish scholars who began it at Alexandria under his patronage. The importance of the Septuagint in the spread of Old Testament teaching among the Jews of the Dispersion, as well as to the Gentile world, cannot be overstressed. The writers of the New Testament show their familiarity with this Greek version of their Holy Scriptures.

Throughout this century also Greek influence penetrated more widely and deeply into the land of Palestine. Greek cities grew up in the region to the east of Jordan, thus forming the *Decapolis*, a district of ten cities to which we find references in Mk. v. 20 and vii. 31. It is said that the Sanhedrin, the aristocratic and powerful council of elders, became organized according to Grecian fashion. The Greek influence had a good side, but it was the attraction of Greek manners and customs, the subtle scepticism of the Grecian outlook, and the selfishness of Grecian pride that were being absorbed by the Jewish leaders. The High Priesthood had degenerated into an office of ceremony and formalism. The Ptolemies found it convenient to regard the High Priest as their resident representative, and the ways of Greece held at least as great attractions for the High Priestly family as did the traditions of Judah.

At this point, therefore, there were clearly two tendencies at work in the land. There were the Hellenizers, those who favoured conformity to Grecian ideas and ways. On the other hand there were still many who clung doggedly to the traditions of their fathers and believed firmly in that separation which Ezra had proclaimed. Jewish hopes for the future lay with the latter tendency, but a trumpet-call was needed to rouse the Separatists, the party of the 'godly' (Heb. *Chasidim*) to action. When the call came the divine instrument was ready. God's champion was Judas Maccabæus.

THE MACCABÆAN REVOLT

As has been stated above, Palestine passed under the control of the Syrian or Seleucid kings in 198 B.C. Antiochus III, the Great, died in the year 187. He was followed by Seleucus Philopator (187-176). On his death, there succeeded to the throne 'a king of fierce countenance' (Dn. viii. 23), whose name has become a by-word for evil. This was Antiochus IV, *Epiphanes*, the Illustrious. The new king was an aggressive Hellenizer and was determined to weld his subjects together by enforcing Greek ways upon them. Robbed of the fruits of victory in a military campaign in Egypt through the intervention of the Romans, whose power was now gradually extending eastwards, he stopped in his rage at Jerusalem on his journey home. There had been trouble arising out of the evil practices of the High Priest, and Antiochus was determined to stamp out Judaism once and for all. The temple was sacked, a statue of the Olympian Zeus was erected in the temple court, and a sow was offered upon the altar of burnt offering, 'the abomination that maketh desolate' of Dn. xi. 31. The year was 167 B.C.

The first serious resistance was offered by an aged priest, Mattathias, of the Hasmonæan family, who slew a Syrian officer who had arrived at the village of Modin to enforce the decrees of the evil Antiochus. The venerable priest's action was the signal for revolt. 'Whosoever,' he cried, 'is zealous of the law and maintaineth the covenant, let him follow me,' as he with his five sons fled to the hills of Judæa. Many of the *Chasidim* followed him, and soon there was an organized body of resistance in the land. When Mattathias died in 166 B.C., the leadership fell to his third son Judas Maccabæus, or Judas the Hammer. By a series of almost incredible victories (and we must remember that for more than three centuries the Jews had been unaccustomed to battle) he drove back the Syrians so that on the twenty-fifth of the Jewish month Chisleu, in 165 B.C., he was able to cleanse the defiled temple and restore the daily sacrifices at Jerusalem. This great event was ever afterwards remembered in the *Feast of the Dedication*, a national festival which appeared now for the first time in Israel's history. We find reference made to the Feast in Jn. x. 22. It is not hard to understand the feelings of the Jews, by that time under the heel of the Romans, as they gathered around Jesus, and stirred by the commemoration of the deliverance wrought by Maccabæus, put the question: 'How long dost thou make us to doubt? If thou be the Christ, tell us plainly.'

THE SONS OF MATTATHIAS

Judas continued the struggle against Syria until his death in battle in 161 B.C., after which the leadership passed to Jonathan, the youngest son, who retired temporarily to the south in order to rally his forces. It was fortunate for him that he assumed the leadership at a time when there was great confusion in Syria over the succession to the throne. As clever in statecraft as his brother Judas had been brave in battle, Jonathan quickly realized how this confusion could be turned to the advantage of his own people.

The rival claimants for the Syrian throne, Demetrius (who had
actually been king since 162 B.C.) and the Pretender, Alexander
Balas, who claimed to be a son of the evil Antiochus IV, vied
with each other for the support of the Maccabæan leader. Alexander Balas came forward with a cross of gold and a purple robe
and offered to appoint Jonathan 'High Priest of the Nation'.

We need to ponder the significance of this offer. Only a few
years previously Jonathan had been a fugitive in the Judæan hills.
Now he was being offered the highest religious office in the land,
an office that for nearly thirteen centuries had followed the
Aaronic line. And this succession was being set aside without so
much as a protest—at the instigation of a Syrian prince, a man
outside the pale so far as Jewry was concerned. Such were the
inevitable results of circumstances. The High Priestly family had
become discredited in the Maccabæan revolt when the sons of
Mattathias had clearly been the nation's outstanding personalities.
In accomplished fact Jonathan was the leader of the nation, and
ever since the return of the exiles the nation had looked for leadership from the High Priest. What more natural now than that
Jonathan, the Hasmonæan, should be made High Priest? Did the
High-priesthood of Melchizedek occur to them in connection with
this transference? We must note, however, that many of the
Chasidim were far from happy about this new development. They
felt that Jonathan's ideas about political independence went unnecessarily beyond the religious aims of the early days of the
struggle. More than ever these people turned their thoughts to
the past, to their lofty traditions and the glories of the law. A
gulf was growing between priest and scribe, eventually to issue in
two distinct and hostile parties.

The otherwise astute Jonathan was ultimately caught in a trap
set by Trypho, the general of Alexander Balas, and put to death
in 142 B.C. Now Simon, the last remaining of the five sons of
Mattathias became leader. He was a capable ruler, and his days
were marked by the growing prosperity of his people. Although
still nominally under Syrian control, Judæa in his time enjoyed
what amounted to a practical independence. The Syrian garrison, which throughout the years had held possession of the
Acra, the temple-fortress, was now forced to surrender; commerce developed through the passing of the port of Joppa into
Simon's control; and the law was given an honoured place in
the land. Jonathan had been appointed High Priest by a heathen
Pretender. Now the position was regularized, and in 140 B.C. the
hereditary High Priesthood was formally vested in the Has-

monæan family. Simon's prosperous period of leadership came to an end when he was treacherously murdered by his son-in-law Ptolemy in 135 B.C.

THE DESCENDANTS OF THE MACCABÆANS

1. *John Hyrcanus* (135-105 B.C.). Jewish influence increased still further during the High Priesthood of Simon's son and successor, John Hyrcanus. Two events in particular deserve attention. The borders of Judæan power now extended northward, southward, and eastward, and during the progress northward the city of Shechem and the Samaritan temple on Mount Gerizim were destroyed. Syria at the time was too busy with its own troubles to be in a position to interfere. It will be remembered that the returning exiles, so proud of their race-purity and Jewish exclusiveness, had rejected the help offered by the mixed inhabitants of Samaria. Opposition eventually deepened into implacable hatred, and a rival temple had been erected on Mount Gerizim; this John Hyrcanus destroyed, and his action intensified the bitterness between the two people. The New Testament reader is familiar with the atmosphere of hostility existing between Jew and Samaritan (Jn. iv. 9). When the woman at Sychar's (Shechem's) well said to the Lord Jesus, 'Our fathers worshipped in this mountain,' she referred to Mount Gerizim, on which the rival sanctuary had formerly stood.

The other great event of the period was the conquest and forcible conversion of the Edomites, a people on the southern border of Judæa. The significance of this will be seen more clearly when we come to the time of Herod. Once the Edomites had been conquered and included in the Jewish nation they became the most ardent of all the Jews. It was a strange irony of history that descendants of the hated Edomites, who had refused the people of Israel a safe passage on their way to the promised land (Nu. xx. 14-21), should rise to such importance in Jewry in later years.

Reference has already been made to the Hellenizing tendencies of the High Priestly party, and to the conservative orthodoxy of the *Chasidim*. The time had now come when two distinct parties emerged. Those who favoured conformity, chiefly those of the High Priestly family and of the classes of nobles, tracing themselves back to Zadok the priest, became known as *Sadducees*—the sons of Zadok. The *Chasidim* drew aside into still greater exclusiveness, determined 'to make a hedge round the law', and became known as the separate ones—*Pharisees*. The word Sadducee refers to a class: the word Pharisee to an organized sect. Both names were destined to play an important part in New Testament times. John Hyrcanus at first leaned towards the Pharisees, even though he was High Priest, but later joined the party of the Sadducees.

2. *Alexander Jannæus* (104-78 B.C.). John Hyrcanus died in 105 B.C. and was succeeded by his eldest son Aristobulus, who after a brief reign as king was followed by his brother Alexander Jannæus. This period marks the decline in the once noble family of Mattathias. Alexander's long reign was one of cruelty, lust of conquest and self-aggrandisement. At one time his territories included more than the original possessions of the twelve tribes. But throughout there were constant domestic troubles, particularly between the Pharisees and the Sadducees, Alexander himself supporting the latter. At the conclusion of a bitter civil war we hear for the first time in Jewish history of death by *crucifixion*, when at an impious revel in Jerusalem Alexander ordered eight hundred of the leading Pharisees to be crucified. Little more than a hundred years remained before *the* cross, 'towering o'er the wrecks of time', would be set up outside the walls of the same city.

3. *Civil war and confusion* (78-65 B.C.) Alexander Jannæus died in 78 B.C., and for some years his widow Alexandra reigned wisely and in comparative peace, her chief trouble coming from her two sons. She had appointed Hyrcanus, the elder, a weak and unambitious character, to the High Priesthood, but when she died, the younger one Aristobulus, who was bold and aggressive, secured the help of Antipater, an Idumæan (or Edomite) who had fought his way up to power in his own country, and seized the throne. In the midst of this struggle the might of Rome appeared on the scene.

THE ROMAN EMPIRE

1. *The Intervention of Pompey.* The Roman general Pompey had been occupied with his eastern conquests, and in the year 65 B.C. his lieutenant Scaurus appeared in Damascus. Both of the brothers Hyrcanus and Aristobulus, immediately appealed for his help. This was granted to Aristobulus, but in the year 63 Pompey himself arrived at Jerusalem and decided that the elder brother Hyrcanus was the legitimate ruler; in addition to which the Roman general knew that an unambitious king would be a useful puppet. After a siege of three months and the massacre of 12,000 Jews, Jerusalem was crushed and, to the horror of its inhabitants, Pompey dared to enter the Holy of Holies inside the temple. But

this time the astonishment was his when, within the veil, he found no idol or object of worship; *vacuam sedem, inania arcana* (a vacant shrine, empty mysteries) wrote Tacitus. It is refreshing to remember that throughout the turmoil and corruption of the centuries the Holy of Holies still bore its impressive witness to the reality of spiritual worship as God had originally intended for His people.

Pompey proceeded to act with typical Roman speed and efficiency. Hyrcanus was allowed to retain the office of High Priest, but could no longer use the title of king. Instead he would be called 'ethnarch'. All her acquired territorities were taken away from Judæa so that the new ethnarch ruled over the tiny kingdom of Judah only; Galilee in the north and Samaria in the centre were now to be separate districts. Jewish independence had been brought to an end. And when Pompey returned to the imperial city and celebrated the greatest triumph Rome had ever seen, one of the captives in that great procession was Aristobulus, once king of the Jews.

2. *Antipater made Roman Procurator.* Hyrcanus was now the ethnarch of Judæa, but the real local power lay in the hands of the Idumæan Antipater. Rome's intervention had meant for him a tremendous gain and he determined to maintain friendly relationships with the mistress of the world. But his plans received a sudden check when Aristobulus with one of his sons, Antigonus, escaped from Rome and renewed the struggle in Palestine. Aristobulus soon after met with an untimely death, but Antigonus survived to make one more vain bid for power.

In 49 B.C. civil war broke out between the Roman generals Pompey and Cæsar. Antipater and Hyrcanus supported their patron Pompey; but when Cæsar conquered Pompey at Pharsalia (48 B.C.), Antipater deserted his cause, and hurried to Rome to offer friendship and help to the victor.

In 47 B.C. Antipater was made a Roman citizen and appointed *procurator* of Judæa, a term with which New Testament readers are familiar in connection with the account of the crucifixion under the procuratorship of the Roman Pontius Pilate. Julius Cæsar showed favour to the Jews, granting them tax remission, religious liberty, and permission to rebuild the walls of Jerusalem that Pompey had destroyed. It was therefore with sincere regret that they learned of his death in 44 B.C. In the next year Antipater himself was poisoned, but he had already made one of his sons, Phasael, governor of Jerusalem, and another, Herod, governor of Galilee. The mention of the name of Herod is a reminder that we are approaching the time of the advent.

3. *The last of the Hasmonæan line.* Alexander Jannæus had left three sons: Hyrcanus who was still High Priest in Jerusalem, Aristobulus whose son Antigonus was still at large, and Alexander who had died, leaving a daughter Mariamne and a son, named also Aristobulus. The general unrest which followed the assassination of Julius Cæsar had drawn Herod and Hyrcanus together, and now this connection was strengthened by Herod's marriage to Mariamne. But Antigonus remained an obstacle to the Idumæan's progress, and in 40 B.C. he entered Jerusalem aided by an army of Parthians. This move was popular with the people, who thought they now saw in his arrival an opportunity to be delivered from Roman oppression. Hyrcanus was cruelly mutilated, and Phasael committed suicide, in prison. Herod himself managed to escape with Mariamne and her brother Aristobulus. Antigonus then assumed the kingship and the High Priesthood for a brief and precarious period.

Meanwhile the crafty Herod made his way directly to Rome, there to secure the support of Antony and Octavian for the claims of the young Aristobulus. But doubtless to his own surprise and delight, the Romans decreed that Herod himself should become the king of the Jews. Herod returned to Jerusalem, and in the year 37 B.C. the city fell to a combined Herodian and Roman army. The brief and unhappy reign of Antigonus was cut short by the Roman executioner. So died the last of the Hasmonæan princes, bringing to an end one of the greatest families in all history. True, there were yet three survivors, but these were not to live very long. The aged Hyrcanus, the young Aristobulus and his sister Mariamne were all soon to fall victims to Herod's murderous suspicion. Of the Hasmonæan family Josephus wrote: 'This family was a splendid and illustrious one, both on account of the nobility of their stock and of the dignity of the High Priesthood, as also for the glorious actions which their ancestors achieved for our nation; but these men lost the government through their dissensions one with another, and so it came to Herod, the son of Antipater, who was of no more than a vulgar family and of no eminent extraction, but one that was subject to other kings.'

4. *Herod the Great rebuilds the temple.* It is beyond the scope o this brief historical sketch to attempt a detailed portrait of king Herod. He has been called 'the Great', and great he was in his vices as well as his personal abilities. Throughout his reign he was hated by the Jews: they saw in him an Edomite and a friend of Rome, and he had replaced the dynasty of the more popular

Hasmonæans. In the early years of his reign he met with constant difficulty from the schemings of his court, and his later years were darkened by trouble from his own sons. Caught up in this mælstrom of evil intrigues, he sank from excess to excess, putting out of the way any who seemed to stand in his path, including even his favourite wife Mariamne. In the conflict between Antony and Octavian for Roman power, Herod's friendship with Antony found him on the losing side. But after Antony's defeat at Actium in 31 B.C. the Idumæan again hastened to greet the victor, and succeeded in gaining his friendship.

Throughout his reign Herod sought to maintain a kingdom at least outwardly peaceful and prosperous. His brilliant organizing gifts were never seen to better advantage than in his public enterprises and magnificent buildings. He rebuilt the temple on a scale that eclipsed even the glories of the days of Solomon (Jn. ii. 20). The existence of the *Herodian* party in New Testament times is an indication that there were some among the people who appreciated his efforts (Mk. iii. 6, xii. 13). On the other hand there was a party called the Zealots (Lk. vi. 15) who went further than the Pharisees in their refusal to swear an oath of allegiance or to pay taxes to this Idumæan monarch or to Cæsar.

Herod's last days were tragic indeed. His body was afflicted by a loathsome disease, and his mind tortured by guilty remembrances and constant fears. Small wonder was it that when 'wise men from the east' appeared in the Judæan capital with the question: 'Where is he that is born king of the Jews?' Herod was alarmed. Was he to be defeated at the eleventh hour, the tyrant who for years had steered a throne past every rock and shoal of hatred and intrigue? The massacre of the innocents at Bethlehem was as nothing when, throughout his reign, the murder of the greatest in the land had been an instrument of Herodian policy.

So we come to the end of this story covering the period from Malachi to Matthew. We have arrived at 'the days of Herod the king' (Mt. ii. 1) when 'there went out a decree from Cæsar Augustus, that all the world should be taxed' (Lk. ii. 1). This Augustus was the Octavian to whom Herod had hurried to ask for friendship after the battle of Actium. And so it happened that while Herod was tossing in pain inside the palace at Jerusalem, Joseph and Mary were making their way southwards from Galilee to Bethlehem, the city of David. God so loved the world that He had sent His only begotten Son.

CHAPTER XVI

THE BACKGROUND OF THE NEW TESTAMENT

IN the days of Herod the king 'there went out a decree from Cæsar Augustus, that all the world should be taxed'. And thus, through the unconscious instrumentality of a Roman emperor, it came to pass that Jesus Christ was born in Bethlehem. 'When the fulness of the time was come,' wrote St. Paul, 'God sent forth His Son.' From apostolic times Christians have believed that world-history, going apparently on its own way, was nevertheless overruled by the providence of God to be a preparation for the gospel. It is true that the Roman empire was for long hostile to Christianity, and persecuted the church for centuries. But in many respects the historical situation at the beginning of our era was definitely favourable to the preaching of a universal faith; and at that point Christ came with the gospel that was to make disciples of all nations.

THE POWER OF ROME

The outstanding fact in the world situation was the political, social, and cultural unification of the Mediterranean world under the dominion of Rome. After long centuries of almost continuous war and social strife, the lands which border on the Mediterranean were at last brought under a strong and stable political order which ensured their peace and prosperity for two hundred years, a quite remarkable and generally beneficent achievement. No doubt this result was due in part to a successful predatory imperialism. It has been suggested that men had fought themselves to a standstill and had reached a position of stalemate. This is not how it appeared either to Virgil or to Paul. To Virgil it seemed that Augustus had achieved the destined mission of Rome, solved to perfection and for ever the political problem of mankind, and even inaugurated the age of gold. Paul was sure at least that 'the powers that be are ordained of God'. In his eyes they were God's ministers for good and for the restraint of evil. Except for the Roman senatorial aristocracy, who lost their power to pillage the provinces for their private gain, everyone hailed with joy the advent of the new regime. Looking back from our detached point of view with our sore experience of a disunited world, we must praise the empire of Rome as having made the world of its day safe for civilization, and as having made possible in practice an œcumenical religion.

With stable government came also the means of safe and easy communication; the land and sea routes, effectively organized and policed, carried not only armies and officials, but also merchants with their wares, and tourists and itinerant teachers with their ideas. There was no restriction on migration from one part of the empire to another. The greater cities were the homes of very mixed populations, and the smaller ones lost their self-sufficiency by being merged in a larger whole. The citizen-patriotism of classical times did not quite disappear, but the trend was now towards individualism and cosmopolitanism.

Unlike Alexander the Great, the Roman emperors did not seek directly to further the unity of the human race, but indirectly their rule actually promoted it. Their policy was to maintain the privileges of Roman citizens, among whom were included the Italian races. Very gradually was Roman citizenship extended to provincials. When, in A.D. 211, it was made universal throughout the empire it became a mark not of privilege, but of subjection. Nevertheless the Stoic idea of humanity as one brotherhood was strongly at work in the minds of thoughtful people. Paul did not introduce it into the world, but without doubt he added to its reality when he preached it in the form: In Christ there is 'neither Jew nor Greek, . . . Barbarian, Scythian, bond nor free' (Col. iii. 11).

The Roman Imperial Government as established by Augustus has been described as 'mildly fascist'. It was certainly a government of conservatism. It frowned upon all novelties as inevitably dangerous. It would be inexorably opposed to any new movement that threatened to turn things upside down. (That, of course, was not how Paul himself would have described his mission!) It suspected all secret societies as possible hotbeds of treason, and prohibited them. The function of a provincial governor was to keep his province quiet by every means. His power, if limited in the case of Roman citizens, was absolute over provincials, who, however, had some protection from sheer tyranny in the fact that he was subject to the supervision of the emperor. At the same time very considerable freedom was allowed. The cities enjoyed a large measure of autonomy under their own elected magistrates, and, provided they kept the peace, had nothing to fear from the proconsul. Apart from payment of tribute, they preserved their ancient laws and customs. Individuals, too, had freedom of movement and freedom of thought. In his extensive missionary travels Paul encountered most of the forms of local government, city magistrates, imperial procurators, senatorial proconsuls. He saw the inside of prisons and was once illegally beaten. But before he stood at Cæsar's judgment seat his testimony was that he found government on the whole protective; a positive aid against the enemies of his mission.

The Roman empire was co-extensive with western civilization. All its people were not on the same level of culture, of course, but educated people everywhere had been brought up on the same literature, were familiar with the same stock of ideas, and lived much in the same way. Unlike the non-Christian world today, where India, China, and Africa present very different problems to the Christian missionary, it was one mission field. This may account, in part at least, for the fact that Paul did not limit his activity to any particular area. His mission was to the empire, i.e. to the western world as a whole. That his work was effective proves that his conception of it was right. How differently the statement 'The field is the world' strikes us today. The most obvious advantage was that he encountered no linguistic barriers anywhere. Greek had long been the *lingua franca* of the Mediterranean world. It was the common tongue of all the eastern provinces. It was the language of the cities of Sicily and South Italy, the old Magna Græcia, as also of Massilia in Gaul. It was the mother tongue of large elements in the population of Rome, and the second language of the educated classes there. Plutarch, on his visit to Rome (*c.* A.D. 90), had no need to learn Latin for his lecturing or social intercourse. Paul wrote to the Romans in Greek, and in Greek Marcus Aurelius meditated. Indeed, it might have seemed that Greek was destined to become the language of the empire which owed so much of its intellectual culture to Greece. It was at least the language of Christianity for two centuries.

THE RELIGIOUS SITUATION

There was, however, no religious unity in the Græco-Roman world, nor did the imperial power dream of imposing one. On the contrary, it not only tolerated but even encouraged the various religions, on the principle that all men everywhere were bound to honour their ancestral gods. The few exceptions to the rule of toleration before Christianity arose were justified on the ground that inhuman rites, such as human sacrifice, must be prohibited. The religions of the empire may be classified into three groups: (1) political religions; (2) mystery religions; and, we may add, (3) philosophic religions.

1. *Political religions.*   These were religions of political communities, and that of Rome itself may be taken as typical. It was the concern of Roman citizens only, wherever they might live. It had been instituted at the origin of the city by Romulus and Numa as a means of keeping the city right with the gods, whose favour was thus secured. The ceremonies were carried out under the supervision of the Pontifex Maximus and the colleges of priests and augurs.   These magistrates need not be believers or theologians, but they generally took the ancestral rites very seriously as important parts of civic duty. Indeed, all Roman life, public and private, was permeated by formal religious observance.   Cicero, who was a professed sceptic, could nevertheless hold the office of augur, and in public willingly conformed to the rules of the Pontiffs. He even claims that the Romans were the most religious of men, because they gave to the gods their due.

It is often said that the Roman state religion as a faith was dead by the end of the Republican period. Among the ruling classes this may have been true.   It certainly has to us more of the appearance of a political device than of a religion. But Augustus thought it worth his while to work for its revival. He even took over the office of Pontifex Maximus, an office which was held by his successors till 382, when it was abolished by the Christian emperor Gratian.   That a religion of this type was still alive is proved by the potency in Ephesus of the cry, 'Great is Diana of the Ephesians.' Any public calamity was apt to be the occasion for an outburst of religious fanaticism.

Another form of political religion is the worship of kings which came into the Greek world with Alexander the Great. It appears in such titles as *Euergetes* (benefactor), and *Soter* (saviour) given to his successors: at its best it represents gratitude for the benefits of law and order secured by political power. But often it is the expression of mere flattery, as in the acclamation of Herod Agrippa as a god by the Tyrians in Acts xii. 22. There is at least a suggestion of it in the name Augustus, who was certainly worshipped as a god, with special temples and priesthoods, in the cities of Asia Minor. In Rome and the Latin west this cult did not take root, though successive emperors were regularly enrolled among the gods after death. Emperor-worship was perhaps regarded as more a gesture of loyalty than a religion, and for that reason it proved the most serious difficulty for Christians. They could not even formally acknowledge the divinity of the emperor and hence they appeared disloyal.

2. *Mystery religions.* Much more recognizable as religions in our sense are the mystery religions of the Hellenistic world. However varied in place of origin and original character, they came to have many features in common. They were personal and voluntary religions, to which individuals devoted themselves by undergoing special rites of initiation, and may be called universal religions in the sense that they appealed to man as man without respect o race, or citizenship, or rank. The benefits which they offered were spiritual rather than material. They promised to the initiate regeneration, redemption from the wheel of existence and the bodily prison-house of the soul, and immortality in union with God. They were based upon a myth of a suffering but finally triumphant deity, in whose sorrows and victory the initiate took part through symbolic rites and pageantry. Such religions made an appeal to the heart and the emotions, which was quite lacking in the political religions; hence their wide popularity. But they were not without an appeal to the head, too, if, as seems evident, some of the philosophers owed much to them.

There is no need to enter into the details of the various mysteries. It will be sufficient to mention two. The ancient Egyptian religion of Mother Isis, whose son Osiris was lost and found, spread over the Greek world during the Hellenistic period, and claimed the philosopher Plutarch as a votary. In 43 B.C., after a long struggle with inveterate Roman prejudice, it won recognition in Rome itself, and was popular among the masses of foreigners and among women. Mithraism, which originated in Persia, was somewhat later in making its mark in the west. Mithras, the unconquered sun, was man's saviour from the power of darkness. To his cult, which dramatized the strenuous battle of good against evil, women were not admitted. Indeed, it became a soldiers' religion, and its traces are found all along the military frontier zone of the empire. It was known in the second century A.D. to Justin Martyr who noted certain resemblances to Christianity, and explained them as malicious travesties of true religion. In the third century it bade fair to become the religion of the soldier-emperors and of the state.

These varied religions were in no sense rivals and did not

normally attack one another, but lived happily side by side. For all their differences, from the Christian point of view, they appeared as, simply, 'heathenism'. Indeed, they tended to borrow ideas and rites one from the other, and so to merge into one. This process, known as syncretism, was at work before the advent of Christianity, but it reached its climax in the religion of Julian the Apostate in the middle of the fourth century. He hoped to find in his artificial amalgamation of religions an effective counterpoise to the victorious church.

3. *Philosophical religion.* Philosophy had had a long history since the classic days of Plato and Aristotle. If less creative, it had come to wield a wider influence. The Platonic and Aristotelian schools remained, but the Stoics and Epicureans, with their rival conceptions of the happy life, captured the popular attention. To counter their easy dogmatisms the successors of Plato abandoned the mysticism of the master, and contented themselves with criticism of the new schools. They professed complete scepticism. Down to *c.* 80 B.C. philosophy was hostile to religion, though in public most philosophers conformed to the state cults. Cicero himself adhered to the school of the Sceptics, but already in his student years a change was coming over the philosophical world. Academics and Stoics wearied of their wordy battles and the way opened for a revival of genuine Platonism. Philosophy was becoming sympathetic to religion once again, and, while critical of the old mythology of the poets, was prepared to offer an apologetic for positive religious faith and practice. It elaborated a natural theology which included the doctrines of monotheism, providence, the immortality of the soul, and a future judgment. It inculcated besides a humanitarian ethic. Indeed, so close was Seneca to Christianity in many of his theological and moral teachings that he was actually claimed by Christians as one of Paul's converts. There is no doubt that for many Platonism paved the way to Christian faith.

We must not, of course, exaggerate the preparedness of the Græco-Roman world for the acceptance of Christianity. It needed three centuries of intensive evangelization and heroic witness-bearing to overcome the pride and self-satisfaction begotten of so mighty and dazzling a civilization. But its external order, its deep spiritual aspirations, and its groping after truth, all assured the presence in it of good soil when the Sower came with His seed which is the word of God. The Sower, however, must come from a very different world, for 'salvation is of the Jews'.

THE JEWS AND THE DISPERSION

We have already seen in the previous chapter that the Romans found Judæa a troublesome province. Its people were non-co-operative and revolt was endemic. They therefore entrusted its government to a dependent king and Herod the Great ruled the lands which had once been king David's empire. On his death (4 B.C.) his kingdom was divided among his sons. Archelaus, the eldest, ruled Judæa until his banishment in A.D. 6, when it passed for a time under the direct rule of Roman procurators, of whom Pontius Pilate is the best known. Herod Antipas ruled in Galilee as tetrarch until A.D. 39. In 41 a political storm, raised by the emperor Caligula who ordered his own statue to be set up for worship in the temple, induced Claudius to return to the expedient of a king, and Herod Agrippa, grandson of Herod the Great, reigned from 41-44, and closed his evil life with a frightful death (Acts xii.). Thereafter there were procurators again (e.g. Felix and Festus of Acts) until the outbreak of the disastrous war which ended with the destruction of the temple in A.D. 70.

The Herods and the procurators did not interfere with the religious practices of the Jews, and left wide religious authority to the Sanhedrin. The Herods even attempted to get themselves accepted as patriotic Jewish kings. They found some support among the Sadducees, the hereditary temple priesthood, who, strangely enough, held aloof from all contemporary religious enthusiasms. At the other end of the scale, the Zealots were violent and fanatical opponents of Roman power. Between the two the bulk of the people admired and followed the Pharisees, though inevitably not in all the details of their legalism. In the synagogues they heard the Law and the Prophets read and expounded and learned to reverence the God of their Fathers, to obey His will, and to trust His promises of salvation through His Messiah. From boyhood Jesus Christ was accustomed to go to the synagogue on the sabbath day, and in the synagogue He first declared His message of the fulfilment of Scripture in Himself. 'He came unto His own, and His own received Him not.' Yet it was in Galilee that He found His first disciples. The soil had been in part prepared for the seed. The messianic hope had pointed to the gospel of the kingdom of God (Jn. i. 45).

Palestine was the mother country of multitudes living outside its boundaries. We know, from the Acts of the Apostles and many other sources, how widely the Jews were spread throughout the Græco-Roman world. Every considerable city had its Jewish colony. In Alexandria and Egypt there are said to have been a million of them. Rome, too, had its Jewish quarter. Their exclusiveness and scorn of idolatry earned for them the hatred of their neighbours, which broke out here and there in anti-semitic riots. Educated people like Tacitus were ready to believe, and even to write down, the most outrageous nonsense about their religious beliefs and practices. Nevertheless the imperial Government gave them legal recognition as a religious community entitled to protection in the exercise of their ancestral customs. Local synagogue authorities were allowed a certain jurisdiction in matters pertaining to the Mosaic law. Gallio, Proconsul of Achæa, knew that in such matters he could not intervene (Acts xviii. 14). The Jews were specifically exempted from the civic cults and from emperor-worship, and from attendance at the law-courts on sabbath days. Nor were they called on for military service. They were thus a people apart, and, even in dispersion, closely bound together by loyalty to the law. They remained also in close touch with Jerusalem, their metropolis, which all hoped to visit at least once in a lifetime.

For all its national exclusiveness, however, the Judaism of the Dispersion was an energetically propagandist faith before the advent of Christianity (Mt. xxiii. 15). The conversion of Roman citizens was illegal, and we hear of several in high station who were put to death for their adherence to Jewish 'atheism'. But this did not affect the subject peoples, and we find the synagogues in Greek-speaking cities surrounded by a fringe of adherents, men and still more women, who, without becoming Jews in the full sense, i.e. accepting all the ritual requirements of the law, were 'worshippers of God'.

THE SEPTUAGINT

As a missionary agency the first place must be given to the old Alexandrian translation of the Hebrew Bible known as the Septuagint, which was read and expounded in the synagogues of the Dispersion. This was not indeed a book for the educated, who were apt to be repelled alike by its style and contents. It was neither literature nor philosophy as generally understood. But it had an attractive power by reason of its very 'barbarity' and exotic wisdom. There was also its great antiquity, its note of authority, and its insistence on righteousness and divine judgment. 'What is Plato,' asked Numenius, 'but Moses speaking Attic Greek?'

JOSEPHUS

For the educated, Josephus, a Jewish priest but also a favourite of the Flavian emperors, rewrote the history of his people in the literary Greek style. He described their beliefs and customs, giving them a Greek colouring. The ritual observances of the law were explained symbolically. The patriarchs became sages, Moses was the founder of an ideal state, and the parties of later Judaism, schools of philosophy. In this way all the wisdom of the Greeks, their monotheism and their ethical ideas and maxims were shown to have their source in Moses who lived at a much earlier date than Homer.

PHILO

But it was in Alexandria where the Jews abounded that their propaganda was most marked, and expressed in an abundant apologetic literature. The outstanding figure was Philo (c. 20 B.C.-A.D. 40). He belonged to a wealthy and influential Jewish family and was a contemporary of Paul, but he makes no reference to Christianity. He was a believing, practising, and patriotic Jew, but he was at the same time profoundly influenced by Greek philosophy. Most of his writings are ostensibly expositions of the Old Testament, but his allegorical method of interpretation enables him to go a long way towards destroying its real meaning. God becomes the perfection of abstract being with none but negative attributes; Philo cannot think of Him as directly related to the world as its Creator or as the Ruler of man's history. He has to find some intermediary agent, and so he develops an ancient Greek conception of God's Logos, God's Word or Wisdom, which he can even call God's Son without thinking of it as personal. With him the Logos is not equivalent to the Christ. Rather it is a stream of potency which imposes form on matter, maintains the universe in being and rules over human history, and shines as the light of reason in human minds. Nevertheless Christian theologians beginning with St. John use the same term in presenting Jesus Christ to the Greek world as the Word and Wisdom of God the Father. Philo's works were preserved by the church as a valuable armoury of weapons, apologetic and dogmatic.

The gospel was first preached in Jewish Palestine where it was at least expected by some as the fulfilment of the Old Testament promises. It would soon have repercussions throughout worldwide Jewry where it would be discussed, accepted, or rejected in every synagogue, and so find access to the Gentile world. The first Christian congregations consisted mainly of Jews and of Gentile adherents of Judaism, who found in Christianity all the truth they had looked for in the synagogue without the entanglements of the ritual law. Among the Gentiles it was welcomed by the humble and simple, and the teachings of philosophy provided Christian teachers and apologists with an instrument with which to win over the learned to the faith.

The more one considers the historical situation at the beginning of our era, both in the Jewish and the Gentile world, the more convinced one becomes of the truth of Paul's word, 'When the fulness of the time was come, God sent forth His Son.'

PART FOUR
THE NEW TESTAMENT

CONTENTS OF PART FOUR

CHAPTER XVII

THE LIFE OF CHRIST

WHAT is intended here is to write a very brief outline of the course of events in the life of Jesus. The standpoint taken is that of the great Christian creeds, which regard Jesus as 'the King of glory', 'the everlasting Son of the Father', and declare that the reason for His appearing upon earth was 'for us men and for our salvation'; and so this article thinks of the life of Jesus as set between the twin miracles of the virgin birth and the resurrection.

The wealth of material contained in the four Gospels may at first present to the student the appearance of a maze, but he will find some helpful guiding clues if he keeps his gaze fixed on certain outstanding events and crucial turning points.

THE BIRTH

Jesus was born at Bethlehem, about six miles S.S.W. of Jerusalem, quite likely not on 25th December, and, it would appear, a few years earlier than our Christian chronology makes out. Two of our Gospels, the first and the third, state that Jesus was born of a virgin, Mary, a devout maiden belonging to the little Galilean village of Nazareth. The virgin birth presents no insuperable difficulty to one who really believes in the full deity of Jesus, and who has thought out all the implications of that. As Denney so cogently puts it, in his *Studies in Theology* (p. 64): 'He came from God, all the apostles believed, in a *sense* in which no other came; does it not follow that He came in a *way* in which no other came?' Those who desire to enquire more fully into all the problems involved here ought to consult Dr. J. Gresham Machen's thoroughgoing work, *The Virgin Birth of Christ.* In his valuable work, *Was Christ born at Bethlehem?* Sir William Ramsay grapples with the various problems connected with Cyrenius (Quirinius) and the Imperial Decree (Lk. ii. 1, 2), and with other problems bearing upon the Birth of Jesus.

THE SILENT YEARS

Jesus spent some thirty years of seclusion at Nazareth, among the mountains of Galilee. Here He lived as one of a poor family, traces of that poverty being found, many think, in the references in His teaching to patched clothes and to the cheapest kind of food, sparrow flesh. He evidently worked as a carpenter there (Mk. vi. 3). There are apocryphal Gospels which recount absurd stories of miracles wrought by Him in His boyhood days (making sparrows of clay and causing them to fly away, etc.), stories which only bring out by contrast the sanity and truthfulness of the Scripture narrative. In the canonical Gospels the only incident that breaks the silence of the thirty years is that recorded in Lk. ii. 42-52. At the age of twelve we see Jesus conscious of a unique relation to God, speaking of God as His Father. The contrast between Mary's 'thy father' and the words 'My Father' on His lips (Lk. ii. 48, 49) deserves consideration.

THE BAPTISM

This is the first important landmark in the ministry of Jesus; it was the official beginning of the ministry, led up to, and prepared for, by the preaching of John the Baptist. All the Gospels stress the importance of the ministry of John. Luke very carefully dates it, indicating, with the painstaking care of an exact historian, its precise place in the framework of world history (Lk. iii. 1, 2). This is the only dated event in the New Testament. The preaching of the Baptist took place, possibly, in A.D. 26-27, and the Baptism of Jesus took place a month or two before the Passover in A.D. 27.

John proclaimed that the time of the fulfilment of the Old Testament prophecies was approaching, and that the Messiah was at the door. He summoned the nation to prepare for His coming by repentance. As the result of his stern preaching in which he spared nobody, Pharisees or soldiers, a deep and widespread revival of religion was brought about (see especially Mt. iii. 5, 6). John could produce a deep sense of sin, but he could not take away sin: that was to be the work of Jesus (Jn. i. 29). He was to baptize with the Holy Spirit and with fire, thus communicating new spiritual life and power to penitent souls. When He was baptized alongside sinners, that was a partial fulfilment of the prophecy regarding the Servant of the Lord, 'He was numbered with the transgressors' (Is. liii. 12; Mt. iii. 15). Here we see Jesus with His face set toward the cross at the very beginning of His ministry. 'The Shadow of the Cross' which Holman Hunt, with real insight, saw cast over the body of Jesus in Nazareth, is over His soul here by the Jordan banks.

'Go to the Jordan,' said Augustine, 'and thou shalt see the Trinity.' The Holy Spirit, in His fulness, came down on Jesus to furnish His humanity with all needed gifts and graces, so as to be the instrument of His deity in the carrying out of the work which He came to do. The words spoken to Him by the Father carry us back to Ps. ii. 7 and Is. xlii. 1, so that the two Old Testament conceptions of the Messiah, as King and as the suffering Servant, are here blended.

THE TEMPTATION

'Jesus, full of the Holy Spirit, . . . was led by the Spirit in the wilderness forty days' (Lk. iv. 1, R.V.), and there endured His mysterious temptation. It is best interpreted in the light of the false messianic ideas of the time. The tempter sought to induce Jesus to be a Messiah on the basis of bread, satisfying the creature needs of man, to the neglect of his deeper needs, the need for spiritual bread; he sought to entice Jesus to use startling, spectacular methods of winning men instead of the method of quiet, spiritual influence; he sought to lure Him away from the hard road that led to the cross and to make Him compromise with evil. Every attack on the soul of Jesus was repulsed, 'every temptation' overcome (Lk. iv. 13, R.V.), and Jesus returned in the power of the Spirit into Galilee (Lk. iv. 14). On His way thither He bound to Himself by the cords of love some of His leading disciples (Jn. i. 35-51). At Cana of Galilee He performed His first miracle (Jn. ii. 1-11).

THE MINISTRY IN JUDÆA

In the fourth Gospel (chapters ii., iii.) we have the story of a ministry of Jesus in Jerusalem and Judæa before He entered on the ministry in Galilee of which the Synoptics have so much to say. In Jerusalem at the Passover Jesus cleansed the temple (Jn. ii. 13-22). We have also in John the report of two famous private interviews with persons almost diametrically opposed in character, one with a noted Jewish teacher (Jn. iii.) and the other with a Samaritan woman (Jn. iv). Though some individuals were thus reached and influenced, the results of this ministry were meagre. It was clear that an extension of the preparatory work of repentance and baptism was necessary. It was when John the Baptist was imprisoned that Jesus entered on His ministry in Galilee, where He addressed Himself to minds that were unsophisticated with the prejudices and supercilious pride of Judæa, where the sacerdotal and learned classes had their headquarters (Mt. iv. 12; Lk. iv. 18).

THE LENGTH OF THE WHOLE MINISTRY

After careful investigation of all the relevant facts, we incline to the old view that the whole ministry lasted three years. Certainly, the theory that it lasted only one year cannot stand close scrutiny; it is not possible to account for the development of faith and unbelief to which the Gospels witness, the missions of the twelve and the seventy, and the different preaching journeys of Jesus, within so brief a space of time. It might be pointed out that the first Gospel indicates two crucial turning points in the ministry which should be carefully noted. In Mt. iv. 17 we read, 'From that time forth Jesus began to preach' (the beginning of the Galilean ministry). In Mt. xvi. 21 we read, 'From that time forth began Jesus to show unto His disciples (at Cæsarea Philippi) that He must suffer.' There is something to be said for the division of the ministry into three periods, which may be called 'the year of obscurity' (spent in Judæa), 'the year of public favour', and 'the year of opposition'.

THE YEAR OF PUBLIC FAVOUR

During this year, spent entirely in Galilee, with the exception of a visit to Jerusalem described in Jn. v., crowds attended Jesus everywhere, attracted by His miracles, but also by His teaching. As to His miracles, we think of the effect produced by one wrought in the very early days in the synagogue at Capernaum. 'What is this? A new teaching! with authority He commandeth even the unclean spirits, and they obey Him' (Mk. i. 27, R.V.). The miracles were signs of the presence and the saving activity of God (Lk. xi. 20). As to the teaching, we think of the profound impression made upon those who listened to the 'manifesto of the king' (Mt. v.-vii.).

Those were wonderful days, and, as the work became more and more exacting, Jesus gathered around Him a band of twelve disciples, the nucleus of a new Israel, and sent them out on missionary campaigns. It seemed sometimes to the disciples in those days as though they were at a continual marriage feast. Yet, there were hints of coming trouble. At a very early period (Lk. v. 17) we read of Pharisees who had come out of every town of Galilee and Judæa and Jerusalem, to watch and to harass Him. Incidentally, that statement bears witness to the fact of an earlier ministry in the south, as described in the fourth Gospel. One day, in the midst of His rejoicing disciples, Jesus spoke some words which must have come to many as an announcement of 'something startling, tragic, like sudden storm in a summer sky' (Mk. ii. 20).

What were the results of this year? There were some good results, as He said to John the Baptist in the message He sent to him in his prison cell at Machærus (Mt. xi. 4, 5). But, He had to upbraid the cities in which most of His mighty works were done, *because they repented not* (Mt. xi. 20). It was on a campaign against sin that He was engaged, and the heart of Jesus was sad because so many refused to repent, though they had in Him a mightier preacher of repentance than Jonah (Mt. xii. 41). Yet, He could rest in the sovereign will of the Father (Mt. xi. 25, 26), and could still go on calling men to come to Him, to find rest in Himself (Mt. xi. 28-30).

It was probably towards the end of this year, when opposition was beginning to become intense, that Jesus began to speak in parables, which concealed, for a time, the deeper things of the kingdom from some, and awakened deeper thought and enquiry in really serious minds. The first parable, that of the Sower, may be regarded, primarily, as describing the results so far of His own ministry.

Towards the end of the year of public favour, some time after the death of the Baptist, there came a clearly marked crisis. The miracle of the feeding of the five thousand *is the only one which is recorded in each of the Gospels*. It had an overwhelming effect on the crowd by the seaside, and they wanted to take Him by force and make Him a king (Jn. vi. 15); they wanted Him to become the leader of a messianic revolt. It seemed to be the crowning hour of success, but Jesus fled from their carnal desires, and, next day, in the synagogue at Capernaum, He told them about the real nature of His vocation. They were looking for a bread-king, but His purpose was to give a better bread, and to give it through His own death (Jn. vi. 35, 51, 53, 54). The result was that there took place a sifting among His followers, and many 'walked no more with Him'. The crowds melted away, and Jesus was left with the Twelve, and one of them was 'a devil' (Jn. vi. 70). There came, however, from the lips of Simon Peter a grand confession of faith (Jn. vi. 68, 69), an anticipation of the great confession which he was to make a few months later at Cæsarea Philippi.

THE YEAR OF OPPOSITION

The opposition that developed against Jesus, and that became ever deeper and more embittered as the days passed, may be put down to His lowly origin, the company He kept, and His disregard of traditions. The difference between Jesus and the religious guides of Israel came out especially with regard to the sabbath, one of God's greatest gifts to man which the Pharisees made to be a burden instead of a blessing.

During the first six months of the final year of His life Jesus seems to have reduced His work of preaching and miracle-working, in order to get away from the crowds and from the growing opposition, and to be alone with the Twelve. The future lay with them, and He gave Himself to training them for it. He engaged in long circuits in the most distant parts of the province of Galilee, travelling to Tyre and Sidon, far in the north-west, to Decapolis on the east, and to Cæsarea Philippi in the extreme north.

Cæsarea Philippi

Cæsarea Philippi was situated at the base of the majestic hill of Hermon, and in its neighbourhood the Jordan has its rise. Here took place something that was of crucial importance. Simon Peter, with various symbols of idolatry in the rocks around him, confessed Jesus as the Messiah, the Son of the Living God. Jesus received the confession with great joy, and recognized in him who made it, and those whose spokesman he was, the nucleus of the future church, the new Israel (Mt. xvi. 17-19). 'From that time forth' (Mt. xvi. 21), Jesus began to speak plainly about His cross. He had previously spoken of His sufferings in veiled, enigmatic language (e.g. Mt. xii. 40; Mk. ii. 20; Jn. iii. 14, vi.), but now He spoke 'openly' (Mk. viii. 32). When Peter tried to turn Jesus away from the path to the cross, Jesus recognized in his blundering appeal an echo of the temptation in the wilderness, Satan hiding this time behind the mistaken and shortsighted love of a disciple (Mt. xvi. 23; Mk. viii. 33).

The Transfiguration

This remarkable event took place almost certainly on Mount Hermon, a week after the happenings at Cæsarea Philippi, and must be studied in close connection with those happenings. Somewhere, amid the solitude of Hermon's fields of snow, the hidden splendour of the Person of Jesus shone forth for some fleeting moments. We are, no doubt, justified in saying that this meant to Jesus Himself a foretaste of future glory, but above all, it brought a message to the three disciples who witnessed it. He was transfigured *before them* (Mt. xvii. 2). This experience would strengthen their faith in the coming days, through an anticipatory vision of what Paul calls 'the body of His glory' (Phil. iii. 21, R.V.). Whatever men might say about 'the scandal of the cross', they had different thoughts about it in heaven.

On Mount Hermon there appeared with Jesus, Moses, as representing the Law, who stood now

> 'On the hills he never trod,
> To talk of the strife which won our life,
> With th' Incarnate Son of God,'

and Elijah, as representing the Prophets. Luke tells us that they spoke of the *exodus* which He was about to accomplish at Jerusalem (ix. 31). 'Exodus' is a great word, looking back to the mighty deliverance from Egypt and pointing forward not only to the cross, but to the resurrection and all the glories that should follow. For a second time the Father spoke to Jesus as at the baptism, with the additional words 'Hear Him' (Mk. ix. 7).

The Journey to Jerusalem

Soon after the transfiguration, Jesus 'steadfastly set His face to go to Jerusalem' (Lk. ix. 51). He sent out the Seventy, to go before Him along the route of His journey (Lk. x. 1). We cannot trace the stages of that journey with exactness, but it seems to have been a slow and lengthened one. We find Him in the southern parts of Galilee, which border on Samaria, where the parable of the Good Samaritan was spoken and the ten lepers were cleansed (Lk. x. 25-37 and xvii. 11-19), and in Peræa, beyond the Jordan (Mk. x. 1; cf. with parallel passages). But Jerusalem was His goal. In those days, as Bengel said, 'He was dwelling in His Passion'. The disciples could not enter into that strange world of thought and were sometimes filled with an overpowering sense of awe (Mk. x. 32). As He walked alone and the disciples followed, He paused, and for the third time told them of His approaching sufferings, and then for the first time revealed the fact that He was to be *crucified* (Mt. xx. 19). Shortly after He spoke the great words about the ransom-price (Mt. xx. 28; Mk. x. 45).

The long section in the third Gospel (Lk. ix. 51-xix. 27), variously called 'the great insertion' and 'the travel document', contains the teaching which was given on the journey to Jerusalem.[1]

Before His last visit to Jerusalem He paid two preliminary visits there, one in September and October, during the Feast of the Tabernacles (Jn. vii. and viii.) and one in December, during the Feast of Dedication (Jn. ix. and x.). On both these occasions He spoke some of His deepest words, and, in connection with the second visit, we have the story of the blind man of Jerusalem, that 'tough reasoner', who was 'cast out', i.e. excommunicated, by the Pharisees (Jn. ix. 34), and to whom Jesus opened a door that no man can shut (Jn. x. 9).

The Arrival in Jerusalem

Shortly before the final entry into Jerusalem, there took place the crowning miracle of Jesus, the raising of Lazarus (Jn. xi). When we come to the final week in the life of Jesus, we find that the events in it are recorded with rich fulness of detail, proving that the Gospels are in entire harmony with the Epistles in regarding the death of Jesus as the all-important event in His career.

On the Sunday He rode into Jerusalem, not in shining armour but seated on an ass's colt, yet in 'lowly pomp', as Israel's King, thus fulfilling the prophecy of Zechariah (ix. 9). On the Monday He cursed the barren fig tree (a symbol of the curse that was coming upon Israel), and for a second time cleansed the temple.

The Tuesday was a great day of controversy with the Pharisees and the Sadducees. He silenced them all, and 'the mass of the people listened with delight to Him' (Mk. xii. 37, Moffatt). Taking His last look at Israel's religion, He discovered in what was so largely a barren wilderness one fair, fragrant flower of devotion and self-sacrifice (Mk. xii. 41-44; Lk. xxi. 1-4). When told of the Greeks who were seeking Him, He entered into a mysterious soul-conflict which was an anticipation of the more severe soul-conflict in Gethsemane (Jn. xii. 21-33). He spoke of His death as the sowing of a seed which would bear 'much fruit', as a magnet which would draw 'all men' unto Himself, and as a judgment of the world, a world-crisis which offered to men the choice of two destinies. Carrying the war into the enemy's camp, He pronounced the terrible 'woes' against the Pharisees (Mt. xxiii.) 'a storm of thunder and lightning passing into a rain of tears', as those words of deepest tenderness and yearning issued from the same lips that had spoken the stern and blistering words

[1] See p. 337.

of judgment, 'O Jerusalem, O Jerusalem! . . .' There followed
the prophecy of the destruction of Jerusalem, the forerunner of
the judgment of the world, and the establishment of Christ's kingdom at His second coming.

On the Thursday evening Jesus observed the Passover feast
alone with His disciples, and made that Old Testament memorial
feast to merge beautifully into the New Testament feast of remembrance and communion; and spoke the great words about
the new covenant which was to be established in His blood, with
the forgiveness of sins as its fundamental blessing, this being the
fulfilment of Jeremiah's prophecy (Je. xxxi. 31-34). John gives us
here some of the most precious portions of the 'table talk' of Jesus
(Jn. xiii.-xvi.), and His High Priestly Prayer (Jn. xvii.).

GETHSEMANE AND CALVARY

Judas, one of the Twelve, sold his Master for thirty pieces of silver,
and his name still speaks to us of the basest treachery. The
mysterious soul-agony of Jesus in Gethsemane was due not primarily to the anticipation of physical agony, which the intervention
of angels might have prevented (Mt. xxvi. 53), but to the burden
of human sin which He was about to bear (1 Pet. ii. 24; 1 Jn. ii.
2), and to the hiding of the Father's face which it entailed. This
was the bitterness of the cup which He must drink (Mk. xiv. 36).

Of the story of the crucifixion there is no need to write in detail,
as it is so well known. It was the most shameful form of death
known then, and it involved excruciating physical agony. But, as
a Puritan divine said, 'The suffering of His soul was the soul of
His suffering,' and that suffering cannot be adequately thought of
unless it be regarded as the enduring of the penalty due to human
sin. The awe-inspiring words of the cry of dereliction, 'My God,
My God, why . . .?', point unmistakably in the same direction.

A sermon exists with the title, 'The Power of Christ even Dying',
based upon Mt. xxvii. 51-53; but an even greater manifestation
of the power of the crucified Jesus was given when, at the eleventh
hour, He opened the kingdom of heaven to a sin-stained man
who was dying on a cross beside Him (Lk. xxiii. 39-43). 'The
Lord has reigned from the tree' (Ps. xcvi. 10) [1].

THE RESURRECTION

The unanimous and unfaltering testimony of all the Gospels is
that, on the morning of the third day, the rock-tomb in Joseph

[1] This reading is found in some of the early Fathers.

L

of Arimathæa's garden was found empty, and they all declare that
the explanation is that Jesus had risen from the dead. The whole
of the New Testament echoes and re-echoes with that triumphant
announcement. It is as certain as any fact in history can be that,
seven weeks after the crucifixion, Peter was preaching Jesus in
Jerusalem as the risen and exalted and reigning Lord. The boldness and assured confidence of Peter and his companions then, as
contrasted with their sadness of heart and cowardice seven weeks
before, demands some kind of explanation, and there is no doubt
as to what their own explanation was. It was the fact of the
resurrection that gave the early church its power, its triumphant
vitality. Great effects demand for their explanation great causes,
causes sufficiently great to explain all that is in the effects.

It may not be easy to trace out the exact course of events in
the history of the different appearances of the risen Lord, in
Jerusalem, and in Galilee. The student will have to reckon also
with the various sceptical theories which have been devised to
account for those appearances, absurd as those theories are seen
to be when they are subjected to close scrutiny.

There is an abundance of literature upon the subject, both old
and new, but those who have experienced the power of the risen
Christ in their own lives will thankfully receive the transparently
honest witness of those who saw Him alive during those forty
days, even if they themselves fail to reconcile every detail of the
circumstances so as to form one harmonious picture.

During a period of forty days the risen Lord appeared from
time to time to His disciples. Then He was 'received up in glory'
(1 Tim. iii. 16, R.V.), and He is now 'enthroned at the right hand
of God, in the glory of the Father'. Christians are now exhorted
to 'seek the things that are above, where Christ is seated on the
right hand of God' (Col. iii. 1, R.V.). They are reminded that,
as they go forth to 'make disciples of all nations', they have the
presence of the living, reigning Lord with them, through the Holy
Spirit. As He said, when He stood 'on the steps of the Throne',
'All authority has been given unto Me in heaven and in earth . . .
and lo! I am with you all the days, until the consummation of the
age' (Mt. xxviii. 18-20, R.V. and R.V. mg.).

CHAPTER XVIII

THE TEACHING OF CHRIST

JESUS was infinitely more than a teacher, yet He was a teacher, and multitudes have been arrested and held by His teaching long before they began to discern deeper elements in His Person and work. The Russian writer, Dostoevsky, in his 'House of the Dead', speaks of a man in prison in Siberia, in the old days of ghastly cruelty, who learned to read the New Testament. When he had read the Sermon on the Mount, he was asked if he liked it, and he answered: 'Oh, yes! Jesus is a holy prophet. Jesus speaks God's words; how good it is!' When he was asked what part he liked best, he said: 'Where He says "Forgive, love, don't hurt others, love even your enemies." Ah, how divinely He speaks!'

To-day men feel, as those felt who heard Jesus speak in Palestine, the uniqueness of what He says. According to the Synoptics, 'the multitudes were astonished at His teaching, for He taught them as one having authority' (Mt. vii. 28, 29, R.V.), and, according to the fourth Gospel, it was said of Him, 'Never man so spake' (Jn. vii. 46, R.V.).

'Never man so spake.' That is true as regards the *manner* of His teaching. It was of such a nature as to gain the ear of the hearer and to arouse in him thoughtful interest. 'He spake of lilies, vines and corn, the sparrow and the raven,' and made them to be teachers of the deepest truth about God and man. He took the commonest objects and incidents around Him, transforming them into vehicles for conveying to the world immortal truth; and the stories which He was continually telling, how they grip the imagination still!

But it is in the *matter* of our Lord's teaching that its uniqueness emerges most clearly. Some of the leading topics of that teaching will now be dealt with.

GOD THE FATHER

Christ came to reveal the Father (Mt. xi. 27; Jn. xiv. 9). There had been heart-stirring anticipations of that conception of God in the Old Testament, as in Ps. ciii. 13 and Is. lxiii. 16, but in the teaching of Jesus that conception is central and all-determining. God is infinitely near, clothing the quick-withering flowers of the field with a beauty surpassing that of Solomon's most gorgeous coronation robes (Mt. vi. 29), feeding at His bountiful table the birds of the air (Mt. vi. 26), present with the dying sparrow as it falls to the ground (Mt. x. 29). Not even the extra sparrow, thrown in, over and above, into the bargain (Mt. x. 29 compared with Lk. xii. 6) is 'forgotten before God'. God is a God of infinite love, ever willing to give 'good things' to His children (Mt. vii. 11), 'kind unto the unthankful and the evil' (Lk. vi. 35). When Jesus tells us about the father who was watching for the return of his lost son and who ran to meet that son and kissed him, while the rags and filth of the far country were still upon him, we are meant to think, 'That is God!' the God who, in Christ, has come more than half way to meet the returning, penitent sinner.

But, the transcendant power and glory of God are also emphasized by Jesus. Here, all the teaching of the Old Testament on such matters is presupposed; it is the background of everything. God is our Father *who is in heaven*, 'the Father of an infinite majesty'. He is good, the only One who can be called good in the full and absolute sense (Mt. xix. 17). He is perfect (Mt. v. 48). He is the 'holy Father' (Jn. xvii. 11), the 'righteous Father' (Jn. xvii. 25). There is something in God which ought to inspire awe. It is God whom we are exhorted to fear (in Mt. x. 28 and Lk. xii. 5), and not the devil.

The Fatherhood of God, according to Jesus, is not a universal Fatherhood. He says to some, in the fourth Gospel, 'Ye are of your father the devil' (viii. 44). In the Synoptics, we hear Him speaking of 'the children of the kingdom' and 'the children of the evil one' (Mt. xiii. 38). He says to His disciples 'Love your enemies . . . that ye may be (i.e. become—*genesthe*) sons of your Father which is in Heaven . . .' (Mt. v. 44, 45). The sons of God are distinguished from others by their faith, love and obedience, and such they become by adoption and grace.

REGARDING HIMSELF

His first recorded words, spoken when He was twelve, are these: 'Wist ye not that I must be about my Father's business' (R.V. —'in my Father's house') (Lk. ii. 49). In these words there is evident a consciousness of His unique relation to God, as God's Son. In the fourth Gospel we have a wealth of teaching from His lips on the Father and the Son, and in that Gospel Jesus quite plainly speaks as God's unique, eternal Son. There is no contradiction whatever between this and His teaching as it is given to us in the Synoptics. The great claims made by Jesus in the Synoptics find their justification in the fuller revelation given in the fourth Gospel of who He really was and is.

In particular note our Lord's claim that He will be the final Judge of men, in that day when He shall send forth *His* angels and gather in *His* elect from the four winds (Mt. xxiv. 31), when He shall sit on the throne of His glory and judge all men (Mt. xxv. 31 ff.). In making such claims, Jesus does indeed 'silently ascend the throne of God'.[1]

In the Synoptics we have those great words of Jesus recorded which contain the essence of the fourth Gospel (Mt. xi. 27; Lk. x. 22). 'The Father' and 'The Son' stand in a mysterious, inscrutable reciprocal relationship to each other: the Father is a mystery to all but the Son, but, more wonderful still, the Son is a mystery to all but the Father. There must be in His being a *metaphysical ground*, an eternal relation to God, for Him to utter such words, which are identical in meaning with the words recorded in Jn. viii. 58, x. 30-38. Such sayings are a flash of revelation out of the unfathomable depths of His eternal consciousness.

The title 'Son of Man' which Jesus used with reference to Himself on about forty distinct occasions, seems to have a double side to it. There are nineteen passages in the Gospels in which it is used in connection with the true and lowly humanity of Jesus, or in connection with His sufferings; there are fifteen passages where it is used in connection with His future glory, as King and Judge. The title rests upon Dn. vii. 13 ff., as can be seen from our Lord's unmistakable allusion to that passage, in His words spoken to the High Priest at His trial (Mt. xxvi. 64; Mk. xiv. 62). In Dn. vii. we have a vision of the Head of the kingdom of God, a superhuman figure, whose natural home is with 'the Ancient of Days'.

There is a good deal of justification for the theory that Jesus chose this title for Himself because it permitted the blending of the two contrasted Old Testament conceptions of the Messiah, that of the suffering Servant of Isaiah and that of the messianic King. The words about 'lifting up' and 'glorifying' in Jn. xii. 23, 32-34 may be a link between the idea of the Son of Man and the suffering Servant.

[1] D. M. M'Intyre, *Christ our Lord*, p. 71.

THE KINGDOM OF GOD

The concept of the 'kingdom of God' is, in the teaching of Jesus, undoubtedly, a many-sided one, and only a few aspects of it can be touched upon here, and what is written may point the way to fuller study of this rich theme.

The fundamental idea in the phrase is that of the rule or reign of God over human hearts and wills. 'The kingdom of God is within you' seems to be the more likely translation of the words of Jesus in Lk. xvii. 21; the words are so understood by both A.V. and R.V., and by Dalman and others. In the Model Prayer, we are taught to pray, 'Thy kingdom come, Thy will be done, as in heaven, so on earth', which seems to mean that the kingdom of God makes progress on earth, in proportion as the will of God is done by men.

The kingdom of God is *present*, in the saving activity of Jesus. 'If I with the finger of God cast out devils, no doubt the kingdom of God is come upon you' (Moff. 'has reached you already') (Lk. xi. 20). As Jesus goes about, healing the sick, casting out demons, saving the worst sinners, God *is here*; 'The royal power of God is already in motion. . . . The forces which will revolutionize heaven and earth are already at work'.[1] The kingdom is a present reality, and that kingdom is destined to grow from small beginnings to vast issues (parables of the Mustard Seed and Leaven). The rule of God is meant to be exercised more and more fully, in all spheres of human activity, in world politics, in trade, in commerce, in literature, in family life, everywhere.

The kingdom is also *future*, in the sense that its final and complete triumph has yet to be revealed. When Jesus speaks of many coming from all parts of the world to the messianic feast in the kingdom of God (Mt. viii. 11; Lk. xiii. 29), it is of the perfected kingdom that He is thinking. To speak theologically, there is 'the kingdom of grace' and there is 'the kingdom of glory'.

The sayings of Jesus preserved in Mt. xvi. 28; Mk. ix. 1; Lk. ix. 27; Mt. xxvi. 64; Mk. xiv. 62; Lk. xxii. 69, can be interpreted of the coming of the kingdom in the church. 'In the early church there were to be many extraordinary manifestations of the Spirit's power, so extraordinary indeed as to anticipate in some respects the phenomena that will be observed at the end of the world. The church actually has within herself the powers of the world to

[1] G. Vos, *The Teaching of Jesus concerning the Kingdom of God and the Church*, pp. 92, 93.

come . . . She forms an intermediate link between the present life and the life of eternity.'[1]

Sometimes the kingdom (or sovereignty) of God means the rich spiritual blessings which are enjoyed by those who are under the rule of God, blessings which are enjoyed here and now, in measure at least, by the 'poor in spirit' (Mt. v. 3). These blessings are so precious a treasure that a man ought to be willing to give up all else in order to possess them (Mt. xiii. 44-46).

MAN AND SIN

Man, as a spiritual being, made for fellowship with God, is worth more than the whole world (Mk. viii. 36). But, man has got out of touch with God and is lost, as the three parables in Lk. xv. declare, lost to the green pastures and the still waters like a strayed sheep; lost to usefulness, like the mislaid coin in the dark and dust; lost to loving fellowship with God, as the prodigal.

Jesus takes a deeply serious view of man's sinful state. Man is sick with a deadly disease (Mt. ix. 12, 13), in bondage, and outside the household of God (Jn. viii. 34 f.). The wrath of God abides on man because of his disobedience (Jn. iii. 36). Jesus may be said to teach a doctrine of Original Sin. 'If ye, *being evil* . . .' (Mt. viii. 11). He does not stay to argue that; He takes it for granted. 'From within, out of the heart of men . . .' (Mt. xv. 19; Mk. vii. 16-23). For this reason man needs more than outward reformation, he needs inward regeneration. 'Except a man be born again, he cannot see the kingdom of God (Jn. iii. 3); 'Whosoever shall not receive the kingdom of God as a little child, he shall not enter therein' (Mk. x. 15). On these words in Mk. Warfield says: 'The children of the kingdom enter it as children enter the world, stripped and naked, infants, for whom all must be done, not who are capable of doing.[2]

Terrible is the plight of man in his sin, but Jesus makes it very plain, by His words and by His whole conduct, that He is here on a mission of mercy to the lost (Lk. xix. 10), that He is here as the physician of sick souls (Lk. v. 31, 32), as the deliverer of the slaves of sin (Lk. iv. 17-21). The salvation which He brings He connects in a special way with His death.

THE MEANING OF HIS DEATH

There are, in the Synoptics, two outstanding sayings of Jesus with regard to the meaning and purpose of His death. The first was

[1] G. Vos, op. cit., p. 156.
[2] Article 'Children' in Hastings *D.C.G.; i.*, 304.

uttered in the course of the final journey to Jerusalem. 'The Son of Man has not come to be served but to serve, and to give His life as a ransom for many' (Mt. xx. 28; Mk. x. 45; Moff.). In these words Jesus identified Himself with the Servant of the Lord of Is. liii. 11, 12, 'by His knowledge shall my righteous Servant justify *many* . . . He bare the sins of *many*'. The meaning of both sayings is the same, and *His* life, the one sinless life, is to be the *redemption-price* that is to pay for the deliverance of the many from sin.

Substitution is clearly taught here. Jesus is to give His life as the redemption-price *instead of* (*anti*) many. In the LXX., *lutron* is used for the ransom-price paid for a slave, Lv. xix. 20; for a captive, Is. xlv. 13; for a life, Ex. xxi. 30; Nu. xxxv. 31. The same word was used in the Greek world of the first century for the purchase money for the emancipation of a slave. It is within the circle of such ideas that the clue must be sought to the meaning of the words of Jesus.[1] He declares that, while His death is the supreme example of service, it is more than that. It is indeed the ransom-price which effects man's deliverance. The Pauline doctrine of the atonement is a commentary on this saying.

The other great saying was uttered in Jerusalem, in connection with the institution of the Lord's Supper. 'This is my blood of the new covenant, which is shed for many for the remission of sins' (Mt. xxvi. 28; cf. Mk. xiv. 24; Lk. xxii. 20; 1 Cor. xi. 25, 26). The words 'for the remission of sins' are found only in Matthew, but there is no valid reason for supposing that they are an interpolation of the Evangelist. Jesus is thinking here of Jeremiah's great prophecy of the new covenant, where we have one of the loftiest peaks of Old Testament revelation (Je. xxxi. 31-34). According to that prophecy, in the new covenant the forgiveness of sins is the fundamental blessing, out of which all the other promised blessings flow, and Jesus announces that He is establishing, at the cost of His life, this new covenant.

The Old Testament ritual had already taught men that there can be no covenant relation between God and men, no fellowship between a holy God and sinners, save on the basis of sacrifice, sacrifice by which sin is atoned for. For the ratification of the old covenant at Sinai, blood was shed (Ex. xxiv. 5-8), and Jesus describes His death as ratifying the new, perfect and eternal covenant, which secures and assures the communion with God of the new humanity, cleansed from its sin.

[1] See James Denney, *The Death of Christ*, Chapter I; H. E. Guillebaud, *Why The Cross?* (I.V.F.).

In the two sayings of Jesus which we have considered here we can find the germ from which the whole teaching of the apostles on the significance of the death of Christ springs and grows.

HUMAN DESTINY

The blessed dead are 'living' (Mt. xxii. 32; Mk. xii. 27). They live *unto* God (Lk. xx. 38). Jesus says that they are *with Him* in paradise (Lk. xxiii. 43). For them there will be 'the resurrection of the just' (Lk. xiv. 14), 'the resurrection of life' (Jn. v. 29). They shall, in the perfected kingdom of God, partake of the messianic feast, of which we read in Is. xxv. 6-8. For them there is 'the Father's House', with its many 'abodes' (Jn. xiv. 2, Moff.).

According to the plain teaching of Jesus, there is also 'a resurrection of judgment' (Jn. v. 29, R.V.); there is the outside of the banqueting hall, with 'the outer darkness', where there shall be *the* weeping and *the* gnashing of teeth, as though weeping and gnashing of teeth in this world were as nothing in comparison (Mt. viii. 12; Lk. xiii. 28, R.V.). The sternest and most terrible language in the Bible on this awful subject comes from the lips of Jesus, who speaks of the worm that dieth not and the fire that is not quenched (Mk. ix. 48; see also Mt. xxv. 46; Mk. iii. 29, R.V.).

The Christian cannot close his eyes to this stern and dark aspect of truth, while at the same time he must always remember that it is a *gospel* which he is called to preach, the good news that salvation is freely offered to the chief of sinners.

THE SECOND ADVENT

The Lord Jesus is ever the 'coming' One. So in effect He acknowledged Himself to be in answer to the messengers from John the Baptist (Mt. xi. 3; Lk. vii. 19; cf. Jn. i. 15). Significant of His messianic character was His coming to Jerusalem (Mt. xxi. 5-9), and of His deity were His words of His coming *into* the world, and the fulness of purpose for which He came (Mk. x. 45; Lk. v. 32; Jn. viii. 42, ix. 39, x. 5, 10. xii. 46, xviii. 37).

He taught that the same messianic character and divine work involved His coming again. In the report of His great apocalyptic discourse He proclaims this in the words of Daniel's prophecy (Mk. xiii. 26; Dn. vii. 13, 14) and, whilst hinting of long delay (Mt. xxv. 19; Mk. xiii. 34), proclaims that it will take place at an unknown time and suddenly (Mk. xiii. 32, 36).

In his record Matthew supplies additional words about the coming (xxiv. 27, 37-39, 42-44) which is called the *parousia*, the expression which came to be applied to it by the early church (1 Cor. xv. 23; 1 Thes. ii. 19, iii. 13, iv. 15, v. 23; 2 Thes. ii. 1; Jas. v. 7, 8; 2 Pet. i. 16, iii. 4, 12; 1 Jn. ii. 28). The purpose of His coming is amplified in His discourses with the disciples at the time of the last supper (Jn. xiv. 3), and He spoke of it again after His resurrection on the shore of the lake (Jn. xxi. 22, 23), and finally from the throne (Rev. xxii. 12, 20).

Even so, come, Lord Jesus.

CHAPTER XIX

THE FOUR GOSPELS AND ACTS

THE WITNESS OF THE APOSTLES

THE four Gospels and the Acts of the Apostles may be called the 'historical' books of the New Testament, i.e. the only five out of the twenty-seven which are cast in narrative form. All five have as their subject-matter the apostolic witness: the four Gospels present the contents of the apostles' witness of preaching and teaching, while the book of Acts describes how some of them went about this work of witness during the thirty years that followed the death of Christ, and what resulted from it.

The four Gospels might with more propriety be called the fourfold gospel. The application of the term 'Gospel' (Gk.: *euangelion*) to each of the four individually is secondary; the titles 'The Gospel according to Matthew', 'The Gospel according to Mark', etc., originally meant that the one and only gospel—the good news of God—was narrated by these four writers. When the four were collected into one book (not long after A.D. 100), that book was known as 'The Gospel', and its four components were distinguished by the additional words, 'According to Matthew', 'According to Mark', etc.

The good news proclaimed by the apostles in the primitive days of the Christian church may be traced in outline in Acts and the Epistles[1]; and this outline is variously expanded and filled in by the four Evangelists. The outline of the message may be summed up thus: 'God has visited and redeemed His people by sending the Messiah at the time of the fulfilment of His purpose as revealed in Old Testament Scripture. Messiah came, as was prophesied, of Israel's race, of Judah's tribe, of David's royal seed, in the person of Jesus the Nazarene, who died on the cross for our sins, was buried, and was raised from the dead the third day thereafter, as the prophets had foretold, and was then exalted to God's right hand, whence He is to return to judge the living and the dead and to inaugurate the visible kingdom of God on earth.'

In this outline of facts about Jesus as the Messiah, chief emphasis was laid upon the crucifixion and resurrection; and this emphasis

---

[1] Cf. Acts ii. 22-36, iii. 13-26, x. 36-43, xiii. 17-41; I Cor. xv. 3-7, etc.

is reflected in the Gospels, where these events occupy what would be a disproportionate amount of space if the writers' purpose were purely biographical. While much of the contents of the Gospels may have served the purpose of illustrative matter in the primitive preaching, the details of the passion and resurrection narratives were told for their own sakes, as essential elements in that preaching. It is generally held, and with good reason, that the passion narrative, from the last supper to the resurrection, was the earliest part of the gospel story to be told consecutively—that, indeed, it was so told from the beginning of the apostolic witness.

It is customary to distinguish preaching (Gk. *kerygma*) from teaching (Gk. *didache*) in the apostolic witness. The former told what Jesus had done; it consisted of narrative, and was aimed in the first instance at reaching non-Christians, to bring them to faith in Christ. The latter repeated the teaching of Jesus, and was imparted mainly to those who already believed the good news. Of our four Gospels, Mk.[1] consists for the most part of narrative, i.e. it reproduces the preaching; while the other three contain preaching and teaching in more nearly equal proportions, variously interwoven with each other.

THE SYNOPTIC QUESTION

It has long been usual to group the first three Gospels together as one group, leaving the fourth by itself. For certain purposes this is a convenient division, although it must not blind us to the fact that all four portray Jesus as a supernatural Being, the Messiah and Son of God. The words in which the purpose of John's Gospel is declared are true of all four: 'These things are written that ye may believe that Jesus is the Christ, the Son of God; and that believing ye may have life in his name' (Jn. xx. 31, R.V.).[2]

The first three Gospels are commonly called the 'synoptic' Gospels, a title apparently first given them by the textual scholar, J. J. Griesbach, towards the end of the eighteenth century. This adjective means literally 'capable of being viewed together', and was applied to these Gospels because they have so much common material, arranged largely in a common order, that it is possible to display them side by side in three parallel columns in what

---

[1] When the *Gospels* are referred to, abbreviations are used (Mt., Mk., Lk., Jn.); when the *evangelists* are referred to, the names are written in full.

[2] On the reliability of the Gospels see F. F. Bruce, *Are the New Testament Documents Reliable?* (I.V.F.), pp. 28 ff.; D. M. M'Intyre, *Some Notes on the Gospels* (I.V.F.).

is called a synopsis, from which one can see at a glance how far two or more of them agree with each other and how far they diverge from each other.

The relation between these three Gospels forms the subject-matter of the 'synoptic problem'. A comparative study of the synoptic Gospels reveals that out of the 1,068 verses of Mt., about 500 contain (in a somewhat compressed form) the substance of 606 out of the 661 verses of Mk., while of the 1,149 verses of Lk., about 320 have parallels in Mk. This appearance of so much Markan material in Mt. and Lk. is usually explained nowadays by the hypothesis that Mark's Gospel (or something very like it) formed one of the chief sources of information for the other two Synoptists. This 'Markan hypothesis' was put forward in 1835 by Lachmann, on the ground that while Mt. and Mk. sometimes agree in order against Lk., and Lk. and Mk. still more frequently against Mt., yet Mt. and Lk. never agree in order against Mk., so that the order of Mk. seems to be the norm from which the others occasionally deviate. Apart from the question of order, it appears probable on grounds of literary criticism that in most of the passages which are common to all three Synoptists Mark's form is earlier than those of the other two. The Greek student should examine the matter for himself with the aid of a good synopsis such as Huck's and the linguistic evidence as marshalled in the second edition of Sir John Hawkins's *Horæ Synopticæ* (1909). Ultimately, the facts behind the Markan hypothesis only show that one of the chief sources of the synoptic tradition is the apostolic preaching as recorded by Mark, and this again is asserted by early Christian writers to consist of the substance of Peter's preaching.[1]

When we compare Mt. and Lk., we find that, apart from the matter which they have in common with Mk., they have nearly 250 verses containing common material not found in Mk. These verses we may distinguish by the symbol Q, but this need not imply that Q at one time existed as a separate document. The Q material consists mainly of Sayings of Jesus, and was probably derived from an early collection of His sayings, perhaps originally compiled in Aramaic by Matthew, and set in a narrative framework. From this collection was probably also derived much of the teaching of Jesus recorded in Mt. alone. This is not the place to enter into detailed arguments; we can but indicate our conclusion, that the common matter of the Synoptic Gospels depends ultimately on the apostolic preaching, especially as uttered by

[1] See p. 329.

Peter and written down by Mark, and the apostolic teaching, probably first committed to writing by Matthew.

The four Evangelists wrote each from his distinctive viewpoint, and the deeds and words of Jesus recorded by each are selected in accordance therewith. Many of the divergences in the reports of the Evangelists can be explained if we consider the special purpose each had in mind. Other differences can readily be accounted for as representing variant renderings of the underlying Aramaic. But just as a well-drawn portrait may give a better impression of a person's appearance than a photograph, so the fourfold Gospel, with all its diversities, presents to the reader a fuller, more all-round impression of the Person and teaching of Christ than could have been given by a single statement however verbally accurate.

The study of 'Form Criticism', so eagerly pursued during the last thirty years, aims at penetrating beyond the putative written sources of the Gospels to the 'forms' or patterns or moulds in which the various types of incidents or sayings were cast in the early oral stage. The value of this approach has frequently been exaggerated; but it has been useful in so far as it has impressed upon us (1) the inadequacy of documentary theories alone to account for the phenomena of our Gospels, (2) the uniform tendency in the first century A.D. to stereotype the 'forms' in which all kinds of religious propaganda were presented, (3) the fact that the portrayal of Jesus as the Son of God pervades every stratum of the Gospels, even the most primitive of them, no matter how we classify and cross-section them. One further result of this method when applied to the recorded Sayings of Jesus is that these are seen to have been regularly cast in poetical form, displaying characteristic Semitic parallelism and rhythms, and (when we try to see behind the Greek the original Aramaic in which He spoke) even rhyme. In this our Lord placed Himself in the succession of the Old Testament prophets, whose oracles were largely given in verse.[1]

THE GOSPEL ACCORDING TO ST. MATTHEW

AUTHORSHIP, DATE AND CIRCUMSTANCES

ALL the Gospels are, strictly speaking, anonymous; none bears its writer's name. The evidence connecting the first Gospel with the name of Matthew is external, and can be traced back to the state-

[1] See C. F. Burney, *The Poetry of our Lord* (Oxford, 1925). See also Introduction to Chapter XI.

ment of Papias, bishop of Phrygian Hierapolis early in the second century (preserved by Eusebius in his *Ecclesiastical History*, iii. 39): 'Matthew compiled the *logia* in the Hebrew tongue, and everyone translated them as best he could.' Papias and all the writers who repeat this information with added details agree that, whatever Matthew wrote, he wrote it in Hebrew (which probably means Aramaic, as it commonly does in the New Testament). The word *logia* means 'sayings' or 'oracles', though Papias' statement need not mean that Matthew compiled a collection of sayings only. (*Logia* is used by Paul in Rom. iii. 2 to denote the Old Testament Scriptures in general.) The evidence seems to suggest that Matthew composed an Aramaic work consisting of Sayings of Jesus set in a narrative framework, and that the Greek translation of this work formed the chief and most characteristic source of our first Gospel, which is thus not unjustifiably known as the Gospel according to Matthew.

The date of Mt. cannot be fixed with certainty; it is a first-century production, as we may infer from the fact of its being quoted by Ignatius early in the second century; and its general tone suggests that it reached its present form not much, if at all, later than the Fall of Jerusalem in A.D. 70. Prof. C. C. Torrey goes so far as to say that there is nothing in any of the four Gospels which demands a date later than A.D. 50. Of all the Gospels, it is most Jewish—even at times Rabbinical—in tone. Its place at the head of the New Testament canon is justified, irrespective of the chronological order of the books, by the way in which it links the gospel story at the outset with the main line of Old Testament history, and that in Old Testament idiom: 'The book of the generation of Jesus the Messiah, the son of David, the son of Abraham' (cf. Gn. v. 1). The descent of Jesus from David in chapter i. is traced along the legal line of succession through the kings of Judah and their heirs, which is not always identical with the line from father to son. Matthew knows about the virgin birth, but *legally* Jesus is the son of Joseph, who is the heir to David's throne.

Yet, if chapter i. presents Jesus as the heir to Jewish hopes, chapter ii. shows Him as the fulfilment of Gentile aspirations; the wise men from the East come to do Him homage in the spirit of the prophecy, 'Gentiles shall come to thy light, and kings to the brightness of thy rising' (Is. lx. 3). This prophecy is not quoted in Mt.; but several others are, and it is to be noted that some of them are introduced to show how the Messiah in His own person recapitulates the history of His people, e.g. the words, 'Out of

Egypt have I called my Son' (Mt. ii. 15), from Hos. xi. 1, where
the original reference is to the nation of Israel.

The early introduction of the Gentiles in chapter ii. indicates
that this Gospel is not exclusively Jewish in its sympathies, and
this is borne out by the closing sentence of Mt., which records the
risen Lord's commission to His disciples to go and make disciples
of *all the nations* (xxviii. 19). The Greek-speaking Jewish Christians,
among whom it seems first to have appeared, will have been those,
in Harnack's words,[1] 'who traced their spiritual descent to St.
Stephen, and from whose midst proceeded those missionaries who
first (in Antioch) preached the gospel to the Gentiles. By such
Christians, who left Palestine after the great catastrophe, the
Gospel of St. Matthew was brought to Asia Minor and other
Christian centres'.

ANALYSIS

i. 1-17.	Genealogy.
i. 18-iv. 11.	Birth, baptism, and temptation of Christ.
iv. 12-25.	Preaching, and call of disciples.
v.-vii.	'The Sermon on the Mount.'
viii.-xvi. 12.	General teaching, preaching and healing, mainly in Galilee.
xvi. 13-xviii.	Peter's confession, the transfiguration, and discourses.
xix. and xx.	Journey to Jerusalem.
xxi.-xxiii.	Christ's entry into Jerusalem. Final warnings and 'woes'.
xxiv. and xxv.	Teaching on 'things to come'.
xxvi.-xxviii.	Betrayal, institution of the Lord's supper, trial, death, resurrection, appearance in Galilee.

CONTENTS

Mt. falls into easily distinguished sections. Its most prominent
feature is its five great groups of discourses, each group being
marked off at the end by some such words as: 'And when Jesus
had finished all these sayings . . .' (vii. 28, xi. 1, xiii. 53, xix. 1,
xxvi. 1). Each of these groups follows a narrative section, so that
the body of the Gospel may be said to consist of five divisions,
each division containing a narrative section followed by a dis-

[1] *Date of the Acts and Synoptic Gospels*, p. 135.

course. These divisions are preceded by the Introduction (chapters i. and ii.), consisting of the genealogy and the nativity narrative, and are followed by chapters xxvi.-xxviii., containing the passion and resurrection narratives.

The fivefold division has been explained (e.g. by Delitzsch) as based on the fivefold arrangement of the law in the Old Testament; Dr. Levertoff finds that 'the sequence of events corresponds chronologically with the Jewish liturgical seasons'.

We may give significant titles to the five discourses as follows:

1. (v.-vii.): The Law of the Kingdom.
2. (x. 5-42): The Preaching of the Kingdom.
3. (xiii. 3-52): The Growth of the Kingdom.
4. (xviii. 3-35): The Fellowship of the Kingdom.
5. (xxiv., xxv.): The Consummation of the Kingdom.

The main theme of all five is the kingdom of God or, as Matthew prefers to call it, the kingdom of the heavens (Aram. *malkutha di-shemayya*), thus preserving literally the Aramaic idiom probably used by our Lord Himself. Indeed, the kingdom is in a special way the distinctive theme of Mt., and Jesus Himself is primarily viewed throughout Mt. as the messianic King.

'The evangelist's purpose,' says Prof. N. B. Stonehouse,[1] 'is to depict Jesus as the messianic King whose history fulfils the Old Testament revelation and whose entrance into a land where a king of the Jews already reigned set up a crisis wherein through divine action the new-born King was preserved and came to dwell in Nazareth.'

The nativity narrative is followed by a description of John the Baptist's ministry and the baptism of Jesus. It is to be noted, as in keeping with the general tendency of this Gospel, that John is here portrayed as a herald of the kingdom; the words which sum up the preaching of Jesus and His disciples are in Mt. ascribed to John as well: 'Repent, for the kingdom of heaven has drawn near' (iii. 2, R.V).

The temptation narrative in iv. 1-16 is followed by a brief summary of the Galilæan ministry, which also is exhibited as a fulfilment of Old Testament prophecy in terms of the oracle of Is. ix. 1, 2. This summary is introduced with the words, 'From that time . . .' (iv. 17), which seem to mark a new departure at this stage of the story; even as they do in xvi. 21 after Peter's confession at Cæsarea Philippi. This summary introduces the Sermon on the Mount, presented in Mt. as a new *Torah*, the primary sense

[1] *The Witness of Matthew and Mark to Christ*, p. 119.

of which is 'instruction'. Christ is the fulfiller of the Old Testament law (v. 17), but in His teaching He fulfils it, not by the casuistic adaptations of the Rabbis, but by extracting the fundamental principle of the Old Testament regulations, and applying these not merely to outward actions but to the thoughts and intents of the heart, the inward springs of conduct. With sovereign authority He proclaims that the prosperity or ruin of men's lives will depend on their response to this teaching of His (vii. 24-27).

The next two chapters (viii. and ix.) are taken up mainly with various healing incidents, in which the King is depicted as exercising His sovereignty in the expulsion of diseases, demons, and even death itself. This healing activity is a further manifestation of the presence of the heavenly kingdom, and the Evangelist finds in it the fulfilment of the Old Testament description of the Servant of the Lord, who 'himself took our infirmities, and bore our diseases' (viii. 17, quoting Is. liii. 4). Interspersed among these incidents are the replies to His would-be followers (viii. 19-22), the Stilling of the Tempest (viii. 23-27), and the Call of Matthew, with the consequent controversies (ix. 9-17). In these, too, the messianic King reveals Himself.

The second discourse, the charge to the Twelve, is introduced by a brief account of the commissioning of the apostles, who are mentioned by name. This discourse as reported here presents markedly primitive characteristics. The promise, 'Ye shall not be gone over the cities of Israel till the Son of Man be come' (x. 23), by its very difficulty shows itself to be early; it was certainly not invented by a writer after the fall of Jerusalem, and it should be taken at its face value, as the charge given by Jesus to His apostles in connection with a mission undertaken by them during His earthly life. Its limitations contrast significantly with the post-resurrection commission of xxviii. 19-20.

As for x. 23, the verse on which Dr. Albert Schweitzer built so disproportionately heavy a structure of 'thorough-going eschatology', we may regard this verse and the similar one in xvi. 28 as fulfilled in the establishment of His church by the risen Lord.

The next narrative section (chapters xi. and xii.) begins with our Lord's answer to John the Baptist's question, and goes on to reveal His attitude to those who rejected His claims, thus leading up to the third discourse-group, consisting of those parables in which are unfolded the mysteries of the kingdom of heaven, showing how from small and unseen beginnings the kingdom suddenly appears in full growth and power.

The following narrative section (xiii. 53-xvii. 27) follows closely

the order of Mk. vi. 14-ix. 32 (see below, p. 331), with expansions
here and there, notably in the story of Peter's confession at
Cæsarea Philippi, where Mt. alone records Christ's words to Peter
commencing 'Blessed art thou, Simon Bar-Jonah . . .' (xvi. 17-
19), which contain the first New Testament reference to the
church (first in order of speaking, not of writing). The second
comes in Mt. xviii. 17, and these are the only occurrences of the
word *ekklesia* in the Gospels. Behind both we should probably
discern the Aramaic *kenishta*, a word used both for the whole
'congregation' of Israel and for an individual synagogue. These
two passages, says Principal W. A. Curtis,[1] 'present no textual
sign of inauthenticity to warrant the suspicion that they are
ecclesiastically motived interpolations inserted to justify the practice and nomenclature of a generation later, and . . . in fact
help to explain the universal acceptance of the name Ecclesia
soon after the Ministry ended.' Besides, Mt. xvi. 17-19, as C. F.
Burney showed,[2] can be turned back literally into rhythmical
Aramaic.

This narrative section ends with the story of the coin in the
fish's mouth, peculiar to Mt. The Master's attitude towards pay-
ing the temple-tax would be treated as a precedent when this
practical question came up for decision in the early Jerusalem
church.

The discourse in chapter xviii. deals with various aspects of
fellowship in the kingdom, beginning with the nature of true
greatness, and going on to deal with the due respect to be paid
to children, the settlement of private strife within the new community, and the universal obligation of unlimited forgiveness lying
on those who have experienced the forgiveness of God.

The following narrative section (xix. 1-xxii. 46) follows the order
of Mk. xi. 1-xii. 37, with the addition of the discussion on marriage
and divorce (xix. 3-12); the parable of the Labourers in the Vineyard (xx. 1-16); the quotation of the prophecy of Zc. ix. 9 in
connection with our Lord's entry into Jerusalem (cf. Jn. xii. 15),
to which prophecy the narrative in Mt. conforms in literal detail
(xxi. 7); the parable of the Two Sons (xxi. 28-32), and that of the
Marriage Feast, to which is appended the incident of the man who
had no wedding garment (xxii. 1-14).

Chapter xxiii. gathers together our Lord's criticisms of the contemporary tendencies in Jewish scribalism, ending with the pronouncement of woe over Jerusalem (spoken by Jesus in the

[1] *Jesus Christ the Teacher*, p. 197.
[2] *The Poetry of our Lord*, p. 117.

character of the divine Wisdom, as we learn from the parallel passage in Lk. xi. 49).

The eschatological discourse of chapter xxiv. (parallel to Mk. xiii.) is expanded by the addition of the eschatological parables of chapter xxv.—the Ten Virgins, the Talents, and the Judgment of the Nations.

The passion narrative of Mt. (xxvi. 1-xxvii. 66) follows closely that of Mk., but adds the incidents of Judas's repentance and suicide, Pilate's wife's dream, Pilate's handwashing, the rising from the dead of many saints after the death of Jesus, and the setting of the watch at the sepulchre.

The resurrection narrative in Mt. alone contains the account of the earthquake, the angel sitting on the stone, the flight and bribing of the guards. It ends with the apostles keeping their appointment with their Lord on the prescribed mountain in Galilee, and their receiving from Him there the world-wide commission of preaching, baptizing, and teaching, coupled with the promise of His presence with them 'all the days, even unto the consummation of the age' (xxviii. 20, R.V.).[1]

THEMES FOR STUDY

1. Trace the manner in which this Gospel links the Old Testament with the New.

2. How far does the Sermon on the Mount relate itself to (i) the law, (ii) the gospel? Is it a rule for Christians? Compare Col. iii. 1-iv. 6.

3. Make a list of passages which point to Christ as messianic King.

4. Matthew is traditionally said to have written to Jews. Study the Gospel from the standpoint of its Jewish background.

5. In what sense can the Gospel be said from the very beginning to lead up to the Great Commission in xxviii. 16-20?

THE GOSPEL ACCORDING TO ST. MARK

AUTHORSHIP, DATE AND CIRCUMSTANCES

THE earliest witness for the second Gospel is to be found in a statement of an unnamed 'elder' reported by Papias:[2] 'Mark,

[1] See article 'The End of the First Gospel', by F. F. Bruce, in *The Evangelical Quarterly*, July 1940.
[2] Eusebius, *Ecclesiastical History*, iii. 39.

having been Peter's interpreter, wrote down accurately all that he mentioned, whether sayings or doings of Christ, not however in order: for he was neither a hearer nor a companion of the Lord; but afterwards, as I said, he accompanied Peter, who adapted his teachings as necessity required, not as though he were making a compilation of the sayings of the Lord. So then Mark made no mistake, writing down in this way some things as he [Peter] mentioned them; for he paid attention to this one thing, not to omit anything that he had heard, nor to include any false statement among them.'

Later writers dot the i's and cross the t's of this testimony, without adding much of independent value to it. The anti-Marcionite Prologue to Mk., which dates from *c.* 170, adds the information that Mark wrote his Gospel 'in the parts of Italy' after Peter's death. This may well be true, at least as regards that form of Mk. which has come down to us; we find, e.g. explanations about Jewish practices which would be unnecessary in Palestine (cf. vii. 3ff.); and the sprinkling of Latin words and constructions in Mark's Greek may possibly point in the same direction.

The external evidence for Peter's authority behind Mk. is supported by some internal evidence. For example, frequently the impersonal third plural of Mk. (presumably reflecting Peter's 'we') is replaced by 'He' in the other Gospels, the writers of which were thinking only of our Lord.[1]

When early writers tell us that Mark was Peter's interpreter, we need not exclude from that word its primary significance of 'translator'; for the Greek of Mk. contains in several places signs of an underlying Aramaic original. Early tradition identifies Mark the Evangelist with John Mark who appears in Acts xii. 12 and later in the New Testament, and there is no reason to doubt this identification.

ANALYSIS

[1] See C. H. Turner, *New Commentary on Holy Scripture*, S.P.C.K., *N.T.*, p. 48.

CONTENTS

Unwarned by Papias' statement that Mk. was not written in
order, some scholars of an earlier generation exaggerated its
chronological continuity and consecutiveness. More recently the
tendency has been in the other direction, to deny the possibility
of tracing in Mk. any chronological development of the ministry
of Jesus. The truth probably lies between these two extremes. Of
special importance is Professor C. H. Dodd's discovery that the
short summaries connecting the various narrative sections which
make up the bulk of Mk. are not merely 'editorial cement', but
prove when put together to form a skeleton outline comparable
to those outlines of the *kerygma* which can be traced in Acts and
the Epistles. This skeleton outline, into which the narrative sections are inserted, provides a measure of chronological sequence
throughout the Gospel, and leads up to the passion narrative,
which formed a unity from the beginning of the apostolic preaching.

The first verse of Mk. gives the title of the work; it is 'the beginning of the good news'. (We may compare Luke's characterization of *his* Gospel as 'all that Jesus *began* both to do and to teach',
Acts i. 1.) The beginning of the good news starts with John's
baptism, which was itself (as Mark points out) the subject of Old
Testament prophecy. The brief record of John's ministry forms
the background for the introduction of Jesus, His baptism, temptation, and appearance in Galilee after John's imprisonment with
the message: 'The time is fulfilled, and the kingdom of God has
drawn near; repent, and believe in the good news' (i. 15). Then
we have the call of the first disciples, followed by a vividly impressive picture of a day's work in Capernaum, no doubt intended
as a sample of the sort of thing that happened everywhere He went
in these early weeks of the Galilæan ministry.

From Mk. ii. 1 to iii. 6 we have a series of those 'pronouncement
stories' which, according to Dibelius, figured so prominently in

the primitive preaching, for which reason he calls them 'paradigms'. These are incidents which lead up to some memorable and impressive pronouncement of Jesus. Many of them, like those in this section, contain an element of controversy; and the prominence of this element at this early stage in Mk. emphasizes the note of conflict which is so marked in this Gospel.

The growing conflict between Jesus and His opponents appears in that He is no longer welcomed to preach in synagogues, as He is no longer *persona grata* with the official teachers. It comes to a head when the deputation from Jerusalem, sent to look into His activities, ascribe His expulsion of demons to the energizing power of Beelzebul, which brings upon them His solemn warning of the danger of sinning against the Holy Spirit, that deliberate shutting of their eyes to the light which was by its very nature irremediable (iii. 22ff.).

At this point (iv. 1ff.) the parables of the kingdom are fittingly introduced. Though the religious leaders of the people refused Him, yet the seed sown would bear fruit, wherever it fell into good ground. As for those who sinned against the light, beholding but not seeing, and hearing but not understanding, to them the whole message of the kingdom was a riddle; but to those who believed was revealed the hitherto unknown mystery of the kingdom.

It is difficult to establish any chronological order or geographical sequence in the next four chapters (v.-viii.), but the arrangement of their contents is not haphazard. It may be remarked that the apparent duplication of incidents in them, culminating in the twofold Feedings of the Thousands, has a theological significance; our Lord repeats in Galilee's Gentile fringe similar actions to those performed in purely Jewish territory. These incidents lead up to the epochal event of Peter's confession at Cæsarea Philippi, which is the dividing-point of this Gospel.

Once we reach Peter's confession (viii. 27ff.), we find again what seems to be a natural chronological sequence. The importance of this event is marked by our Lord's warning His disciples for the first time of His impending arrest and death (viii. 31)—a warning repeated in ix. 31 and x. 33ff. In face of this warning He issues His cross-bearing challenge to those who would follow Him—a challenge to be weighed in the light of His coming kingdom, of which the three disciples are given a glimpse on the Mount of Transfiguration (ix. 1-13).

Chapter x. begins with our Lord's departure from Galilee to Transjordan and Judæa, and in verse 32 we see Him treading with determination the fateful road to Jerusalem. The request by

James and John for preferential treatment in the kingdom elicits
from Him a lesson on the true greatness, in which He points to
Himself as an example to be followed; 'for even the Son of Man
came not to be ministered unto, but to minister, and to give His
life a ransom for many' (x. 45)—words in which we hear an
echo of the great Servant-oracle of Is. liii., in terms of which Jesus
so constantly interpreted His life-mission.

Then comes the entry into Jerusalem (xi. 1ff.), while the Passover crowds hail Him as the Coming One.   The story moves
swiftly to its climax; everything recorded is significant—the curs-
ing and withering of the barren fig tree (an acted parable of the
imminent ruin of the nation), the cleansing of the temple, and
the parable of the Vineyard, where His messianic claim is as plain
as could be without His actually saying 'I am the Messiah'. Then,
in chapter xii., we have the famous group of controversial incidents, where the Herodians and Sadducees receive replies to their
awkward questions, one of the scribes hears with delight the Lord's
summary of the law in the two comprehensive commandments
of love, and the Lord Himself asks about Messiah's relation to
David, since in Ps. cx. He is called David's Lord.

The eschatological discourse in chapter xiii. (the only discourse
of any length preserved in Mk.) raises several problems. It possibly circulated in writing before Mark's Gospel itself, perhaps in
connection with the crisis of A.D. 40, when Caligula attempted to
have his image set up in the temple at Jerusalem. At such a time
it was but natural that Christ's words about the Abomination of
Desolation should be remembered and recorded. We may trace
the influence of this discourse in Paul's description of 'the Man of
Sin' in 2 Thes. ii. 4, and in the Apocalypse.

With chapter xiv. the passion narrative proper begins, and it
is carried rapidly to its *dénouement* on the cross—and at the empty
tomb.   The narrative includes the anointing at Bethany, the
betrayal, the preparing and eating of the last passover, the revelation of the traitor's presence, the institution of the Lord's supper
(a further reminiscence of Is. liii. may be detected in xiv. 24), the
prediction of the scattering of the disciples and the promise to lead
them forth to Galilee after the resurrection, Peter's boast and the
Lord's warning. Then come the agony in the Garden, the arrest,
the trial before the Sanhedrin, where sentence of death is passed
after the Lord's plain claim to be the Messiah—a claim made in
terms of Ps. cx. 1 and Dn. vii. 13. He is then taken to Pilate who,
upon the crowd's preferring Barabbas, hands Jesus over for crucifixion; and at last the story of the cross is told, in unrelieved

starkness and grimness, until the cry with which Jesus dies causes even the pagan centurion to acknowledge His divinity.

An interesting intrusion into the passion narrative is the remark about the young man who witnessed the arrest (xiv. 51f.); no better explanation of this has been offered than that the young man was the evangelist himself. In that case part at least of the passion narrative may come to us on first-hand evidence.

The last twelve verses of Mk. seem to be an early catechetical summary of the resurrection appearances of Jesus as related in the apostolic preaching, which was appended to this Gospel. It is commonly supposed that the original ending of Mk. was lost; but Dr. Stonehouse argues ably for the appropriateness of xvi. 8 as an ending for the Gospel story as Mark conceived it; the empty tomb, interpreted by the young man in white as signalizing the resurrection of its temporary Tenant, and the consequent awe of the women, bringing the record to an end on a fitting note.[1]

THEMES FOR STUDY

1. What witness does the Gospel bear to Christ as (i) the Son of Man and (ii) the Son of God?

2. What internal evidence is there of Peter's authority behind St. Mark?

3. Trace the note of conflict and controversy throughout the Gospel.

4. The 'Servant of the Lord' is pictured in Is. xlii., xlix., l., lii. 13- liii. Find correspondences between these prophecies and Jesus Christ as seen in this Gospel.

5. Miracles have been called 'parables in action'. Extract the teaching from those recorded by St. Mark.

THE GOSPEL ACCORDING TO ST. LUKE

AUTHORSHIP, DATE AND CIRCUMSTANCES

THE third Gospel and the Acts of the Apostles are ascribed, according to a tradition which we can confidently accept, to that companion of Paul whom in Col. iv. 14 he calls 'Luke, the beloved physician'. These two books should be regarded as two volumes

[1] See article 'The End of the Second Gospel', by F. F. Bruce, in *The Evangelical Quarterly*, July 1945.

of a history of Christian origins, written for the benefit of one Theophilus, to add to his assurance of the truth of the gospel narrative.

It is likely that Acts was written not very long after the date of the last event recorded in it, the end of Paul's two years' detention in Rome (Acts xxviii. 30). The optimistic note on which the history ends seems to indicate a date before the Neronian persecution of A.D. 64. The Gospel was certainly written earlier, but how much earlier it is not possible to say.

Luke was a Gentile who inherited the tradition of Greek historical and biographical writing. His quality as a historian is high; Sir W. M. Ramsay[1] summed it up by saying that 'Luke's history is unsurpassed in respect of its trustworthiness' and that he 'should be placed along with the very greatest of historians'. He alone of the Evangelists sets the gospel story within the framework of world-history, as appears, e.g. from his list of synchronisms in Lk. iii. 1f., and from his frequent reference to emperors and imperial officials and vassal kings. In him, too, as distinct from the other Evangelists, we can discern something of a biographical interest in Christ, as appears from the greater detail of his infancy and boyhood narratives. Even so, the kernel of his Gospel, as of the others, is the apostolic preaching.

Some older theologians pointed out that while Matthew presents Jesus as the King of Israel, Mark as the Servant of the Lord, and John as the Son of God, Luke portrays Him as the Son of Man; and there is much truth in this. For example, while the Matthæan genealogy traces the lineage of Jesus back through David to Abraham, Luke traces it back through David (but not via the kings of Judah) to Adam; and the wide human sympathy of our Lord is emphasized throughout this Gospel. Luke loves to display His interest in humble and unprivileged people—women, Samaritans, the poor. The note struck in the *Magnificat*, 'He hath filled the hungry with good things; and the rich He hath sent empty away' (i. 53), is maintained throughout. The nature of true riches is also revealed, for 'a man's life does not consist in the abundance of his possessions' (xii. 15). Further teaching in Lk. on what we may call 'the economics of the kingdom of God' is to be found in the parables of the Rich Fool (xii. 16ff.), the Unjust Steward (xvi. 1ff.), and Dives and Lazarus (xvi. 19ff.), and in our Lord's advice to His host in xiv. 12-14.

In addition to the Markan source and the Logia (see above, p. 321), Luke had access to other valuable information; about half

---

[1] *Bearing of Recent Discovery on the Trustworthiness of the New Testament*, pp. 81, 222.

the material in his Gospel is not found in the others. To his special sources we owe the nativity narratives of chapters i. and ii., probably, as Sanday said, 'the oldest evangelical fragment, or document, of the New Testament, and in any case the most archaic thing in the whole volume'; and several other well-known incidents and parables, most of which have been included by Luke in his long non-Markan section, ix. 51-xviii. 14. He may have acquired his information for chapters i. and ii. in Jerusalem, which he visited with Paul in A.D. 57 (Acts xxi. 15ff.), when he probably met some of the Twelve, and of 'the eyewitnesses from the beginning' (i. 2), and perhaps the mother of our Lord. It has been argued, with considerable show of probability, that much of his other special material was acquired in the house of Philip the evangelist at Cæsarea (cf. Acts xxi. 8ff., etc.).

The literary art with which Luke weaves the various parts of his narrative together makes it more difficult to keep the order of his Gospel in mind than that, say, of the more schematized Mt.

ANALYSIS

i. and ii.   The birth and childhood of our Lord and the Baptist.

iii. 1-iv. 13.   The preaching of John; the baptism and temptation of the Lord.

iv. 14-ix. 50.   The ministry in Galilee.

ix. 51-xix. 28.   Journeyings towards Jerusalem; ministry outside Galilee.

xix. 29-xxi.   Last days of public teaching.

xxii.-xxiv.   The last supper, the arrest, trial, death, and resurrection of the Lord.

CONTENTS

The first four verses of this Gospel are intended as a prologue not to the Gospel only, but to the whole of Luke's history. While the primary purpose of this history was to supply Theophilus with an orderly account of the facts of the Christian faith, we can trace several subsidiary motives, one of which is to show that from the beginning the Christian movement was innocent of any offence against the law of the empire. This motive is more prominent in Acts; but it appears in Lk. in the agreement between Herod Antipas and Pontius Pilate that nothing worthy of death had been pone by Jesus (xxiii. 14f.).

While the nativity chapters have a markedly Hebraic atmosphere, yet even in them the wider expansion of the gospel is anticipated. Not only had God visited and redeemed His people; the Child born in Bethlehem was to be a light to lighten the Gentiles as well as to be the glory of Israel. Similarly the angels in the *Gloria in Excelsis* announce peace on earth to men who are the objects of God's good pleasure; there are no national limitations here. But at the same time as they adumbrate the extension of the good news to the Gentiles, these chapters emphasize that it is firmly rooted in the Old Testament revelation. The words in which the aged Simeon hails the new-born Messiah echo the Servant-prophecy of Isaiah, in a passage (Is. xlix. 6) which is later quoted by Paul when, at Pisidian Antioch, he turns from the Jews to preach to the Gentiles (Acts xiii. 47).

The same note is struck in chapter iv., where the account of our Lord's address in the Nazareth synagogue places the foreground of His public ministry the programme of the kingdom contained in that address. The 'text' of the address was the opening passage of Is. lxi. which, while not actually one of the Servant Songs, is animated by the same spirit; and the address itself emphasized the wider aspect of the divine visitation, the gospel's extension to the Gentiles and acceptance by them as foreshadowed by the Old Testament incidents of the widow of Zarephath and Naaman the Syrian.

The story of the miraculous draught of fishes with which chapter v. begins is peculiar to Lk., and is followed by a block of material (v. 12-vi. 19) parallel to Mk. i. 40-iii. 19. Then comes the Lukan version of the Great Sermon which is reported in an expanded form in Mt. v.-vii. Luke's version of this seems, in part, to have been derived from a source other than Matthew's. From this source, for example, the woes which follow Luke's shorter version of the Beatitudes (Lk. vi. 20-26), seem to have been derived.

The report of the Sermon is followed, as in Mt., by the healing of the centurion's servant (vii. 2ff.); and this is followed in turn by the raising of the young man of Nain, the inquiry from the Baptist, the incident of the sinful woman in Simon's house, and a note of the women who supported Christ with their substance as He went from place to place.

The next section (viii. 4-56) is parallel to Mk. iv. 1-v. 43 for the most part; ix. 1-17 records the Mission of the Twelve and the Feeding of the Five Thousand (cf. Mk. vi. 7-44). Luke omits the death of John the Baptist, which comes as a parenthesis in Mk. vi. 17-29, but he does mention Herod's curiosity about Jesus (ix.

7-9). Mk. vi. 45-viii. 26 has no parallel in Lk., a fact which is commonly referred to as 'the great omission'. Lk. ix. 18-50 is parallel to Mk. viii. 27-ix. 40, including the confession at Cæsarea Philippi and the transfiguration.

Then comes the long non-Markan section, Lk. ix. 51-xviii. 14, sometimes called the 'larger interpolation' or the 'Peræan section' or the 'travel document', all of which names are open to greater or less objection. This section includes most of the parables and narratives peculiar to Lk.; to it we are indebted for the parables of the Good Samaritan, the Rich Fool, the Great Supper, the Prodigal Son, the Unjust Steward, Dives and Lazarus, the Importunate Widow, the Pharisee and the Publican. It commences with a time-note (ix. 51), referring no doubt to the occasion in or about September of A.D. 29, when our Lord left Galilee for the last time.

After this long section Luke follows the Markan narrative again for the account of the last journey to Jerusalem and the events of Holy Week, with some passages peculiar to himself, such as the story of Zacchæus (xix. 1-10); the parable of the Pounds (xix. 11-27) (which is similar to, but not identical with, the Matthæan parable of the Talents); and the lament over the city (xx. 41-44). The Lukan version of the eschatological discourse (xxi.) has some variant phraseology which has been thought, but unnecessarily, to indicate a date after the Fall of Jerusalem in A.D. 70. To be sure, in verse 20 the Markan reference to the 'abomination of desolation' is replaced by the words, 'But when you see Jerusalem encompassed by armies'; either these words were part of the original discourse or Luke, writing for Gentiles, is interpreting for them an expression which they might find meaningless. The surrounding of Jerusalem by hostile armies was a well-marked feature of the Old Testament programme of the End-time.

Luke's passion narrative, too, agrees with the Markan account in the main, with additions here and there, such as the institution of the Lord's supper and the following talk (xxii. 24-38), the appearing before Herod (xxiii. 7ff.), the incident of the weeping women on the Via Dolorosa (xxiii. 27-31), the narrative of the repentant thief (xxiii. 39-43); and among the resurrection appearances (all of which are Judæan in Lk.), we are indebted to this Gospel for the immortal story of the Emmaus road (xxiv. 13-35).

Luke ends his Gospel as he began it, with the note of fulfilment of Old Testament prophecy: 'Thus it is written, that the Messiah

should suffer, and rise from the dead the third day; and that in
His name repentance for remission of sins should be proclaimed
to all the nations, beginning at Jerusalem' (xxiv. 46f.). Though
writing as a Gentile for Gentiles, Luke cannot but be true to the
facts, and he insists on the integrity of Christianity with the Old
Testament revelation out of which it sprang.

THEMES FOR STUDY

1. Collect the teaching of the Gospel concerning prayer and
praise.

2. What indications are there that the author was a Gentile,
interested in the spread of the gospel through the world?

3. Note how our Lord's teaching takes on a different form when
addressed to the Scribes, to outsiders, and to simple folk.

4. Show how prominence is given to the doctrine of free grace
and other points in the teaching of St. Paul.

5. Show how the main themes of the Gospel first find mention
in the two first chapters.

THE GOSPEL ACCORDING TO ST. JOHN

AUTHORSHIP, DATE AND CIRCUMSTANCES

'I AM accustomed,' wrote John Calvin in his Argument to the
fourth Gospel, 'to call this Gospel the key, which opens the door
to the understanding of the others.' In more recent times Archbishop William Temple re-echoed this sentiment: 'Let the Synoptists repeat for us as closely as possible the very words He spoke;
but let St. John tune our ears to hear them.'

Yet this Gospel has frequently been called in question because
of its differences from the others. Differences there are; but if we
take the fourth Gospel on its own merits, it is difficult to avoid
the conclusion that it was either written by an eyewitness or else
draws upon the reminiscences of an eyewitness. An impartial
critic, the Rabbinic scholar Israel Abrahams,[1] recorded his conviction that it 'enshrines a genuine tradition of an aspect of Jesus'
teaching which has not found a place in the Synoptics'; and elsewhere[2] drew attention to 'the cumulative strength of the argu-

[1] *Studies in Pharisaism and the Gospels*, First Series, p. 12.

[2] *Cambridge Biblical Essays*, p. 181.

ments adduced by Jewish writers favourable to the authenticity of the discourses in the fourth Gospel, especially in relation to the circumstances under which they are reported to have been spoken'.

The almost unanimous consensus of early Christian writers whose views on the subject of its authorship have been preserved is that this Gospel was written towards the end of his life (c. 90-100) by John the Apostle, the son of Zebedee. The Gospel is quoted or alluded to from the early years of the second century onwards—by Ignatius, Basilides, Justin Martyr, Tatian, etc. One of the earliest fragments of any New Testament writing is a papyrus fragment of Jn., found in Egypt in 1917, and belonging to the first half of the second century. In the last quarter of the second century Irenæus (who had connections both with Asia Minor and with Gaul), Clement of Alexandria, Theophilus of Antioch, Tertullian of Carthage, and the gnostic Heracleon in Italy, together with the Muratorian Canon and the anti-Marcionite Gospel Prologues (both emanating from Rome) attest the generally held belief that the Evangelist was the Apostle John.

The internal evidence points to the identification of this apostle with 'the disciple whom Jesus loved', of whom we read in xxi. 24: 'This is the disciple who bears witness of these things and wrote these things; and we know that his witness is true.' The people who say 'we know' seem to have been John's disciples who took down the Gospel at John's dictation and published it after his death; this view agrees with the earliest external evidence. It would not make much practical difference if we were to suppose that the whole Gospel was penned by a disciple at the dictation and on the authority of John the Apostle.

The existence of 'John the elder', who is frequently mentioned in this connection nowadays, was inferred by Eusebius from the following remark of Papias concerning his sources of information: On any occasion when a person came in my way who had been a follower of the elders, I would inquire about the discourses of the elders—what Andrew, or Peter, or Philip, or Thomas, or James, or John, or Matthew, or any of the Lord's disciples said, and what Aristion and the elder John, the disciples of the Lord, say.' Eusebius, looking for a non-apostolic writer to whom he might ascribe the book of Revelation, connected these words with a report mentioned by Dionysius, bishop of Alexandria (c. 270), that two tombs were pointed out at Ephesus as commemorating John and concluded that Papias here mentioned two Johns, first the apostle and then one whom he calls 'the elder'. Bishop

Lightfoot agreed that Papias intended two different persons, though holding firmly to the apostolic authorship of the Gospel.[1] Many modern scholars, however, also think that this shadowy figure of this 'Presbyter John' was the evangelist. But 'belief in two Johns is not necessitated by the statement of Papias'[2]; and Zahn and others hold that 'the elder John' was the apostle, who had just been included in a list of 'elders' and 'disciples of the Lord'; the change of tense from 'said' to 'say' indicating that whereas John, like others of the twelve, belonged to the older generation, he was, like Aristion, still alive at the time. This interpretation is rendered the more probable by the fact that Eusebius himself in his 'Chronicle' refers to Papias as 'a hearer of John the divine and apostle'.[3]

ANALYSIS

[1] See *Biblical Essays*, p. 53.

[2] So Prof. C. E. Raven, *Jesus and the Gospel of Love*, p. 220, note.

[3] See also F. F. Bruce, *Are the New Testament Documents Reliable?* (I.V.F.) pp. 47-59; H. P. V. Nunn, *The Fourth Gospel* (Tyndale Press), pp. 22-25; and Chapters XXI and XXII under *The Epistles of John* and *Revelation*.

CONTENTS

The Christology of Jn. is not essentially different from that of Mk.; in both, Jesus is the Messiah, the Son of God, sent by the Father. And Mt. and Lk. both preserve a *logion* which has been termed 'the fourth Gospel in a nutshell', so thoroughly 'Johannine' is it in thought and phraseology (Mt. xi. 27; Lk. x. 22). The early existence of this high Christology in the Palestinian and adjoining churches, expressed in phraseology not unlike John's, is further evidenced by the first-century collection of Christian hymns known curiously as the 'Odes of Solomon'. The same high Christology appears independently in the Pauline Epistles and the Epistle to the Hebrews; indeed, it has been argued that the famous Christological passage in Phil. ii. 6ff. is an early Palestinian hymn.

The Prologue to Jn. narrates how the 'Word' which was with God in the beginning (cf. Prov. viii. 22), sharing His essence and acting as His mediator in creation, became flesh and set among men His dwelling-place, from which the divine glory shone forth. 'We beheld His glory,' says the writer; and this is one of the key-notes of the Gospel; the wondrous works wrought by Christ are in Jn. regularly called 'signs'—signs, that is, of the glory hidden from outward sight but visible to faith. Such signs are: the changing of the water into wine (ii. 1-11); the cleansing of the temple (ii. 13-22); the healing of the nobleman's son (iv. 46-54); the healing of the paralytic at the pool of Bethesda (v. 1-16); the feeding of the multitude (vi. 1-14); the walking on the sea (vi. 15-21); the healing of the blind man (ix. 1-38); the raising of Lazarus (xi. 1-46), and lastly, the 'sign' predicted by Himself in ii. 18ff., His resurrection. That was, of course, the culminating manifestation of His glory; and it is noteworthy that, among the others, the word 'glory' is specially associated with the first and the last, the house of feasting (ii. 11) and the place of mourning (xi. 4, 40).

The purpose of Jn. is expressed in xx. 31, R.V.: 'These things are written, that ye may believe that Jesus is the Christ, the Son of God, and that believing ye may have life in His name'; and the succession of testimonies to Him is a marked feature throughout the Gospel—beginning with that of John the Baptist (i. 26-34), and going on through those of Andrew (i. 41), Philip (i. 45), Nathanael (i. 49), Nicodemus (iii. 2), the Samaritan woman (iv. 19, 29), the men of Sychar (iv. 42), the Galilæan multitude (vi. 14), Peter (vi. 68f.), and others, until we reach the crowning con-

M

fession of Thomas, 'My Lord and my God' (xx. 28), with the
answering final Beatitude on all believers since then: 'Blessed are
they that have not seen, and yet have believed.' Indeed, witness-
ing and believing are two further key-words of this Gospel.

These testimonies, however, together with the self-revelations
of Jesus in this Gospel (e.g. iv. 26, ix. 37), constitute one of the
chief difficulties arising out of a comparison of Jn. with the
Synoptics. The impression we get from *them* is that Jesus did not
declare Himself to be the Messiah until Peter at Cæsarea Philippi
confessed Him as such. This, however, is an obstacle in the way
of accepting John's account as historical only if we regard the
impression received from the other Evangelists (Mark in particular) as so complete and watertight that no other impression
can be historically justified. But a wiser method of proceeding is
to allow the Synoptic and Johannine impressions to be modified
by each other. If we do this, we may agree that while the testimony of John the Baptist led the disciples to acclaim Jesus as
Messiah in the early spring-tide of His ministry, the disillusioning
experiences of His rejection by the religious leaders of the people
and the conflict of the facts with their preconceived ideas of the
Messiah's rôle might well have made them change their minds,
had not a higher than a merely human witness (Mt. xvi. 17)
convinced them that their Master was indeed the One whom
John had proclaimed Him to be, the Son of God.

The fact that John deals mainly with our Lord's Judæan activity, in contradistinction to the Galilæan setting of the Synoptists,
may have something to do with this problem; 'That He should
in His dealings with the simpler and more revolutionary people
of Galilee refuse to blaze abroad His Messiahship is natural in
view of His concept of its character,'[1] says Professor C. E. Raven.
In Jerusalem, on the other hand, He had to challenge the people
to accept His claims, and even there He did so in such a manner
as to leave them in doubt; for in the December preceding the
passion an attempt was made in the temple to get an un-
ambiguous answer: 'How long will you keep us in suspense? If
you are the Messiah, tell us plainly' (Jn. x. 24).

This geographical factor also helps to explain the difference in
His manner of speech in Jn. as contrasted with the Synoptists.
Many of the discourses in Jn. are conducted with skilled theo-
logical disputants, and, as we have seen, Jewish scholars have
recognized in them the current forms of Rabbinical dialectic.
Our Lord knew how to talk to varying audiences in varying forms

[1] *Jesus and the Gospel of Love*, p. 216.

of speech. Not but what something may be said for the view that this Evangelist has 'transposed into another key' the speeches which he reports and, in any case, they were originally delivered in a Semitic tongue.

Where Jn. is compared with the Synoptics in the matter of chronology, it is found that it is the only Gospel which presents anything approaching a chronological scheme of the Ministry, a scheme which several scholars are willing to accept who nevertheless decline to extend this recognition of historicity to other parts of this Gospel. Thus, where there appear to be chronological discrepancies between Jn. and the others, we may feel safe in taking Jn. as normative, and interpreting the Synoptic data in the light of Jn.'s more explicit statements. This is so, for example, in such vexed questions as the single or dual cleansing of the temple and the date of the last passover in relation to the day of the crucifixion.

In connection with the crucifixion, another startling divergence is the part played by the raising of Lazarus, on which the Synoptists are silent. F. C. Burkitt denied the historicity of this miracle; it simply could not be fitted into the Markan scheme. Few nowadays would ascribe to Mark's order quite that degree of completeness; and it may be better to try to fit the Markan and other Synoptic evidence into the Johannine framework. When one makes this attempt, a wonderfully convincing picture of the course of events of our Lord's ministry results.

The Galilæan ministry recorded by the Synoptists can be fitted in between Jn. v. and vii.; it lasted a year, ending with the October preceding the passion. The events of Jn. i.-v. deal with an earlier ministry, before the Baptist's imprisonment, with which event the ministry related by the Synoptists begins (Mk. i. 14).

In spite of the many differences between Jn. and the others, this Gospel no less than they contains as its kernel the same apostolic preaching. 'In the Fourth Gospel,' says Professor Dodd,[1] 'we can discern, no less clearly than in Matthew and Luke, the fixed outline of the historical section of the *kerygma* as we have it in Acts x. and xiii.: the ministry of John the Baptist, the "anointing" of Jesus with the Holy Spirit, His teaching and works of mercy and power in Galilee; His ministry in Judæa and Jerusalem, His arrest and trial before Pilate, His crucifixion, burial and resurrection.'

The first resurrection-appearances recorded in Jn. (those of chapter xx.) are located in Jerusalem; and xx. 31 seems a natural

[1] *The Apostolic Preaching and its Developments*, pp. 164, 165.

ending for the Gospel. The last chapter may have been added later by those who published the Gospel (the 'we' of xxi. 24?) as the record of a further appearance—and that a Galilæan one— which they had heard related by the Evangelist. However this may be, many Christians in all ages, reading this 'spiritual Gospel', as Clement of Alexandria called it, have been constrained, apart from all the critical questions raised by it, to re-echo the testimony of those earliest witnesses and say of the writer, '*We know that his witness is true.*'

THEMES FOR STUDY

1. What do we learn from the Gospel about John the son of Zebedee, and what indications are there that he himself was the author?

2. Examine the Gospel in the light of xx. 31, and show how both belief and unbelief progress throughout.

3. Make a list of the 'signs' as narrated. To what do they point?

4. What is there in this Gospel to prove our Lord's divinity?

5. Make a list of our Lord's post-resurrection appearances in the four Gospels (i) on the first day, (ii) afterwards in Judæa, and (iii) in Galilee. Note how the teaching then imparted leads on to the apostolic testimony.

THE ACTS OF THE APOSTLES

AUTHORSHIP, DATE AND CIRCUMSTANCES

THIS book, called since the second century 'The Acts of the Apostles', is, as we have seen (pp. 333 f.), the continuation of the history of Christian beginnings, the first part of which is the third Gospel.

It commences with a reference by Luke to the former part of his history, which he describes as concerned with 'all that Jesus began both to do and to teach', from which a natural inference would be that the second part deals with what Jesus *continued* to do and teach after His ascension, by His Spirit in the apostles. Certainly great emphasis is laid in Acts on the part played by the Holy Spirit from the Day of Pentecost onwards.

The book cannot justly be called, as one early document (the Muratorian Canon) calls it, 'the Acts of *all* the apostles'; it is restricted chiefly to the progress of the gospel along the road from Jerusalem to Rome, the chief agent in this sphere being the apostle Paul. On certain occasions Luke himself was present at the events he narrates; he indicates this by passing from the third person to the first person plural. The passages characterized by this change are therefore called the 'we' passages; they are three in number: xvi. 10-17, xx. 5-xxi. 18, xxvii. 1-xxviii. 16.

Luke had ample access to first-rate sources of information in the course of his journeys with Paul, especially if the second-century tradition is true which represents him as a native of Syrian Antioch.[1]

An obvious purpose in Acts—and indeed in the whole Lukan history—is the apologetic one. Luke shows how the responsible authorities throughout the empire admit that Christianity is not contrary to the law. The Cypriot proconsul is favourable to Paul and Barnabas (xiii. 7-12); the Philippian prætors apologize for their unwarranted ill-treatment of Paul and Silas (xvi. 35-40); the Asiarchs in Ephesus are Paul's friends (xix. 31), and the town clerk of that city defends him against the popular accusations (xix. 35-40). Gallio, the proconsul of Achaia, refuses to hear the charges brought against Paul by the Corinthian Jews, regarding them as not within the competence of Roman law (xviii. 12-17). At Cæsarea, the procurators Felix and Festus and the vassal king Herod Agrippa II state their belief in his innocence (xxiv. 22ff., xxv. 14ff., xxvi. 31f.).

Why, then, was the progress of Christianity attended by so much trouble? Luke, by way of answer, points to the Jews throughout the empire. All the attacks on the Christians which he records were instigated by Jews, with the exception of the beating and imprisonment at Philippi and the riot at Ephesus, both of which were occasioned by the threat of the gospel to certain Gentile property-interests. From one city to another Paul and his companions go, offering the good news 'to the Jew first' in synagogue after synagogue; but almost invariably their message is refused there, and they turn to the Gentiles, so that while Acts records the advance of the gospel in the Gentile communities of the empire, it records *pari passu* its rejection by the majority of the Jewish communities, a rejection which is summed up at the end of the book by Paul in a quotation from Is. vi. 9f., words already quoted by Christ Himself in the same sense.

[1] See also p. 334

ANALYSIS

CONTENTS

The first five chapters contain a series of cameos depicting primitive church life in Jerusalem. After Christ's ascension, the apostles and other believers in Jerusalem, one hundred and twenty strong, await in that city the promise of the Spirit, meanwhile electing Matthias to the vacancy in the Twelve caused by Judas's defection and suicide. The descent of the Spirit on the day of Pentecost (ii. 1ff.) is accompanied by a manifestation of 'speaking with tongues', and when crowds have been attracted by this phenomenon, Peter seizes the opportunity to proclaim Jesus as the Messiah, crucified at the instance of the Jewish rulers, but raised from the dead and exalted by God to His right hand; and such is the power accompanying his words that three thousand, convicted of the guilt of Messiah's death, believe the good news and express their repentance in baptism, and form the first Christian church.

The movement spreads, and the apostles enjoy popular favour, which increases with the healing of a lame man in the temple courts (iii. 1 ff.), so much so that the Sadducean authorities try in vain to check the apostles' activity (iv. 1 ff.). The numbers increase, and the brighter and darker sides of the practice of pooling their wealth for the common good are illustrated on the one hand by the generosity of Barnabas (iv. 36 f.) and on the other by the sad fate of Ananias and Sapphira (v. 1-11). This last incident, not improbable amid the prevalent enthusiasm, acts as a deterrent to those who would lightheartedly join the believers, but even so the new movement goes on from strength to strength.

Chapter vi. brings us into a new atmosphere, where the Hellenistic members of the church make their weight felt. Among the seven officers appointed to preside over the daily distribution from the common stock, Stephen stands out as exceptionally farsighted in his comprehension of the breach between the old faith and the new. In many ways he anticipated the outlook of Paul and the writer to the Hebrews. His consequent declaration that the temple worship had been superseded by Christ, a view bound to rouse the anger of the Jerusalem Jews, enabled the authorities to prosecute him on a popular charge, and his speech recorded in chapter vii. is not so much a defence as an elaboration of his position, in which he develops two theses: (1) the people of God are a pilgrim people; therefore the movable tent in the wilderness is a fitter shrine than the stationary temple in Jerusalem; (2) Israel has been consistently rebellious throughout her history, and has attained the pinnacle of rebellion by the murder of 'the just One'. Whether Stephen's subsequent stoning was an act of lynch-law or an excess of jurisdiction is disputed; at any rate it was the signal for a thoroughgoing campaign of suppression, led by the young rabbi Saul of Tarsus (viii. 1 ff.). The Jerusalem church was scattered throughout Palestine and even beyond it (though the fact that the Twelve remained in Jerusalem may indicate that they had not yet forfeited their popularity). The dispersion meant the further broadcasting of the gospel; one early feature being the initiative taken by Philip, another member of the Seven, in evangelizing Samaria (viii. 5 ff.).

The conversion of Saul, which Luke narrates next (ix. 1-30), was in his eyes an event of the first importance; in spite of his limited space he records it in some detail three times (here and in xxii. 3-21, xxvi. 4-18). The persecution seems to have died down with the conversion of the chief persecutor (ix. 31), but the good it did lived after it; Peter's evangelization of the half-Gentile cities of western Palestine, Lydda and Joppa (ix. 32-43), put him in the way of taking the momentous step of visiting a Gentile household in Cæsarea to proclaim the gospel there (x. 1 ff.). Not long afterwards the Hellenistic Christians, who had gone so far afield as Antioch, did the same thing there on a wider scale (xi. 19-21), so that this church was from an early date predominantly Gentile. The Jewish element in Jerusalem did not accept Peter's innovation without question (xi. 1 ff.), and though he satisfied them, possibly the Twelve lost favour with the Jewish population; it may be no accident that soon after this Herod Agrippa I (king of Judæa,

41-44) had James executed, and, 'because he saw it pleased the Jews', imprisoned Peter with a like object in view (xii.).

News of the advance at Antioch came to the apostles, who despatched Barnabas to see what was taking place there (xi. 22 ff.). Barnabas was so pleased at the proportions of the good work that he sent to Tarsus for Saul to come and join him in Antioch. Shortly afterwards both Barnabas and Saul were sent as delegates from Antioch to Jerusalem with gifts to the poverty-stricken metropolitan church in view of an impending famine (we are told by Suetonius that the reign of Claudius, 41-54, was marked by persistent unfruitful seasons).

Antioch now became the centre for the wider expansion of Christianity. From there Barnabas and Saul went forth to evangelize Cyprus and parts of Asia Minor and during this journey founded those churches in the Roman province of Galatia to which the Epistle to the Galatians is addressed (xiii., xiv.). On their return from this tour they found that the question of the terms on which Gentiles might be admitted to full church membership was being warmly disputed (xv. 1 ff.). The Antiochene practice (followed by Paul[1] and Barnabas in their missionary journeys) was to receive Gentiles to fellowship on the same terms as Jews, without requiring them to be circumcised (like Jewish proselytes) or imposing the Mosaic ceremonial law upon them; the stricter members of the Jewish-Christian church of Jerusalem insisted that these conditions be required. At the ensuing Council in Jerusalem, to which Paul and Barnabas led an Antiochene delegation to discuss this matter, it was decided that no such conditions be imposed on Gentile converts, but that in order to facilitate ordinary social intercourse and table-fellowship between Gentile and Jewish Christians, the former should be urged to avoid meat which had been consecrated to idols or from which the blood had not been drained, and to observe the high Jewish code of morals. Once the main principle had been safeguarded, Paul was ready to go all lengths in conciliation; and the conditions of the decree were such as he himself in his Epistles enjoins upon his readers.

We come next to two missionary tours based on Antioch—one made by Barnabas and his cousin Mark to Cyprus (xv. 39), the other by Paul and Silas, a Jerusalem Christian, to Asia Minor (xv. 40 ff.). Paul and Silas visited the churches formed on the previous visit, delivering them the apostolic decree as a charter of Christian freedom. At Lystra they took into their company

[1] From xiii. 9 onwards Luke uses the Roman cognomen Paul instead of the Jewish name Saul.

Timothy, the son of a Jewish mother and pagan father, who had been brought up in the Jewish faith. Prevented from taking the main road westward to Ephesus by the guidance of the Holy Spirit (xvi. 6), they struck northward until they reached the coast at Troas, from which, accompanied by Luke, they took ship across the Ægean and landed at Neapolis (mod. Kavalla). From here they went inland to Philippi, a Roman colony, and after founding a church in that city they went on to Thessalonica (xvii. 1), another Macedonian town, where another church was formed as a result of three sabbaths' preaching in the synagogue.[1] Forced to leave Thessalonica through the representations made by local Jews to the magistrates (politarchs), they divided their forces and went south. Paul's stay at Athens (xvii. 15 ff.) is full of interesting detail and accurate local colour, as also is his speech to the Areopagus, a sample of a method of presenting Christianity to the Gentile world which was to become widespread.[2]

From Athens he went on to Corinth, another Roman colony (xviii. 1 ff.), and was rejoined by Silas and Timothy, and here they worked for eighteen months. At the end of that time Paul paid a short visit to Palestine (xviii. 21-23), and then returned to the Ægean, this time settling in Ephesus, where he spent two and a half years, evangelizing not only that city itself, but also its populous hinterland, to such good purpose as to threaten the prevalent cult of Ephesian Artemis (xix.). The Ephesian ministry was followed by a visit to Macedonia and Greece (xx. 1-3), and then Paul and his company returned to Jerusalem (bearing, as we know from the Epistles, the money collected in the new Gentile churches for the relief of the poor of the Jerusalem church).

This visit to Jerusalem led to a riot in which Paul was accused of violating the sanctity of the temple (xxi. 27 ff.), and when he was rescued by the Roman garrison from lynching at the hands of the mob, he spent two years in detention at the procurator's headquarters in Cæsarea (xxiv. 27), until, afraid that Festus would give him up to the Jews to ingratiate himself with them, he appealed to the emperor (xxv. 11), and was sent to Rome, although the Palestinian authorities agreed that he might otherwise have been set free (xxvi. 31 f.).

The story of the voyage to Rome (xxvii.) is one of the finest pieces of descriptive writing in the New Testment and a document of first-rate importance for our knowledge of ancient seafaring. Shipwrecked at Malta, the ship's company and passengers

---

[1] See also p. 378.
[2] See *The Speeches in the Acts*, by F. F. Bruce (Tyndale Press), pp. 14-18.

spent the winter of 59-60 there (xxviii. 1-11). Paul arrived at
Rome in the following spring, and there the narrative leaves him,
spending two years in the heart of the empire, making known the
gospel to all and sundry who came to his lodging, without let or
hindrance (xxviii. 30 f.). 'The victory of the Word of God,'
says Bengel, 'Paul at Rome, the climax of the gospel, the end of
the Acts. . . . Here thou hast thy form, O church: it is thine to
keep it, and to guard the deposit.'

THEMES FOR STUDY

1. Trace the missionary development of the church in Judæa,
Samaria and beyond. How far was it spontaneous, and how far
planned?

2. Trace the working of the Holy Spirit, comparing it with the
teaching in St. Luke's Gospel and in Jn. xiv.-xvi.

3. What lessons does this book contain on (i) prayer, (ii)
courage under persecution, and (iii) the brotherhood of believers?

4. How was Paul prepared for his life-work by (i) natural and
spiritual gifts, and (ii) by his early experiences?

5. Collect together the teaching contained in the speeches as it
relates (i) to Christians and (ii) to non-Christians.

CHAPTER XX

THE EPISTLES OF PAUL

OUT of twenty-seven books of the New Testament no less than twenty-one are letters, thirteen of which are certainly, and one other (Hebrews) possibly, written by Paul. Called forth by the needs and circumstances of actual persons and communities, which determined their content, they make their own unique contribution to the completeness of Holy Scripture. It is without question due to the over-ruling providence of God that so much of revealed truth has come down to us in this form, woven like so much of the divine revelation into a historical context.

The man whose letters compose so much of the New Testament was a free-born Roman citizen, a Jew of Tarsus, a Hebrew of the Hebrews, brought up at the feet of Gamaliel, but becoming a bond-slave and a missionary of Jesus Christ; such are the descriptions he gives of himself. His Lord calls him 'a chosen vessel unto me, to bear my name before the Gentiles, and kings, and the children of Israel' (Acts ix. 15). In his letters and in the Acts his many-sided character is revealed; strong of will in spite of a weak body; zealous at one time for the law, then for the gospel; untiring in his labours, ready to live or die for Christ; undoubtedly a Jew, glorying in the Scriptures, the fathers, and the promises (Rom. iii. 1, 2, ix. 4, 5), yet the apostle of the Gentiles, magnifying his office (Rom. xi. 13).

Paul was intensely human. His affection and tender feeling knew no bounds of race or social position, being shown equally to his Jewish kinsfolk and to his Gentile converts, to Onesimus the slave and to Philemon his master. The salutations contained in his letters reveal a loving and individual appreciation of his companions and fellow-Christians.

But that which chiefly qualified him to be an evangelist and a teacher, as he well knew, was the grace and calling of God (1 Cor. xv. 9-11). This was the source of his abundant and successful labours, as a result of which we have stored up in these letters such treasures of experience and teaching in the ways and the truth of God.

THE PAULINE TEACHING

The aim of Paul's letters was essentially practical. They were not composed as literature, nor designed to set up a system, but were written to encourage and help and to guide those to whom they were addressed.

From the day of his conversion Christ was Paul's very life (Gal. ii. 20), and he writes to those who like himself are now 'in Christ' (Col. i. 2). Although his Epistles are conversational in style and related to the circumstances of everyday life, Christ is always their theme, the living Lord and mighty Saviour. Paul's exhortations to the simplest duties are therefore based upon the sublime principles of salvation, faith, spiritual privilege and power, all derived from his own experience of the exalted yet indwelling Christ.

The wonderfully clear teaching in Galatians on salvation through Christ crucified, justification by faith, and Christian liberty, all bear upon the actual danger in which the churches of Galatia stood of falling back into bondage to the Mosaic law. The relationship between Jews and Gentiles in the great Roman metropolis gives the opportunity for a grand exposition of the principles of justification and sanctification applicable to Jew and Greek alike (Rom. i.-xi.), which is followed by practical exhortations founded upon them. Likewise, when the Christians in Corinth seek for advice concerning marriage, attendance at heathen feasts or the resurrection of the body, they receive answers definite and practical enough, yet all centred in Christ, so that Christ in life, and life in Christ is everywhere being taught.

A comparison of Paul's letters with the Gospels, with the speeches in Acts i.-xii., and with the rest of the Epistles will show that they contain no essential doctrine which cannot be found elsewhere. Luther once said that 'John's Gospel, the Epistles of Paul, especially Romans, Galatians and Ephesians, and 1 Peter —these are the books which show thee Christ, and teach all that is needful and blessed for thee to know'; and with this we might agree without denying the value and importance of the other Scriptures.

'Pauline doctrine' is, in fact, nothing but the doctrine of the primitive church. Based upon the facts of Christ's birth, crucifixion, resurrection, and ascension, the revelation concerning Christ's Person and work was ministered in the Spirit by Paul just as it was by the other apostles and evangelists (1 Cor. xv. 11).

OUTLINE OF THE LIFE OF PAUL

The following outline is given to help towards a better understanding of the time and circumstances of each Epistle as related to the events in Paul's life and in the progressive spread and development of the churches. The dating can only be taken as approximate.

A.D.

33   Paul's conversion (Acts ix. 1-9). For events preceding his conversion see Acts xxii. 3-5, xxvi. 4-5; 1 Tim. i. 12-16. For those immediately following see Acts ix. 19-30, xxii. 17-21, xxvi. 19, 20; Gal. i. 15-20.

33-46   Paul in Tarsus, Syria and Cilicia (Acts ix. 30; Gal. i. 21; 2 Cor. xii. 2, 3), including stay in Antioch (Acts xi. 25, 26).

46   Visit to Jerusalem (Acts xi. 27-30, xii. 25; Gal. ii. 1-10).

47   *First missionary journey:* Antioch, Cyprus, Antioch in Pisidia, Iconium, Lystra, and Derbe (Acts xiii., xiv.).

49   Dissensions with Jewish party at Antioch (Gal. ii. 11-14).

     Writes *Galatians*, from Antioch.

50   Paul visits Jerusalem and is present at the Christian Council (Acts xv. 1-35).

51   *Second missionary journey:* Antioch, Cilicia, S. Galatia, Troas, Philippi, Thessalonica, Berea, Athens, and Corinth (Acts xv. 36-xviii. 1).

51-53   Stay in Corinth (Acts xviii. 1-18).

     Writes *1* and *2 Thessalonians*.

53   Return via Ephesus and Cæsarea to Jerusalem, and again to Antioch (Acts xviii. 18-22).

     Third missionary journey: Antioch, Phrygia, and Galatia to Ephesus (Acts xviii. 23, 24).

53-56   Stay in Ephesus (Acts xix. 1-xx. 1).

     Writes *1* and *2 Corinthians*.

56-57   *Continuation of third journey:* Macedonia, Greece, Corinth, Philippi, Miletus (Conference with Ephesian elders), Tyre, Ptolemais, Cæsarea, Jerusalem (Acts xx. 1- xxi. 17).

     Writes *Romans*, from Corinth.

57-59   Arrest in Jerusalem, two years' imprisonment in Cæsarea (Acts xxi. 18- xxvi. 32).

59-60 Journey to Crete, Malta, Rhegium, and Rome (Acts xxvii.).

60-62 In Rome awaiting trial, under guard (Acts xxviii.). Writes *Colossians, Philemon, Ephesians, Philippians.*

62-65 Paul released (?), revisits churches. Writes *1 Timothy, Titus.*

66 or 67 Imprisonment in Rome. Writes *2 Timothy* shortly before his death.

ROMANS

AUTHORSHIP, DATE AND CIRCUMSTANCES

ALL of this Epistle may confidently be accepted as the work of Paul. There is, however, reason for asking whether chapters xv. and xvi. were part of the original Epistle. The doxology (xvi. 25-27) is found in some MSS. at the end of chapter xiv. or xv., and some scholars have suggested that chapter xvi. belonged originally to a letter written not to Rome, but to Ephesus. This hypothesis may, however, be rejected as 'not proven'; and the sub-section xv. 1-13 so continues the thought of xiv. that it seems more likely to have been an original part of the whole than something added later. A possible explanation of the manuscript variations is that the Epistle, because of its general character, although written originally as we have it to Rome, was used at a later time by other churches, with the local and personal references omitted.

The Epistle was written from Corinth during Paul's third journey, not long after he finished his prolonged sojourn in Ephesus, just before he took to Jerusalem the collection for the poor saints, and when he was hoping for the first time to visit Rome on his way to Spain, i.e. about A.D. 56 or 57 (Acts xix. 21, xx. 2, 3; Rom. xv. 23-28). Since Paul commends Phœbe to his readers (xvi. 1, 2), it would appear that she was about to go to Rome. She has commonly been regarded, from early times, as the bearer of the Epistle. See xvi. 27, A.V. footnote.

The church in Rome

Rome was the centre of the civilized world, the great metropolis of a vast empire. Paul was a Roman citizen, and was able to speak of 'the powers that be' as ministers of God for good (xiii. 1-6). There were already many Christians in Rome. There is no clear evidence how the gospel was first brought there, and the tradition that Peter founded the church there is unworthy of credence. Paul would not have written as he does to a church founded by Peter (xv. 20-24). It is probable that individuals, who had become Christians in Palestine, Syria, Asia Minor, Macedonia or Greece, travelled to Rome and thus introduced Christianity there. Aquila and Priscilla were probably Christians before they were forced to leave Rome in A.D. 51 (Acts xviii. 1, 2). Before this Epistle was written they had returned to Rome, and were active in Christian service there (xvi. 3-5). It is evident that the church in Rome contained both Jews and Gentiles and was a mixed community both socially and racially. Paul bases his right to address them on his apostleship to the Gentiles (xv. 15, 16; cf. i. 5, 6, xi. 13); and on the other hand, knowledge of the Old Testament and of Jewish ideas is generally assumed, and some of the problems dealt with are such as imply the immediate presence of Jews.

Occasion and purpose of writing

1. The immediate reason why Paul wrote this letter was because he hoped before long to visit Rome. His plan was to use Rome as a base for fresh evangelism in Spain. So he wrote to acquaint the Roman Christians with his desires (xv. 23, 24).

2. He was probably not stirred to write by reports about conditions in Rome itself, though Paul's knowledge of the Christians there, gained perhaps from Aquila and Priscilla, may have determined his selections of some points for special mention (e.g. in xiv. 1-xv. 13).

3. He had for long wished to visit Rome and see the Christians there. Now, though he hoped to do so soon, there was real uncertainty what might happen to him on his coming visit to Jerusalem (xv. 25, 30-32), and so, lest he should never see them in person, he may have been the more eager to use this opportunity to minister to them in writing.

4. Also, the fact that he was writing to Christians in the chief city of the Roman empire, and that he realized that his remaining days might be numbered, may well have been used to stir Paul to seek to set forth a comprehensive statement of the truths of the gospel. This statement finds a parallel and supplement in the Epistle to the Ephesians.

ANALYSIS

i. 1-15. Introduction. Personal reference.
i. 16, 17. Main theme. The gospel. What it is and does.

i. 18-v.   Justification for sinners. God's way of righteousness. Man's universal need. All have sinned. God's free gift, through Christ's atoning death, on condition of faith. The consequences: peace with God, present grace, future glory.

vi.-viii.   Consequent full salvation for believers in Christ. The call to live unto God. The power to overcome the flesh—the Spirit of Christ. The assurrance of present victory and final redemption.

ix.-xi.   Vindication of the divine providence in relation to the problem of Israel's unbelief. God's will is sovereign. Israel has refused God's way. God is still working for good—to have mercy upon all.

xii.-xv. 13.   Practical moral application to everyday life. The call to consecration. Christians' social obligations as members of a church and as citizens. Guidance on matters in which judgment differs. The one supreme governing principle—love.

xv. 14-xvi.   Personal conclusion. Paul's work and plans. Warning against false teachers. Greetings and benedictions.

CONTENTS

The central part of this letter (i. 16-xv. 13) may almost be described as a treatise contained within a letter. The main subject throughout is the gospel of Jesus Christ. (See i. 1-3, 16, xvi. 25.) In the introductory summary (i. 16, 17) the gospel is declared to concern Christ, to be 'of God', i.e. divine in origin, to be a mighty divine activity working to save, bringing inestimable benefit to all, Jew and Gentile alike, on the sole condition of individual faith.

Detailed exposition of this gospel follows. Paul first shows the need for such a saving work of God (i. 18-iii. 20). For all men are exposed to judgment. The divine wrath is revealed against all unrighteousness, and there is none righteous, no, not one. Some reject the witness of creation to the Creator, worship idols, and become morally corrupt both in thought and deed. Others stand condemned by the witness of their own conscience. In judging others they acknowledge a moral standard by which they themselves stand condemned. The Jew, though he has had the advantage of special God-given privileges, is not on that account guiltless. Rather by his knowledge his responsibility is increased; and he is the more clearly guilty.

Next (iii. 21-v.) Paul sets forth the new way of justification as a free gift of God, through the expiatory death of Jesus Christ, to all who believe. It is essentially new, for none could be justified by the works of the law. But its principle had already been foreshadowed in the types and promises of the Old Testament revelation, and as is shown in the case of Abraham, faith on man's part is the one indispensable condition of enjoying the divine blessing. Those who believe are at once reconciled to God: they experience present fellowship and saving grace, and rejoice in the sure hope of final deliverance and entrance into glory. What the human race lost in Adam is much more than restored in Christ. The reign of sin is superseded by the reign of grace.

In the following six chapters (vi.-xi.) Paul proceeds to set forth the glorious fulness of the gospel by answering two main questions. Is this gospel great enough (1) to provide a full salvation in the face of evils, both in the flesh within and in the world without, and (2) to embrace and explain the puzzling problems of experience and history—as forcibly represented by the Jewish rejection of the Christ?

(1) In chapters vi.-viii. Paul shows that the full gospel is sufficient not only to give man a standing in grace but also to change his conduct, making him a doer of righteousness and assuring him of victory in the face of opposing circumstances. The Spirit of Christ, whom Christ gives to all who are His, sets the believer free, establishes him in assurance and hope, and enables him to live as a child of God. In this confidence that God is working for them, Christians know that, come what may, all is well; for the day of full physical redemption is coming; and meanwhile nothing can separate them from the love of God. (2) In chapters ix.-xi. Paul vindicates the divine providence. Because God is God He can and does act as He will. Nevertheless His doings are not arbitrary or merciless. Israel has obstinately refused to enter into God's way of righteousness by faith in Christ, so their exclusion is their own fault. Yet Israel's unbelief and rejection have been used of God to serve a beneficial end—the bringing in of the Gentiles. Further, Israel's fall does not exclude them from the hope of restoration through the same gospel of mercy to the disobedient, for God does not go back on His promises. The simple sufficiency of the gospel is shown in its central principle of free forgiveness of sin. Jew and Gentile alike are now all shown to be

sinners—only that God may have mercy upon all alike. So the providence of God is all embracing. To Him be glory for ever.

In the next section (xii.-xv. 13) Paul turns to moral exhortation. He indicates the practical application of the gospel to the every-day life of the believer. Experience of the mercies of God demands the response of full consecration. Christians ought to offer their bodies in living sacrifice to do God's will as it is now revealed to their renewed understanding. There are two main directions in which the Christian is called to function socially: (1) as a member of the church, the body of Christ, (2) as a citizen or member of the state. In the one he should fulfil his service in humility and love. In the other he should, under the guidance and constraint of his own conscience, submit to the powers that be as ordained of God, and support every effort to promote justice in the com-munity. Love should be for him the one supreme governing principle of all his action; and he should find in the prospect of the approaching day of salvation an additional motive for living a disciplined life. Paul then makes special reference to practical matters of immediate concern to the Roman Christians—pointing out to the two parties who differed on points of Christian practice how to order their conduct and relationships according to the law of love, following the example of Christ.

In conclusion (xv. 14-xvi.) Paul returns to the style of a letter. He refers to his plans, and indicates in particular his hope of visiting Rome, and asks for the prayers of the Roman Christians. Various personal greetings and benedictions follow; also a warn-ing against false teachers.

THEMES FOR STUDY

1. Make a careful summary of the contents of the gospel as expounded by Paul in chapters i.-viii.

2. Study the character of, and the steps in, the life of faith.

3. Collect all the references to the Holy Spirit, and set out in order what can be learnt about His Person and work from these statements.

4. Study chapters ix.-xi. in the light of the subsequent history of the Jews and of missionary effort.

5. What ruling principles should govern a Christian's practical conduct and social relationships?

I CORINTHIANS

AUTHORSHIP, DATE AND CIRCUMSTANCES

Of the Pauline authorship of this Epistle no serious question has ever been raised. The beauty and strength of the apostle's character breathe through the letter, and it is impossible to imagine that any other hand than his could have written words of such far-sighted wisdom. External evidence of the authenticity of the book is found before the close of the first century in Clement of Rome's Epistle to the Corinthians, where it is quoted by name; and it was employed almost certainly by Ignatius (c. 110) and Polycarp (c. 115) as well as possibly by Hermas (c. 120). The details of the Epistle coincide in minute particulars with the record of the Acts, with what is known otherwise of the conditions in the church and city of Corinth, and with the presuppositions of Paul's doctrine and experience as expressed in Galatians and Romans.

(a) The state of society in Corinth

By reason of its geographical position, linking the western Mediterranean with the Ægean sea, Corinth had in the first century A.D. assumed an important mercantile position in the Roman Empire. It was the metropolis of the province of Achaia, holding the keys of commerce, and swarming with a cosmopolitan population. The Isthmian games were famous throughout the empire, the poets sang of the wealth of Corinth, and her buildings were among the finest of the ancient world. But along with this cultural and material prosperity Corinth was infamous for vice and corruption. To 'Corinthianize' was to lead an immoral life.

(b) St. Paul and Corinth

As was his custom, the apostle sought to spread the gospel in a centre in which he could touch men from various lands, and Corinth, with its large and mixed Jewish colony, presented him with a great challenge and opportunity. Here he arrived from Athens in the course of his second missionary journey (Acts xv. 36-41, xviii. 1), about the year A.D. 51. Having joined forces with Aquila and Priscilla, two Jews recently expelled from Rome by Claudius (Acts xviii. 2-3; cf. 1 Cor. xvi. 19), he began to preach in the synagogue, but later, because of continued opposition, turned to the Gentiles (Acts xviii. 5-11). In the course of more than eighteen months, with the help of Silas and Timothy (Acts

xviii. 5, 11; cf. 2 Cor. i. 19), and by clear and simple declaration of the gospel (1 Cor. i. 14-17, 21-24, ii. 1-5), the infant church was established, chiefly, but not exclusively, among the lower classes (1 Cor. i. 26-28; Acts xviii. 8). Later on, opposition from the Jews became stronger (Acts xviii. 12-17), and Paul eventually departed with Priscilla and Aquila, whom he left in Ephesus on his way back to Antioch (Acts xviii. 18-22). About this time Paul may have written an earlier letter to the Corinthians, now lost, in which he warned them of the seriousness of immorality in the church (see 1 Cor. v. 9, R.V., and 10, R.V. margin, though some interpret these words as referring to this Epistle). Shortly after Paul's departure from Antioch on his third missionary journey (Acts xviii. 23) an Alexandrian Jew named Apollos came to Ephesus, and having received further instruction from Priscilla and Aquila went over to Corinth to help the church there (Acts xviii. 24-28; cf. 1 Cor. iii. 6). Meanwhile Paul arrived back in Ephesus for a stay of two years (Acts xix. 1, 10). Here he received a letter from Corinth asking for advice on certain problems (1 Cor. vii. 1) possibly brought by Apollos (1 Cor. xvi. 12), and news of dissensions and evils in the Corinthian church brought by Chloe's family (1 Cor. i. 11, v. 1, xi. 18). Although he had already sent Timothy to Corinth via Macedonia (Acts xix. 22; 1 Cor. iv. 17, xvi. 10), he felt it necessary to write at once, possibly sending this letter by Titus (2 Cor. ii. 13, vii. 6, viii. 6). That the letter was written from Ephesus is indicated by references to Aquila and Priscilla (xvi. 19), who were at Ephesus at the time (Acts xviii. 19), and to his opportunities in that city (xv. 32, xvi. 8, 9). The date of this stay in Ephesus is probably A.D. 53-56.

ANALYSIS

i. 1-9.   Greeting and thanksgiving.

i. 10-iv. Deprecation of divisions in the church, due to their failure to understand what is true wisdom and the relation of Christian leaders to each other and to the church (cf. xi. 17-19, xii. 14-31, xvi. 14).

v.-vi.   Demand for effective judgment, in the fellowship of the church, on a member guilty of gross immorality.

vii.   Replies to their questions about marriage.

viii.-xi. 1. Christian liberty and self-restraint in eating meat offered to idols. Paul's own example—no compromise with idolatry (cf. iv. 1-5).

xi. 2-34.   Order in Christian assemblies (cf. xiv. 27-36).

xii.-xiv.   The place of spiritual gifts, and the supreme value of love.

xv.   The resurrection of the dead.

xvi.   Instructions for a collection for Jerusalem, future plans (cf. iv. 18-21, xi. 34), and farewell messages.

CONTENTS

In a great cosmopolitan city such as Corinth differences of background and temperament were bound to endanger the spiritual unity of the church (cf. Acts xviii. 12). The church was divided into several factions (i. 11, 12), of which the most disturbing party claimed (with little justification, cf. xvi. 12) the leadership of the learned Apollos (i. 12, iii. 4-6, iv. 6; cf. Acts xviii. 24-28). This group, in a manner similar to the later Gnostic heretics, claimed a deeper knowledge of the truth (i. 19-ii. 5, iii. 18-23, iv. 6-10, 18, 19, v. 2, viii. 1-3, 10, 11, xii. 8, xiv. 2, 20, 37), making this supposed intellectual superiority an excuse for physical licence (iii. 1, 16-17, v. 1-13, vi.) and opposition to apostolic authority (iv. 1-5, 18, 19, ix. 3, xi. 16, xiv. 37, xv. 12, xvi. 22). It is important to note the grounds on which St. Paul asserts his own authority as the founder of the church in Corinth (ii. 16, iii. 10, iv. 14-21, v. 3-5, xi. 1, 2, 16, 34, xiv. 18, 37, xv. 1-3). Further insight into the circumstances and difficulties of the early church is provided by references to the celebration of the Lord's supper (xi. 17-34), and the dangers of Christian emancipation being confused with Corinthian immorality (vi. 12-20, xi. 2-16). But, besides such interesting historical details, St. Paul throughout approaches local problems with reference to fundamental spiritual principles, applicable equally to our day, and includes passages of great doctrinal importance.

THEMES FOR STUDY

1. Study the principles by which Christian liberty is to be combined with consideration of the weaknesses of other men's consciences (cf. viii.-x. with Rom. xiv.).

2. The Epistle indicates clearly the true relation between Christian workers and those among whom they live and serve (iii. 5-11, iv. 1-16, xii.-xiv.). To what extent are these principles understood and applied in the church to-day?

3. Seek out incidents from the life of Christ to illustrate the fulfilment of the Christian conception of love delineated in chapter xiii.

4. Which points of chapter xv. 1-11 are confirmed by the Gospel narratives of the resurrection, and which are additional to them? Compare this outline of 'the gospel' with chapters i.-iii. and with Paul's speeches in Acts xiii. 16-41 and xvii. 22-31. What place should the resurrection occupy in present-day evangelistic preaching?

II CORINTHIANS

AUTHORSHIP, DATE AND CIRCUMSTANCES

THE second Epistle to the Corinthians came into circulation less rapidly than the first, and was apparently unknown to Clement of Rome at the end of the first century. Shortly afterwards it was probably used by Polycarp (c. 115), accepted by Marcion (c. 140), included in the Muratorian Canon (c. 170), and quoted as Pauline by Irenæus (c. 180). The genuineness of the whole letter is amply proved by internal evidence. No imitator could, or would have wished, to invent the complex relationships between Paul and the Corinthians, or the intimate and personal expressions of love and fear which it contains. Some have suggested that the passage vi. 14-vii. 1, which introduces an entirely new subject, and interrupts the sequence of thought between vi. 13 and vii. 2, is a misplaced fragment of the epistle mentioned in 1 Cor. v. 9. But the break may be due to an interruption in Paul's thought. Absolute unanimity in the MS. evidence forbids the possibility of a later interpolation, and arguments based on differences of vocabulary may be equally applied to sections of undoubted authenticity. The suggestion that x.-xiii. represents an earlier 'severe' letter equally lacks all MS. evidence. There is no reason why the effect described in ii. 3, 4 and vii. 8-12 should not have been caused by parts of 1 Corinthians (especially iii.-vi.), and 2 Cor. x.-xiii. contains no mention of the demand for punishment of the offender (cf. 2 Cor. ii. 5-11).

After writing 1 Corinthians Paul remained in Ephesus for a while until the uproar over the goddess Diana made his departure imperative (Acts xix. 22-41, xx. 1). It is uncertain whether he made a second visit to Corinth before writing the second Epistle, as is suggested by xii. 14 and xiii. 1, 2, and during which he may have been personally insulted (ii. 5-11, vii. 12, xi. 20). His explanation of why he refrained from making an earlier visit in i. 17-ii. 4 may indicate that xii. 14 and xiii. 1, 2 refer only to an unfulfilled intention (see R.V. margin). On reaching Troas (ii. 12, 13) he was so much troubled by the possible effects of his previous letter, that he went on to Macedonia, where he met Titus with good news of the results of his earlier correspondence (vii. 5-16). After visiting several Macedonian churches (viii. 1, ix. 2) he appears to have been rejoined by Timothy (i. 1) at Philippi, where this Epistle was probably written. Shortly afterwards he proceeded to Corinth (Acts xx. 2, 3; cf. 2 Cor. ix. 4, x. 2, 11, xii. 14, 20, 21, xiii. 1, 2), at which time the letter to the Romans was written (cf. Rom. xvi. 1, 2, 21, 23).

ANALYSIS

i. 1-11.   Greeting and thanksgiving.

i. 12-ii. 11.   Explanation of the delay in his visit, and forgiveness of the offender.

ii. 12-iv. 6.   Declaration of his integrity as a minister of the new covenant.

iv. 7-vi. 10.   The weakness and impermanence of the body: Paul's compensation for his sufferings.

vi. 11-vii. 16.   His relief at their response to his letter, and plea for their separation from evil (cf. 1 Cor. x. 14-22).

viii.-ix.   Appeal for their support of the Jerusalem collection, after the example of Macedonia.

x.-xii. 13.   His authority based not on physical ability, but on his affection for them and his sufferings in Christ's name.

xii. 14-xiii.   Final declaration of affection, warning against apostasy, and farewell.

CONTENTS

This Epistle, perhaps more than any other, affords us an insight into the heart of its author. We feel with him the tremendous relief experienced at the favourable response of the Corinthians to his earlier letter of rebuke (ii. 3-14, vii. 4-16; cf. 1 Cor. v. 1-8), and we glimpse the depths of his love for the church (i. 6, 15-ii. 4, 10, iv. 5, 15, v. 13, vi. 11-13, vii. 2-4, xi. 1, 2, 7-11, xii. 11-20, xiii. 9, 10) together with his restored confidence in them (i. 7, 14,

15, ii. 3, iii. 2-4, vii. 4, 16, viii. 24, ix. 2-4). Nevertheless, the dangers of division and apostasy at Corinth were not past (xi. 3, xii. 20, 21, xiii. 5-7, 11). Some members were opposed to the apostle's authority, accusing him of fickleness (i. 17-20) and of misusing the funds intended for Jerusalem (viii. 20, 21, xi. 8-12, xii. 13-18; cf. 1 Cor. ix. 1-17). They even made capital out of his physical disabilities (x. 1-3, 10, xi. 6, 29, 30, xii. 5-10, xiii. 3, 4). These men possessed testimonials of some sort (iii. 1, v. 12, x. 12, 17, 18), laid stress on some outward observance (v. 12, x. 7, xi. 18), perverted the gospel (ii. 17, xi. 4), and sought to bring the church 'into bondage'. The similarity of these characteristics to those associated with the Judaizers of Galatia (Gal. i. 6-9, iv. 1-v. 1, vi. 13) suggests that the party in Corinth claiming to be 'of Christ' may have been a group which accepted Jesus only as a Jewish Messiah (1 Cor. i. 12, 13; cf. 2 Cor. iii. 1-18, x. 7, xi. 13-15, 22, 23). Against this faction Paul reasserts the grounds of his authority as an apostle, combining expressions of affection with strong protestations of his spiritual leadership (i. 12-14, 24, iii. 1-3, 6, 12, iv. 1-6, v. 11-13, 20-vi. 10, vii. 2-4, viii. 8-10, 23, x. 8-18, xi. 5, 16-xii. 13, xiii. 10). In this he appears to have been successful, for Clement of Rome could speak forty years later of the soundness of the Corinthian church in knowledge, in freedom from factions, and in the blameless lives of their women.

THEMES FOR STUDY

1. Study all the references to the death of Christ, and from them deduce Paul's teaching on the atonement. See especially v. 14-21.

2. From the references to Paul's own physical weakness and sufferings frame a Christian philosophy of suffering and its place in God's purpose (cf. i. 3-11, iii. 4, 5, iv. 5-v. 10, vi. 4-10, vii. 5, 6, xi. 16-xii. 10, xiii. 3-10).

3. What lessons about Christian stewardship are contained in viii. and ix. (cf. 1 Cor. xvi.)?

4. What should be the attitude of the believer towards fellow Christians who have gone astray either in doctrine or in practice?

GALATIANS

AUTHORSHIP, DATE AND CIRCUMSTANCES

No scholar has seriously disputed that Paul was the author of this Epistle. Nor has it been divided up into fragments and segments, as has been the fate of so many books of the Bible. This unanimity with regard to the authorship and unity of the Epistle is not due to external testimony; for it was very little quoted by the early fathers. But it is due to the character of the letter itself, which is so impregnated with intense personal feeling that it could not have been the work of a forger or an editor. Also the question with which it deals belongs to a very early stage in the history of the church.

The Epistle is addressed to the churches of Galatia, and the readers are described as Galatians. In the first century A.D. the word 'Galatia' had two meanings. Galatia in the ethnological sense was the district in central Asia Minor (round about modern Ankara) which had been occupied in the third century B.C. by Gallic tribes, invaders from central Europe. In 25 B.C. the Romans incorporated this kingdom of Galatia into their empire, and formed the province of Galatia, which included, besides the Galatian kingdom, large areas to the south which had never been settled by the Gallic tribes, though some parts had been subject to their suzerainty. Of these new districts the chief towns were Pisidian Antioch, Iconium, and Lystra. The question, therefore, that needs to be settled is whether Paul wrote to the churches of Galatia proper or to the churches in the south.

We know from Acts that Paul visited south Galatia on his first missionary journey A.D. 47 (Acts xiii.). From Luke's preference for ethnological terms, and from the grammar, it is probable that Acts xvi. 6 records a visit of the apostle to north Galatia; and it was formerly thought that Paul wrote his letter to the churches of this district when on his third missionary journey, about the same time as he wrote the Epistle to the Romans, which would be *after* the council of Acts xv. Against this date, however, is the fact that at this council the matter troubling the Galatian church, namely, circumcision, was decided; yet in this letter, Paul makes no reference to the council nor to its decrees, which so strongly supported his position, and which he himself had delivered to those to whom he was now writing (Acts xvi. 4), and which were intended to settle the matter once and for all. The inference is that the letter was written *before* the decrees were promulgated. If this is so, the letter must have been sent to south Galatia, as Acts records no visit to the north till after the council, and the recipients would be those churches Paul had founded on his first missionary journey. On this view, which is probably correct, Galatians is Paul's earliest Epistle (see pp. 348, 353).

The occasion which drew forth from the apostle this vigorous letter was an attack made by some Jewish-minded Christians on the gospel which Paul had delivered to the Galatian churches. These false teachers taught that the gospel as preached by Paul was only the first step in the Christian life, and that his converts needed to enter into a fuller blessing through obedience to the law of Moses (iii. 3). The arguments of the false teachers had a certain amount of speciousness. They could point to the church at Jerusalem where the Christians were zealous in observing the Mosaic law (Acts xxi. 20). They accused Paul of inconsistency, as he kept the law without requiring his converts to do so. Their line of attack was to undermine Paul's authority by saying that he taught a different gospel from the Twelve, and that he had no right to do this, as his authority was derived from them. Such assertions obviously succeeded in misleading the majority of Paul's Galatian converts. The situation was crucial. For what had happened in Galatia could happen in any church founded by the apostle. He, therefore, sent off this letter post haste.

ANALYSIS

i.-ii. Paul vindicates his apostleship by an appeal to his personal history and experience.

iii.-v. 1. Paul proves the truth of his gospel by showing the superiority of faith to law.

v. 2-vi. 10. An exposition of the gospel and its practical application.

vi. 11-18. Autobiographical conclusion.

CONTENTS

Paul claims that his commission to preach the gospel came direct from the Lord and was not mediated through the Twelve. He proves this by showing the paucity of his relationships with them. Further, in what contacts he had with them in Jerusalem and Antioch, his gospel had been approved. He and they were agreed as to the gospel, which was that righteousness comes through Christ, not through the law. This is confirmed by the gift of the Spirit (a very real phenomenon), which was the result of the gospel, not the law. Also, God's dealings with Abraham show that the gospel of divine promise, given to faith, is antecedent and superior to the law. Paul continues to press home his case, by exposition, by personal appeal, and by a detailed argument (iv.

21-v. 1) couched in the Jewish legalistic style, directed against those who 'desire to be under the law'. This argument is conclusive. 'What saith the Scripture? Cast out the bond woman and her son.' Thus those who favour the law are confuted. The gospel is faith working through love. The whole law is fulfilled in one word, Thou shalt love thy neighbour as thyself. So then as we have opportunity let us do good unto all men, especially unto those who are of the household of faith.

'How can a man be just with God?' This age-old problem was the problem of Paul and his contemporaries. The apostle acknowledged that if a man could keep the law of God perfectly, he would be righteous in the sight of God (iii. 12, 21). But he knew from his own experience and from Scripture that it was impossible for humans to do this (ii. 16). One slip meant that a man's righteousness was fatally marred (cf. Jas. ii. 10). Through the gospel, however, Paul learned that by faith in Jesus Christ a man might be found righteous before God (ii. 16; Acts xiii. 39), not by his own works of righteousness but through the righteousness of Christ Jesus (Phil. iii. 9). Being united with Christ through faith, the Christian participates in the righteousness of Christ, and inherits the promise of the Spirit.

The abiding value of the Epistle is its exposition of the nature of Christianity. It shows the gulf between legalism and the religion of the Spirit. Legalistic religion, since it dispenses with regeneration, is attractive and intelligible to the natural man. But it is the subtle and persistent enemy of true Christian faith. Over against it, Paul affirms that regeneration is the fundamental of Christianity (vi. 15), and that love is the practical expression of this change of heart (v. 6). Further, this new life is entered into and enjoyed not by doing works prescribed by the law, but by putting all one's faith in the living Christ, who, as Paul puts it, 'loved me and gave Himself for me' (ii. 20). From this Epistle the Christian church continually needs to relearn what Martin Luther so decisively discovered, namely, that 'the just shall live by faith' (iii. 11).

THEMES FOR STUDY

1. What does Paul here declare about himself and his past history? And why does he give such details?

2. What is the gospel which Paul preached? Collect and summarize carefully the evidence of this Epistle.

3. What arguments does Paul here use to prove that blessing is to be obtained solely by faith in Christ and not by works of law?

4. What can we learn from this epistle about
   (i) the way in which the Holy Spirit is received?
   (ii) the results of this gift of God?

EPHESIANS

AUTHORSHIP, DATE AND CIRCUMSTANCES

THAT Paul wrote this letter is well attested by external evidence. It is probably the Epistle most frequently quoted by the early writers of the church. It is mentioned in Marcion's list, in the Muratorian Fragment, and by Irenæus.

In recent times some scholars have questioned the Pauline authorship, using arguments from internal evidence, but these are subjective and inconclusive, and by no means sufficient to overthrow all that there is to be said on the other side.

Again, the similarity of style between Colossians and Ephesians has led some to conclude that one is an imitation of the other, and not written by Paul; but they are not agreed as to which is original. The truth appears to be that both are genuine, being composed at the same time and sent by Tychicus (vi. 21, 22; Col. iv. 7-9).

The absence of personal greetings to a church where Paul had spent over two years, and the fact that some ancient manuscripts omit the words 'in Ephesus' in i. 1, have led to the supposition that this Epistle was intended for other churches in the province of Asia, as well as the church in Ephesus, and that in some copies a space was left for other names to be substituted. Lightfoot suggested that the letter referred to in Col. iv. 16 as 'the epistle from Laodicea', which the Colossians were also to read, may have been such a copy of this Epistle.

Ephesus was connected with the sea by an inland waterway, and was famous for its temple of Diana (Acts xix. 27) and its theatre (1 Cor. xv. 32). It was the capital of the province of Asia, and the centre of the Roman administration. It was a populous, prosperous, and impressive city. Paul had founded the church there.

The Epistle's place of origin is most probably Rome, and the date, during Paul's imprisonment there, about A.D. 61 or 62, when Epaphras had arrived with news of the Colossian church. In support of this Paul speaks of himself as 'a prisoner' (iii. 1, iv. 1); and as the Acts of the Apostles ends with Paul a prisoner at Rome, it seems to be the obvious place of imprisonment. He was able to hire his own dwelling there, and had a reasonable amount of liberty to teach and preach (Acts xxviii. 30; Eph. vi. 19, 20 and Col. iv. 3, 4); the most suitable place for Cæsar's household would be Rome (Phil. iv. 22). A runaway slave, especially if he had robbed his master (Phm. 18), would be more likely to hide in Rome—the London of that day—than elsewhere. Expectation soon to be released (Phil. ii. 23, 24; Phm. 22) could not have been entertained in Cæsarea, since he had appealed to go to Rome, and would not be free for a long time. Style and subject matter show a development in Paul's thought, which indicates a lapse of considerable time after the writing of his earlier Epistles. The phrase 'I am an ambassador' (vi. 20) may convey a suggestion of presence in the imperial city.

ANALYSIS

i. 1, 2. Greeting.

i. 3-14. An expanded doxology. God's purpose in Christ.

i. 15-iii. 21. An expanded prayer—with much parenthesis.

    i. 15-ii. 10. God's power manifested in raising Christ, and in raising us in Him.

    ii. 11-22. The position of the Gentiles, formerly aliens, now through Christ made one with Jews as fellow citizens in God's house.

    iii. 1-13. The mystery of the gospel, and Paul's part in its proclamation.

    iii. 14-21. The concluding prayer and doxology.

iv. 1-vi. 20. Exhortation based on the previous teaching.

    iv. 1-16. The unity in diversity of the church as Christ's body.

    iv. 17-24. Contrast between the old life and the new.

    iv. 25-v. 5. The way to live the new life.

    v. 6-21. Contrast between darkness and light.

    v. 22-vi. 9. Consequent Christian duties—in the family and household.

    vi. 10-20. The call to put on the armour of God and to live as soldiers of Christ.

vi. 21-24. Conclusion.

CONTENTS

This letter contains some of the most sublime thought, pious exhortation, affectionate admonition, depth of doctrine, and animated fervour of style to be found in the New Testament. It is full of closely interlaced doctrinal arguments on the character and greatness of Christ and His church. The first part (i.-iii.) is a sustained and expanded prayer. The second part (iv.-vi.) is an exhortation concerning the Christian's walk and manner of life.

God's eternal purpose of love is world-wide redemption through Christ, the one Head of redeemed creation. By union with Christ believers are sealed by the Holy Spirit, the pledge of future glory. In Christ the Gentiles who were afar off are made nigh. This great truth has been entrusted to Paul; he has been especially commissioned to declare this 'mystery' to the Gentiles; he has, therefore, the Gentiles especially at heart, and his prayer is for them. He has no place for self, all glory is due to God through Christ.

This great privilege of membership in Christ and fellowship with the saints must be displayed in life and act. They must remember that they are parts of the one Lord, with one faith and baptism, one God and Father of all, who rules over, acts through, and dwells in all. Each Christian has his own special gift to be used for the good of the whole body. In the earlier Epistles Paul seems to think chiefly of the various churches in the different localities, each of them largely independent of the rest. But here there emerges the thought of the one church, invisible, spiritual, an all-embracing fellowship including all believers, past, present, and to come. The church is the body of which Christ is the head; it is the bride of Christ, the object of His special love without which He is incomplete.

In the practical section Paul denounces the old Gentile vices, and indicates that the new Christlike nature must be sought. Christian virtues must be cultivated. They must walk in the light, using this short life wisely with soberness, thankfulness, and humility. They must pay regard to family concerns; the slave must serve as unto Christ, the master must remember that he also has a Master (iv. 17-vi. 9).

The enemy is spiritual and 'the whole armour of God' is absolutely necessary for the conflict. They must pray without ceasing, remembering Paul especially; Tychicus will report to them of his estate. A farewell blessing is adjoined—'to all them that love our Lord Jesus Christ in sincerity'.

THEMES FOR STUDY

1. God 'hath blessed us with all spiritual blessings in Christ' (i. 3). How does the Epistle show this to be true? Make a list of the blessings.

2. What support does this letter give for our belief in the Trinity?

3. God's eternal purpose is manifested in Christ. In what ways does the Epistle confirm this?

4. How can the Christian best seek to establish international brotherhood and peace?

5. Discover all you can about the origin, method of establishment, membership, calling, and ultimate destiny of the church.

PHILIPPIANS

AUTHORSHIP, DATE AND CIRCUMSTANCES

THE genuineness of the Epistle is not open to doubt. It is unquestionably Pauline. Its tone is transparently sincere, and its contents offer no motive for a forger. External testimony is good. Clement of Rome (A.D. 90) knew the Epistle, and Ignatius (A.D. 110) quoted it. On account of the sudden change of tone some have wondered whether the section beginning at iii. 2 might be part of another letter of Paul's. But there is no unanimity of opinion as to where such a supposed interpolation ends. It is, therefore, much more reasonable to regard the Epistle as it stands as a unity. The fresh beginning and sudden denunciation, which do appear at iii. 2, can best be accounted for by some reminiscence of Jewish opposition suddenly coming to the forefront of Paul's mind.

Philippi, in eastern Macedonia, was situated eight miles from the sea, athwart the Egnatian Way, which led from the Bosphorus to the Adriatic on the way to Rome. It had been constituted a Roman colony by Augustus to mark his victory won nearby, and many veterans from the army had settled there. Like most colonists they were very proud of their connection with the mother city. Traces of this are seen in Acts xvi. 21 and Phil. iii. 20, R.V. St. Paul's first visit to Philippi was the result of the vision he experienced at Troas. His converts included Lydia of Thyatira and a prison jailer (Acts xvi. 9-40). He made several subsequent visits (Acts xx. 1, 6; Phil. ii. 24; 1 Tim. i. 3), and always retained a tender affection for the Philippian church.

The Epistle was written from prison (i. 7). From Acts we know that Paul was imprisoned at Cæsarea and at Rome, in addition to the night he spent in the Philippian jail. Clement of Rome says Paul was imprisoned several times; and Paul himself, writing in *c.* A.D. 55, tells the Corinthians that he had been 'in prisons more frequent' (2 Cor. xi. 23), when the only previous imprisonment that Luke records was that at Philippi. So it is plain that Paul was imprisoned on more occasions than is recorded in the Acts, and recently it has been suggested that one of these was during his two to three years' stay at Ephesus. The Scripture references are 1 Cor. xv. 30-32; 2 Cor. i. 8, 9, vi. 9; Acts xx. 19; and they are corroborated by certain external evidence.

Where, then, was the Epistle written? Not from Cæsarea, for Paul was expecting speedy release (ii. 24), but at Cæsarea he knew he had to journey to Rome. The frequent comings and goings between Paul and the Philippians referred to in the Epistle (ii. 19, 25, iv. 14-18) are thought to favour Ephesus as the place of origin as being less distant from Philippi than Rome. On the other hand, travelling was both safe and easy and communication simple and certain in the Roman world in the days of the empire. It is therefore quite possible, and, on the whole, more natural and reasonable to hold to the traditional view that Rome was the place where Paul wrote this Epistle, especially as the references to 'the whole Prætorium' (i. 13, R.V.) and to Cæsar's 'household' (iv. 22) are more likely to imply Rome than anywhere else.

ANALYSIS

i. 1, 2.	Greeting.
i. 3-11.	Thanksgiving and prayer for the Philippians.
i. 12-26.	Account of how things are with Paul.
i. 27-ii. 16.	Practical exhortations to live worthily as Christians, and to realize unity through humility—following the example of Christ.
ii. 17-30.	Expected movements of Paul and his friends, Timothy and Epaphroditus.
iii. 1.	Call to rejoice in the Lord.
iii. 2-iv. 1.	Warnings against enemies of spiritual progress, which develop into a declaration of Paul's aim in life. Call to stand fast in the Lord.
iv. 2-9.	Further exhortations—to unity, joy, prayer, etc.
iv. 10-20.	Thankful reference to the Philippians' gifts.
iv. 21-23.	Farewell.

CONTENTS

Paul had decided to send Epaphroditus back to Philippi (ii. 25-30), and he wrote this letter for him to take to the Philippians (1) to thank them for their gift (iv. 10-19); (2) to give them news about himself (i. 12-26, ii. 17-24); (3) to encourage them to find in Christ continual joy and peace of mind (ii. 14, 18, 28, iii. 1, iv. 4-7); (4) to exhort them to unity—by putting aside party spirit and vainglory, and putting on humility and the spirit of self-forgetful service (i. 27-30, ii. 1-5, iv. 2, 3); (5) to warn them against various spiritual enemies—the self-righteous, the self-satisfied, and the self-indulgent (iii. 2-21).

This is much the most affectionate and joyful of Paul's letters. It gives a vivid picture of the unfailing trust and characteristic cheerfulness of the great apostle. It emphasizes the joy, peace, and hope which the Christian is meant to have in all circumstances. Its outstanding message is the need for unity among Christians, a unity to be achieved through humility and love, and the following of the example of Jesus Christ.

Here Paul is seen as the man he was. There is no trace of jealousy when he contemplates the success of other Christian preachers; no fear as he faces death, but only a joyful anticipation; no regret as he reviews his life and recalls the advantages, dear to humans, which he has given up in order to win Christ. In Paul's thanks for the Philippians' generosity we glimpse the tender feelings which existed between him and his Philippian friends. We notice also the delicate balance between his acknowledgment of their gifts and his affirmation of his reliance on Christ for all things.

The Epistle contains two important doctrinal passages, both introduced somewhat incidentally in illustration of more practical themes. In ii. 5-11, as part of an exhortation to humility, Paul speaks of Christ's pre-existence and full Deity, the humiliation of His incarnation and death, and His consequent exaltation and Lordship. In iii. 7-14, in describing the satisfaction which he has found and still seeks in Christ, Paul declares very plainly that the principle of salvation is not by the self-righteousness of works of one's own doing, but by the gift of God, a gift given to all who by faith are found 'in Christ'.

THEMES FOR STUDY

1. Collect the teaching of the Epistle on (i) prayer, (ii) contentment and joy, (iii) unity.

N

2. What ought to be a Christian's ambition for himself? Make a list of (i) things to be coveted, (ii) things to be avoided, in one's life as a member of a company of Christians.

3. Note in detail how the believer's relationship to the Lord should make a difference to (i) his own condition, (ii) his attitude to circumstances, (iii) his relationship to people.

4. What Christian virtues were exemplified by the conduct of (i) Timothy and (ii) Epaphroditus?

COLOSSIANS

AUTHORSHIP, DATE AND CIRCUMSTANCES

MODERN scholarship tends more and more to confirm the traditional opinion that Paul was the author. This is attested by early Christian writers, including Irenæus, Clement of Alexandria, and Tertullian. The parallelism between the letters to the Colossians and to the Ephesians is easily explained if, as seems certain, Paul was writing both Epistles at the same time.

The unquestionable genuineness of the Epistle to Philemon should be regarded as a guarantee for the authenticity of the letter to the Colossians, particularly as Onesimus is commended in both letters (Col. iv. 9; Phm. 16)—a detail which has no bearing upon the particular problem at Colossæ, and which would be out of place in this letter, unless it were written by Paul at the time when Onesimus was returning to Colossæ.

The vocabulary and style of this letter would naturally be somewhat different from those of Paul's other letters, since he was dealing with some entirely new problems; and his use of particular words in this Epistle, not used elsewhere by him, may mean that he is using the very words used by Epaphras to describe the Colossian troubles.

Colossæ, Laodicea, and Hierapolis were situated on the River Lycus in Phrygia about one hundred miles on the road inland from Ephesus. The people were chiefly Phrygian natives, generally superstitious and fanatical; there was a proportion of Greek traders, like all Greeks keen on speculation (cf. Acts xvii. 21); and a considerable Jewish element which wielded a strong influence upon the inhabitants. Paul had never visited these cities (ii. 1), but they had apparently received the gospel through Epaphras (iv.

12, 13), himself a Colossian; he now joined Paul in Rome and gave a report both of the progress and the dangers of the Christian churches in the Lycus valley.

The conclusion that Ephesians, Colossians, and Philemon were despatched from Rome by Paul by the same messenger at the same time fixes the date at about A.D. 62. Epaphras had reported to Paul a peculiar type of heresy arising at Colossæ, with which he had evidently not been able to cope, so he sought the advice of the apostle. Paul decided to write to the Colossians himself. Because Epaphras himself had been detained in Rome a prisoner, Paul's letter had to be sent to the Colossians by the hand of Tychicus, who was accompanied by Onesimus, a converted runaway slave who was returning to Colossæ to his master Philemon (Col. iv. 7-9; Phm. 23).

ANALYSIS

i. 1, 2. Greeting.

i. 3-14. Thanksgiving and prayer for the Colossians.

i. 15-ii. 3. The true wisdom—wholly in Christ. His Person; their experience; the apostle's ministry.

ii. 4-iii. 4. Warnings against a false wisdom.

iii. 5-iv. 6. Practical exhortations.

iv. 7-18. Personal references, greetings, etc.

CONTENTS

Paul, on behalf of himself and Timothy, greets the church of Colossæ. He rejoices at the report of their steadfastness in faith, hope, and love. Praise of Epaphras is given; he has proved himself a worthy substitute in their place. The joy at the news brought has impelled Paul to pray that they might have clearer knowledge and spiritual discernment (i. 1-12).

In order to counter the false teaching, Paul expounds positively the truth about Christ. Christ is the visible representation of the invisible God; He created all things; He is the Head of the church. God has chosen to reconcile all things to Himself through Christ (i. 13-20).

This reconciliation the Colossians themselves have experienced; it is a sure foundation, they must hold fast to it. Even the minister of Christ must find his joy amid suffering, in being steadfast to the message and experience of 'Christ in you, the hope of glory' (i. 20-29).

Deep concern is then expressed for the churches in the Lycus valley (ii. 1). Plausible teachers may attempt to mislead them; they must remember that they have received Christ and act in vital union with Him. Christ is the fulness of God; in Him they are complete; baptism was their circumcision. The cross of Christ is where He triumphed over all evil; they have been given life in Him. No room is left for Jewish observances or angelic mediation; obedience to outward rules leaves sin and self unconquered; they must rise above these things. Christ is all and in all; in Him there are no divisions, no sects, no cliques (ii. and iii. 1-11).

The Epistle passes on from the rebuke of the heretical teaching to describe the life of the true Christian. A new life, in union with Christ, involves the putting away of every kind of sin and the putting on of holiness; all Christlike qualities are to be appropriated. Everything must be done to God's glory in Christ's name (iii. 12-17).

Practical advice is given to the husband, wife, and child; to masters and slaves. He desires their prayers that again he may have full liberty to preach the gospel. They are requested to allow the Laodiceans to read the Epistle; in turn they must read 'the Epistle from Laodicea' (iii. 18-iv. 18). Either this Epistle is now lost or is our present Ephesians.[1]

The Colossian heresy

The precise dangers against which Paul warns the Colossians, and the doctrine of the false teachers, can be gathered from the Epistle itself. There was insistence upon Jewish observances being kept rigidly (ii. 16-20); with this there was mingled a 'philosophy'— a common catchword of the day (ii. 8)—and a worshipping of angels (ii. 18). There was also an ascetic neglect of the body (ii. 23). All this was taught as a 'mystery' to the initiated ones, and under the seal of secrecy (ii. 20). All these tenets are common to the heresy known as Gnosticism, which became active at the end of the first century, and there is no doubt that similar ideas were abroad well before that date. It combined elements of the popular religion of Asia Minor, including the cult of Cybele and magical rites, with certain notions about the creation and the universe current in Jewish circles, and with ideas drawn from Greek philosophy.

Such teaching Paul countered by asserting that (1) the gospel is the true wisdom (ii. 2-4); (2) Christ is the only and all-sufficient Mediator (i. 15-20); (3) ascetic practices are wrong and useless

[1] See under *Ephesians*, p. 368ff..

(ii. 20-23); (4) the right remedy is a new life 'in Christ' (iii. 1-5); (5) this gospel is unto all, and is not a secret reserved for a select few (i. 26-28, iii. 11).

The Christology

The abiding value of this Epistle is to be found in its teaching about the person and the work of Christ. This teaching is shown to provide a complete answer to the questions raised by the Colossian heresy. Christ is the one absolute Mediator between God and the whole creation. On the one side, Godward, He is 'very God', the image of the invisible God, possessing the fulness of the Godhead (i. 15, 19, ii. 9). On the other side, manward, in relation to the natural creation, He is the Lord of the universe. All things are of Him, and through Him, and to Him. 'In Him' they have come into being; 'in Him' they continue to hold together; 'in Him' they will find their consummation (i. 15-17). Further, in relation to the spiritual creation, He is the Head of the church. Through the blood of His cross all things are reconciled to God. In Him the church is rooted, built up, and made complete. Every member of the body is in direct and living communication with Him as the Head. He joins all the members to God and to one another (i. 18-22, ii. 13-15, 19). So in all things He has the pre-eminence (i. 18).

THEMES FOR STUDY

1. What was the nature of the false teaching at Colossæ, and how did Paul combat it? Are corresponding heresies abroad to-day?

2. Which do you think matters most: a system of doctrine or a practical expression of one's faith? How are the two related?

3. Carefully collect and systematize all the evidence provided by this Epistle concerning the person and work of Christ.

4. Why does Paul regard it as a retrograde step for a Christian to be occupied with ceremonial observances?

I THESSALONIANS

AUTHORSHIP, DATE AND CIRCUMSTANCES

THE external evidence in support of Paul's authorship is very strong. The Epistle was included in Marcion's list and in the Muratorian Fragment. Irenæus quoted it by name. The internal evidence is equally convincing. The personal references are inexplicable, if not genuine. Its differences of statement from those in the Acts indicate the independent authorship of the two writings, but provide no adequate ground for doubting the genuineness of this Epistle. From it, as from first-hand evidence, we may learn something of the sort of man Paul was, and of the kind of letters he wrote.

The Epistle was written in Corinth, probably in the year A.D. 51 (Acts xviii.). Paul and Silas left Philippi after their release from imprisonment and came to Thessalonica (the modern Salonika), a large commercial centre and the capital of one of the four divisions of Macedonia. For three sabbath days Paul preached in the Jewish synagogue (see Acts xvii. 2-4 for the content of his message). It may be inferred from 1 Thes. i. 9 and ii. 14 that he stayed on among the Gentiles, since there was a considerable Gentile following in the Thessalonian church. The Jews who refused to accept the preaching stirred up opposition, and Paul was obliged to leave the city. After a stay in Berœa and a visit to Athens, he settled for eighteen months in Corinth. He sent Timothy to Thessalonica to secure news of the church, and it was Timothy's report brought to him in Corinth that led to the writing of this Epistle.

The church at Thessalonica probably consisted mainly of Gentiles. The predominant atmosphere of the city was one of idolatry and immorality. The unbelieving Jews, jealous of the success of Paul, were casting doubts upon his claim to apostleship, and were pointing to his sudden departure and failure to return as a sign of his lack of care for the church. They declared that his gospel was a delusion and insinuated that he preached from motives of personal gain. Timothy must have reported a spirit of unrest in the church caused by the expectation of the imminent return of Christ, and the existence of a fear that those Christians who had died would not share in the coming glories of the *Parousia*. It appears also that there was lack of respect for the leaders of the church and that some of the Gentile converts had not broken free from immorality. In reading this Epistle one should remember that it was written by a missionary to an infant church.

ANALYSIS

    i.   Salutation. Thanksgiving for their conversion and conduct.

  ii. 1-12.   Vindication of his preaching and manner of life.

CONTENTS

The first three chapters of the Epistle are full of personal reference, the last two are more doctrinal. Paul begins by reminding his readers of his message and the nature of his ministry, and recalls their love and faith. His deep affection for the church wells up in thanksgiving and fervent prayer. Chapters iv. and v. are devoted to the answering of certain points raised by Timothy's report. Paul recalls various elements in his teaching (iv. 1, 2, v. 2), and adds further comments. He deals with the weaknesses in the life of the church, and gives a number of general exhortations. The whole is concluded with a commendation of them to God, and renewed expression of love.[1]

THEMES FOR STUDY

1. Read Acts xvii. 1-9 to see how what is there narrated adds to the understanding of the Epistle.

2. Extract from chapters i.-iii. the character of Paul, the evangelist and pastor.

3. Examine the weak points revealed in the church of the Thessalonians, and how Paul prayed for them.

4. Discover in detail how the Christian believer should exhibit in practice his faith, his love, and his hope.

5. What has this Epistle to teach us about (i) the certainty and manner of Christ's second coming, and (ii) how this hope should affect the Christian's life? Compare with 1 Cor. xv.

II THESSALONIANS

AUTHORSHIP, DATE AND CIRCUMSTANCES

THE external evidence for the authenticity of 2 Thessalonians is even stronger than that for the first Epistle. In addition to mention

[1] See also under 2 *Thessalonians* below.

by Marcion, the Muratorian Fragment, and Irenæus, it seems to
have been known to Polycarp, Ignatius, and Justin. After A.D.
200 it was universally accepted. Some modern scholars find difficulty on internal grounds. For instance, they regard the eschatological teaching as inconsistent with that of the first Epistle. But
the difference is one of emphasis; here Paul is correcting misunderstanding of what he wrote in 1 Thessalonians by indicating
other aspects which are complementary, not contradictory. The
inadequacy and artificiality of such criticism is shown by the fact
that some have advanced the similarities and others the differences
between the two Epistles as reasons for doubting the Pauline
authorship of 2 Thessalonians. Nor have any satisfactory reasons
for the composition of a spurious letter been suggested. The best
scholars are therefore convinced of the genuineness of both Epistles.

The second Epistle was written from Corinth, probably only
a month or two later than the first Epistle. The underlying situation appears to be the same.

ANALYSIS

CONTENTS

Serious misunderstanding had arisen among the Thessalonian
Christians concerning the second coming of Christ. Because they
thought that this event was imminent some had in their excitement thrown up their work, and were living in idleness, expecting
the brethren to support them. Alarm lest they had missed the
day of the Lord was also caused by the assertion of others that
Christ had already come. The life of the Christians was consequently very unsettled. They were tending to bring reproach upon
the cause of Christ. So Paul wrote to explain further the truth
about the time of Christ's coming, and to rebuke the restless and
the idle. He also used the opportunity to encourage those suffering
persecution by the expectation of righteous judgment and true
recompense when the Lord does come.

Christ's Second Coming

This subject is the outstanding theme of 1 and 2 Thessalonians. Paul's appeals and warnings continually have this great hope in mind. Clearly, therefore, it was an important part of the original gospel. In particular it provided an appropriate introduction for the gospel of salvation to Gentile minds. Also, the radical conflict between the two empires of Christ and of Cæsar, which was already becoming more manifest, was but an expression of a deeper war between God and Satan himself—a warfare which in 2 Thessalonians is recognized as coming to a head in the supreme manifestation of the power of Satan in a man of sin, a lawless one, or anti-Christ, and in his complete overthrow and judgment at the final manifestation of the power of God in the coming, or the revelation from heaven, of the Lord Jesus.

To describe this consummation Paul avails himself freely, as our Lord did in His great eschatological discourse, of figurative language already current among the Jews (cf. Mt. xxiv. 4, 24, 30, 31 with 1 Thes. iv. 16, 17 and 2 Thes. ii. 3, 9-11). Such language is partly cryptic, and could best be understood by those for whom it was written; some of the references may have had an immediate meaning for them which we cannot fully identify. We can, however, learn something of the great principles of the divine purpose. In order to obtain a balanced view of the second advent the teaching of these two chapters should be carefully compared with that in Mt. xxiv., 1 Cor. xv., and Rev. i., xix., xx. Nothing happens out of its time. Evil will be fully manifested in a deliberate rebellion or falling away (Gk. *apostasia*) from God. Finally, the sovereignty of God will be displayed in the overthrow of evil thus fully manifested, in the return of Christ, and in the gathering together with Him of His elect in glory. It is, therefore, for us to live, as the early Christian so clearly did, inspired by the hope, and constrained by the awe, of this prospect.

THEMES FOR STUDY

1. From 1 and 2 Thessalonians and Mt. xxiv. construct your own interpretation of the signs and events accompanying Christ's return.

2. For what does Paul (i) give thanks, and (ii) pray in 2 Thessalonians?

3. What can we learn about the effectual calling, over-ruling providence, and eternal faithfulness of God? What difference ought these things to make to our lives?

THE PASTORAL EPISTLES

THE three Epistles which form the last group of St. Paul's writings in the New Testament, comprising 1 and 2 Timothy and Titus, are generally known as the Pastoral Epistles. They are called by this name because they deal largely, though not exclusively, with the pastoral work of the church and the duties of the Christian minister. The title is more applicable to 1 Timothy and Titus than to 2 Timothy, the latter being largely personal in character, although inextricably bound up with the other two.

AUTHORSHIP, DATE AND CIRCUMSTANCES

The Pauline authorship of these Epistles has been the subject of a great deal of controversy during the last hundred years, some critics going so far as to attribute them to an unknown author in the middle of the second century; but it is significant that this extreme view has now been generally abandoned, and those scholars who are still reluctant to accept the Epistles in their present form as being the work of St Paul usually admit that they do incorporate a number of the apostle's thoughts, and even some fragments of his actual writings. On the other side, many of the ablest New Testament scholars, while admitting the difficulties involved, have vigorously defended the Pauline authorship of the Pastorals and exposed the weakness of the critical position. The external evidence for the authenticity of the Epistles is remarkably good. 'There is not a shred of historical evidence against the letters. The witness of the early church to their place in the New Testament canon and their Pauline authorship is as clear, full, and unhesitating as that given to the other Epistles.'[1] They are quoted or referred to in the second century by Ignatius, Polycarp, Irenæus, Tertullian, and Clement of Alexandria, all of whom regarded them as genuine apostolic writings.

In fact, the controversy is entirely a modern one; from the second century to the nineteenth no one ever doubted that they were written by St. Paul. If these Epistles were indeed second-century forgeries, we might well inquire how it happened that the age which produced so consummate a literary artist produced no one capable even of suspecting him. The following objections have been raised.

1. It is objected that no place can be found for them in the life of St. Paul as recorded in the Acts, and that the journeys to which

[1] G. G. Findlay, *The Epistles of Paul*, p. 211.

the apostle makes reference in the Pastorals are inconsistent with the movements ascribed to him in Luke's narrative. This difficulty is entirely removed if we accept the traditional view that Paul's life did not end with his first imprisonment at Rome (Acts xxviii.), but that he was released and continued his missionary travels for a further period. If so, and if these Epistles belong to this last period of his life, they are of particular value for the light which they cast on the apostle's closing years.

2. It is asserted that the language of the Pastorals is non-Pauline: that they contain many words not found in any other of the apostle's writings; and also that the style is different. This argument is double-edged, for an imitator, we may assume, would have taken care to avoid this. The new words can be fully accounted for by Paul's versatility of style and by the new subjects dealt with. None of them implies a later date, and nearly half of them occur in the Septuagint. Similar differences of style and vocabulary can be found in the earlier Pauline Epistles.

3. The other objections raised against the authenticity of the Pastorals, such as those based upon the references to heresy, doctrine, and church organization, present no special difficulty and on the whole argue *for*, rather than against, an early date for the Epistles. It is alleged, for instance, that the view of the ministry presented in the Epistles is too developed to suit the time when Paul wrote, and requires a second-century date. But the contrary is true. The passages 1 Tim. iii. 1-7 and Titus i. 5-9 prove decisively that when these Epistles were written the 'bishops' and 'elders' (or presbyters) were the same persons and that the offices were regarded as identical, whereas in the second century the two offices were differentiated, as the Ignatian letters (*c.* A.D. 110) prove.

Accepting, then, Paul's authorship of these letters, and his release from his first imprisonment (Acts xxviii.) as most consonant with the facts, it appears that he enjoyed three or four years of further missionary service. During this time it is possible that he realized his hopes of reaching Spain (Rom. xv. 24), and probable that he fulfilled his promises of visiting Colossæ (Phm. 22) and of revisiting Philippi (Phil. ii. 24).

It is quite certain that in the course of these travels he paid a missionary visit to the island of Crete in company with Titus, and that on his departure he left Titus behind to 'set in order the things that were wanting and appoint elders in every city' (Tit. i. 5). In like manner he placed Timothy in charge of the

church at Ephesus (1 Tim. i. 3), though it is unlikely that Paul
himself ever visited Ephesus again (see Acts xx. 25). Probably
the tearful farewell referred to in 2 Tim. i. 4 took place at Miletus
(cf. 2 Tim. iv. 20). Thence the apostle crossed over to Macedonia
via Troas (2 Tim. iv. 13); and it was from there, probably in the
summer of A.D. 64, that he wrote his first letter to Timothy.

At much the same time, it would seem, he also wrote to Titus
in Crete, mentioning in the course of his letter his plan of proceeding to Nicopolis for the winter and requesting Titus to join
him there (Tit. iii. 12). However, before his plans could proceed
further, he was re-arrested and taken as a prisoner to Rome; and
it was from a Roman dungeon, shortly before his martyrdom[1]
(A.D. 66 or 67), that the apostle addressed his second letter to
Timothy, with the urgent plea: 'Do thy diligence to come shortly
unto me' (2 Tim. iv. 9).

From the above it will be clear that the *chronological* order of
the Epistles is: 1 Timothy—Titus—2 Timothy. It is in this order
that we shall now consider them separately.

1 Timothy

Timothy was converted as a youth during Paul's first visit to
Lystra, and later, on the occasion of the second visit, was chosen
to become the apostle's assistant and travelling companion (Acts
xvi. 1-3). From this last reference we learn that his father was a
Greek, and from 2 Tim. i. 5 and iii. 15 that his mother was a pious
Jewess. As was the case with Paul and Barnabas (Acts xiii. 1-3),
Timothy's commission appears to have been accompanied by
prophecy (1 Tim. i. 18), and Paul also refers to the laying on of
hands then or at some other time (1 Tim. iv. 14; 2 Tim. i. 6).
The 'good confession' which he witnessed (1 Tim. vi. 12) may
have been made on that occasion, or else may appropriately be
referred to his baptism.

ANALYSIS

i. Introduction. Exhortation to faithfulness in view of false
    teachers, enforced by a reference to Paul's own ministry.
ii. Directions regarding public prayer, with special reference to
    the place of women in the church worship.
iii. Qualifications for the Christian ministry.

[1] See pp. 353 f.

iv.   Warnings against heretical teachers and counsel regarding Timothy's personal life.

v.   Instructions as to his behaviour towards particular classes in the church, special attention being paid to Christian widows.

vi.   Final warnings and exhortations.

CONTENTS

Paul wrote to Timothy to encourage him in the faith, bidding him to war a good warfare (i. 18, 19), and that he might know how men ought to behave themselves in the church of the living God (iii. 15).   Instructions are given on the ordering of public prayer, the choice of fit men for the ministry, the care of Christian widows, and the attitude to be adopted towards different classes of members; while again and again he emphasizes the need for sound doctrine and holy living.   It is evident from the references here and in Tit. i. that the persons referred to as 'bishops' (*episcopoi*, 'overseers', R.V. margin) and 'elders' (*presbuteroi*) are one and the same.   Alford, Lightfoot, and others have pointed out that bishops in the modern sense are unknown in the New Testament.

Paul also wrote to put Timothy on his guard against certain false teachers, who were spreading errors and causing dissensions in the church at Ephesus (i. 3-7, iv. 1-3, vi. 3-10, 20, 21).   The heresy was in all probability an early form of Gnosticism not unlike that dealt with in the epistle to the Colossians.   Incidentally, this is further proof of the early date of the Epistle.   In view of this danger, Timothy must maintain a faithful ministry and 'guard the deposit' of the gospel (vi. 20).   A third purpose of Paul's in writing, namely, encouragement, was particularly called for in Timothy's case, owing to the difficult and responsible task allotted him and to his timid and reserved nature (i. 18, 19, iv. 12-16, vi. 11, 12, 20).

Titus

Our information about Titus is derived entirely from this Epistle, Galatians, and 2 Corinthians; his name never occurring in the Acts.   He was of purely Gentile descent (Gal. ii. 3), owing his conversion to Paul (Tit. i. 4) and becoming in due course one of his missionary companions.   Three times he was sent to Corinth as the apostle's delegate to supervise the collection for the Jeru-

salem Christians (2 Cor. viii. 6, xii. 18), and the difficult and
delicate nature of this mission reveals the measure of Paul's confidence in his ability. Nothing is known after this until we find
him entrusted with another exacting task, the oversight of the
church in Crete after Paul's visit to the island. It was this circum-
stance that called forth the present Epistle. The last reference to
him in the New Testament is found in 2 Tim. iv. 10.

ANALYSIS

i. Introduction. Instructions about the appointment of elders
in view of the presence of an unruly element in the Cretan
church.

ii. Practical counsel concerning Christian conduct in relation to
family life, the appeal being based upon the grace of God
in man's salvation.

iii. Exhortations regarding civil and social life, with final warnings against heretics, and personal greetings.

CONTENTS

Paul's visit to Crete had evidently been a short one, and Titus
had been left behind to consolidate and extend the work (i. 5).
Hence the purpose of this letter, written soon after Paul's departure, was to give Titus authority and instructions concerning
the organization of church life in Crete, more especially in view
of peculiar difficulties inherent in the situation (i. 10-16, iii. 9-11).
Though the greater part of the Epistle is thus occupied with such
practical matters as ministerial duties and social relations, there
are three great doctrinal passages which contain notable summaries of the gospel in all the glory of its saving and sanctifying
appeal, namely, i. 1-3, ii. 11-14, iii. 3-7.

2 Timothy

ANALYSIS

i. Introduction. Exhortations to courage and fidelity.

ii. Counsels on personal discipline and public duty.

iii. The coming apostasy, and consequent need for a loyal
adherence to the inspired Scriptures.

iv. The last solemn charge to Timothy, accompanied by parting
counsels and requests.

CONTENTS

When Paul wrote his second letter to Timothy he was again a prisoner at Rome, courageously awaiting the end (iv. 6-8). He urges Timothy to do his utmost to come to him with all speed, and to bring with him his cloke (for winter is drawing on), together with certain books and parchments (iv. 9-13). The whole Epistle is a fervent appeal for loyalty to Christ and His gospel, with further warnings against perils of a moral and doctrinal character (ii. 14-iii. 9).

THEMES FOR STUDY

1. Reconstruct from the Acts and Epistles a 'life' of Timothy.

2. Contrast the characters of Timothy and Titus. What reasons are there for believing that Timothy was the younger of the two men, that he was a less robust character than Titus, and that Paul cherished for him a special affection?

3. Note and study the five 'faithful sayings' in these Epistles.

4. Make a list of Paul's friends mentioned in these Epistles, and follow with a reference Bible what is said of them elsewhere.

5. Study the warnings against false doctrines, and apply them to modern heresies and evils.

6. Note the following words for study: (i) 'Saviour' and 'salvation'; (ii) 'knowledge'; (iii) 'good works'; (iv) 'sound'; (v) 'godliness'; (vi) 'soberminded' (see R.V.).

7. From the references in the Epistles construct pictures of (i) the ideal minister; (ii) the ideal church member.

8. Study the important doctrinal passages in these Epistles and note especially their Pauline character, e.g. 1 Tim. ii. 3-7, iii. 16; Tit. ii. 11-14, iii. 4-7; 2 Tim. i. 9-11, iii. 16-17.

9. Note the references to the second coming of our Lord in each of these three Epistles, and consider their bearing upon the modern theory that St. Paul abandoned belief in this doctrine towards the end of his life.

PHILEMON

AUTHORSHIP, DATE AND CIRCUMSTANCES

THIS Epistle is unquestionably the work of Paul. Historical reality is stamped upon every sentence; the vivacity and directness of the writing make doubt as to its genuineness well-nigh impossible. External evidence shows that it was included in the earliest lists of Paul's Epistles.

Paul was in captivity at the time of writing (verse 10), and the letter was sent from Rome (see Ephesians) about A.D. 62, when Paul was awaiting his trial. During this period he came into contact with Onesimus, a runaway slave of a former Colossian convert of his, Philemon. This Onesimus became a convert to the Christian faith, and Paul determined to send Onesimus back to his master with this letter to beg Philemon to forgive him.

Under the Roman empire by far the greater number of residents were slaves. These had no relationships, no judicial rights. The slave was absolutely at his master's disposal; for the smallest offence he might be scourged, mutilated, crucified, thrown to the wild beasts. This majority of the population was only kept in check by the fear of these dreadful tortures.

CONTENTS

The Epistle to Philemon is unique among the Epistles of Paul inasmuch as it is addressed to an individual about a private matter. As an example of simple dignity, fine courtesy, and personal affection it stands unrivalled.

After salutation to Philemon, Apphia, Archippus, and to the church in his house, the apostle expresses thankfulness to God for the steadfastness of Philemon's faith. He then indicates his main purpose in writing, something which he might boldly have enjoined, but which he prefers to plead as a favour, namely, the begging of pardon for Onesimus.

This Epistle illustrates the refining influence of the gospel. The Saul of anti-Christian prejudice, with the roughness of his original nature, persecuting and outraging the church and dragging even women to prison (Acts viii. 3, ix. 1), is shown by this Epistle to have been transformed by the Spirit into an outstanding example of true gentility and loving consideration.

The name Onesimus means 'profitable'. Formerly he had been untrue to his name, for he had stolen from his master's goods and escaped; now he returns to be profitable not for a season only, but for ever. Paul would have desired his presence himself, for Onesimus had been of help to him; but he returns him as a duty, not for punishment, but for the profit of Philemon; not just as a slave now, but as a 'brother beloved', a fellow Christian. The debts of Onesimus may be put to Paul's account, nevertheless Philemon's debt to Paul can never be repaid. Paul longs for release that he may spend a season with Philemon, enjoins his prayer, and ends the Epistle with special greeting from others known to Philemon, and now also in Rome.

The apostle never commands the liberation of slaves as a Christian duty, but boldly enunciates a principle which must in the end prove fatal to slavery.

THEMES FOR STUDY

1. Should we judge our fellows by social class or spiritual standing?

2. 'The word "emancipation" seems to be trembling on the apostle's lips, and yet he does not utter it.' Which is more important, the enjoining of a command or the unfolding of a principle?

3. Compare Paul's manner in Acts viii. and ix. with that displayed in this Epistle. Can you find a similar change displayed in other New Testament characters?

HEBREWS

AUTHORSHIP, DATE AND CIRCUMSTANCES

THE Epistle of Clement of Rome, c. A.D. 95, quotes this Epistle freely as canonical and as having apostolic authority behind it, but Clement does not name the author. In the African branch of the western church, Tertullian says: 'There is extant an Epistle addressed to the Hebrews by Barnabas.' He then identifies it as our epistle to the Hebrews by quoting Heb. vi. 4-8.

In the early eastern church at the end of the second century Clement of Alexandria affirms that Paul wrote it in Hebrew and that Luke carefully translated it into Greek. Origen, a little later, writes: 'I should say that the thoughts are the apostle's, but the language and composition belong to someone else.' Later belief in Alexandria was more definite, and ultimately belief in the full Pauline authorship spread throughout the church, the strong influence of Jerome and Augustine, towards the end of the fourth century, swinging the western church round to that view.

There is a marked difference of literary style which distinguishes this Epistle from the undoubted Epistles of Paul, a difference which makes itself felt at once in the stately, finely-balanced, and richly sonorous opening verses; and this difference was felt and commented upon in the early church by Greek scholars like Origen.

It is closer to the literary classical Greek than that found in any other New Testament book, with the possible exception of Luke and Acts. Luther and Calvin questioned the Pauline authorship, and noted the contrast between Heb. ii. 3 and Gal. i. where Paul places himself on an equality with the first disciples, but the truth is that we do not know who the author was. Delitzsch makes the felicitous remark that this Epistle comes to us like its own Melchizedek, 'without father, without mother'. Like him, it marches forth in lonely royal and sacerdotal dignity, and like him it is without pedigree.

It must have been written a considerable time before A.D. 95, since Clement quotes it as a document whose authority had been long established. Indeed, it must have been written before A.D. 70. Although it is the ritual of the tabernacle in the wilderness, and not of the temple, to which the writer refers, the most natural way to understand the Epistle is to think of the temple as still standing, with its sacrifices still in vogue. Had the terrible tragedy of the year 70, when Jerusalem and the temple were laid in ruins, belonged to the past at the time of writing, the author could hardly have failed to refer to so stupendous a judgment of God upon the ancient ritual. We may then regard the letter as having been written on the eve of a stern and epoch-making crisis, a day of judgment fast approaching for the Jewish people (viii. 13, x. 25, xii. 26 ff.). The bloody Neronian persecution began c. A.D. 65, and, possibly, the letter should be dated a little before then, as, once that persecution had started, it could no longer be said of the readers, 'Ye have not yet resisted unto blood . . .' (xii. 4).

The Epistle may have been addressed to Jerusalem, Alexandria, or to a group of Christians somewhere in Italy, perhaps in Rome. The latter theory has much to recommend it. The most natural interpretation of the words 'They of Italy salute you' (xiii. 24) seems to be that there were some Italian Christians with the writer at the time of writing who took advantage of the occasion to send greetings to their fellow believers in the homeland. Moreover, the first time we hear of this letter it is in the possession of the Christians of Rome, Clement of Rome, as we have seen, making frequent use of it c. A.D. 95.

The people addressed were Jews who had professed Christianity for a considerable time (v. 12). But they had not grown in grace as they should have done; they were still in the A B C class in the school of Christ (v. 12-14). They had ceased to make progress in the Christian life (vi. 1-4). As there could be no standing still, they were in great danger of drifting back to Judaism, swept by strong currents of subtle influence in the world around them (ii. 1). There was grave danger lest 'an evil heart of unbelief' should develop in some of them (iii. 12). Conscious of the spiritual perils threatening his readers, the author addresses to them many grave warnings and exhortations (ii. 1, iii. 6, 14, vi. 9, 11, 12, xii. 1 ff., etc.). If only, he argues, they would see the real glory of Christ and His salvation, all their doubts would vanish. They would then no longer drift out across perilous seas, but would be 'borne along' by the mighty tide of the Spirit to perfection (vi. 1).

ANALYSIS

i. 1-ii. 4.	The person and dignity of Christ.
ii. 5-iv. 13.	Christ, whose suffering was necessary for our redemption, is greater than Moses and Joshua.
iv. 14-x.	Christ's priestly office.
iv. 14-v. 10.	Christ's priesthood like that of Melchisedek.
v. 11-vi.	The urgency of continuing in faith.
vii. 1-viii. 6.	His priesthood eternal, not like that of Aaron.
viii. 7-x. 18.	The old and new covenants contrasted.
x. 19-39.	The urgency of continuing in faith.
xi.	The example of the Old Testament saints in faith.
xii.	Exhortation to faith, patience, and godliness.
xiii.	Call to holiness, praise, and good works.

CONTENTS

The writer's thesis is the superiority of Christianity to Judaism. The key-word may be said to be 'better', which occurs thirteen times: a better covenant, better promises, better sacrifices, etc.

The superiority of the revelation made in Christ is, in the opening verses, said to consist in this: that this revelation has been made 'in a Son', this Son is He who is the effulgence of the glory of God and the exact representation of His being. Showing how Christ is better than the angels, better than Moses, better than Joshua (iv. 8), better than the Aaronic priests, the writer demonstrates the superiority, the reality, and the perfection of the work of Christ. This comparison occupies the first seven chapters.

Then, after a brief summary of what he has already written

(viii. 1), he proceeds to prove the superiority of the new covenant to the old, which is decaying and ready to vanish away (viii. 6-13), the doom and destruction of the temple and its ritual being now near at hand. Various points should be noted in the argument that follows. The author takes his readers back to the first covenant delivered at Sinai, to the tabernacle, to the time when the people were approaching the promised land. The sacrifices and priesthood then inaugurated were now to end, they were but a 'shadow' of the one sacrifice for sins for ever. Henceforth there was no need of a sacerdotal ministry, for the way of access was open to all through the all-sufficient sacrifice on Calvary. No other sacrifice was needed, and none could be offered (ix. 24-28, x. 18, 26). Henceforth our High Priest is in heaven, and through Him we offer our sacrifices of praise (xiii. 10-15). Thus throughout the Epistle the reader's thoughts are carried from earth to heaven (iii. 1, iv. 14, v. 4, vii. 26, viii. 1, 5, ix. 22-24, xi. 16, xii. 22). In a closely-knit argument he exhibits the superiority of the God-pitched tabernacle and the eternal salvation accomplished therein to the first, man-pitched tabernacle and its services (ix. 1-x. 18). 'Eternal redemption' (ix. 12) has been accomplished by Christ through the sacrifice of Himself; that word 'eternal' is one of the great words of the Epistle. Having proved the perfect and eternal character of the religion of Christ, the writer addresses a strong appeal to his readers to 'possess their possessions', to draw near unto God in full assurance of *faith*, to hold fast the confession of their *hope*, and to provoke one another unto *love* (x. 19-25), and enforces this by solemn warnings (x. 26-31) and by reminders of their 'first love' (x. 32-39). He causes to pass before their eyes that noble procession of the heroes of faith, and directs their gaze here finally to Jesus, the pioneer and perfecter of faith (xii. 1-4). Their trials are but the chastening of the Lord, which will one day bear rich fruit and lead on to a glorious salvation (xii. 5-29).

In the last chapter we have a number of practical precepts and a beautifully comprehensive benediction which stresses again one of the main themes of the Epistle, the 'eternal covenant', with 'our Lord Jesus', in His incomparable dignity and glory, as its Mediator (xiii. 20, 21).

THEMES FOR STUDY

1. Collect references to the perfection and eternal nature of the work of Christ.

2. Note all references to the Old Testament and the evidence they bear to its place, purpose and value.

3. What is the teaching of the Epistle upon (i) heaven; (ii) the need of continual advance in the Christian life; (iii) atonement for sin?

4. Study the teaching about the end of all mediation by human priests between the soul and God.

CHAPTER XXI

THE CATHOLIC EPISTLES

JAMES

AUTHORSHIP, DATE AND CIRCUMSTANCES

MOST scholars are agreed in ascribing this Epistle to James, the 'brother of the Lord' (Gal. i. 19), rather than to James the son of Zebedee, or to the other apostle, James the son of Alphæus. The reasons are as follows: James, the brother of John, was killed by Herod, as narrated in Acts xii. 2, and would hardly have had time to write such an Epistle. The second apostle named James is mentioned only in the lists of the apostles, and possibly in the list of the women round the cross which refers to 'Mary, the mother of James the less and of Joses' (Mk. xv. 40). One who made so little impression in the gospel narrative does not seem to correspond to the strong personality that is felt to be behind this Epistle. But from what we know about James, the brother of the Lord, who presided over the church in Jerusalem, he seems the most likely author.

The earliest direct reference to the Epistle as the 'Epistle of James' is by Origen (c. 200), though he declares himself uncertain as to who this James was. Indirect references to the Epistle are thought to be contained in many second-century writings prior to the time of Origen, right back to Clement of Rome, who wrote at the end of the first century. These references, however, are indirect, and simply reflect phrases occurring in the Epistle. It would seem, then, that the Epistle was not widely studied in the early church, and indeed Eusebius tells us that it was not universally accepted. When we study the Epistle ourselves, however, and consider its nature, we can perhaps find a reason for this neglect among Gentile Christians, for the Epistle is best understood as addressed to Jewish Christians, and this fits in with the view that the author was James the brother of the Lord.

The names of the individuals who composed the family of Jesus are given in Mt. xiii. 55 as James, Joses, Simon and Judas (or Jude), two of whom are believed to be the authors of Epistles in the New Testament. Although the evangelist uses the regular word for 'brother' in this verse, yet many commentators find cause to modify its natural meaning.

The Greek church holds that the four 'brethren' are to be considered as half-brethren—sons of Joseph by a former marriage; the Roman Catholic church regards them as cousins—sons of a sister of the Virgin Mary; it has been left to some Protestant commentators to admit the full natural meaning of the word 'brother'. Perhaps an open mind might be kept, but it may be noted that St. Paul also used the ordinary word for *brother* to describe James' relation to our Lord in Gal. i. 19.

It would seem that James and the other brethren of the Lord did not recognize Christ as the Messiah, certainly during the early part of His ministry (see Mk. iii. 21, margin; Jn. vii. 5), but the risen Lord is said by St. Paul in 1 Cor. xv. 7 to have appeared unto 'James'; and as James the brother of the Lord is explicitly mentioned by the same writer in Gal. i. 19 in a way which implies his importance in the church in Jerusalem, it is natural to conclude that he was converted to Christ later on, and became the head of the Christian community there by common consent. Thus it would be this James who presided over the first council of the church, recorded in Acts xv., and also over the council referred to in Acts xxi. 18-25. Writers outside the New Testament, such as Josephus and Clement of Alexandria and Hegesippus (both of the latter being quoted by Eusebius), also bear witness to a leading personality named James. From these sources we learn that he was surnamed the Just, and was eventually put to death by the Jews. The date of his death is said by Hegesippus to have been just before the siege of Jerusalem (A.D. 70), but by Josephus about ten years earlier.

The date of the Epistle is quite indeterminate from external references, and almost equally so from consideration of its contents. Reasoning from this latter evidence, however, many scholars place it early—in the forties of the first century. This would best account for the absence of any reference to the council mentioned in Acts xv., whilst the possible reference to persecution in ii. 15-18 would be explained by the events recorded in Acts ix. and xii. A few argue for the late sixties in order to leave time for the question discussed at the council described in Acts xv. to have died down; but the early date on the whole is preferable.

Since the Epistle is addressed to 'the twelve tribes which are scattered abroad', it appears that James was led to write to his fellow Israelites in the faith, many of whom would visit Jerusalem for the feasts, and would be glad to receive instructions of this kind which showed what it meant to be a Christian in daily life; that Christianity is not a matter of words only, but leads to a righteousness which 'exceeds that of the Scribes and Pharisees'.

ANALYSIS

i. 1-18.   The endurance of trials.
i. 19-27.   Hearing and doing God's word.
ii. 1-13.   Respect of persons.
ii. 14-26.   The relation between faith and works.
iii. 1-12.   Control of the tongue.
iii. 13-18.   Earthly and heavenly wisdom.
    iv.   The wickedness of strife, worldliness, and evil-speaking.
v. 1-11.   The sins of the rich; comfort and counsel for patient sufferers.
v. 12-20.   Oaths; the power of prayer; the blessedness of converting others.

CONTENTS

It has been said that there is no Epistle which contains in a small compass so many allusions to the teaching of Christ as contained in the Gospels. The Epistle, in fact, gives many of the sayings of Christ in a form which a free reference to them by one who intimately knew the Lord would take. Examples are: Jas. i. 2, Mt. v. 11; Jas. ii. 5, Mt. v. 3; Jas. iii. 12, Mt. vii. 16; Jas. v. 12, Mt. v. 34-37; also cf. Jas. iv. 6 with Mt. xviii. 4; Jas. v. 1 with Lk. vi. 24. This extensive—though indirect—use of Christ's teaching makes the Epistle one of the most interesting and important in the New Testament.

Then, again, the personality of the writer is revealed in the teaching of this Epistle in a striking manner. We should conclude that he was a man who would not suffer fools gladly, though essentially kindly in disposition ('my beloved brethren', Jas. i. 16); one who had no use for religious profession not accompanied by a good life (i. 23); one who had a deep mistrust of riches (i. 10 and v. 1-3), and was a great sympathizer with the poor (ii. 5); who regarded control of one's tongue as the greatest virtue (iii. 5); and who looked upon suffering for Christ's sake as joyous (i. 2 and v. 11).

The writer's beliefs are equally strong and clear. He regards God as the 'eternal changeless One' from whom come all good gifts (i. 17), and under whose providence is every detail of life (iv. 15). He holds a strong belief in prayer (v. 16), and looks for the coming of Christ (v. 7). He urges them to seek the conversion of evil doers, and to exercise the love which prefers to throw a cover

over sins, rather than bring them out into the light (v. 19, see Pr. x. 12).

The Epistle is probably best known for its teaching (apparently contradictory to Paul's), on the nature of, and relation between, *faith* and *works*. Paul says, 'We are therefore justified by faith' (see Rom. v. 1); James says, 'By works a man is justified and not by faith only' (ii. 24). A closer study of both writers, however, reveals basic agreement. Paul, equally with James, urges his readers to good works, but as the natural outcome and 'fruit' of their faith (Rom. xii.; Gal. v. 18, 22, 23; Eph. ii. 10; Tit. ii. 7), and not allowing that the works of the law constitute a *claim* for justification.

James asserts strongly the need of faith, but maintains that a living faith, as distinguished from a dead orthodoxy, must evidence itself in good works (ii. 14-26). The teachings of Paul and James are therefore not contradictory to one another, though often paradoxical statements may be drawn from them. A study of the meaning of *inspiration* as evidenced by the Scriptures themselves would take these distinctions into account.

Some striking aphorisms are contained in the Epistle which merit attention: 'A double-minded man is unstable in all his ways' (i. 8); 'The wrath of man worketh not the righteousness of God' (i. 20); 'The friendship of the world is enmity with God' (iv. 4); 'Resist the devil and he will flee from you' (iv. 7); 'The effectual fervent prayer of a righteous man availeth much' (v. 16); also there are some memorable similes (see i. 6, iii. 3, 4, iv. 14).

THEMES FOR STUDY

1. What is the relation between faith and works in the life of the elect?

2. What parallels and differences are found between James and 1 Peter?

3. How much of Christ's life and teaching can be found in this Epistle? What passages echo the Sermon on the Mount?

I PETER

AUTHORSHIP, DATE AND CIRCUMSTANCES

THE external evidence for the genuineness of the Epistle is strong and unimpeachable. 'There is no book of the New Testament which has earlier, stronger or better attestation' (Dr. C. Bigg). It is quoted as the work of the apostle by writers so far apart as

Clement of Alexandria, Irenæus in Gaul, and Tertullian from North Africa. Eusebius says that it was known and cited by Papias and Polycarp, and the reference in 2 Pet. iii. 1 is proof that 1 Peter was known and accepted before the close of the first century. The objection that Christians were not persecuted *as Christians* (1 Pet. iv. 16) until much later, is fully met by the answer that popular persecution, as distinct from that by the imperial power, had existed from the beginning. Nor can any argument be founded on Peter's ignorance of Greek, seeing that he had Mark and Silvanus with him (v. 12, 13).

The main outlines of the apostle's life and work may be traced as follows: Jn. i. 35-42 tells of his first meeting with Christ, Lk. v. 1-11 gives the fullest record of his call, Mt. xvi. 13-20 of his great confession, Jn. xiii. 6-9 the Lord's washing of his feet, Mt. xxvi. the incidents leading up to his great denial, and Jn. xxi. his Master's last words to him before His ascension. In the Acts he is the chief figure in the first twelve chapters, and we get other glimpses of him in Gal. i., ii.; Acts xv. and 1 Cor. ix. 5. It is probable that he met with his death in Rome about A.D. 67. The Epistle moves in the same circle of ideas as that of Acts i.-xii.; Peter's life and his Epistles mutually confirm each other.

The apostle writes to the 'scattered' Christians in the provinces named in i. 1; and those addressed include Gentiles as well as Jews (see i. 14, ii. 10, iii. 6, iv. 3). These brethren were suffering persecution, and that from the heathen (iv. 4, 5). They appear to have been visited previously by Silvanus (v. 12). He is probable the same as the 'Silas' of Acts xv. 22, 32, 40 and the 'Silvanus' of 1 Thes. i. 1; 2 Thes. i. 1; 2 Cor. i. 19. This would account for his acquaintance with Peter and his interest in the Christian churches of Asia, some of which he had formerly visited in Paul's company. Mark also was with him (v. 13), and the presence of these two is sufficient to account for the acquaintance with the Pauline Epistles which is generally recognized, copies of which they may have brought with them (2 Pet. iii. 15). It is possible that the parallels with Rom. xii., xiii. may be derived in both Epistles from current catechisms for the instruction of converts.

The Epistle was written from 'Babylon' (v. 13), and contains a greeting from the lady ('she', R.V.) in that place, which may refer to some well-known individual or to the church (A.V.). The Roman church, which asserts (what is certainly not true) that Peter was first bishop of Rome, treats 'Babylon' as a metaphorical name of the great city, an opinion also held by many others.

This was the traditional view, but the reasons against it are serious. No obvious reason can be alleged for *not* saying Rome if that was what he meant, nor for introducing a metaphorical meaning in the middle of simple and matter-of-fact sayings. If Peter was martyred at Rome, the interval between his arrival and his death could scarcely have been long enough to allow for the writing of both Epistles; nor do the contents of the Epistles fit in well with this hypothesis. Finally, the order in which the provinces are named, from east to west, favours an eastern place of origin.

Many Protestant writers, following Erasmus and Calvin, believe that Babylon on the Euphrates is intended. This is open to other objections; there is no ancient tradition that Peter ever visited these parts, nor was it likely that Mark and Silas would also be found there. The ancient city had long perished, and the Jewish colony which had settled near by is stated by Josephus to have removed in large numbers to Seleucia during the reign of Caligula.[1]

A third alternative, held by the Coptic church and adopted by Bishop Pearson and some others, is that Babylon on the Nile (to-day known as Old Cairo) was intended, the site of a very ancient Jewish colony, and mentioned by Strabo as the station of a Roman legion, where the ruins of the ancient Roman fort and wall can still be seen. Here the holy family is said to have passed the sojourn in Egypt, and here a Christian community existed from very early times. Whether the reference to the elect lady in v. 13 is to a person or to the church it would be more apposite in connection with a small body of Christians than with the great metropolis. This hypothesis is supported by the fact that various traditions connect the name of Mark also with Egypt. He is said to have been there in A.D. 61-62 before joining Paul in Rome, and to have appointed his convert Annianus as bishop of Alexandria.[2]

Of the churches addressed, Pontus was the birthplace of Aquila and Asia his subsequent home (Acts xviii. 2; 1 Cor. xvi. 19; 2 Tim. iv. 19); while Pontus, Cappadocia, and Asia were all represented on the day of Pentecost. The regions bordering on the Black Sea were remote from the great routes between Rome and Palestine, and having heard of their trials, the apostle sends to them by the willing hands of Silvanus these wonderful words of comfort, testimony and exhortation.

[1] Salmon, *Introduction to the New Testament*, p. 440.
[2] See Swete, *St. Mark*, p. xix.

ANALYSIS

    i. The privilege and destiny of believers; the cost and purpose of their redemption.

   ii. 1-10. The church as a temple with Christ as the chief cornerstone.

ii. 11-iii. 7. Social duties of the Christian citizen, servant, wife, and husband.

  iii. 8-iv. Fellowship with Christ in prayer and service, in trial and reproach.

    v. Duties of seniors and juniors. Salutations.

CONTENTS

The Epistle derives peculiar value from the fact that its writer was an eyewitness (2 Pet. i. 16) to the power and majesty of Christ. This gives force to his plain teaching on the atonement (i. 11-19, ii. 21-24, iii. 18, iv. 13), resurrection (i. 3, ii. 7, iii. 18, 21), and the second advent (i. 5, 7, iii. 22, iv. 5, 13, v. 4). The teaching regarding the new birth (i. 18-25, ii. 2) and the church as the company of believers (ii. 4-10) is equally simple and definite. Having thus set forth these doctrines in plain terms (i. 1-ii. 11) the rest of the letter is given up to practical exhortation. It is the Epistle *par excellence* for the practical man who has to stand up boldly for his Lord in the way that Peter did after Pentecost.

For the relationship with 2 Peter see that Epistle.

THEMES FOR STUDY

1. Study the person, life, and work of Christ as portrayed in this Epistle.

2. Note correspondences between Peter's life and speeches and his teaching in this Epistle.

3. What light is thrown on the problem of suffering and its relation to the sufferings of Christ?

4. Compare the passage ii. 4-10 with Ps. cxviii. 22; Is. viii. 14, xxviii. 16; Mt. xvi. 18. What inferences can be drawn from the comparison?

5. What lines of Christian conduct, as set out in Rom. xii., xiii., find an echo in this Epistle?

II PETER

AUTHORSHIP, DATE AND CIRCUMSTANCES

THE right of this Epistle to a place in the canon was long in doubt. Origen quoted it as Peter's and spoke of 'the two trumpets of his Epistles', but noted that the second was doubted by some. Eusebius classed 2 Peter with James and Jude as 'questioned' (*antilegomena*), but yet acknowledged by most people.[1]

Its brevity and the circumstances of its origin may account for the paucity of references to it in the first two centuries, and to its slow progress to recognition afterwards. In the second and third centuries, when many spurious writings appeared (including an Apocalypse supposed to be by Peter), the great Christian scholars were rightly cautious as to what they received as Holy Scripture, and this may give us confidence in their ultimate judgment. In the fourth century Jerome records that many denied it to be by Peter owing to the difference of style from that of the former Epistle; but he accepted it as genuine and put down the difference of style to Peter having used two different 'interpreters' to write for him. From the end of the fourth century onwards it secured universal acceptance.

The internal evidence is strongly in its favour, not even excepting the differences of expression which have been the chief ground for doubt. Some of these may be attributable, as Jerome thought, to the use of different amanuenses; others are certainly due to difference of occasion and subject. A detailed examination of the differences, and of the many and subtle similarities which exist, shows them to be such as no forger of that time would have employed. There are many parallels to the first Epistle and to Peter's speeches in the Acts.[2] Peter was known in Jerusalem by his own name Simeon (Acts xv. 14), and the use of this in 2 Pet. i. 1 (R.V.) would be natural for him, whereas an impersonator would have copied from 1 Pet. i. 1. The double use (2 Pet. ii. 14, 18, R.V.) of the expression 'enticing' (literally 'setting a bait') is reminiscent of his previous calling, and the use of the words 'tabernacle' and 'decease' together (i. 14, 15) corresponds with Luke's account of the transfiguration, which itself reflects Peter's thoughts and words (Lk. ix. 31, 33); the reference to Christ's prophecy in 2 Pet. i. 14 and its record in Jn. xxi. 18, 19 afford each other mutual confirmation.

---

[1] *H.E.* iii. 25.
[2] A list of these is given by Alford's Commentary. See also Bigg in the *Int. Crit. Comm.*

No doubt need be entertained, therefore, regarding the genuineness and inspiration of this letter. It is consistent with the character of the apostle whose name it bears; it slowly but surely won its way to acceptance by the early church; it has stood the test of criticism; and equally with other books of the New Testament it bears the impress of the Spirit and speaks the word of God to each listening soul.

The Epistle appears to have been addressed to the same Christians as the earlier one (iii. 1), but not limited to them, and at a time when Peter's death (see Jn. xxi. 18) appeared imminent (i. 14) The date would therefore be A.D. 66 or 67. The news had reached him, as it came to Paul about the same time (see 1 Tim. iv. 1, 2, vi. 5, 20; 2 Tim. iv. 1-7), of the teachers, who by false doctrine and evil example, were troubling the infant church, and he writes to warn and strengthen his readers in the knowledge of the truth and in expectancy of the return of their Lord.

The second chapter displays a marked similarity to the Epistle of Jude (see verses 2, 4, 6, 11, 17). Dr. Bigg makes the interesting suggestion 'that the errors denounced from both Epistles took their origin from Corinth, that the disorder was spreading, that St. Peter took alarm and wrote his second Epistle, sending a copy to St. Jude with a warning of the urgency of the danger, and that St. Jude at once issued a similar letter to the churches in which he was personally interested'.[1] This, or some similar explanation, receives support from Jd. 3, 4. It is a natural inference that the two Epistles were written about the same time.

ANALYSIS

i. Christians are expected to make their calling and election sure, for the gospel message is well founded.

ii. Warning against evildoers and false teachers.

iii. The manner and certainty of the Lord's return.

CONTENTS

The keynotes of the Epistle are holiness of life, the knowledge of the truth, and the expected coming of the Lord. The apostle begins with encouragement to progress in the Christian life, both in knowledge and in all the virtues, the new revelation in Christ being linked with that which came of old through the prophets.

This is followed by the contrasted picture of how false doctrine

[1] *International Critical Commentary.*

is accompanied by presumption and evil living, which cannot go unpunished, as illustrated in the Old Testament.

Looking to the future, Peter dwells with expectation on the coming of the Lord, which adds incentive to his appeals for blameless living and increase in the knowledge of God through the Scriptures. The style, like that of the first Epistle, is graphic and full of energy.

The reference to Paul's Epistles which is implicit in the earlier letter is explicit here, and the important truth is propounded that they can be classed with the other inspired Scriptures.

THEMES FOR STUDY

1. Compare the various dangers against which Peter warns his readers with those which threaten the church and the individual at the present time.

2. Apply to the present day the teaching of 2 Peter regarding errors in doctrine and how they are to be avoided.

3. What lessons are contained in this Epistle regarding holiness of life, the second advent and the inspiration of Holy Scripture? Compare them with the teaching of 1 Peter.

I, II and III JOHN

AUTHORSHIP, DATE AND CIRCUMSTANCES

THE three Epistles called after St. John have been, all down history, ascribed with fair unanimity to the apostle John. There might have been no question about the identification of this John were it not for one sentence in the famous passage of Papias recorded by Eusebius.[1]

Scholars generally are agreed that the author of the Gospel also wrote at least the first Epistle, owing to their affinity in thought and language. The early reception of this Epistle into the canon is evidence that from the first it was regarded as the work of the apostle; and the characteristic features of the three Epistles, the tone of authority, the exhortation to avoid false teachers, the insistence on love, and the use of the expression 'little children' are all in closest accord with what tradition relates of the last days of the aged son of Zebedee.[2] They exhibit a notable difference in

[1] See Chapter XIX.
[2] See Westcott, *Gospel of St. John*, p. 24.

spiritual quality, and in the sense of authority they convey, from the non-canonical writings of the second century.

1 John

ANALYSIS

i. Walking in the light, forgiveness and cleansing.
ii. Christ our Advocate; counsel to fathers, young men, and children.
iii. Children of God, love evidenced in action.
iv. The spirit of truth and of error, the love of God.
v. Faith, prayer, and things known.

CONTENTS

The circumstances suggested by a reading of this Epistle are such as were known to exist late in the apostolic age. A settled Christian community is assumed—'the darkness is past and the true light now shineth' (ii. 8)—but Christians need to be reminded that *they ought to love one another*; in other words, secular standards of community life have already taken hold of the Christian church. Again, false teachers have arisen and a deeper spirit is now discernible in the false teaching, which St. John describes as *anti-Christ*. This deeper movement includes the denial that *Christ has come in the flesh* (iv. 1-3), and seems akin to the well-known Gnostic heresies which came to fruition in the second century. A date in the last decade of the first century would fit in with these conditions and with the traditional belief regarding its origin.

2 and 3 John

ANALYSIS

2 John Exhortations to love, and warning against false teachers.
3 John Gaius praised for hospitality, Diotrephes blamed for self-assertion.

CONTENTS

These two short documents may be taken together, because they resemble each other in many respects. Both are probably addressed to *individuals*, though to individuals who are surrounded by other Christian believers (verse 1 in each Epistle, and verse 6 in 3 John). In both the apostle expresses the desire to speak further 'face to face', and hopes to see his correspondents shortly (2 Jn. 12 and 3 Jn. 14). And in both the need for Christian love is stressed as in the first Epistle also (2 Jn. 5 and 3 Jn. 8).

In the second Epistle reference is made to the rise of new teaching which denies that 'Jesus Christ is come in the flesh' (verse 7), and the writer declares 'This is a deceiver and an anti-Christ'. This warning reminds us of the first Epistle, and links this one on to it as from the same author; and so all three Epistles may be ascribed to the apostle John, and taken as having been written late in the apostolic age.

The personal character of John shines through these short documents. A man at once kindly and fatherly, and yet most sensitive to evil and quick to rebuke it. Is not such a character a reflection of the divine character itself, as revealed in Scripture as a whole?

THEMES FOR STUDY

1. What is the teaching of the first Epistle on forgiveness of, and victory over, sin? With v. 5 compare Rev. ii. 7, xxi. 7.

2. With 1 Jn. i. 6 compare 1 Jn. ii. 4 and iii. 4, also Jn. xiv. 17, xvi. 13, xvii. 17. What is the relation between truth in doctrine and practice?

3. With 1 Jn. iv. 1-3 compare the teaching concerning 'anti-Christ' in 2 Thes. ii.; 1 Tim. iv.; 2 Pet. iii.; Rev. xiii. What do you learn from these to illustrate the first of these passages?

4. Study the attitude which should be adopted towards men who deliberately falsify the doctrine of Christ (2 Jn. 9, 10) or are self-seeking (3 Jn. 9). Compare 1 Tim. vi. 5; 2 Tim. ii. 16-18; Tit. iii. 10.

5. What can be learned from these and Paul's Epistles as to the proper exercise of Christian hospitality?

JUDE

AUTHORSHIP, DATE AND CIRCUMSTANCES

THE Epistle of Jude is one of the shortest letters in the New Testament, but it has an interest all its own. First, let us inquire about the author. We read: 'Judas, a servant of Jesus Christ, and brother of James' (verse 1). This is the author's account of himself, and leads us to believe that he is one of the four brethren of the Lord, James being especially mentioned because of his important position in the church at Jerusalem.

It is noteworthy that in Lk. vi. 16, where the Greek simply says 'Judas of James', the Authorized Version has inserted *brother*, thus making an identification between Judas the faithful apostle and Judas the writer of this Epistle. This is hardly warranted, and the Revised Version translates 'son', which represents the more probable inference. Thus the writer of the Epistle is not one of the apostles, and this is in harmony with verse 17, which speaks of the apostles as of a company to which the writer does not seem to belong. The words in 2 Pet. iii. 2, though similar, do not convey quite the same impression.

There is ample evidence to the existence of this Epistle and its ascription to Judas, the Lord's brother, in second century writers such as Tertullian and Clement of Alexandria; it is mentioned in the list given in the Muratorian Fragment, and is also included in the old Latin version of the New Testament.

As we read the Epistle we see that it cannot be placed early in the apostolic age, because reference is made to the apostles as men who had already delivered their message, and also because signs of evil in the church are becoming manifest. On the other hand, if Jude was written before 2 Peter, it would have to be not later than the year 67. There is an account in the writings of Hegesippus (preserved by Eusebius) that two grandsons of Jude, who were farmers, were summoned to appear before the emperor Domitian (A.D. 81-96), who questioned them about the 'kingdom' to which they belonged; this would be consistent with a date about A.D. 65.

ANALYSIS

1-4. Greeting. Purpose of the Epistle.

5-19. Warning against evil teachers, and of the judgment that awaits them.

20-25. Concluding exhortation and doxology.

CONTENTS

The Epistle is sent to the faithful in the local churches to warn them against new teachers ('men crept in unawares', verse 4), who are likely to lead them astray. Jude urges them to 'contend for the faith which was once delivered to the saints' (verse 3). Yet such defence of the faith must be undertaken in a certain spirit, not in a 'railing' manner (verse 9), but rather through the power of the Holy Ghost—'building up yourselves on your most holy faith, praying in the Holy Ghost' (verse 20). This message is equally applicable to the present day.

There are two statements in this Epistle which do not appear elsewhere in the Bible, but are found in two non-canonical writings of the first century. The first of these (verse 9) is found in a work entitled *The Assumption of Moses*, known to us through quotation by certain Greek fathers, and in an incomplete Latin version. The second (verse 14) might be a loose quotation from a work known as the *Book of Enoch*, but the date of both of these books is uncertain. We naturally ask, 'Does Jude's use of these statements confirm them as authentic, or was he merely using current ideas to teach spiritual lessons?' Either view can be held consistently with a full belief in the inspiration of Jude. We can recall how St. Paul on occasion made use of even current pagan literature to do the same thing (see Acts xvii. 28; Tit. i. 12).

THEMES FOR STUDY

1. What is the content of the 'faith once delivered to the saints'? (cf. 1 Cor. xv. 3; 1 Tim. iii. 16).

2. Compare Jude and 2 Tim. ii. for guidance as to how to deal with false teachers.

4. The keeping power of Christ (cf. Rom. viii. 38, 39).

CHAPTER XXII

REVELATION

AUTHORSHIP, DATE AND CIRCUMSTANCES

THE book of Revelation was written by a Hebrew Christian of Palestine who, after a period of exile in the isle of Patmos, settled in Asia Minor. His name was John (Rev. i. 1). Early tradition identifies him with the apostle of that name, though this might represent only a conjecture based on the information which the book itself provides. It is to be noted, however, that in this book, above others in the New Testament, human authorship is of little account. The book is 'the Revelation of *Jesus Christ* which *God* gave Him . . . and He sent and signified it by His angel unto His servant John' (i. 1).

The evidence for regarding the apostle John as the author is weighty, viz.:

1. The testimony to the apostle's authorship by the early fathers (Justin, Irenæus, Hippolytus, Tertullian, Origen).

2. The correspondence of the character of John in the Synoptic Gospels with the character assumed by the seer.

3. The unquestioned authority over the churches of Asia Minor possessed by the author, whose simple designation of himself as 'John' presupposes there was no other Christian leader named John in that area with whom he could be confused.

The main objections which have been raised are:

1. The marked differences of style and diction between the Revelation and the Gospel and Epistles of John.

2. The difference of doctrine in Revelation from that in the Gospel and Epistles of John.

3. A tradition of the early martyrdom of the apostle John.
The two latter may, on adequate grounds of scholarship, be dismissed.[1] The only serious objection is the first, which to many is conclusive against identical authorship of the books in question. Swete insists on divorcing the problem of the authorship of Revelation from that of the Gospel and Epistles, holding that John probably wrote the former but not the latter. It is possible that John

[1] See H. P. V. Nunn, *The Son of Zebedee.*

was the authority behind the Gospel, in an even closer fashion than Peter was behind Mark, and that he wrote the Revelation himself.

Gwatkin[1] thinks that 'we may safely say that its difference from the Gospel is very much what we should expect if it was written soon after John's arrival in Asia, while the Gospel dates from quieter times, perhaps twenty years later, when his thoughts were ripened and his Greek was improved'; adding that Hegesippus and Irenæus are much more likely to be mistaken on the date than on the author. The extent of Semitic influence on the language employed is an important factor; if John wrote the Revelation in Aramaic in Nero's days, and someone else translated it, while he himself later wrote the Gospel in his own Greek, the difficulty would disappear. It is not without significance that Swete, writing in 1906, declined to register a final verdict on this matter owing to insufficient evidence, and Kiddle, writing in 1941, did the same.[2]

The book reveals that a persecution, unparalleled in intensity and scope, is about to fall on the churches. This distress will especially come upon the Christians of Asia Minor, but will also ultimately embrace the churches of all lands (cf. the universal appeal in the promises to the conquerors in ii. 7, 11, 17, etc., and elsewhere). The fact of the banishment of John, a prominent Christian leader, from a Roman province, probably implies a decree issued by the imperial Government against Christians generally, with the intention of suppressing Christianity in the empire. The prophecies reveal a deification of the emperor and a compulsion of all to worship him. Such conditions obtained in Asia Minor at the close of Domitian's reign, c. A.D. 95. This agrees with the main stream of Patristic testimony, which assigns the book to this date.

Eusebius[3] says that Domitian sent Christians into exile for their adhesion to their faith, e.g. his own niece Flavia Domitilla and many other Christians were banished to the island of Pontia. Pliny wrote to the emperor Trajan (c. 112) that in Bithynia Christians had apostatized about twenty years earlier, i.e. c. A.D. 92. If the 'angels' of the churches addressed in chapters ii. and iii. are to be taken as 'overseers', as is maintained by some, this would tell in favour of a later date.

---

[1] *Early Church History*, Vol. I, p. 110.

[2] See also under the *Gospel* and *Epistles of John*, and *Canon of the New Testament*, pp. 338 ff., 403 ff., 32 ff.

[3] *Eccl. Hist.*, III, 18, 4.

All this evidence points to *c.* A.D. 95 as the date of writing, when the air was full of foreboding to Christians about to face at the peril of their lives the question: 'Christ or Cæsar?' Nevertheless, Lightfoot and other able scholars have favoured a Neronic date. Prof. Ramsay points out that it was not the vision of a day, but 'embodied the contemplation and the insight of years', during which 'the long drawn out living death in Patmos was the necessary training through which he must pass who should write the fourth Gospel'.[1] The outlook of the writer on the world would necessarily be that at the commencement of his exile, which may have lasted many years.

ANALYSIS

In the following analysis the judgments of God are regarded as three series, which, in some measure at least, are parallel, each series concluding with a sight of the kingdom about to come and enlarging on certain matters requiring to be more thoroughly understood.

i. 1-3.	Title.
i. 4-20.	Prologue. Vision of the ascended Christ.
ii., iii.	Letters to the churches.
iv., v.	Vision of God on the throne and of the Lamb.
vi.-xix.	Judgments of God.
vi.-viii. 5.	The seven seals, including the sealing of the 144,000 and the triumph of the great multitude.
viii. 6-xi. 19.	The seven trumpets, including the vision of the angel with the little book, the measuring of the temple, and the testimony of the two witnesses.
xii.-xiv.	The woman with the Man-Child, the dragon and two beasts, the triumph of the 144,000, the fall of Babylon, the harvest and vintage of the earth.
xv., xvi.	The seven bowls; leading to the end.
xvii.-xix.	The fall of Babylon and messianic judgment at Armageddon.

[1] *Letters to the Seven Churches*, p. 89.

CONTENTS

The book is cast in the form of an encyclical letter, with an 'address' (i. 1-3) and 'signature' (xxii. 16-21). No letter was ever more carefully planned. It issues a trumpet-call to faith, courage and endurance, seeing that Christ is seated on the throne. It demands of Christians that they examine themselves, repent for their failures, and renew their dedication to Christ, even though it lead to martyrdom. For their encouragement, some of the most gracious promises in Holy Writ are given for those who endure and thus overcome. This is the purpose of the letters to the churches. The visions which follow bid them look up and see their Lord and God seated on the throne of the universe, guiding the destinies of the nations, through all terrors, to the establishment of the kingdom of God on earth and the introduction of the final state in the new heavens and earth. The prophet thus points, not *away from* distresses, which are the lot of followers of the Lamb, but *through* them to the ultimate triumph of God, in which, if they remain faithful, they shall share.

It exhibits the stark terror of the judgment of God against sinners; let that truth occupy its due proportion in our thinking. It reveals the sure fulfilment of the purposes of God; let that not lead to slothful optimism but to confident labour. It is pre-eminently the book of worship; let us capture its spirit now and sing its matchless song with joy. It vibrates with the sound of victory and triumph; let that give us steadfastness to overcome. It tells of Christ's speedy return; let that fill us with expectation and hope.

Interpretation

The Revelation has been the subject of different systems of interpretation. During the first three centuries the early return of Christ was expected, to be followed by a millennial reign of Christ for a literal thousand years. The persecuting power portrayed in chapters xiii.-xvii. was assumed to be pagan Rome, and the symbols were given a spiritual interpretation. Hippolytus saw the Christian church in the woman of chapter xii., and, in

the ten horns of chapter xiii., ten kingdoms which should arise
to replace the Roman empire.

The Reformation saw the development of three systems known
as the *Præterist, Historical,* and *Futurist,* all of which find advocates
to-day. The first of these regards the prophecy as finally fulfilled
in the circumstances of the time when it appeared. It is adopted
by the Roman church, and at the other extreme by the rationalistic critics. The *Historical* system was adopted by the Reformers
generally, and later by Sir Isaac Newton and Bengel; it identifies
papal Rome as the persecuting power, and sees the various judgments progressively fulfilled in the course of history. The *Futurist*
school sees in chapters ii. and iii. an outline picture of the church's
history, and awaits a fulfilment of the remainder, of a more or
less literal character, in connection with the second advent of
Christ.

The following points should be borne in mind: ·

1. The book was as truly written for the needs of its original
readers as any other letter of the New Testament. Its historical
situation must therefore never be forgotten.

2. On the other hand, the burden of the book is the glorious
consummation of all things in the *Parousia* and the establishment
of the universal kingdom of God. This final reference must not
be obscured by the frequently repeated 'shortly' in regard to
things to come. The imminence of the kingdom of God runs
throughout Scripture and partakes of the nature of prophecy. The
major part of the book is, therefore, as yet unfulfilled, and, *pace*
some modern commentators, is yet to be fulfilled (cf. 1 Cor. xiv.
22, 'Prophecy is not for the unbelieving but for the believing').

3. Inasmuch as God does not act on caprice, there are to be
discerned in the prophecies expressions of those principles which
ever obtain, both in the lives of individuals and nations. There
are occasions in history when we can identify such secondary fulfilments of John's words, and here the historical method of interpretation finds some justification.

The place of Revelation in the Bible

The fittingness of the Apocalypse to conclude the canonical
writings is obvious in view of its theme. That position would be
equally merited, however, by reason of its unique use of the other
Scriptures. John hardly speaks without making some allusion to
an Old Testament Scripture. He is particularly indebted to
Daniel, and almost equally to Isaiah and Ezekiel; references to
Exodus, Psalms, Jeremiah, Joel, and Zechariah can also be found

(see Swete, *Apocalypse*, cxl.-clviii.). It is usually thought he had the Synoptic Gospels before him; certainly he knew their material, the great eschatological discourse of our Lord being one of his major foundation stones. Traces of Paul's and of other Epistles have been found. Its difficulties and the extravagant theories of some interpreters have led to the neglect of this closing book of the Bible by some Christians.

But it cannot be ignored without loss. It supplements the Gospels and Epistles, teaching the same truths, but flooding them with fresh light and colour. John knew himself to be a prophet and foresaw that his words would last to the end of time. Of all the oracles he uttered none is more true to experience than the benediction he himself had felt, 'Blessed is he that readeth, and they that hear the words of the prophecy, and keep the things which are written therein; for the time is at hand' (i. 3).

THEMES FOR STUDY

1. What can be learned from chapters i. and xxii. of the person of Christ? Trace these characteristics throughout the book.

2. From chapters ii. and iii. deduce the purpose of the writer as it concerned the churches originally addressed, and note the working out of this purpose in what follows.

3. Compare chapters iv. and v. with Is. vi., Ezk. i. and Rom. viii., noting the recurrent symbolism. What is taught here concerning the relationship between the creation and the Creator?

4. Study the promises, assurances and conditions of victory.

5. Observe the prophecies in Dn. i., vii. and ix., and in Mt. xxiv. What light does the book of Revelation throw upon those parts of these prophecies which have been already fulfilled, and on those which are still future?

6. Study the features of this Scripture which specially qualify it to be the closing book of the Bible.

CHAPTER XXIII

THE PROGRESS AND FULNESS OF CHRISTIAN DOCTRINE

THERE are three things to note about Christian doctrine itself before its progress and fulness can be appreciated.

CHRISTIAN DOCTRINE AS REVELATION[1]

Christian doctrine, as it is here viewed, is not the teaching of men, but the revelation of God. The uniqueness of the religion of Jesus Christ is just this fact, that it reveals God as seeking man rather than man as seeking God. God spake to man, but man heard only after the divine voice had broken silence. Christianity lays the emphasis upon the divine quest for man rather than upon the human quest for God. The initiative is altogether in the divine hand. Christian doctrine has its origin in the sovereign grace of God, who condescended to reveal Himself to the fallen race of mankind. Revelation, being thus communion between God and man, is not apart from human elements and factors. In the construction and presentation of Christian doctrine man has always his part to play, but he is supremely a recipient. He listens when the 'Thus saith the Lord' arrests him. He is not a creator of truth. Truth is external to him until he absorbs it.

CHRISTIAN DOCTRINE AS THE WORD OF GOD

The repository of Christian doctrine is the Bible. Like other faiths Christianity possesses its documents and standards, and these are collected in the canonical writings of the Old and New Testament. It is claimed that these Scriptures are the Word of God, that they are divinely inspired and that they contain the gospel of Jesus Christ, the good news of salvation from sin. No other book in the world points out to men the way of escape from sin, furnishes the secret of self-realization, and inspires with the hope of eternal life.

In any estimate of Christian doctrine as deposited in the Word of God it is to be specially noted that it presents itself, not as

---

[1] See also Chapter I.

theoretical truth, but as practical power. God drew near to man not with a philosophy of life alone, but in a redeeming activity. In other words revelation is an historical process and the Bible is the record of that saving intervention within human affairs. It is what God did that is the foundation of scriptural revelation. 'He made known His ways unto Moses; His acts unto the children of Israel' (Ps. ciii. 7). All this saving activity which transcends the mere unveiling of objective truth and forms the data of Christian doctrine is preserved for us in the Word of God.

CHRISTIAN DOCTRINE AS AN ORGANIC UNITY

This is another way of saying that one main stream of grace runs through all the history of redemption and all the pages of the Bible. There is a very definite continuity between the Old and the New Testaments, which has been recognized from the days of the primitive church. The one covenant is the complement of the other. Both are essential for the understanding of the full revelation of Jesus Christ. The one centres in Sinai; the other in Calvary.

This view of scriptural revelation is vital, for on no other hypothesis can any development of doctrine be traced. It presupposes one guiding hand down throughout the ages of man, and one superintending mind throughout all human history. There can be no radical difference between the teaching of the two dispensations. The revelation is born of the one Spirit of truth; the Scriptures are inspired by the one Holy Ghost. There may be many kinds and degrees of inspiration that the human mind has experienced, but the inspiration of the Bible is unique in this, that, among all writings purporting to possess inspiration, the Word of God alone is a means of grace by divine appointment. It is a living Word appealing to the whole personality of man. Received by faith as well as reason it operates in the soul or self unto salvation and sanctification. The inspiration of the Scriptures has stood the test of time and its true doctrine has wrought efficaciously in the lives of many witnesses.

To accept this integrity of revelation, this wholeness of Christian doctrine, is to avoid any disparagement of the Old Testament and any false emphasis upon any aspect of truth as it emerges from the historical stream. The continuity and unity of truth as revealed in the Word of God provide a true perspective of the complete manifestation and work of Jesus Christ. The assertion of two Gods, one in the Old and the other in the New Testament, or the view of a development within the divine nature and a consequent growth in the character of God, arises from a complete misunderstanding of the method of the approach of the one living and true God, even the God and Father of our Lord Jesus Christ, to His creatures ruined by the fall.

Granted these premises, that Christian doctrine is primarily a divine product, not *of* man although *through* man, that it is deposited by supernatural agency in the Word of God, and that it is an organic whole, the ground has been cleared to advance to the consideration of its progress and fulness.

Christian doctrine developed *pari passu* with the redemptive movement in history. The progress was not a revival of learning increasing in strength and light from age to age. Emphatically revelation demanded an awakened and enlarged mental outlook, but the vision of truth was not woven on the loom of human thought. The rebirth of Israel into a world-wide spiritual nation was an idea beyond the unaided powers of man. The hope of salvation from sin had not even a seed within the human mind until it was planted there by the redeeming intervention of God. As it is written, 'Eye hath not seen, nor ear heard, neither have entered into the heart of man the things which God hath prepared for them that love Him' (1 Cor. ii. 9). The development of Christian doctrine was not first in the sphere of subjective contemplation, but in that of objective revelation. God was ever a step in advance of His people, and guided them along the pilgrimage of His saving purpose.

LAWS OF PROGRESS

There are some well-defined laws of progress which have governed this historical unveiling of divine truth, and are still operative.

(a) *Christian doctrine progresses through election*

The truth passes from generation to generation through chosen channels. The Psalmist can sing of his legacy of spiritual knowledge from those who had been in the secret of the Lord before him. 'Thou hast given me the heritage of those that fear Thy name' (Ps. lxi. 5). It is recorded that in the infancy of the race, when God approached the antediluvians with His way of life, they rejected the path of righteousness. Two morally diverse branches of the human race very early became manifest, and revelation passed through the generation of Seth. This elect line was almost obliterated; in the days of righteous Noah the race was given a fresh start, the ungodly ancestry being annihilated.

This, however, did not suffice. Again a line was separated through which God could make Himself and His redeeming purpose known. The descent of Shem was chosen. Faithful Abraham became the father of Israel, the elect people, whose destiny it was to give the world the knowledge of God and prepare a possible environment for the incarnation of His Son our Saviour. In nothing amidst the redemptive activity of God is the principle of election more evinced than in the selection of race, tribe, family, and persons for the coming of the Messiah. According to the same law is the truth transmitted in every age. Elect souls are led by the Spirit of God into the full understanding of the mystery of the kingdom.

(b) Christian doctrine progresses according to human capacity

Increasing light can be given only in proportion to increasing ability to receive. This capacity for reception is constantly under the divine supervision in relation both to nations and individuals. It regulates revelation. The law operates right down the story of the human race and was openly enunciated and practised by Jesus Himself. 'And with many such parables spake He the word unto them as they were able to hear it' (Mk. iv. 33). With infinite patience God dealt with His chosen people. The Pentateuch recounts the rebellion of the Exodus nation and its discipline. The slave people were transformed but slowly into a free people with a mind liberated to apprehend God. From the awful Mount of Sinai the divine commandments were promulgated. This law, adapted to a settled community, remained the abiding ideal of ethics and religion. The period of the Judges was one of retrogression when the tribes in this and that locality lapsed into sin, superstition, and ignorance. It was the drama of the wilderness history repeated. All through the monarchy, united and divided, God educated His people, and through bitter and sweet experience made them the medium of His revelation. Gradually the truth dawned upon the Hebrew nation that they were in the moulding hand of God, and the tragic experience of the exile opened the door for a flood of light—the lessons of spirituality, sacrifice and universalism. It appears that in the post-exilic period the rigorous exclusiveness of the law held sway, but in the divine providence it was a process of racial and religious preservation, wherein the progressive gains of revelation were conserved. In the fulness of time, when the disciplined nation was ready, or as ready as could be, for the coming of the Messiah, and when the heathen nations were weary of their gods, Jesus came as the 'light of the world'.

(c) Christian doctrine progresses through personality

Another leading law in the development of revelation is its transmission through personality. Great souls were born from time to
time, Abraham, Moses, or David, the gifts of God to the human
race. These were light-holders who reflected the truth of the past
and radiated new rays for their own age, until the goal of revelation was reached in the divine Person who was the light of the
world. He in turn entrusted His entire teaching to chosen disciples,
who taught others, so forming a chain of life and light. Jesus did
not express His mind in a book or crystallize His teaching in a
creed. The only writing of His about which we are told consists
of some words in the sand, and what they were nobody knows
(Jn. viii. 6, 8). He wrote upon the lives of men, who in their turn
influenced others.

These three principles—of election, human capacity and transmission through personality—mark a process which had a very
definite starting point and goal. 'In the beginning God' is a
fundamental axiom of the Christian faith, while all along the way
of revelation it is a personal God who regulates the increasing
light, ever contingent upon the degree of human capacity.   The
climax is reached in the entrance into human life of the heaven-
sent incarnate Son of God.

DIRECTIONS OF DEVELOPMENT

It is possible to mark some main lines of progress wherein Christian
doctrine advanced from age to age. Some ideas were worked out
in life and ran parallel to the divine redemptive activity, and
some were obviously guides on the way to full revelation.

(a) The gospel message

An outstanding example of the progress and fulness of Christian
doctrine is the growth of the gospel message right through the Old
Testament to the New Testament declaration of the way of salvation. It begins with the *Protevangelium* in Gn. iii. 15: 'And I
will put enmity between thee and the woman, and between thy
seed and her seed; it shall bruise thy head, and thou shalt bruise
his heel.' Gradually the theme is developed, always associating
the deliverance from sin with the person of a Deliverer. It is true
that the salvation envisaged at first was both material and
national; but later it was transformed into something personal and
spiritual. It is remarkable how the early preaching of the apostles
grew out of the Old Testament ideas and rooted itself in the

revelation given to the fathers. Recent study of the primitive preaching confirms this development. Derived from the four speeches of Peter (Acts ii.-iv.) the contents of the early gospel message have been summarized thus:

1. The age of fulfilment has dawned: 'This is that which was spoken by the prophet' (Acts ii. 16); 'The things which God foreshewed by the mouth of all the prophets, . . . He thus fulfilled' (Acts iii. 18, R.V.); 'All the prophets from Samuel and them that followed after . . . told of these days' (Acts iii. 24, R.V.).

2. The historical Jesus is the medium of this realization according to the determinate counsel and foreknowledge of God.

3. The resurrection and ascension of Jesus verifies His Lordship as messianic Head of the new Israel. 'Therefore let all the house of Israel know assuredly, that God hath made that same Jesus . . . both Lord and Christ' (Acts ii. 36).

4. The Holy Spirit in the church is the sign of Christ's present power and glory (Acts ii. 17-21, 33; cf. Joel ii. 28-32).

5. The messianic age will shortly reach its consummation in the return of Christ (Acts iii. 21).

6. The message always closes with an appeal for repentance and offer of forgiveness and of the Holy Spirit and promise of salvation (Acts ii. 38-39; cf. Joel ii. 32; Is. lvii. 19).[1]

This apostolic gospel message is the enlargement of the preaching of Jesus as recorded in the four Evangels (Mk. i. 14-15). The Pauline doctrine is the development of the early *kerygma* (preaching), emphasizing the deity of our Lord, the value of His atoning death, and His continual intercession at God's right hand.

(b) The law

The function of the law in its widest sense is didactic; the *Torah* of God is instruction. In its more legal essence it reveals the mortal nature of sin, and is openly declared to be a schoolmaster to bring us to Christ. In the older Scottish theology a 'law-work' was reckoned an indispensable preliminary to any saving experience. Jesus is most emphatic that His purpose on earth is not to destroy, but to fulfil the law. In all His public ministry He reverenced this revelation of right thinking, and right living, and right access to God. His summary of the moral law is memorable: 'Thou shalt love the Lord thy God with all thy heart, and with all thy soul, and with all thy mind. . . . Thou shalt love thy neighbour as

[1] See C. H. Dodd, *The Apostolic Preaching and its Developments*.

thyself' (Mt. xxii. 37, 39). In presenting this perfect law Jesus did three things:

1. Assumed authority to re-interpret its meaning first hand. He Himself was the criterion of moral values. 'But I say unto you.'

2. Gave a deeper meaning to the old law so as to include inner motive as well as outward act.

3. Extended the law to cover other acts not included in the ritual, making the law co-extensive with daily life.

The New Testament writers, including the apostle Paul, accept the supersession of the law by Christ, yet fight against antinomianism.

(c) Prophecy

As Jesus fulfilled the law so also did He the prophets. The progress of prophecy throughout the ages is a study in itself. There were great prophets before the canonical writers of the eighth century B.C. appeared, e.g. Samuel, Elijah, Elisha. These men of God fulfilled the true function of a prophet by speaking in the name, and by the authority, of God in their day and generation. They were the heralds of the men whose words are preserved for us in the Scriptures. With one voice all the prophets announced the spirituality of religion. To them we owe the understanding of worship of God and walk with God. T. W. Manson[1] has pointed out that there were three primary conceptions in the religion of Israel.

1. The conception of one living God revealed in history.

2. The consciousness of God's covenanted 'election' of Israel to be His people.

3. The inseparability of morality and religion.

In the highest sense Jesus perfected this prophetic revelation.

1. He was in His own person God in human history, appearing at a definite hour in a definite place, and living through a definite period of time.

2. He called His own unto Himself by an election of grace (Jn. xv. 16).

3. He founded a kingdom of His own, distinct from the kingdoms of this world. He ever insisted by His life and death that the spiritual life expressed itself in moral living, and that religion was

---

[1] *Companion to the Bible*, p. 317

nothing if not practical. He taught that Christianity was not a philosophy, but a 'way' of life.

(d) Sacrifice

A red line of progress runs through the Old and New Testaments and comes to its climax at Calvary. There are some scholars who deny this continuity of the idea of sacrifice in the Scriptures. Their view is that sacrifice is alien to the stream of revelation and pagan in origin; and that the prophets above all else delivered spiritual Israel from its bondage. These are alleged to have constantly assailed the temple cult and to have condemned the whole ritual of sacrifice. Such passages as Is. i. 11; Je. vii. 21-23; Am. v. 25-27 are adduced as evidence of this attitude, and therefore the connection between the supreme sacrifice of the cross and the ancient ritual of the Old Testament is denied.

Such repudiation—that Christ was not the perfect Priest and the perfect Victim at one and the same time—has a direct bearing on the interpretation of the death of Jesus, and leads to a defective doctrine of the atonement. The Old Testament prophetic attitude to sacrifice may, on the contrary, be stated thus:

1. The ethical prophets were one with the priests as members of the same body and expressed the same mind of God. They themselves observed the law and the temple cult. They differed from the priests only in function.

2. They inveighed not against the sacrificial system, but against its abuse. They did not wish to abolish, but to reform, the ritual.

3. They never viewed the sacrifices as ends in themselves, but as symbolic of some deeper truth. The golden passional of Is. liii. is the example *par excellence* of the quest for the permanent reality and the light of a sure fulfilment.

(e) The Personal Christ

This is the central line of progress into which flowed all the streams of gospel, law, prophecy, sacrifice, and all other doctrines. The unity of Christian doctrine lies not in a principle, but in a Person. It is true that the messianic hope in its early dawn—and still later in its noonday—was more prominently associated with the kingdom than with the King; yet these two ideas are inseparable. It was realized at length that the kingdom could not come without the King. It became prominent in His own Person.[1] It is similar with the evangelical message. Its centre lies in the Saviour, the Son of God and the Son of Man, a divine-human Person. The law likewise found its fulfilment only in the perfect obedience of

[1] See Chapter XIV, *The Messianic Hope*, pp. 265 ff.

the historic Jesus, and its full revelation was reached in His life and work. Similarly the threads of prophecy are unravelled only by the divine Prophet, who was the ultimate spokesman for God. Again sacrifice was perfected and potent in the unblemished offering at Calvary. Because Christ in His own Person is supreme in the revelation of both the old and the new covenants He has rightly been called 'The Key of Scripture'.

The law and the prophets, the history, poetry and wisdom o the Old Testament all find their consummation in the life and work of Jesus Christ. In Christ, 'are hid all the treasures of wisdom and knowledge'; 'For in Him dwelleth all the fulness of the God-head bodily' (Col. ii. 3, 9). Jesus expressed this complete 'ful-ness' in three distinct modes: in what He said, in what He did, and in what He was. His teaching, His actions, and His character spoke the same language, and bore a common testimony.

THE FINALITY OF CHRISTIAN DOCTRINE

The fulness of Christian doctrine involves the postulate of the absoluteness of the religion of Jesus. To assert that Christ fulfils all the revelation of the Scriptures and is in Himself the fulness of Christian teaching is to declare that there can be nothing be-yond. It is just this finality which offends many thinkers to-day. Why should Christ consummate all spiritual wisdom? Simply because He is the Son of God. The very finality of Jesus demands acceptance by faith of a high Christology. Hebrews was written to prove that Christianity fulfilled the highest ideals of Judaism, which must on this account pass away. Jesus, however, is the same yesterday, to-day, and for ever. The absoluteness of Jesus belongs to His pre-existence and His eternal nature. 'The finality of Jesus is an expression of the faith that in the life, the words, the dying and rising again of Jesus Christ, the eternal love of God gathered up the whole of itself into the unique fact of Christ. The fact of Christ is the act of God. What happened in the death and resurrection of Jesus though it happened at one point in history, is a timeless thing.'[1]

To claim finality for Christian doctrine is not equivalent to accepting a closed system of revelation. Jesus Himself declared that the function of the Paraclete would be to lead the disciples into all truth. Although Christ's work of redemption is finished, and the written Word complete, the fulness of doctrine will only be known when all the will of God shall be done (Jn. vii. 17).

[1] Dr. R. H. Strachan, *The Historic Jesus in the New Testament*, p. 72.

INDEX

INDEX

A detailed analysis of each chapter will be found in the Contents pages placed at the beginning of each Part.

425

Malachi, the prophet, 114, 242, 255, 259 f., 287

Malachi to Matthew, 276-287. See analysis of Chapter XV

Man, antiquity of, 83, 127. See also under *Creation* and *Fall*
Destiny of, 317

Manuscripts. See under *Text, Old Testament* and *New Testament*

Marcion, the heretic, 34 f., 362, 368, 377, 380

Mark, the Evangelist, 328 ff.
The Gospel according to, 319 ff., 328-333

Marston, Sir Charles, quoted, 135, 138, 157, 164

maschil, Heb. instruction, 193

mashal, Heb. proverb, 199

mashiach, Heb. anointed, 265

Massoretes, the, 20

Massoretic text of the Old Testament, 20 f., 38, 120

Mattathias. See under *Maccabees*

Matthew, the Evangelist, 224, 322 ff.
The Gospel according to, 319 ff., 322-328

Medes, the, 102

megilloth, Heb. rolls, 27, 31, 225

Melchizedek, 129, 141, 268, 282, 390

Melito, Bishop of Sardis, 35, 38

Messiah, Messianic hope, 127, 132, 152, 167 171, 190, 197 f., 208, 211, 215, 218, 220, 222 f., 228, 238, 245, 256, 258 ff., 265-275, 294, 302 f., 313, 319 f., 323, 332, 336 f., 341 f., 346, 364, 394, 416 f. See analysis of Chapter XIV

Micah, the book of, 211, 248-251
The prophet, 199, 248 ff.

michtam, Heb. epigram, 193

midrash, Heb. commentary, 177

Miracles, 13, 43, 57-68, 304. See analysis of Chapter V
In Exodus, 134 f.
In Jonah, 247
In Joshua, 158 f.
In the New Testament, 58, 304 f., 308
Rejection of, 40, 43 f., 63 f.

Mithraism, 292

Moabite stone, the, 97

Modern criticism, 40-56. See analysis of Chapter IV

Monarchy, the, 94 f., 109 f., 169, 192 207, 210, 417. See also under *Kingdom*

Monotheism, 40, 46 ff., 55, 81

Moses, 89, 108 f., 115 ff., 169, 191, 207, 209 f., 240, 245, 249, 261, 268, 272, 307, 391, 418
As lawgiver, 26, 136 ff., 144. See also under *Law*

Muratorian fragment, 339, 345, 362, 368, 377, 380, 406
Contents of, 35

Musical directions for Psalms, 193 f.

nabi, Heb. prophet, 207

nagid, Heb. leader, 169

Nahum, the book of, 211, 252
The prophet, 223, 252 ff.

Names, the divine, 47 f., 50, 53, 117 f., 129, 131, 188, 194, 213, 217

Nazirites, 143, 162, 171

nebiim, Heb. prophets, 26

Nebuchadnezzar, king, 100 f., 113, 180, 220, 227, 235 f., 271 f.

neginoth, Heb. strings, 193

Nehemiah, 29 f., 102, 113, 179 ff., 195, 276
The book of, 175 f., 179-182, 232

nehiloth, Heb. wind instruments, 193

Nero, 34, 334, 390, 409 f.

New Testament, the, 22 ff. See also under *Bible*
Background, 288-297
Canon, 32 ff.
Date of writing, 34. See also Introductions to separate books
MSS., 22 ff.
Relation to Old Testament, 4, 13 f., 71, 107, 152, 191, 196, 238, 259 f., 276, 415
Translations and commentaries, 35
Types of text, 22 ff.
Versions of, 24 f.

Nineveh, 100, 223, 247 f., 252

Numbers, the book of, 143-146. See also under *Pentateuch*

Nunn, H. P. V., quoted, 340, 408

OBADIAH, the book of, 211, 246, 247
The prophet, 246 f.

Obelisk, the black, 97